Frommer's®

Kauai

4th Edition

by Jeanette Foster

WILEY

Wiley Publishing, Inc.

ABOUT THE AUTHOR

A resident of the Big Island, **Jeanette Foster** has skied the slopes of Mauna Kea—during a Fourth of July ski meet no less—and gone scuba diving with manta rays off the Kona Coast. A prolific writer widely published in travel, sports, and adventure magazines, she's also the editor of *Zagat's Survey to Hawaii's Top Restaurants.* In addition to writing this guide, Jeanette is the author of *Frommer's Hawaii; Frommer's Hawaii with Kids; Frommer's Maui; Frommer's Portable Big Island; Frommer's Honolulu, Waikiki & Oahu; Frommer's Maui Day by Day; Frommer's Honolulu & Oahu Day by Day;* and *Frommer's Hawaii Day by Day.*

Published by:

WILEY PUBLISHING, INC.

111 River St.
Hoboken, NJ 07030-5774

ISBN 978-0-470-55125-7

Editor: Christine Ryan
Production Editor: Jana M. Stefanciosa
Cartographer: Andrew Dolan
Photo Editor: Richard Fox
Production by Wiley Indianapolis Composition Services
Front cover photo: The Na Pali Coast © Frans Lanting / Corbis
Back cover photo: Pakala Beach © Douglas Peebles Photography / Alamy Images

For information on our other products and services or to obtain technical support, please contact our Customer Care Department within the U.S. at 877/762-2974, outside the U.S. at 317/572-3993 or fax 317/572-4002.

Wiley also publishes its books in a variety of electronic formats. Some content that appears in print may not be available in electronic formats.

Manufactured in the United States of America

5 4 3 2 1

CONTENTS

LIST OF MAPS vi

1 BEST OF KAUAI 1

1 The Best Beaches 1
2 The Best Kauai Experiences 4
3 The Best Adventures 5
4 The Best of Natural Hawaii 5
5 The Best of Underwater Hawaii. 6
6 The Best Golf Courses 6
7 The Best Luxury Hotels & Resorts 7
8 The Best Moderately Priced Accommodations. 8
9 The Best Inexpensive Accommodations. 10
10 The Best Bed & Breakfasts 10
11 The Best Restaurants 11
12 The Best Shops & Galleries 13
Pampering in Paradise 14
13 The Best Spas 15

2 HAWAII IN DEPTH 16

1 History 101 16
2 Hawaii Today 19
3 Life & Language. 20
4 A Taste of Hawaii. 21
5 The Natural World: An Environmental Guide to the Islands 24
6 Hawaii in Popular Culture: Books, Film & Music 33

3 PLANNING YOUR TRIP TO KAUAI 38

1 When to Go. 38
What to Pack 39
That Long Flight to Hawaii: How to Stay Comfortable 40
Kauai Calendar of Events 42
Honoring the Dead: Obon Festival. 45
2 Entry Requirements 47
3 Getting There & Getting Around 48
Coping with Jet Lag 51
4 Money & Costs. 53
What Things Cost in Kauai 55
5 Health 55
What to Do If Your Luggage Is Delayed or (Gasp!) Lost. 56
Don't Get Burned: Smart Tanning Tips. 58
6 Safety. 60

7 Specialized Travel Resources 62
8 Getting Married on Kauai 63
9 Sustainable Tourism...............65
General Resources for Green Travel 68
10 The Active Vacation Planner.......69
Fun for Less: Don't Leave Home Without a Gold Card 71
11 Money-Saving Package Deals 71
12 Staying Connected................73
The Welcoming Lei.................74
13 Tips on Accommodations.........75
Hawaii on the Web.................79

4 SUGGESTED KAUAI ITINERARIES 80

The Island in Brief..................80
Niihau: The Forbidden Island 82
1 One Week on Kauai 84
2 Two Weeks on Kauai 87
3 Kauai for Families 90
4 Kauai for the Adventurous 93

5 WHERE TO STAY 96

1 Lihue & Environs 96
Family-Friendly Hotels.............98
2 The Poipu Resort Area........... 101
Construction in Poipu 104
The King of Condos 107
What's the Story on "Cleaning Fees?" 108
3 Western Kauai.................. 115
4 The Coconut Coast.............. 116
A Rose by Any Other Name: Timeshares 118
5 The North Shore 125

6 WHERE TO DINE 132

1 Lihue & Environs 132
Plate Lunch Palaces.............. 134
2 The Poipu Resort Area........... 138
Family-Friendly Restaurants 142
Where's All the Bottom Fish on the Menu?.................... 145
3 Western Kauai.................... 146
Icy-Cold Dessert.................. 147
4 The Coconut Coast.............. 148
Vegetarian-Friendly Restaurants 150
5 The North Shore 154
A Hawaiian Feast: The Luau 156

7 FUN IN THE SURF & SUN 161

1 Beaches.......................... 161
Safety in the Surf................. 165
Frommer's Favorite Kauai Experiences...................... 166
2 Watersports...................... 171
Especially for Kids 176
3 Hiking & Camping 177
Hiking Safety 184
4 Other Outdoor Pursuits 191

8 EXPLORING KAUAI 198

1 Lihue & Environs 198

Discovering the Legendary "Little People" 201

2 The Poipu Resort Area........... 202

3 Western Kauai.................... 203

Taking to the Skies—It's More Than Just a Helicopter Ride 206

4 The Coconut Coast.............. 208

Make a Pilgrimage to a Hindu Temple 209

5 Paradise Found: The North Shore 210

Hollywood Loves Kauai........... 212

9 SHOPPING 215

1 Green Markets & Fruit Stands.... 215

Fruity Smoothies & Other Exotic Treats 216

2 Lihue & Environs 217

3 The Poipu Resort Area........... 218

Up and "Rumming:" Koloa Rum Company Tasting Room.......... 219

Niihau Shell Lei: The Island's Most Prized Artwork.............. 220

4 Western Kauai................... 221

Ultimate Kauai Souvenir: The Red Dirt Shirt 222

5 The Coconut Coast.............. 222

6 The North Shore 224

10 KAUAI AFTER DARK 226

1 Lihue 226

2 Poipu Resort Area............... 226

It Begins with Sunset............ 227

3 West Side 227

4 Coconut Coast.................. 228

5 The North Shore 228

Watch for the Green Flash 229

11 FAST FACTS 230

1 Fast Facts: Kauai................. 230

2 Airline, Hotel & Car Rental Websites........................ 235

INDEX 236

General Index................... 236

Accommodations Index......... 245

Restaurant Index................ 246

LIST OF MAPS

Kauai 3
One Week on Kauai. 85
Two Weeks on Kauai. 89
Kauai for Families 91
Kauai for the Adventurous 95
Where to Stay in Lihue. 97
Where to Stay in the Poipu Resort Area 103
Where to Stay on the Coconut Coast 117
Where to Stay on Kauai's North Shore 127
Where to Dine in Lihue 133
Where to Dine in the Poipu Resort Area 139
Where to Dine on the Coconut Coast 149
Where to Dine on Kauai's North Shore 155
Kauai Beaches 163
Kauai Hiking Trails. 179
Kauai Cabins & Campgrounds. . . . 181
Kauai Golf Courses 193
Kauai Attractions. 199

HOW TO CONTACT US

In researching this book, we discovered many wonderful places—hotels, restaurants, shops, and more. We're sure you'll find others. Please tell us about them, so we can share the information with your fellow travelers in upcoming editions. If you were disappointed with a recommendation, we'd love to know that, too. Please write to:

Frommer's Kauai, 4th Edition
Wiley Publishing, Inc. • 111 River St. • Hoboken, NJ 07030-5774

AN ADDITIONAL NOTE

Please be advised that travel information is subject to change at any time—and this is especially true of prices. We therefore suggest that you write or call ahead for confirmation when making your travel plans. The authors, editors, and publisher cannot be held responsible for the experiences of readers while traveling. Your safety is important to us, however, so we encourage you to stay alert and be aware of your surroundings. Keep a close eye on cameras, purses, and wallets, all favorite targets of thieves and pickpockets.

FROMMER'S STAR RATINGS, ICONS & ABBREVIATIONS

Every hotel, restaurant, and attraction listing in this guide has been ranked for quality, value, service, amenities, and special features using a **star-rating system.** In country, state, and regional guides, we also rate towns and regions to help you narrow down your choices and budget your time accordingly. Hotels and restaurants are rated on a scale of zero (recommended) to three stars (exceptional). Attractions, shopping, nightlife, towns, and regions are rated according to the following scale: zero stars (recommended), one star (highly recommended), two stars (very highly recommended), and three stars (must-see).

In addition to the star-rating system, we also use **seven feature icons** that point you to the great deals, in-the-know advice, and unique experiences that separate travelers from tourists. Throughout the book, look for:

Finds	Special finds—those places only insiders know about
Fun Facts	Fun facts—details that make travelers more informed and their trips more fun
Kids	Best bets for kids and advice for the whole family
Moments	Special moments—those experiences that memories are made of
Overrated	Places or experiences not worth your time or money
Tips	Insider tips—great ways to save time and money
Value	Great values—where to get the best deals

The following **abbreviations** are used for credit cards:

AE	American Express	**DISC**	Discover	**V**	Visa
DC	Diners Club	**MC**	MasterCard		

TRAVEL RESOURCES AT FROMMERS.COM

Frommer's travel resources don't end with this guide. Frommer's website, **www.frommers.com**, has travel information on more than 4,000 destinations. We update features regularly, giving you access to the most current trip-planning information and the best airfare, lodging, and car-rental bargains. You can also listen to podcasts, connect with other Frommers.com members through our active-reader forums, share your travel photos, read blogs from guidebook editors and fellow travelers, and much more.

1

Best of Kauai

On any list of the world's most spectacular islands, Kauai ranks right up there with Bora Bora, Huahine, and Rarotonga. All the elements are here: moody rainforests, majestic cliffs, jagged peaks, emerald valleys, palm trees swaying in the breeze, daily rainbows, and some of the most spectacular golden beaches you'll find anywhere. Soft tropical air, sunrise bird song, essences of ginger and plumeria, golden sunsets, sparkling waterfalls—you don't just go to Kauai, you absorb it with every sense. It may get more than its fair share of tropical downpours, but that's what makes it so lush and green—and creates an abundance of rainbows.

Kauai is essentially a single large shield volcano that rises 3 miles above the sea floor. The island lies 90 miles across the open ocean from Oahu, but it seems at least a half century removed in time. It's often called "the separate kingdom" because it stood alone and resisted King Kamehameha's efforts to unite Hawaii. In the end, a royal kidnapping was required to take the Garden Isle: After King Kamehameha died, his son, Liholiho, ascended the throne. He gained control of Kauai by luring Kauai's king, Kaumualii, aboard the royal yacht and sailing to Oahu; once there, Kaumualii was forced to marry Kaahumanu, Kamehameha's widow, thereby uniting the islands.

A law on Kauai states that no building may exceed the height of a coconut tree—between three and four stories. As a result, the island itself, not its palatial beach hotels, is the attention grabber. There's no real nightlife here, no opulent shopping malls. But there is the beauty of the verdant jungle, the endless succession of spectacular beaches, the grandeur of Waimea Canyon, and the drama of the Na Pali Coast. Even Princeville, an opulent marble-and-glass luxury hotel, does little more than frame the natural glory of Hanalei's spectacular 4,000-foot-high Namolokama mountain range.

This is the place for active visitors: There are watersports galore; miles of trails through rainforests and along ocean cliffs for hikers, bikers, and horseback riders; and golf options that range from championship links to funky local courses where chickens roam the greens and balls wind up embedded in coconut trees. But Kauai is also great for those who need to relax and heal jangled nerves. Here you'll find miles of sandy beaches, perfect for just sitting and meditating. There are also quiet spots in the forest where you can listen to the rain dance on the leaves, as well as an endless supply of laid-back, lazy days that end with the sun sinking into the Pacific amid a blaze of glorious tropical color.

1 THE BEST BEACHES

- **Kalapaki Beach:** Kalapaki is the best beach not only in Lihue but also on the entire east coast. Any town would pay a fortune to have a beach like Kalapaki, one of Kauai's best, in its backyard. But little Lihue turns its back on Kalapaki; there's not even a sign pointing the way through the labyrinth of traffic to this graceful half moon of golden sand at the foot of the Kauai Marriott Resort & Beach Club. Fifty yards wide and a quarter mile long, Kalapaki is protected by a jetty, making it very safe for swimmers. The waves are good for surfing when there's a winter swell, and the view from the sand—of the steepled, 2,200-foot peaks of the majestic Haupu Ridge that shield Nawiliwili Bay—is awesome. See p. 161.

- **Poipu Beach Park:** Big, wide Poipu is actually two beaches in one; it's divided by a sandbar, called a tombolo. On the left, a lava-rock jetty protects a sandy-bottomed pool that's perfect for children; on the right, the open bay attracts swimmers, snorkelers, and surfers. You'll find excellent swimming, small tide pools to explore, great reefs for snorkeling and diving, good fishing, nice waves for surfers, and a steady wind for windsurfers. See p. 164.
- **Polihale State Park:** This mini-Sahara on the western end of the island is Hawaii's biggest beach: 17 miles long and as wide as three football fields. This is a wonderful place to get away from it all, but don't forget your flip-flops—the midday sand is hotter than a lava flow. The golden sands wrap around Kauai's northwestern shore from the Kekaha plantation town, just beyond Waimea, to where the ridges of the Na Pali Coast begin. The state park includes ancient Hawaiian *heiau* (temple) and burial sites, a view of the "forbidden" island of Niihau, and the famed **Barking Sands Beach,** where footfalls sound like a barking dog. (Scientists say that the grains of sand are perforated with tiny echo chambers, which emit a "barking" sound when they rub together.) See p. 168.
- **Anini Beach County Park:** Kauai's safest beach for swimming and windsurfing, Anini is also one of the island's most beautiful: It sits on a blue lagoon at the foot of emerald cliffs, looking more like Tahiti than almost any other strand in the islands. This 3-mile-long, gold-sand beach is shielded from the open ocean by the longest, widest fringing reef in Hawaii. With shallow water 4 to 5 feet deep, it's also the very best snorkeling spot on Kauai, even for beginners. On the northwest side, a channel in the reef runs out to the deep blue water with a 60-foot drop that attracts divers. Beachcombers love it, too: Seashells, cowries, and sometimes even rare Niihau shells can be found here. See p. 169.
- **Hanalei Beach:** Gentle waves roll across the face of half-moon Hanalei Bay, running up to the wide, golden sand. Sheer volcanic ridges laced by waterfalls rise to 4,000 feet on the other side, 3 miles inland. Is there any beach with a better location? Celebrated in song and hula and featured on travel posters, this beach owes its natural beauty to its age—it's an ancient sunken valley with post-erosional cliffs. Hanalei Bay indents the coast a full mile inland and runs 2 miles point to point, with coral reefs on either side and a patch of coral in the middle—plus a sunken ship that belonged to a king, so divers love it. Swimming is excellent year-round, especially in summer, when Hanalei Bay becomes a big, placid lake. The aquamarine water is also great for bodyboarding, surfing, fishing, windsurfing, canoe paddling, kayaking, and boating. (There's a boat ramp on the west bank of the Hanalei River.) See p. 169.
- **Haena Beach:** Backed by verdant cliffs, this curvaceous North Shore beach has starred as paradise in many a movie. It's easy to see why Hollywood loves Haena Beach, with its grainy golden sand and translucent turquoise waters. Summer months bring calm waters for swimming and snorkeling, while winter brings mighty waves for surfers. There are plenty of facilities on hand, including picnic tables, restrooms, and showers. See p. 170.

Kauai

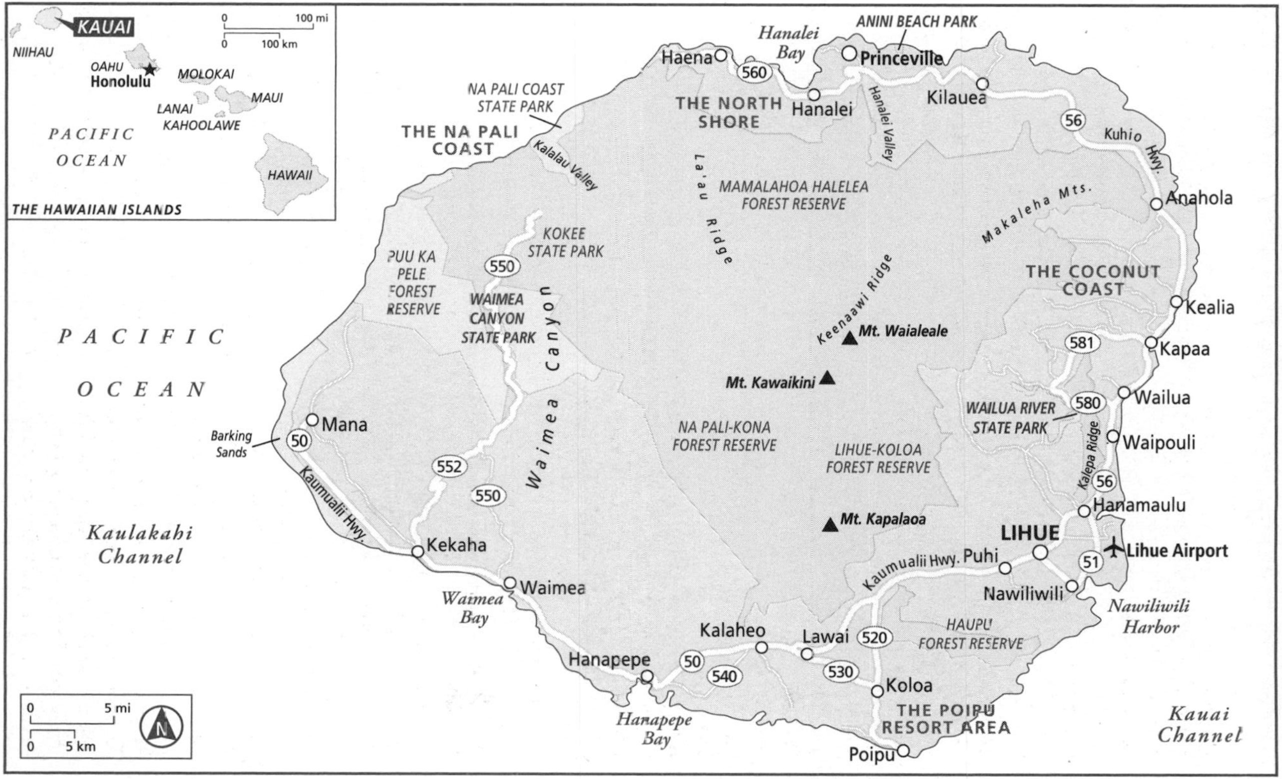
KAUAI
NIIHAU
OAHU
Honolulu
MOLOKAI
MAUI
LANAI
KAHOOLAWE
HAWAII
PACIFIC OCEAN
THE HAWAIIAN ISLANDS
0 100 mi
0 100 km
PACIFIC OCEAN
Kaulakahi Channel
Kauai Channel
Hanalei Bay
ANINI BEACH PARK
Haena
560
Princeville
Kilauea
Hanalei
Hanalei Valley
THE NORTH SHORE
NA PALI COAST STATE PARK
THE NA PALI COAST
Kalalau Valley
La'au Ridge
MAMALAHOA HALELEA FOREST RESERVE
56
Kuhio Hwy.
Makaleha Mts.
Anahola
KOKEE STATE PARK
550
PUU KA PELE FOREST RESERVE
WAIMEA CANYON STATE PARK
Waimea Canyon
THE COCONUT COAST
Kealia
Keenaawi Ridge
Mt. Waialeale
581
Kapaa
Mt. Kawaikini
Wailua
580
WAILUA RIVER STATE PARK
Waipouli
Kalepa Ridge
NA PALI-KONA FOREST RESERVE
LIHUE-KOLOA FOREST RESERVE
Mana
Barking Sands
50
Kaumualii Hwy.
552
550
Hanamaulu
Mt. Kapalaoa
LIHUE
Lihue Airport
Kekaha
Puhi
51
Waimea
Nawiliwili
Nawiliwili Harbor
Waimea Bay
HAUPU FOREST RESERVE
Kalaheo
Lawai
520
Hanapepe
50
540
530
Koloa
THE POIPU RESORT AREA
Hanapepe Bay
Poipu
0 5 mi
0 5 km

2 THE BEST KAUAI EXPERIENCES

- **Hitting the Beach:** A beach is a beach is a beach, right? Not on Kauai. With 50 miles of beaches, Kauai offers ocean experiences in all shapes and forms. You can go to a different beach every day during your vacations and still not get tired of seeing them. See chapter 7.
- **Taking the Plunge:** Rent a mask, fins, and snorkel, and enter a magical underwater world. Facedown, you'll float like a leaf on a pond, watching brilliant fish dart here and there in water clear as day; a slow-moving turtle may even stop by to check you out. Faceup, you'll contemplate green-velvet cathedral-like cliffs under a blue sky, with long-tailed tropical birds riding the trade winds. See chapter 7.
- **Meeting Local Folks:** If you go to Kauai and see only people like the ones back home, you might as well not have come. Extend yourself—leave your hotel, go out and meet the locals, and learn about Hawaii and its people. Just smile and say "Howzit?"—which means "How is it?" ("It's good," is the usual response—and you may make a new friend.) Hawaii is remarkably cosmopolitan; every ethnic group in the world seems to be represented here. There's a huge diversity of food, culture, language, and customs.
- **Feeling History Come Alive:** It is possible to walk back in history on Kauai. You can see ancient, ancient history, from the times when the *menehune* were around, at the **Menehune Ditch** and **Menehune Fishpond.** Or experience Hawaiian history at the **Kauai Museum,** the archaeological sites at **Wailua River State Park,** and the **Ka Ulu O Laka** *heiau.* For more recent history since the arrival of Captain Cook, check out the **Grove Farm Homestead Museum, Kilohana,** and the **Waioli Mission House Museum.** See chapter 8.
- **Exploring the Grand Canyon of the Pacific:** The great gaping gulch known as Waimea Canyon is quite a sight. This valley, known for its reddish lava beds, reminds everyone who sees it of the Grand Canyon. Kauai's version is bursting with ever-changing color, just like its namesake, but it's smaller—only a mile wide, 3,567 feet deep, and 12 miles long. A massive earthquake sent streams into the single river that ultimately carved this picturesque canyon. Today, the Waimea River—a silver thread of water in the gorge that's sometimes a trickle, often a torrent, but always there—keeps cutting the canyon deeper and wider, and nobody can say what the result will be 100 million years from now. See chapter 8.
- **Watching the Hula:** The Coconut Marketplace, on Kuhio Highway (Hwy. 56) between mile markers 6 and 7, hosts free shows every Wednesday at 5pm. Arrive early to get a good seat for the hour-long performances of both *kahiko* (ancient) and *auwana* (modern) hula. The real showstoppers are the *keiki* (children) who perform. Don't forget your camera! See chapter 10.
- **Bidding the Sun Aloha:** Polihale State Park hugs Kauai's western shore for some 17 miles. It's a great place to bring a picnic dinner, stretch out on the sand, and toast the sun as it sinks into the Pacific, illuminating the island of Niihau in the distance. Queen's Pond has facilities for camping as well as restrooms, showers, picnic tables, and pavilions. See chapter 7.
- **Soaring over the Na Pali Coast:** This is the only way to see the spectacular, surreal beauty of Kauai. Your helicopter will dip low over razor-thin cliffs, flutter

past sparkling waterfalls, and swoop down into the canyons and valleys of the fabled Na Pali Coast. The only problem is that there's too much beauty to absorb, and it all goes by in a rush. See chapter 8.

3 THE BEST ADVENTURES

- **Take a Helicopter Tour of the Island:** Don't leave Kauai without seeing it from a helicopter. It's expensive but worth the splurge. You can take home memories of the thrilling ride up and over the Kalalau Valley on Kauai's wild North Shore and into the 5,200-foot vertical temple of Mount Waialeale, the most sacred place on the island and the wettest spot on Earth. (In some cases, you can even take home a video of your ride.) See p. 206.
- **Explore the Na Pali Coast by Water:** Unless you're willing to make an arduous 22-mile hike (see chapter 7), there are only two ways to see Na Pali: by helicopter (p. 205) or by boat. Picture yourself cruising the rugged Na Pali coastline in a 42-foot ketch-rigged yacht under full sail, watching the sunset as you enjoy a tropical cocktail, or speeding through the aquamarine water in a 40-foot trimaran as porpoises play off the bow. See p. 171.
- **Duck Underwater:** You haven't really seen Hawaii until you have seen the magical world underwater. Beneath those blue waves is an entire universe in itself. You'll see schools of rainbow-colored fish, dazzling corals, graceful manta rays, lumbering turtles, and quick-moving silvery game fish. If you are really lucky, you may see playful dolphins or the frequent winter visitors to Hawaii, humpback whales. See chapter 7.
- **Hike Until You Drop:** Kauai is made for hiking, from the numerous trails in Waimea Canyon to the high forests of Kokee to the interior trails that give the island its special beauty. See chapter 7.

4 THE BEST OF NATURAL HAWAII

- **Waterfalls:** Rushing waterfalls thundering downward into sparkling freshwater pools are some of Hawaii's most beautiful natural wonders. Kauai is loaded with waterfalls, especially along the North Shore and in the Wailua area, where you'll find 40-foot **Opaekaa Falls,** probably the best-looking drive-up waterfall on Kauai. With scenic mountain peaks in the background and a restored Hawaiian village on the nearby riverbank, the Opaekaa Falls are what the tourist bureau folks call an eye-popping photo op. See p. 210.
- **Gardens:** The islands are redolent with the sweet scent of flowers. For a glimpse of the full breadth and beauty of Hawaii's spectacular range of tropical flora, we suggest spending an afternoon at a lush garden. **Na Aina Kai Botanical Gardens,** on some 240 acres sprinkled with about 70 life-size (some larger than life-size) whimsical bronze statues, lies hidden off the beaten path of the North Shore. Other great gardens are **Allerton Garden** in Poipu and **Limahuli** outside of Hanalei. See chapters 7 and 8.
- **National Wildlife Refuges:** Kauai has three wildlife refuges: **Kilauea Point,** which protects seabirds; **Huleia,** which shelters endemic Hawaiian birds and

wetlands; and **Hanalei,** which maintains a sheltered area for Hawaiian birds and the watershed. See p. 196, 162, and 196.

- **The Grand Canyon of the Pacific—Waimea Canyon:** This valley, known for its reddish lava beds, reminds everyone who sees it of Arizona's Grand Canyon. Kauai's version is bursting with ever-changing color, just like its namesake, but it's smaller—only a mile wide, 3,567 feet deep, and 12 miles long. All this grandeur was caused by a massive earthquake that sent existing streams flowing into a single river, which then carved this picturesque canyon. You can stop by the road to view the canyon, hike down into it, or swoop through it by helicopter. See p. 205.

5 THE BEST OF UNDERWATER HAWAII

- **Caverns:** Located off the Poipu Beach resort area, this site consists of a series of lava tubes interconnected by a chain of archways. A constant parade of fish streams by (even shy lionfish are spotted lurking in crevices), brightly hued Hawaiian lobsters hide in the lava's tiny holes, and turtles swim past. See p. 174.
- **Hanalei Beach:** Divers love this area because it has an ancient sunken valley with post-erosional cliffs. Hanalei Bay indents the coast a full mile inland and runs 2 miles point to point, with coral reefs on either side and a patch of coral in the middle—plus a sunken ship that belonged to a king, which means excellent diving. See p. 169.
- **Oceanarium:** Northwest of Hanalei Bay you'll find this kaleidoscopic marine world in a horseshoe-shaped cove. From the rare (long-handed spiny lobsters) to the more common (taape, conger eels, and nudibranchs), the resident population is one of the more diverse on the island. The topography, which features pinnacles, ridges, and archways, is covered with cup corals, black-coral trees, and nooks and crannies enough for a dozen dives. See p. 174.
- **Haena Beach Park:** In summer when the water calms down, this golden sand beach becomes a giant aquarium, great for snorkeling amid clouds of tropical fish. See p. 188.
- **Kee Beach:** Where the road ends on the North Shore, you'll find a dandy little reddish-gold-sand beach almost too beautiful to be real. It borders a reef-protected cove at the foot of fluted volcanic cliffs. Swimming and snorkeling are safe inside the reef, where long-nosed butterfly fish flit about and schools of *taape* (blue stripe snapper) swarm over the coral. See p. 170.

6 THE BEST GOLF COURSES

- **Kauai Lagoons Golf Courses** (**✆ 800/634-6400**): Choose between two excellent Jack Nicklaus–designed courses: the **Mokihana Course** (formerly known as the Lagoons Course), for the recreational golfer; or the **Kauai Kiele Championship Course,** for the low handicapper. The 6,942-yard, par-72 Mokihana is a links-style course with a bunker that's a little less severe than Kiele's; emphasis is on the short game. The Kiele is a mixture of tournament-quality challenge and high-traffic playability. It winds up with one of Hawaii's most difficult holes, a 431-yard, par-4 played straightaway to an island green. See p. 191.

- **Puakea Golf Course** (✆ **866/773-5554**): This former Grove Farm sugar plantation opened up 18 holes in 2003 to rave reviews. The course was in the middle of construction when Hurricane Iniki slammed into it in 1992, rearranging the greens from golf-course designer Robin Nelson's original plan. The first 9 (actually the first 10) holes finally opened in 1997 to many kudos; *Sports Illustrated* named Puakea one of the 10 best 9-hole golf courses in the U.S. The final 8 holes were finished last year. See p. 191.
- **Poipu Bay Golf Course** (✆ **808/742-8711**): This 6,959-yard, par-72 course with a links-style layout is the home of the PGA Grand Slam of Golf. Designed by Robert Trent Jones, Jr., this challenging course features undulating greens and water hazards on 8 of the holes. The par-4 16th hole has the coastline weaving along the entire left side. You can take the safe route to the right and maybe make par (but more likely bogey), or you can try to take it tight against the ocean and possibly make it in 2. See p. 194.
- **Kiahuna Golf Club** (✆ **808/742-9595**): This par-70, 6,353-yard Robert Trent Jones, Jr.–designed course plays around four large archaeological sites, ranging from an ancient Hawaiian temple to the remains of a Portuguese home and crypt built in the early 1800s. This Scottish-style course has rolling terrain, undulating greens, 70 sand bunkers, and near-constant winds. At any given time, about half the players on the course are Kauai residents, the other half visitors. See p. 192.
- **Princeville Golf Club** (✆ **808/826-5070**): Here you'll find 45 of the best tropical holes of golf in the world, all the work of Robert Trent Jones, Jr. They range along green bluffs below sharp mountain peaks and offer stunning views in every direction. One of the top three courses in Hawaii, the 18-hole Prince provides a round of golf few ever forget; it winds along 390 acres of scenic tableland bisected by tropical jungles, waterfalls, streams, and ravines. See p. 194.

7 THE BEST LUXURY HOTELS & RESORTS

- **Grand Hyatt Kauai Resort & Spa** (✆ **800/55-HYATT**): This Art Deco beach hotel recalls Hawaii in the 1920s—before the Crash—when gentlemen in blue blazers and ladies in summer frocks came to the islands to learn to surf and play the ukulele. The Hyatt's architecture and location on the sunny side of Kauai make this the island's best hotel. The beach is a bit too rough for swimming, but the saltwater swimming pool is the biggest on the island. An old-fashioned reading room by the sea houses club chairs, billiards, and a bar well stocked with cognac and port. Golf, horseback riding, and the shops of Koloa, a plantation town offering numerous boutiques, are nearby diversions. See p. 101.
- **Kauai Marriott Resort & Beach Club** (✆ **800/220-2925**): Water flows throughout this resort: lagoons, waterfalls, fountains, a 5-acre circular swimming pool (some 26,000 sq. ft., the largest on the island), and a terrific stretch of beach. The lagoons are home to six islands that serve as an exotic minizoo, which still lends an air of fantasy to the place and, along with the enormous pool and children's program, makes the resort popular with families. See p. 96.

- **Ko'a Kea Hotel & Resort** (✆ **877/806-2288**): Just opened in 2009 is this oasis—a small boutique hotel on one of the most beautiful stretches of beach in Poipu, with luxurious accommodations and first-class amenities (including an espresso maker in your room). In the footprints of the former Poipu Beach Hotel (which was destroyed by Hurricane Iniki in 1992), the 121-room hotel offers a central location in Poipu for dining, shopping, and activities, but you may feel so relaxed on the manicured grounds and so happy with the beach out front that you won't want to leave. See p. 102.
- **Sheraton Kauai Resort** (✆ **800/782-9488**): This modern Sheraton (since 1997) has the feeling of Old Hawaii and a dynamite location on one of Kauai's best beaches. It features buildings on both the ocean side and the mountain side of the road. The horseshoe-shaped, Polynesian-style lobby has shell chandeliers dangling from the ceiling. You have a choice of three buildings: one nestled in tropical gardens with koi-filled ponds; one facing the palm-fringed, white-sand beach (our favorite); and one looking across green grass to the ocean, with great sunset views. The rooms overlook either the tropical gardens or the rolling surf. See p. 102.
- **St. Regis Resort Princeville** (✆ **800/826-4400**): As we went to press, this jewel in the Sheraton crown was set to reopen at the end of 2009. Formerly the Princeville Resort, the property was a palace full of marble and chandeliers reminiscent of a European castle, but after the multi-million dollar massive interior renovation, it has been reborn as a luxurious reflection of the island. With the new opening come four new restaurants, a new spa, and St. Regis butler service for the suites. The location still enjoys one of the world's finest settings, between Hanalei Bay and Kauai's dramatic mountain peaks. See p. 125.
- **Outrigger Waipouli Beach Resort & Spa** (✆ **800/OUTRIGGER**): Stay in the lap of luxury at this $200-million condominium project on 13 acres (between the historic towns of Wailua and Kapaa). It's right on the beach and within walking distance to restaurants, shops, and recreational activities. The resort, which opened in 2007, has hotel rooms, as well as 1-and 2-bedroom condo units. Each unit is furnished with top-of-the-line materials like granite countertops; stainless steel appliances by Sub-Zero, Wolf, and Fisher/Paykel; double dishwasher; full-size washer and dryer; whirlpool bathtub in the master bathroom; and 37-inch flatscreen TVs in the living room and bedrooms. The resort features a long list of amenities, such as complimentary high-speed Internet access; a 4,000-square-foot Aveda spa; fitness center; and a 300,000-gallon heated saltwater fantasy pool, with flowing river, garden, dual serpentine waterslides, sand-bottom children's pool, and three sand-bottom whirlpool tubs. See p. 119.

8 THE BEST MODERATELY PRICED ACCOMMODATIONS

- **Aloha Sunrise Inn/Aloha Sunset Inn** (✆ **888/828-1008**): Hidden on the North Shore, these two unique cottages nestle on a quiet 7-acre farm. They come fully furnished with all the great videos you've been meaning to watch and an excellent CD library. The cottages are close to activities, restaurants, and shopping, yet isolated enough to offer the peace and quiet of Old Hawaii. Rates start at $185. See p. 126.

- **Garden Isle Cottages Oceanfront** (✆ **800/742-6711**): The site is spectacular: a 13-foot cliff overlooking historic Koloa Landing and an ocean inlet (where you can see turtles swimming). Nestled in a tropical garden setting, these one-bedroom apartments have an island feel, with rattan furniture, batiks, and original art on the walls—and great views. This is a quiet, peaceful place to stay in the heart of the Poipu area, within walking distance of beaches, golfing, tennis, shopping, and restaurants. Rates start at $216. See p. 106.
- **Hanalei Surf Board House** (✆ **808/826-9825**): If you are looking for a moderately priced ($195 a night), adorable studio just a block from the beach in Hanalei, get on the phone and book this right now. If you have a great sense of humor and enjoy whimsical little touches in the decor, you will love this place. See p. 129.
- **Hideaway Cove Poipu Beach** (✆ **886/849-2426**): Just a block from the beach and next door to an excellent restaurant are these gorgeous condominiums in a plantation setting. Amenities are top-drawer, and no expense was spared in the decor. Living areas are spacious, kitchens come with the best appliances and granite-top counters, and the outdoor lanais are big. You get all of this in a lush, landscaped tropical jungle at an affordable price (from $185 a night). See p. 106.
- **Kauai Banyan Inn** (✆ **888/786-3855**): Off the beaten path, but still just a 10-minute drive to the beach, this four-unit inn has the amenities of a much more expensive property (kitchenette, views, in-room massage) at budget prices (from $130). See p. 109.
- **Kauai Country Inn** (✆ **808/821-0207**): Fabulous location (nestled in the rolling hills behind Kapaa), terrific prices (from $129 a night), wonderful accommodations (big suites, hardwood floors, kitchen or kitchenette, your own private computer, comfy beds, and great views), and friendly hosts make this a "must-book" place. See p. 122.
- **Poipu Kapili Resort** (✆ **800/443-7714**): This quiet, upscale oceanfront cluster of condos is outstanding in every area. We like the home-away-from-home comforts and special touches: a video and book library, a spacious pool, several barbecues, tennis courts lit for night play, and an herb garden. (You're welcome to take samples if you're cooking.) A golf course is located nearby. Starting at $250 a night. See p. 107.
- **Wailua Bayview** (✆ **800/882-9007**): Located right on the ocean, these spacious one-bedroom apartments offer excellent value. The bedrooms are roomy, and the sofa bed in the living room allows you to sleep up to four. On-site facilities include a pool and barbecue area. Restaurants, bars, shopping, golfing, and tennis are nearby. A deal, starting from $163 a night. See p. 124.
- **Waimea Plantation Cottages** (✆ **866/77-HAWAII**): This beachfront vacation retreat is like no other in the islands: Among groves of towering coco palms sit clusters of restored sugar-plantation cottages, dating from the 1880s to the 1930s and bearing the names of their original plantation-worker dwellers. The lovely cottages have been transformed into cozy, comfortable guest units with period rattan and wicker furniture and fabrics from the 1930s, sugar's heyday on Kauai. Each has a furnished lanai and a fully equipped modern kitchen and bathroom; some units are oceanfront. Facilities include an oceanfront pool, tennis courts, and laundry. The seclusion of the village makes it a nice place for kids to wander and explore, away from traffic. Prices start at $197/night. See p. 116.

9 THE BEST INEXPENSIVE ACCOMMODATIONS

- **Brennecke's Beach Bungalow** (✆ **888/393-4646**): Attention honeymooners (or honeymooner wannabes): This is your place—so close to Poipu Beach that you can see it from your private lanai (about a 45-second walk from the front door to the waves). Tucked into a large two-story house is this private-entrance studio decorated with bamboo floors, maple cabinets, and lots of Hawaiian decor. This studio also has a small kitchenette (microwave, toaster oven, blender, coffeemaker, and fridge), cozy sitting area, and a comfortable bed. Outdoors there's a beach shower, barbecue area, and a big, green lawn. Restaurants, dining, tennis, and golf are just minutes away. Starting at $150 per night. See p. 108.
- **Ellie's Koloa House** (✆ **808/635-0054**): This two-bedroom/two-bathroom home, surrounded by tropical gardens, is for the traveler who wants a "real" Hawaii experience living in a residential area among locals. The house (with full kitchen) has antique furniture re-covered in old Hawaiian print fabric, with paddle fans to keep the house cool, TV, washer and dryer, and barbecue. Just a mile and a half to the beach and within walking distance to Koloa town's shops and restaurants. Prices are $125 and up. See p. 109.
- **Garden Island Inn** (✆ **800/648-0154**): Centrally located (a couple of miles from the airport, walking distance to the beach), this small inn has comfortable accommodations at budget prices (from $99). See p. 100.
- **Kalaheo Inn** (✆ **888/332-6023**): What a deal! This boutique inn, located in the community of Kalaheo (10 min. to the beach, walking distance to great restaurants) is comfy, clean, and terrific for families. Prices start at $83. See p. 114.
- **Kauai Cove** (✆ **800/624-9945**): These immaculate cottages, located just 300 feet from Koloa Landing and next to Waikomo Stream, are the perfect private getaway. Each studio has a full kitchen, a private lanai (with barbecue grill), and a big bamboo four-poster bed. The cozy rooms feature beautiful hardwood floors, tropical decor, and cathedral ceilings. The cottages are close enough for walks to sandy beaches, great restaurants, and shopping, yet far enough off the beaten path that privacy and quiet are assured. From $99 a night. See p. 110.

10 THE BEST BED & BREAKFASTS

- **Hale Ho'o Maha** (✆ **800/851-0291**): Kirby Guyer and her husband Toby custom-designed this B&B located on the North Shore in the Hanalei area known as Wainiha. Overlooking the mountains, waterfalls, and pristine Wainiha Bay, the Hawaiian antiques–filled home is just 110 steps to the beach (and a 10-min. drive to golf courses, shops, restaurants, and two riding stables). This spacious five-bedroom/five-and-a-half-bathroom home features an elevator (something you don't often see on Kauai). Guests are welcome to use the gourmet kitchen, gas barbecue, washer/dryer, refrigerator with ice maker/water, and TV/VCR/DVD in the "great room." Use of the boogie boards and snorkel equipment, beach chairs, towels, and coolers is all complimentary. See p. 128.

- **Lani-keha** (✆ **800/821-4898**): Step back in time to the 1940s, when Hawaiian families lived in open, airy, rambling homes on large plots of land lush with fruit trees and sweet-smelling flowers. This gracious age is still alive and well in Lani-keha, a *kamaaina* (old-timer) home with an open living/game/writing/dining room and oversize picture windows to take in the views. Bedrooms come with private bathrooms. The house is elegant yet casual, with old-style rattan furniture—practicality and comfort outweigh design aesthetics. See p. 124.
- **Marjorie's Kauai Inn** (✆ **800/717-8838**): This quiet property, perched on the side of a hill, is just 10 minutes from Poipu Beach and 5 minutes from Old Koloa Town. From its large lanai it offers stunning views over rolling pastures and the Lawai Valley. Every unit has a kitchenette with dining table, ceiling fan, and lanai. The new Sunset View unit has a separate sitting area and a futon sofa for extra guests. On the hillside is a huge, 50-foot swimming pool, perfect for lap swimming. Former owner Marjorie Ketcher has sold her popular inn to new owners, Mike and Alexis, who have kept the motto "do one fun thing a day." A treasure-trove of beach toys, from snorkeling gear to kayaks, and even bicycles and bike racks for cars, help guests achieve that goal. See p. 110.
- **The Palmwood** (✆ **562/688-3433**): This is a unique property: tranquil (located atop a hill of a 4-acre estate), fabulous views (360-degree view of the rolling hills of Moloa'a Valley and out to the ocean), and unbelievably beautiful rooms and surrounding landscaping. From the stone entryway to the leather/palm-wood chairs (so comfortable you will be hard-pressed to leave them) to the sound of water falling—this is the lap of luxury. The amenities at this tiny inn include flat-screen TVs, large lanais, hot tub, and Japanese Zen gardens outside (with barbecue area). Enjoy a full breakfast (such as crab cakes with banana bread and sliced mango) then relax in the free-form hammock. It's pricey (from $280) but worth every penny. See p. 126.
- **Rosewood Bed & Breakfast** (✆ **808/822-5216**): This lovingly restored century-old plantation home, set amid tropical flowers, lily ponds, and waterfalls, has accommodations to suit everyone. There's a Laura Ashley–style room in the main house, and two private cottages on the grounds. There's also a bunkhouse with three separate small rooms with a shared shower and toilet. See p. 123.

11 THE BEST RESTAURANTS

- **Bar Acuda** (✆ **808/826-7081**): After starting two successful restaurants in San Francisco (The Slow Club and 42°), chef/owner Jim Moffat moved to the tiny town of Hanalei and opened this sleek, romantic restaurant specializing in his favorite tapas dishes from the Southern European regions along the 42° latitude (southern France, Italy, Spain, and Portugal). In an atmosphere of candlelight and exotic mouthwatering aromas coming from the open exhibition kitchen, wonderful food and terrific service make this a must-stop. See p. 154.

- **The Beach House** (✆ **808/742-1424**): Though there has been a major cosmetic overhaul at this beachfront magnet in Lawai, the food is as good as ever. The Beach House remains the south shore's premier spot for sunset drinks, appetizers, and dinner—a treat for all the senses. See p. 138.
- **Caffè Coco** (✆ **808/822-7990**): This gets our vote for the most charming ambience on Kauai. Caffè Coco is just off the main road at the edge of a cane field in Wailua, its backyard shaded by fruit trees, with a view of Sleeping Giant Mountain. Gourmet fare is cooked to order—and at cafe prices. The food is excellent, with vegetarian and other healthful delights such as spanakopita, homemade chai, Greek salad, fish wraps, macadamia nut–black sesame ahi with wasabi cream, and an excellent tofu-and-roast-veggie wrap. See p. 148.
- **Dondero's** (✆ **808/742-1234**): This is one of your best bets for a romantic dinner on Kauai. Dine either under the stars overlooking the ocean or tucked away at an intimate table surrounded by inlaid marble floors, ornate imported floor tiles, and Franciscan murals. All this atmosphere comes with the best Italian cuisine on the island, served with efficiency. It's hard to have a bad experience here. Dinners are pricey and worth every penny. See p. 138.
- **Duke's Canoe Club** (✆ **808/246-9599**): Tropical atmosphere overlooking the ocean, great fresh fish at attractive prices, and dependably good meals. Don't miss the wallet-pleasing drink prices at happy hour. See p. 150.
- **Hanapepe Café** (✆ **808/335-5011**): Now under new management, Hanapepe maintains the same wholesome cuisine in a casual, winning ambience that has drawn foodies for a decade. During lunchtime the place is packed with businesspeople who drive 30 minutes to eat here. On the Friday-night dinner menu, such Italian specialties as lasagna quattro formaggio with spinach, mushrooms, and four cheeses steal the show. There's no liquor license, but you can bring your own wine. See p. 146.
- **Kilauea Fish Market** (✆ **808/828-6244**): Perfect for a takeout lunch or dinner on the beach, this tiny deli (with a handful of tables outside) pumps out incredibly delicious meals (even dishes for vegetarians) with fresh, healthy, locally grown and caught ingredients. See p. 160.
- **Mediterranean Gourmet** (✆ **808/826-9875**): This "hidden" restaurant, located next door to the Hanalei Colony Resort, nearly at the end of the road, was awarded "Best New Restaurant" on Kauai by a local magazine and is very deserving of the distinction. The oceanfront location is the perfect backdrop for chef/owner Imad Beydoun's Middle Eastern dishes, which he embellishes with an island twist. See p. 158.
- **Mermaids Café** (✆ **808/821-2026**): This tiny sidewalk cafe, with brisk takeout and a handful of tables on Kapaa's main drag, serves healthy, organic, home-cooked meals. Mermaids uses kaffir lime, lemon grass, local lemons (Meyers when available), and organic herbs, when possible, to make the sauces and beverages to go with its toothsome dishes. See p. 152.
- **Postcards Café** (✆ **808/826-1191**): The charming plantation-style building that used to be the Hanalei Museum is now Hanalei's gourmet central. Postcards is known for its use of healthful ingredients, fresh from the island and creatively prepared and presented. See p. 159.
- **Roy's Poipu Bar & Grill** (✆ **808/742-5000**): This is a loud, lively room with ceiling fans, marble tables, works by local artists, and a menu tailor-made for

foodies. The signature touches of Roy Yamaguchi (of Roy's restaurants in Oahu, Big Island, Maui, Tokyo, New York, and Guam) are abundantly present: an excellent, progressive, and affordable wine selection; fresh local ingredients prepared with a nod to Europe, Asia, and the Pacific. See p. 140.

- **Tidepool Restaurant** (✆ **808/742-1234**): An ultraromantic setting (literally hanging over the water), fabulous creative cuisine, and quick, efficient service with a smile make this restaurant in the Grand Hyatt a standout. See p. 141.

12 THE BEST SHOPS & GALLERIES

- **Banana Patch Studio** (✆ **808/335-5944**): This place has the best prices on the island for anything artsy and cute, such as tropical plates and cups, hand-painted tiles, artwork, handmade soaps, pillows with tropical designs, and jewelry. Plus, they will pack and ship for you anywhere. See p. 221.
- **Bambulei** (✆ **808/823-8641**): Celebrate the charm and style of 1930s and 1940s collectibles in this treasure-trove at the edge of a cane field. Fabulous one-of-a-kind vintage finds—Mandarin dresses with hand-sewn sequins, 1940s *pake* muumuus in mint condition, Peking lacquerware, and Bakelite jewelry—fill this jewel of a boutique, owned by two women with a passion for the past. See p. 222.
- **Koloa Rum Company Tasting Room, Retail Store & Gallery** (✆ **808/742-1616**): Kauai's first rum distillery makes white, gold, dark, and, on occasion, specialty flavors rum (like coconut and vanilla). They use high-grade molasses and sugar from Hawaii's only remaining sugar company (Gay & Robinson) and pure water from Mount Waialeale (one of the wettest spots on Earth). Enjoy a sample in the tasting room, browse the retail store (where the rum and other Kauai-made products are sold), and check out the historical display on the history of rum and sugar cane in Kauai. See p. 219.
- **Kong Lung** (✆ **808/828-1822**): You'll be surprised by what you find inside this 1922 stone building. It's a showcase of design, style, and quality, with items ranging from dinnerware, books, jewelry, and clothing to the finest sake and tea sets on the island. Throw in a lacquer bowl or two, a pair of beaded sandals, and a silk dress from the women's section, and the party's on at "Gump's of the Pacific." See p. 224.
- **Ola's** (✆ **808/826-6937**): Fine crafts from across the country find their way to this temple of good taste: lamps, vases, blown glass, drumsticks, jewelry, hard-to-find books, and the peerless paintings of award-winning artist Doug Britt. See p. 224.
- **Tropical Flowers by Charles** (✆ **800/699-7984**): Charles is a flower genius who grows a range of tropical blossoms, including some very rare and unusual varieties. Prices are extremely reasonable. See p. 221.
- **Yellowfish Trading Company** (✆ **808/826-1227**): Surprise yourself at Yellowfish Trading Company, where vintage bark cloth and that one-of-a-kind 1940s rattan sofa are among owner Gritt Benton's short-lived pleasures. The collectibles—1930s lampshades, '40s vases, '50s lunchboxes, antique silk piano shawls—move quickly. See p. 225.

Pampering in Paradise

Kauai's spas have raised the art of relaxation and healing to a new level. The traditional Greco-Roman–style spas, with lots of marble and big tubs in closed rooms, have evolved into airy, open facilities that embrace the Tropics. Spa-goers in Kauai are looking for a sense of place, steeped in the culture. They want to hear the sound of the ocean, smell the salt air, and feel the caress of the warm breeze. They want to experience Hawaiian products and traditional treatments they can get only in the islands.

The spas, once nearly exclusively patronized by women, are now attracting more male clients. There are special massages for children and pregnant women, and some spas have created programs to nurture and relax brides on their big day.

Today's spas offer a wide diversity of treatments. There is no longer plain, ordinary massage, but Hawaiian lomilomi, Swedish, aromatherapy (with sweet-smelling oils), craniosacral (massaging the head), shiatsu (no oil, just deep thumb pressure on acupuncture points), Thai (another oil-less massage involving stretching), and hot stone (with heated, and sometimes cold, rocks). There are even side-by-side massages for couples. The truly decadent might even try a duo massage—not one, but *two* massage therapists working on you at once.

Massages are just the beginning. Body treatments, for the entire body or for just the face, involve a variety of herbal wraps, masks, or scrubs using a range of ingredients from seaweed to salt to mud, with or without accompanying aromatherapy, lights, and music.

After you have been rubbed and scrubbed, most spas offer an array of water treatments—a sort of hydromassage in a tub with jets and an assortment of colored crystals, oils, and scents.

Those are just the traditional treatments. Most spas also offer a range of alternative healthcare like acupuncture and chiropractic, and more exotic treatments like ayurvedic and siddha from India or reiki from Japan.

Once your body has been pampered, spas also offer a range of fitness facilities (weight-training equipment, racquetball, tennis, golf) and classes (yoga, aerobics, step, spinning, stretch, tai chi, kickboxing, aquacize). Several even offer adventure fitness packages (from bicycling to snorkeling). For the nonadventurous, most spas have salons, dedicated to hair and nail care and makeup.

If all this sounds a bit overwhelming, not to worry, all the spas in Hawaii have individual consultants who will help design an appropriate treatment program to fit your individual needs.

Of course, all this pampering doesn't come cheap. Massages are generally $95 to $195 for 50 minutes and $150 to $250 for 80 minutes; body treatments are in the $150 to $250 range; and alternative healthcare treatments can be has high as $200 to $300. But you may think it's worth the expense to banish your tension and stress.

13 THE BEST SPAS

- **ANARA Spa at the Grand Hyatt Kauai** (✆ **808/240-6440**): Get rid of stress and be pampered in a Hawaiian atmosphere where the spirit of aloha reigns. An elegant 25,000-square-foot spa, ANARA (A New Age Restorative Approach) focuses on Hawaiian culture and healing, with some 16 treatment rooms, a lap pool, fitness facilities, lava rock showers that open to the tropical air, outdoor whirlpools, a 24-head Swiss shower, Turkish steam rooms, Finnish saunas, and botanical soaking tubs. The menu of treatments includes a four-handed massage (two therapists at once), which is not to be missed. See p. 101.
- **Hanalei Day Spa** (✆ **808/826-6621**): Located on the grounds of the Hanalei Colony Resort in Haena, this small but wonderfully effective spa not only has a full menu of massages, body treatments, and body wraps, but also specializes in ayurvedic treatments to soothe and comfort your weary body. Spa owner and ayurveda practitioner Darci Frankel is a recognized expert in the field of ayurvedic treatments. See p. 128.
- **Princeville Health Club & Spa, Princeville Resort** (✆ **808/826-5030**): This spa offers good value. Not only are the treatments a full 60 minutes (versus the standard 50 min. in most spas), but prices are also quite a bit lower than what many spas charge. Just a short 7-minute drive from the Princeville Hotel, this 10,000-square-foot boutique spa has such amenities as an 82-foot heated lap pool, outdoor whirlpool, sauna, steam room, five treatment rooms (plus massage cabanas poolside at the hotel), exercise classes, a weight room, a cardio room, and even babysitting services. See p. 125.

2 Hawaii in Depth

Today, other tropical islands are closing in on the 50th state's position as the world's premier beach destination. But Hawaii isn't just another pretty place in the sun. There's an undeniable quality ingrained in the local culture and lifestyle—the quick smiles to strangers, the feeling of family, the automatic extension of courtesy and tolerance. It's the aloha spirit.

1 HISTORY 101

Paddling outrigger canoes, the first ancestors of today's Hawaiians followed the stars and birds across a trackless sea to Hawaii, which they called "the land of raging fire." Those first settlers were part of the great Polynesian migration that settled the vast triangle of islands stretching from New Zealand in the southwest to Easter Island in the east to Hawaii in the north. No one is sure exactly when they came to Hawaii from Tahiti and the Marquesas Islands, some 2,500 miles to the south, but a dog-bone fishhook found at the southernmost tip of the Big Island has been carbon-dated to A.D. 700.

An entire Hawaiian culture arose from these settlers. Each island became a separate kingdom. The inhabitants built temples, fishponds, and aqueducts to irrigate taro plantations. Sailors became farmers and fishermen. The *alii* (high-ranking chiefs) created a caste system and established taboos. Ritual human sacrifices were common.

THE "FATAL CATASTROPHE" No ancient Hawaiian ever imagined that a *haole* (a white person; literally, one with "no breath") would ever appear on one of these "floating islands." But then one day, in 1779, just such a person sailed into Waimea Bay on Kauai, where he was welcomed as the god Lono.

The man was 50-year-old Captain James Cook, already famous in Britain for "discovering" much of the South Pacific. Now on his third great voyage of exploration, Cook had set sail from Tahiti northward across uncharted waters to find the mythical Northwest Passage that was said to link the Pacific and Atlantic oceans. On his way, Cook stumbled upon the Hawaiian Islands quite by chance. He named them the Sandwich Islands, for the Earl of Sandwich, first lord of the admiralty, who had bankrolled the expedition.

Overnight, Stone-Age Hawaii entered the age of iron. Gifts were presented and objects traded: nails for fresh water, pigs, and the affections of Hawaiian women. The sailors brought syphilis, measles, and other diseases to which the Hawaiians had no natural immunity, thereby unwittingly wreaking havoc on the native population.

After his unsuccessful attempt to find the Northwest Passage, Cook returned to Kealakekua Bay on the Big Island, where a fight broke out over an alleged theft, and the great navigator was killed by a blow to the head. After this "fatal catastrophe," the British survivors sailed home. But Hawaii was now on the sea charts. French, Russian, American, and other traders on the fur route between Canada's Hudson Bay Company and China anchored in Hawaii to get fresh water. More trade—and more disastrous liaisons—ensued.

Two more sea captains left indelible marks on the islands: The first was American John Kendrick, who, in 1791, stripped Hawaii of its sandalwood and sailed to China. The second captain was Englishman George Vancouver, who, in 1793, left cows and sheep, which spread out to the high-tide lines. King Kamehameha I sent to Mexico and Spain for cowboys to round up the wild livestock, thus beginning the islands' *paniolo* (Hawaiian cowboy) tradition.

The tightly woven Hawaiian society, enforced by royalty and religious edicts, began to unravel after the death in 1819 of King Kamehameha I, who had used guns seized from a British ship to unite the islands under his rule. One of his successors, Queen Kaahumanu, abolished the old taboos, thus opening the door for religion of another form.

STAYING TO DO WELL In April 1820, God-fearing missionaries arrived from New England, bent on converting the pagans. Intent on instilling their brand of rock-ribbed Christianity on the islands, the missionaries clothed the natives, banned them from dancing the hula, and nearly dismantled their ancient culture. They tried to keep the whalers and sailors out of the bawdy houses, where a flood of whiskey quenched fleet-size thirsts, and the virtue of native women was never safe. They taught reading and writing, created the 12-letter Hawaiian alphabet, started a printing press, and began recording the islands' history, until then only an oral account in remembered chants.

Children of the missionaries became the islands' business leaders and politicians. They married Hawaiians and stayed on in the islands, causing one wag to remark that the missionaries "came to do good and stayed to do well." In 1848, King Kamehameha III proclaimed the Great Mahele (division), which enabled commoners and, eventually, foreigners to own crown land. In two generations, more than 80% of all private land was in *haole* hands. Sugar planters imported waves of immigrants to work the fields as contract laborers. The first Chinese came in 1852, followed by Portuguese in 1878, and Japanese in 1885.

King David Kalakaua was elected to the throne in 1874. This popular "Merrie Monarch" built Iolani Palace in 1882, threw extravagant parties, and lifted the prohibitions on the hula and other native arts. For this, he was much loved. He also gave Pearl Harbor to the United States; it became the westernmost bastion of the U.S. Navy. In 1891, King Kalakaua visited chilly San Francisco, caught a cold, and died in the royal suite of the Sheraton Palace. His sister, Queen Liliuokalani, assumed the throne.

A SAD FAREWELL On January 17, 1893, a group of American sugar planters and missionary descendants, with the support of gun-toting U.S. Marines, imprisoned Queen Liliuokalani in her own palace, where she penned the sorrowful lyric "Aloha Oe," Hawaii's song of farewell. The monarchy was dead.

A new republic was established, controlled by Sanford Dole, a powerful sugarcane planter. In 1898, through annexation, Hawaii became an American territory ruled by Dole. His fellow sugar-cane planters, known as the Big Five, controlled banking, shipping, hardware, and every other facet of economic life on the islands.

Oahu's central Ewa Plain soon filled with row crops. The Dole family planted pineapple on its vast acreage. Planters imported more contract laborers from Puerto Rico (1900), Korea (1903), and the Philippines (1907–31). Most of the new immigrants stayed on to establish families and become a part of the islands. Meanwhile, the native Hawaiians became a landless minority.

For nearly a century on Hawaii, sugar was king, generously subsidized by the

U.S. government. The sugar planters dominated the territory's economy, shaped its social fabric, and kept the islands in a colonial-plantation era with bosses and field hands. But the workers eventually went on strike for higher wages and improved working conditions, and the planters found themselves unable to compete with cheap Third World labor costs.

THE TOURISTS ARRIVE Tourism proper began in the 1860s. Kilauea Volcano was one of the world's prime attractions for adventure travelers, who rode on horseback 29 miles from Hilo to peer into the boiling hellfire. In 1865, a grass version of Volcano House was built on the Halemaumau Crater rim to shelter visitors; it was Hawaii's first tourist hotel. But tourism really got off the ground with the demise of the plantation era.

In 1901, W. C. Peacock built the elegant Beaux Arts Moana Hotel on Waikiki Beach, and W. C. Weedon convinced Honolulu businessmen to bankroll his plan to advertise Hawaii in San Francisco. Armed with a stereopticon and tinted photos of Waikiki, Weedon sailed off, in 1902, for 6 months of lecture tours to introduce "those remarkable people and the beautiful lands of Hawaii." He drew packed houses. A tourism-promotion bureau was formed in 1903, and about 2,000 visitors came to Hawaii that year.

Steamships were Hawaii's tourism lifeline. It took 4½ days to sail from San Francisco to Honolulu. Streamers, leis, and pomp welcomed each Matson liner at downtown's Aloha Tower. Well-heeled visitors brought trunks, servants, even their Rolls-Royces, and stayed for months. Hawaii amused the idle rich with personal tours, floral parades, and shows spotlighting that naughty dance, the hula.

Beginning in 1935, and running for the next 40 years, Webley Edwards' weekly live radio show, "Hawaii Calls," planted the sounds of Waikiki—surf, sliding steel guitar, sweet Hawaiian harmonies, drumbeats—in the hearts of millions of listeners in the United States, Australia, and Canada.

By 1936, visitors could fly to Honolulu from San Francisco on the *Hawaii Clipper*, a seven-passenger Pan American Martin M-130 flying boat, for $360 one-way. The flight took 21 hours, 33 minutes. Modern tourism was born, with five flying boats providing daily service. The 1941 visitor count was a brisk 31,846 through December 6.

WORLD WAR II & ITS AFTERMATH On December 7, 1941, Japanese Zeros came out of the rising sun to bomb American warships based at Pearl Harbor. This was the "day of infamy" that plunged the United States into World War II.

The aftermath of the attack brought immediate changes to the islands. Martial law was declared, stripping the Big Five cartel of its absolute power in a single day. Feared to be spies, Japanese Americans and German Americans were interned in Hawaii as well as in California. Hawaii was "blacked out" at night, Waikiki Beach was strung with barbed wire, and Aloha Tower was painted in camouflage. Only young men bound for the Pacific came to Hawaii during the war years. Many came back to graves in a cemetery called Punchbowl.

The postwar years saw the beginnings of Hawaii's faux culture. Harry Yee invented the Blue Hawaii cocktail and dropped in a tiny Japanese parasol. Vic Bergeron created the mai tai, a rum and fresh-lime-juice drink, and opened Trader Vic's, America's first theme restaurant that featured the art, decor, and food of Polynesia. Arthur Godfrey picked up a ukulele and began singing *hapa-haole* tunes on early TV shows. Burt Lancaster and Deborah Kerr made love in the surf at Hanauma Bay in 1954's *From Here to Eternity.* In 1955, Henry J. Kaiser built the Hilton Hawaiian Village, and the 11-story high-rise Princess Kaiulani Hotel opened on a site where the real princess once played. Hawaii greeted 109,000 visitors that year.

STATEHOOD In 1959, Hawaii became the 50th of the United States. That year also saw the arrival of the first jet airliners, which brought 250,000 tourists to the fledgling state. The personal touch that had defined aloha gave way to the sheer force of numbers. Waikiki's room count virtually doubled in 2 years, from 16,000 units in 1969 to 31,000 in 1971; more followed before city fathers finally clamped a growth lid on the world's most famous resort. By 1980, annual arrivals had reached four million.

In the early 1980s, the Japanese began traveling overseas in record numbers, and they brought lots of yen to spend. Their effect on sales in Hawaii was phenomenal: European boutiques opened branches in Honolulu, and duty-free shopping became the main supporter of Honolulu International Airport. Japanese investors competed for the chance to own or build part of Hawaii. Hotels sold so fast and at such unbelievable prices that heads began to spin with dollar signs.

In 1986, Hawaii's visitor count passed five million. Just 2 years later, it went over six million. Expensive fantasy megaresorts bloomed on the neighbor islands like giant artificial flowers, swelling the luxury market with ever-swankier accommodations.

The highest visitor count ever recorded was 6.9 million in 1990, but the bubble burst in early 1991, with the Gulf War and worldwide recessions. In 1992, Hurricane Iniki devastated Kauai, which is only now staggering back to its feet. Airfare wars sent Americans to Mexico and the Caribbean. Overbuilt with luxury hotels, Hawaii slashed its room rates, giving middle-class consumers access to high-end digs at affordable prices—a trend that continues as Hawaii struggles to stay atop the tourism heap.

2 HAWAII TODAY

A CULTURAL RENAISSANCE A conch shell sounds, a young man in a bright feather cape chants, torch lights flicker at sunset on Waikiki Beach, and hula dancers begin telling their graceful centuries-old stories. It's a cultural scene out of the past come to life once again—for Hawaii is enjoying a renaissance of hula, chant, and other aspects of its ancient culture.

The biggest, longest, and most elaborate celebrations of Hawaiian culture are the Aloha Festivals, which encompass more than 500 cultural events from August through October. "Our goal is to teach and share our culture," says Gloriann Akau, who manages the Big Island's Aloha Festivals. "In 1946, after the war, Hawaiians needed an identity. We were lost and needed to regroup. When we started to celebrate our culture, we began to feel proud. We have a wonderful culture that had been buried for a number of years. This brought it out again. Self-esteem is more important than making a lot of money."

In 1985, native Hawaiian educator, author, and *kupuna* George Kanahele started integrating Hawaiian values into hotels like the Big Island's Mauna Lani and Maui's Kaanapali Beach Hotel. (A *kupuna* is a respected elder with leadership qualities.) "You have the responsibility to preserve and enhance the Hawaiian culture, not because it's going to make money for you, but because it's the right thing to do," Kanahele said. "Ultimately, the only thing unique about Hawaii is its Hawaiianness. Hawaiianness is our competitive edge."

From general managers to maids, resort employees went through hours of Hawaiian cultural training. They held focus groups to discuss the meaning of *aloha*—the Hawaiian concept of unconditional love—and applied it to their work and their lives. Now many hotels have joined the movement and instituted Hawaiian programs. No longer content with teaching hula as a joke, resorts now employ a real *kumu hula* (hula teacher) to instruct visitors, and have a *kupuna* take guests on treks to visit *heiau* (temples) and ancient petroglyph sites.

THE QUESTION OF SOVEREIGNTY The Hawaiian cultural renaissance has also made its way into politics. Many *kanaka maoli* (native people) are demanding restoration of rights taken away more than a century ago when the U.S. overthrew the Hawaiian monarchy. Their demands were not lost on President Bill Clinton, who was picketed at a Democratic political fundraiser at Waikiki Beach in July 1993. Four months later, Clinton signed a document stating that the U.S. Congress "apologizes to Native Hawaiians on behalf of the people of the United States for the overthrow of the Kingdom of Hawaii on January 17, 1893, with the participation of agents and citizens of the United States, and deprivation of the rights of Native Hawaiians to self-determination."

But even neo-nationalists aren't convinced that complete self-determination is possible. Each of the 30 identifiable sovereignty organizations (and more than 100 splinter groups) has a different stated goal, ranging from total independence to nation-within-a-nation status, similar to that of Native Indians. In 1993 the state legislature created a Hawaiian Sovereignty Advisory Commission to "determine the will of the native Hawaiian people." The commission plans to pose the sovereignty question in a referendum open to anyone over 18 with Hawaiian blood, no matter where they live. The question still remains unanswered.

3 LIFE & LANGUAGE

Plantations brought so many different people to Hawaii that the state is now a rainbow of ethnic groups. Living here are Caucasians, African Americans, American Indians, Eskimos, Japanese, Chinese, Filipinos, Koreans, Tahitians, Vietnamese, Hawaiians, Samoans, Tongans, and other Asian and Pacific islanders. Add a few Canadians, Dutch, English, French, Germans, Irish, Italians, Portuguese, Scottish, Puerto Ricans, and Spaniards. Everyone's a minority here.

THE HAWAIIAN LANGUAGE

Almost everyone here speaks English, so except for pronouncing the names of places, you should have no trouble communicating in Hawaii.

But many folks in Hawaii now speak Hawaiian as well, for the ancient language is making a comeback. All visitors will hear the words *aloha* and *mahalo* (thank you). If you've just arrived, you're a *malihini.* Someone who's been here a long time is a *kamaaina.* When you finish a job or your meal, you are *pau* (over). On Friday, it's *pau hana,* work over. You put *pupu* (Hawaii's version of hors d'oeuvres) in your mouth when you go *pau hana.*

The Hawaiian alphabet, created by the New England missionaries, has only 12 letters: the five regular vowels (a, e, i, o, and u) and seven consonants (h, k, l, m, n, p, and w). The vowels are pronounced in the Roman fashion, that is, *ah, ay, ee, oh,* and *oo* (as in "too")—not *ay, ee, eye, oh,* and *you,* as in English. For example, *huhu* is pronounced *who-who.* Most vowels are sounded separately, though some are pronounced together, as in Kalakaua: *Kah-lah-cow-ah.*

WHAT HAOLE MEANS When Hawaiians first saw Western visitors, they called the pale-skinned, frail men *haole,* because they looked so out of breath. In Hawaiian, *ha* means *breath,* and *ole* means an absence of what precedes it. In other words, a lifeless-looking person. Today, the term *haole* is generally a synonym for Caucasian or foreigner and is used casually without any intended disrespect. However, if uttered by an angry stranger who adds certain adjectives (like "stupid"), the term can be construed as a mild racial slur.

SOME HAWAIIAN WORDS Here are some basic Hawaiian words that you'll often hear in Hawaii and see throughout this book. For a more complete list of Hawaiian words, point your Web browser to **www.geocities.com/~olelo/hltableofcontents.html**.

akamai smart

alii Hawaiian royalty

aloha greeting or farewell

halau school

hale house or building

heiau Hawaiian temple or place of worship

hui club, assembly

kahuna priest or expert

kamaaina old-timer

kapa tapa, bark cloth

kapu taboo, forbidden

keiki child

lanai porch or veranda

lomilomi massage

mahalo thank you

makai a direction, toward the sea

malihini stranger, newcomer

mana spirit power

mauka a direction, toward the mountains

muumuu loose-fitting gown or dress

nene official state bird, a goose

ono delicious

pali cliff

paniolo Hawaiian cowboy(s)

wiki quick

PIDGIN: 'EH FO'REAL, BRAH

If you venture beyond the tourist areas, you might hear another local tongue: pidgin English. A conglomeration of slang and words from the Hawaiian language, pidgin developed as a method sugar planters used to communicate with their Chinese laborers in the 1800s.

"Broke da mouth" (tastes really good) is the favorite pidgin phrase and one you might hear; "'Eh fo'real, brah" means "It's true, brother." You could be invited to hear an elder "talk story" (relating myths and memories) or to enjoy local treats like "shave ice" (a tropical snow cone) and "crack seed" (highly seasoned preserved fruit). But since pidgin is really the province of the locals, your visit to Hawaii is likely to pass without your hearing much pidgin at all.

4 A TASTE OF HAWAII

TRIED & TRUE: HAWAII REGIONAL CUISINE

Hawaii's tried-and-true baseline remains Hawaii Regional Cuisine (HRC), established in the mid-1980s in a culinary revolution that catapulted Hawaii into the global epicurean arena. The international training, creative vigor, fresh ingredients, and cross-cultural menus of the 12 original HRC chefs have made the islands a dining destination applauded and emulated nationwide. (In a tip of the toque to island tradition, *ahi*—a word ubiquitous in Hawaii—has replaced *tuna* on many chic New York menus.) And other options have proliferated at all levels of the local dining spectrum: Waves of new Asian residents have transplanted the traditions of their homelands to the fertile soil of Hawaii, resulting in unforgettable taste treats true to their Thai, Vietnamese, Japanese, Chinese, and Indo-Pacific roots. When combined with the bountiful, fresh harvests from sea and land for which Hawaii is known, these ethnic and culinary traditions take on renewed vigor and a cross-cultural, uniquely Hawaiian quality.

Hawaii Regional Cuisine has evolved as Hawaii's singular cooking style, what some say is this country's current gastronomic, as well as geographic, frontier. It highlights the fresh seafood and produce of Hawaii's rich waters and volcanic soil, the cultural traditions of Hawaii's ethnic groups, and the skills of well-trained chefs who broke ranks with their European predecessors to forge new ground in the 50th state.

Fresh ingredients are foremost here. Farmers and fishermen work together to provide steady supplies of just-harvested seafood, seaweed, fern shoots, vine-ripened tomatoes, goat cheese, lamb, herbs, taro, gourmet lettuces, and countless harvests from land and sea. These ingredients wind up in myriad forms on ever-changing menus, prepared in Asian and Western culinary styles. Exotic fruits introduced by recent Southeast Asian emigrants—such as sapodilla, soursop, and *rambutan*—are beginning to appear regularly in Chinatown markets. Aquacultural seafood, from seaweed to salmon to lobster, is a staple on many menus. Additionally, fresh-fruit sauces (mango, litchi, papaya, pineapple, guava), ginger-sesame-wasabi flavorings, corn cakes with sake sauces, tamarind and fish sauces, coconut-chile accents, tropical-fruit vinaigrettes, and other local and newly arrived seasonings from Southeast Asia and the Pacific impart unique qualities to the preparations.

Here's a sampling of what you can expect to find on a Hawaii Regional menu: seared Hawaiian fish with lilikoi-shrimp butter; taro-crab cakes; Pahoa corn cakes; Molokai sweet-potato or breadfruit vichyssoise; Ka'u orange sauce and Kahua Ranch lamb; fern shoots from Waipio Valley; Maui onion soup and Hawaiian bouillabaisse, with fresh snapper, Kona crab, and fresh aquacultural shrimp; blackened ahi summer rolls; herb-crusted onaga; and gourmet Waimanalo greens, picked that day. You may also encounter locally made cheeses, squash, and taro risottos, Polynesian imu-baked foods, and guava-smoked meats. If there's pasta or risotto or rack of lamb on the menu, it could be *nori* (red algae) linguine with *opihi* (limpet) sauce, or risotto with local seafood served in taro cups, or rack of lamb in cabernet and *hoisin* sauce (fermented soybean, garlic, and spices). Watch for ponzu sauce, too; it's lemony and zesty, a welcome new staple on local menus.

PLATE LUNCHES & MORE: LOCAL FOOD

At the other end of the spectrum is the vast and endearing world of "local food." By that, we mean plate lunches and poke, shave ice and saimin, bento lunches and manapua—cultural hybrids all.

Reflecting a polyglot population of many styles and ethnicities, Hawaii's idiosyncratic dining scene is eminently inclusive. Consider Surfer Chic: Barefoot in the sand, in a swimsuit, you chow down on a **plate lunch** ordered from a lunch wagon, consisting of fried mahimahi, "two scoops rice," macaroni salad, and a few leaves of green, typically julienned cabbage. (Generally, teriyaki beef and shoyu chicken are options.) Heavy gravy is often the condiment of choice, accompanied by a soft drink in a paper cup. Like **saimin**—the local version of noodles in broth topped with scrambled eggs, green onions, and, sometimes, pork—the plate lunch is Hawaii's version of high camp.

Because this is Hawaii, at least a few licks of *poi*—cooked, pounded taro (the traditional Hawaiian staple crop)—and other examples of indigenous cuisine are a must. Other **native foods** include those from before and after Western contact, such as *laulau* (pork, chicken, or fish steamed in ti leaves), *kalua* pork (pork cooked in a Polynesian underground oven known here as an *imu*), *lomi* salmon (salted salmon with tomatoes and green onions), squid *luau* (cooked in coconut milk and taro tops), *poke* (cubed raw fish seasoned with onions and seaweed and the occasional sprinkling of roasted *kukui* nuts), *haupia* (creamy coconut pudding), and *kulolo* (steamed pudding of coconut, brown sugar, and taro).

Bento, another popular quick meal available throughout Hawaii, is a compact, boxed assortment of picnic fare usually consisting of neatly arranged sections of rice, pickled vegetables, and fried chicken, beef, or pork. Increasingly, however, the bento is becoming more health-conscious, as in macrobiotic bento lunches or vegetarian brown-rice bentos. A derivative of the modest lunch box for Japanese immigrants who once labored in the sugar and pineapple fields, bentos are dispensed everywhere, from department stores to corner delis and supermarkets.

Also from the plantations come **manapua,** a bready, doughy sphere filled with tasty fillings of sweetened pork or sweet beans. In the old days, the Chinese "manapua man" would make his rounds with bamboo containers balanced on a rod over his shoulders. Today you'll find white or whole-wheat manapua containing chicken, vegetables, curry, and other savory fillings.

The daintier Chinese delicacy **dim sum** is made of translucent wrappers filled with fresh seafood, pork hash, and vegetables, served for breakfast and lunch in Chinatown restaurants. The Hong Kong–style dumplings are ordered fresh and hot from bamboo steamers from invariably brusque servers who move their carts from table to table. Much like hailing a taxi in Manhattan, you have to be quick and loud for dim sum.

For dessert or a snack, particularly on Oahu's north shore, the prevailing choice is **shave ice,** the island version of a snow cone. Particularly on hot, humid days, long lines of shave-ice lovers gather for the rainbow-colored cones heaped with finely shaved ice and topped with sweet tropical syrups. (The sweet-sour *li hing mui* flavor is a current rage.) The fast-melting mounds, which require prompt, efficient consumption, are quite the local summer ritual for sweet tooths.

AHI, ONO & OPAKAPAKA: A HAWAIIAN SEAFOOD PRIMER

The seafood in Hawaii has been described as the best in the world. In Janice Wald Henderson's pivotal book *The New Cuisine of Hawaii,* acclaimed chef Nobuyuki Matsuhisa (chef/owner of Matsuhisa in Beverly Hills and Nobu in Manhattan and London) writes, "As a chef who specializes in fresh seafood, I am in awe of the quality of Hawaii's fish; it is unparalleled anywhere else in the world." And why not? Without a doubt, the islands' surrounding waters, including the waters of the remote northwestern Hawaiian Islands, and a growing aquaculture industry contribute to the high quality of the seafood here.

The reputable restaurants in Hawaii buy fresh fish daily at predawn auctions or from local fishermen. Some chefs even catch their ingredients themselves. "Still wiggling" or "just off the hook" are the ultimate terms for freshness in Hawaii. The fish can then be grilled over *kiawe* (mesquite) or prepared in innumerable other ways.

Although most menus include the Western description for the fresh fish used, most often the local nomenclature is listed, turning dinner for the uninitiated into a confusing, quasi-foreign experience. To help familiarize you with the menu language of Hawaii, here's a basic glossary of island fish:

ahi yellowfin or bigeye tuna, important for its use in sashimi and poke at sushi bars and in Hawaii Regional Cuisine

aku skipjack tuna, heavily used by local families in home cooking and poke

ehu red snapper, delicate and sumptuous, yet lesser known than opakapaka

hapuupuu grouper, a sea bass whose use is expanding from ethnic to nonethnic restaurants

hebi spearfish, mildly flavored, and frequently featured as the "catch of the day" in upscale restaurants

kajiki Pacific blue marlin, also called *au,* with a firm flesh and high fat content that make it a plausible substitute for tuna in some raw fish dishes and as a grilled item on menus

kumu goatfish, a luxury item on Chinese and upscale menus, served *en papillote* or steamed whole, Asian-style, with sesame oil, scallions, ginger, and garlic

mahimahi dolphin fish (the game fish, not the mammal) or dorado, a classic sweet, white-fleshed fish requiring vigilance among purists, because it's often disguised as fresh when it's actually "fresh-frozen"—a big difference

monchong bigscale or sickle pomfret, an exotic, tasty fish, scarce but gaining a higher profile on Hawaiian Island menus

nairagi striped marlin, also called *au;* good as sashimi and in poke, and often substituted for ahi in raw-fish products

onaga ruby snapper, a luxury fish, versatile, moist, and flaky

ono wahoo, firmer and drier than the snappers, often served grilled and in sandwiches

opah moonfish, rich and fatty, and versatile—cooked, raw, smoked, and broiled

opakapaka pink snapper, light, flaky, and luxurious, suited for sashimi, poaching, sautéing, and baking; the best-known upscale fish

papio jack trevally, light, firm, and flavorful, and favored in island cookery

shutome broadbill swordfish, of beeflike texture and rich flavor

tombo albacore tuna, with a high fat content, suitable for grilling and sautéing

uhu parrotfish, most often encountered steamed, Chinese-style

uku gray snapper of clear, pale-pink flesh, delicately flavored and moist

ulua large jack trevally, firm-fleshed and versatile

5 THE NATURAL WORLD: AN ENVIRONMENTAL GUIDE TO THE ISLANDS

The first Hawaiian Islands were born of violent volcanic eruptions that took place deep beneath the ocean's surface, about 70 million years ago—more than 200 million years after the major continental landmasses had been formed. As soon as the islands emerged, Mother Nature's fury began to carve beauty from barren rock. Untiring volcanoes spewed forth rivers of fire that cooled into stone. Severe tropical storms, some with hurricane-force winds, battered and blasted the cooling lava rock into a series of shapes. Ferocious earthquakes flattened, shattered, and reshaped the islands into precipitous valleys, jagged cliffs, and recumbent flatlands. Monstrous surf and gigantic tidal waves rearranged and polished the lands above and below the reaches of the tide.

It took millions of years for nature to shape the familiar form of Diamond Head on Oahu, Maui's majestic peak of Haleakala, the waterfalls of Molokai's northern side, the reefs of Hulopoe Bay on Lanai, and the lush rainforests of the Big Island. The result is an island chain like no other—a tropical landscape rich in unique flora and fauna, surrounded by a vibrant underwater world.

THE ISLAND LANDSCAPES

OAHU Oahu is the third-largest island in Hawaii (behind the Big Island and Maui). As the home of Honolulu, it's also the most urban island, with a population of nearly 900,000. Oahu is defined by two mountain ranges: the Waianae Ridge in the west, and the jagged Koolau in the east, which form a backdrop for Honolulu. These ranges divide the island into three different environments. The windward (eastern) side is lush with greenery, ferns, tropical plants, and waterfalls. On the leeward (western) side, the area between the Waianae Ridge and the ocean is drier, with sparse vegetation, little rainfall, and an arid landscape. Between the two mountain ranges lies the central Ewa Valley; it's moderate in temperature and vibrant with tropical plants, agricultural fields, and trees.

HAWAII, THE BIG ISLAND By far the largest island at some 4,034 square miles (and still growing), the Big Island is twice the size of all the other islands combined. Here you'll find every type of climate zone existing in Hawaii. It's not uncommon for there to be 12 feet of snow on the two largest mountain peaks, 13,796-foot Mauna Kea and 13,680-foot Mauna Loa. These mountains are the tallest in the state; what's more, when measured from their true base on the ocean floor, they reach 32,000 feet, making them the tallest mountains in the world. The 4,077-foot Kilauea Volcano has been continuously erupting since January 3, 1983, and has added more than 600 acres of new land to the Big Island since then. Just a few miles from the barely cooled barren lava lies a pristine rainforest. On the southern end of the island is an arid desert. The rest of the island contains tropical terrain; white-, black-, and even green-sand beaches; windswept grasslands; and productive farming and ranching areas growing tropical fruits, macadamia nuts, coffee, and ornamental flowers.

MAUI When two volcanoes—Mauna Kahalawai, a 5,277-foot ancient volcano in the West Maui Mountains, and 10,000-foot Haleakala—flowed together a million or so years ago, the event created a "Valley Isle" with a range of climates from arid desert to tropical rainforest. This 728-square-mile island is the only place in the world where you can drive from sea level to 10,000 feet in just 38 miles, passing from tropical beaches through sugar and pineapple plantations and rolling grassy hills up past the timber line to the lunarlike surface of the top of Haleakala. In addition to 33 miles of public beaches on the south and west shores, Maui is home to the arid lands of Kihei, the swampy bogs of the West Maui Mountains, the rainforest of Hana, and the desert of Kaupo.

MOLOKAI Roughly the shape and size of Manhattan, Molokai is 37 miles long and 10 miles wide, with a "thumb" protruding out of the North Shore. The North Shore begins on the west, with miles of white-sand beaches that fringe a desertlike landscape. The thumb—the Kalaupapa Peninsula—is cut off by a fence of cliffs, some 2,000 feet tall, that line the remainder of the north side. Molokai can be divided into two areas: the dry west end; and the rainy, tropical east and north ends. Its highest point is Mount Kamakou, at 4,970 feet.

LANAI This small, kidney bean–shaped island—only 13 miles wide by 17 miles long—rises sharply out of the ocean, with cliffs on the west side that rise to a high point of 3,370 feet. Lanai slopes down to sea level on the east and south sides. The only town, Lanai City, sits in the clouds at 1,600 feet. The island's peak is covered with Norfolk pines and is usually shrouded in clouds, while the arid beaches survive on minimal rainfall. One area in particular stands out: the Garden of the Gods, just 7 miles from Lanai City, where oddly strewn boulders lie in the amber- and ocher-colored dirt and bizarre stone formations dot the landscape. The ancient Hawaiians formed romantic legends explaining this enigma, but modern-day scientists still debate its origins.

KAUAI This compact island, 25 miles long by 33 miles wide, has Mount Waialeale, the island's highest point at nearly 5,000 feet and the Earth's wettest spot, with more than 400 inches of rain annually. Just west of Mount Waialeale is the barren landscape of Waimea Canyon, dubbed "the Grand Canyon of the Pacific"—the result of the once 10,000-foot-tall Olokele shield volcano, which collapsed and formed a *caldera* (crater) some 3,600 feet deep and 14 miles across. Peaks and craters aren't Kauai's only distinctive landscape features, though: Miles of white-sand beaches rim most of the island, with majestic 2,700-foot cliffs—the spectacular Na Pali Coast—completing the circle. Lush tropical jungle inhabits the north side of the island, while balmy, palm tree–lined beaches are located in the south.

THE FLORA OF THE ISLANDS

Hawaii is filled with sweet-smelling flowers, lush vegetation, and exotic plant life.

AFRICAN TULIP TREES Even from afar, you can see the flaming red flowers on these large trees, which can grow to be more than 50 feet tall. The buds hold water, and Hawaiian children use the flowers as water pistols.

ANGEL'S TRUMPETS These small trees can grow up to 20 feet tall, with an abundance of large (up to 10-in. diameter) pendants—white or pink flowers that resemble, well, trumpets. The Hawaiians call them *nana-honua,* which means "earth gazing." The flowers, which bloom continually from early spring to late fall, have a musky scent. ***Warning:*** All parts of the plant are poisonous and contain a strong narcotic.

ANTHURIUMS Anthuriums originally came from the tropical Americas and the Caribbean islands. There are more than 550 species, but the most popular are the heart-shaped red, orange, pink, white, and purple flowers with tail-like spathes. Look for the heart-shaped green leaves in shaded areas. These exotic plants have no scent but will last several weeks as cut flowers. Anthuriums are particularly prevalent on the Big Island.

BANYAN TREES Among the world's largest trees, banyans have branches that grow out and away from the trunk, forming descending roots that grow down to the ground to feed and form additional trunks, making the tree very stable during tropical storms. The banyan in the courtyard next to the old courthouse in Lahaina, Maui, is an excellent example of a spreading banyan—it covers ⅔ acre.

BIRDS-OF-PARADISE These natives of Africa have become something of a trademark of Hawaii. They're easily recognizable by the orange and blue flowers nestled in gray-green bracts, looking somewhat like birds in flight.

BOUGAINVILLEA Originally from Brazil, these vines feature colorful, tissue-thin bracts, ranging in color from majestic purple to fiery orange, that hide tiny white flowers. A good place to spot them is on the Big Island, along the Queen Kaahumanu Highway stretching from Kona Airport to Kailua-Kona.

BREADFRUIT TREES A large tree—more than 60 feet tall—with broad, sculpted, dark-green leaves, the famous breadfruit produces a round, head-size green fruit that's a staple in the diets of all Polynesians. When roasted or baked, the whitish-yellow meat tastes somewhat like a sweet potato.

BROMELIADS There are more than 1,400 species of bromeliads, of which the pineapple plant is the best known. "Bromes," as they're affectionately called, are generally spiky plants ranging in size from a few inches to several feet in diameter. They're popular not only for their unusual foliage, but also for their strange and wonderful flowers. Used widely in landscaping and interior decoration, especially in resort areas, bromeliads are found on every island.

COFFEE Hawaii is the only state that produces coffee commercially. Coffee is an evergreen shrub with shiny, waxy, dark-green pointed leaves. The flower is a small, fragrant white blossom that develops into half-inch berries that turn bright red when ripe. Look for coffee at elevations above 1,500 feet on the Kona side of the Big Island and on large coffee plantations on Kauai, Molokai, Oahu, and Maui.

GINGER White and yellow ginger flowers are perhaps the most fragrant in Hawaii. Usually found in clumps growing 4 to 7 feet tall in areas blessed by rain, these sweet-smelling, 3-inch-wide flowers are composed of three dainty petal-like stamens and three long, thin petals. Ginger was introduced to Hawaii in the 19th century from the Indonesia-Malaysia area. Look for white and yellow ginger from late spring to fall. If you see ginger on the side of the road, stop and pick a few blossoms—your car will be filled with a divine fragrance the rest of the day.

Other members of the ginger family frequently seen in Hawaii include red, shell, and torch ginger. Red ginger consists of tall green stalks with foot-long red "flower heads." The red "petals" are actually bracts, which protect the 1-inch-long white flowers. Red ginger, which does not share the heavenly smell of white ginger, lasts a week or longer when cut. Look for red ginger from spring through late fall. Shell ginger, which originated in India and Burma, thrives in cool, wet mountain forests. These plants, with their pearly white, clamshell-like blossoms, bloom from spring to fall.

Perhaps the most exotic ginger is the red or pink torch ginger. Cultivated in Malaysia as seasoning, torch ginger rises directly out of the ground. The flower stalks, which are about 5 to 8 inches in length, resemble the fire of a lighted torch. This is one of the few types of ginger that can bloom year-round.

HELICONIA Some 80 species of the colorful heliconia family came to Hawaii from the Caribbean and Central and South America. The bright yellow, red, green, and orange bracts overlap and appear to unfold like origami birds. The most obvious heliconia to spot is the lobster claw, which resembles a string of boiled crustacean pincers. Another prolific heliconia is the parrot's beak: Growing to about hip height, it's composed of bright-orange flower bracts with black tips. Look for parrot's beaks in spring and summer.

HIBISCUS The 4- to 6-inch hibiscus flowers bloom year-round and come in a range of colors, from lily white to lipstick red. The flowers resemble crepe paper, with stamens and pistils protruding spire-like from the center. Hibiscus hedges can grow up to 15 feet tall. The yellow hibiscus is Hawaii's official state flower.

JACARANDA Beginning around March and sometimes lasting until early May, these huge lacy-leaved trees metamorphose into large clusters of spectacular lavender-blue sprays. The bell-shaped flowers drop quickly, leaving a majestic purple carpet beneath the tree.

MACADAMIA A transplant from Australia, macadamia nuts have become a commercial crop in recent decades in Hawaii, especially on the Big Island and Maui. The large trees—up to 60 feet tall—bear a hard-shelled nut encased in a leathery husk, which splits open and dries when the nut is ripe.

MONKEYPOD TREES The monkeypod is one of Hawaii's most majestic trees; it grows more than 80 feet tall and 100 feet across. Seen near older homes and in parks, the leaves of the monkeypod drop in February and March. Its wood is a favorite of woodworking artisans.

NIGHT-BLOOMING CEREUS Look along rock walls for this spectacular night-blooming flower. Originally from Central America, this vinelike member of the cactus family has green scalloped edges and produces foot-long white flowers that open as darkness falls and wither as the sun rises. The plant also bears an edible red fruit.

ORCHIDS To many minds, nothing says Hawaii more than orchids. The most widely grown variety—and the major source of flowers for leis and garnish for tropical libations—is the vanda orchid. The vandas used in Hawaii's commercial flower industry are generally lavender or white, but they grow in a rainbow of colors, shapes, and sizes. The orchids used for corsages are the large, delicate cattleya; the ones used in floral arrangements—you'll probably see them in your hotel lobby—are usually dendrobiums. On the Big Island, don't pass up a chance to wander through the numerous orchid farms around Hilo.

PANDANUS (HALA) Called *hala* by Hawaiians, pandanus is native to Polynesia. Thanks to its thick trunk, stiltlike supporting roots, and crown of long, swordlike leaves, the hala tree is easy to recognize. In what is quickly becoming a dying art, Hawaiians weave the *lau* (leaves) of the hala into hats, baskets, mats, bags, and the like.

PLUMERIA Also known as frangipani, this sweet-smelling, five-petal flower, found in clusters on trees, is the most popular choice of lei makers. The Singapore plumeria has five creamy-white petals, with a touch of yellow in the center. Another popular variety, *ruba*—with flowers from soft pink to flaming red—is also used in leis. When picking plumeria, be careful of the sap from the flower—it's poisonous and can stain clothes.

PROTEA Originally from South Africa, this unusual oversize shrub comes in more than 40 different varieties. The flowers of one species resemble pincushions; those of another look like a bouquet of feathers. Once dried, proteas will last for years.

SILVERSWORD This very uncommon and unusual plant is seen only on the Big Island and in the Haleakala Crater on Maui. The rare relative of the sunflower family blooms between July and September. The silversword in bloom is a fountain of red-petaled, daisylike flowers that turn silver soon after blooming.

TARO Around pools, near streams, and in neatly planted fields, you'll see these green heart-shaped leaves, whose dense roots are a Polynesian staple. The ancient Hawaiians pounded the roots into poi. Originally from Sri Lanka, taro not only is a food crop, but is also grown for ornamental reasons.

THE FAUNA OF THE ISLANDS

When the first Polynesians arrived in Hawaii between A.D. 500 and 800, scientists say they found some 67 varieties of endemic Hawaiian birds, a third of which are now believed to be extinct. They did not find any reptiles, amphibians, mosquitoes, lice, fleas, or even a cockroach.

There were only two endemic mammals: the hoary bat and the monk seal. The **hoary bat** must have accidentally blown to Hawaii at some point, from either North or South America. It can still be seen during its early evening forays, especially around the Kilauea Crater on the Big Island.

The **Hawaiian monk seal,** a relative of warm-water seals found in the Caribbean and the Mediterranean, was nearly slaughtered into extinction for its skin and oil during the 19th century. These seals have recently experienced a minor population explosion; sometimes they even turn up at various beaches throughout the state. They're protected under federal law by the Marine Mammals Protection Act. If you're fortunate enough to see a monk seal, just look; don't disturb one of Hawaii's living treasures.

The first Polynesians brought a few animals from home: dogs, pigs, and chickens (all were for eating), as well as rats (stowaways). All four species are still found in the Hawaiian wild today.

Birds

More species of native birds have become extinct in Hawaii in the last 200 years than anywhere else on the planet. Of 67 native species, 23 are extinct and 30 are endangered. Even the Hawaiian crow, the **alala,** is threatened.

The **ae'o,** or Hawaiian stilt—a 16-inch-long bird with a black head, black coat, white underside, and long pink legs—can be found in protected wetlands like the Kanaha Wildlife Sanctuary on Maui (where it shares its natural habitat with the Hawaiian coot), the Kealia Pond on Maui, and the Hanalei National Wildlife Refuge on Kauai, which is also home to the Hawaiian duck. Other areas in which you can see protected birds are the Kipuka Puaulu (Bird Park) and the Olaa Rain Forest, both in Hawaii Volcanoes National Park on the Big Island, and at Goat Island bird refuge off Oahu, where you can see wedge-tailed shearwaters nesting.

Another great birding venue is Kokee State Park on Kauai. Various native birds that have been spotted include some of the 22 species of the native honey creepers. Frequently seen are the **apapane** (a red bird with black wings and a curved black bill), **iiwi** (also red with black wings but with orange legs and a salmon-colored bill), **amakihi** (a plain olive-green bird with a long, straight bill), and **anianiau** (a tiny yellow bird with a thin, curved bill). Also in the forest is the **'elepaio,** a small gray flycatcher with an orange breast and an erect tail. The most common native bird at Kokee—and the most easily seen—is the **moa,** or red jungle fowl, a chicken brought to Hawaii by the Polynesians.

To get a good glimpse of the seabirds that frequent Hawaii, drive to Kilauea Point on Kauai's North Shore. Here you can easily spot **red-** and **white-footed boobies, wedge-tailed shearwaters, frigate birds, red-tailed tropic birds,** and the **Laysan albatross.**

Hawaii's state bird is the **nene.** It's being brought back from the brink of extinction through strenuous protection laws and captive breeding. A relative of the Canada goose, the nene stands about 2 feet high and has a black head and yellow cheeks. The approximately 500 nene in existence can be seen in only three places: on Maui at Haleakala National Park, and on the Big Island at Mauna Kea State Recreation Area bird sanctuary and on the slopes of Mauna Kea.

The Hawaiian short-eared owl, the **pueo,** which grows to between 12 and 17 inches, can be seen at dawn and dusk on Kauai, Maui, and the Big Island. According to legend, spotting a pueo is a good omen.

Leapin' Lizards!

Geckos are harmless, soft-skinned, insect-eating lizards that come equipped with suction pads on their feet, enabling them to climb walls and windows to reach tasty insects such as mosquitoes and cockroaches. You'll see them on windows outside a lighted room at night or hear their cheerful chirp.

Sea Life

Approximately 680 species of fish are known to inhabit the waters around the Hawaiian Islands. Of those, approximately 450 species stay close to the reef and inshore areas.

CORAL The reefs surrounding Hawaii are made up of various coral and algae. The living coral grows through sunlight that feeds a specialized algae, which, in turn, allows the development of the coral's calcareous skeleton. The reef, which takes thousands of years to develop, attracts and supports fish and crustaceans, which use it for food and habitat. Mother Nature can batter the reef with a strong storm, but humans have proven far more destructive.

The corals most frequently seen in Hawaii are hard, rocklike formations named for their familiar shapes: antler, cauliflower, finger, plate, and razor coral. Some coral appears soft, such as tube coral; it can be found in the ceilings of caves. Black coral, which resembles winter-bare trees or shrubs, is found at depths of more than 100 feet.

REEF FISH Of the approximately 450 types of reef fish here, about 27% are native to Hawaii and are found nowhere else in the world. During the millions of years it took for the islands to sprout up from the sea, ocean currents—mainly from Southeast Asia—carried thousands of marine animals and plants to Hawaii's reef; of those, approximately 100 species adapted and thrived. You're likely to spot one or more of the following fish while underwater.

Angelfish can be distinguished by the spine, located low on the gill plate. These fish are very shy; several species live in colonies close to coral.

Blennies are small, elongated fish, ranging from 2 to 10 inches long, with the majority in the 3- to 4-inch range. Blennies are so small that they can live in tide pools; you might have a hard time spotting one.

Butterfly fish, among the most colorful of the reef fish, are usually seen in pairs (scientists believe they mate for life) and appear to spend most of their day feeding. There are 22 species of butterfly fish, of which three (bluestripe, lemon or milletseed, and multiband or pebbled butterfly fish) are endemic. Most butterfly fish have a dark band through the eye and a spot near the tail resembling an eye, meant to confuse their predators (moray eels love to lunch on them).

Moray and **conger eels** are the most common eels seen in Hawaii. Morays are usually docile except when provoked or when there's food around. Unfortunately, some morays have been fed by divers and now associate divers with food; thus, they can become aggressive. But most morays like to keep to themselves. While morays may look menacing, conger eels look downright happy, with big lips and pectoral fins (situated so that they look like big ears) that give them the appearance of a perpetually smiling face. Conger eels have crushing teeth so they can feed on crustaceans; because they're sloppy eaters, they usually live with shrimp and crabs that feed off the crumbs they leave.

Parrotfish, one of the largest and most colorful of the reef fish, can grow up to 40 inches long. They're easy to spot—their front teeth are fused together, protruding like buck teeth that allow them to feed by scraping algae from rocks and coral. The rocks and coral pass through the parrotfish's system, resulting in fine sand. In fact, most of the white sand found in Hawaii is parrotfish waste; one large parrotfish can produce a ton of sand a year. Native parrotfish species include yellowbar, regal, and spectacled.

Scorpion fish are what scientists call "ambush predators:" They hide under camouflaged exteriors and ambush their prey. Several kinds sport a venomous dorsal spine. These fish don't have a gas bladder, so when they stop swimming, they sink—that's why you usually find them "resting" on ledges and on the ocean bottom. They're not aggressive, but be very careful where you put your hands and feet in the water so as to avoid those venomous spines.

Surgeonfish, sometimes called *tang,* get their name from the scalpel-like spines located on each side of the body near the base of the tail. Several surgeonfish, such as the brightly colored yellow tang, are boldly colored; others are adorned in more conservative shades of gray, brown, or black. The only endemic surgeonfish—and the most abundant in Hawaiian waters—is the convict tang, a pale white fish with vertical black stripes (similar to a convict's uniform).

Wrasses are a very diverse family of fish, ranging in length from 2 to 15 inches. Wrasses can change gender from female to male. Some have brilliant coloration that changes as they age. Several types of wrasse are endemic to Hawaii: Hawaiian cleaner, shortnose, belted, and gray (or old woman).

GAME FISH Hawaii is known around the globe as *the* place for big-game fish—marlin, swordfish, and tuna. Six kinds of **billfish** are found in the offshore waters around the islands: Pacific blue marlin, black marlin, sailfish, broadbill swordfish, striped marlin, and shortbill spearfish. Hawaii billfish range in size from the 20-pound shortbill spearfish and striped marlin to the 1,805-pound Pacific blue marlin, the largest marlin ever caught with rod and reel in the world.

Tuna ranges in size from small (1 lb. or less) mackerel tuna used as bait (Hawaiians call them *oioi*) to 250-pound yellowfin ahi tuna. Other local species of tuna are big-eye, albacore, kawakawa, and skipjack.

Other types of fish, also excellent for eating, include **mahimahi** (also known as dolphin fish or dorado), in the 20- to 70-pound range; **rainbow runner,** from 15 to 30 pounds; and **wahoo** (ono), from 15 to 80 pounds. Shoreline fishermen are always on the lookout for **trevally** (the state record for a giant trevally is 191 lb.), **bonefish, ladyfish, threadfin, leatherfish,** and **goatfish.** Bottom fishermen pursue a range of **snapper**—red, pink, gray, and others—as well as **sea bass** (the state record is a whopping 563 lb.) and **amberjack** (which weigh up to 100 lb.).

WHALES Humpback whales are popular visitors who come to Hawaii to mate and calve every year, beginning in November and staying until spring—April or so—when they return to Alaska. On every island, you can take winter whale-watching cruises that will let you observe these magnificent leviathans up close. You can also spot them from shore—humpbacks grow to up to 45 feet long, so when one breaches (jumps out of the water), you can see it for miles.

Humpbacks are among the biggest whales found in Hawaiian waters, but other whales—such as pilot, sperm, false killer, melon-headed, pygmy killer, and beaked—can be seen year-round, especially in the calm waters off the Big Island's Kona Coast.

SHARKS Yes, there *are* sharks in Hawaii, but you more than likely won't see one unless you're specifically looking. About 40 different species of sharks inhabit the waters surrounding Hawaii, ranging from the totally harmless whale shark (at 60 ft., the world's largest fish), which has no teeth and is so docile that it frequently lets divers ride on its back, to the not-so-docile, extremely uncommon great white shark. The most common sharks seen in Hawaii are white-tip or gray reef sharks (about 5 ft. long) and black-tip reef sharks (about 6 ft. long).

HAWAII'S ECOSYSTEM PROBLEMS

Officials at Hawaii Volcanoes National Park on the Big Island saw a potential problem a few decades ago with people taking a few rocks home with them as souvenirs. To prevent this problem from escalating, the park rangers created a legend that the fiery volcano goddess, Pele, did not like people taking anything (rocks, chunks of lava) from her home, and bad luck would befall anyone disobeying her wishes. There used to be a display case in the park's visitor center filled with letters from people who had taken rocks from the volcano, relating stories of all the bad luck that followed. Most of the letters begged Pele's forgiveness and instructed the rangers to please return the rock to the exact location that was its original home.

Unfortunately, Hawaii's other ecosystem problems can't be handled as easily.

MARINE LIFE Hawaii's beautiful and abundant marine life has attracted so many visitors that they threaten to overwhelm it. A great example of this is Oahu's **Hanauma Bay.** Crowds flock to this marine preserve, which features calm, protected swimming and snorkeling areas loaded with tropical reef fish. Its popularity has forced government officials to limit admissions and charge an entrance fee. Commercial tour operators have also been restricted.

Another marine-life conservation area that suffers from overuse is **Molokini,** a small crater off the coast of Maui. Twenty-five years ago, one or two small six-passenger boats made the trip once a day to Molokini; today it's not uncommon to sight 20 or more boats, each carrying 20 to 49 passengers, moored inside the tiny crater. One tour operator has claimed that, on some days, it's so crowded that you can actually see a slick of suntan oil floating on the surface of the water.

Hawaii's **reefs** have faced increasing impact over the years as well. Runoff of soil and chemicals from construction, agriculture, and erosion can blanket and choke a reef, which needs sunlight to survive. Human contact with the reef can also upset the ecosystem. Coral, the basis of the reef system, is very fragile; snorkelers and divers grabbing onto it can break off pieces that took decades to form. Feeding the fish can also upset the balance of the ecosystem (not to mention upsetting the digestive systems of the fish). In areas where they're fed, the normally shy reef fish become more aggressive, surrounding divers and demanding food.

FLORA The rainforests are among Hawaii's most fragile environments. Any intrusion—from hikers carrying seeds on their shoes to the rooting of wild boars—can upset the delicate balance of these complete ecosystems. In recent years, development has moved closer and closer to the rainforests. On the Big Island, people have protested the invasion of bulldozers and the drilling of geothermal wells in the Wao Kele O Puna rainforest for years.

FAUNA The biggest impact on the fauna in Hawaii is the decimation of native birds by feral animals, which have destroyed the bird's habitats, and by mongooses that have eaten the birds' eggs and young. Government officials are vigilant about snakes because of the potential damage they can do to the remaining bird life.

A recent pest introduced to Hawaii is the coqui frog. That loud noise you hear after dark, especially on the eastern side of the Big Island and various parts of Maui, including the Kapalua Resort area and on the windward side of the island, is the cry of the male coqui frog looking for a mate. A native of Puerto Rico, where the frogs are kept in check by snakes, the coqui frog came to Hawaii in some plant material, found no natural enemies, and has spread across the Big Island and Maui. A chorus of several hundred coqui frogs is deafening (it's been measured at 163 decibels, or the noise level of a jet engine from 100 ft.). In some places, like Akaka Falls, on the Big Island, there are so many frogs that they are now chirping during daylight hours.

6 HAWAII IN POPULAR CULTURE: BOOKS, FILM & MUSIC

In addition to the books discussed below, those planning an extended trip to Hawaii should check out *Frommer's Hawaii; Frommer's Hawaii Day by Day; Frommer's Honolulu, Waikiki & Oahu; Frommer's Honolulu & Oahu Day by Day; Frommer's Maui; Frommer's Maui Day by Day;* and *Frommer's Hawaii with Kids* (all published by Wiley Publishing, Inc.).

BOOKS

Fiction

The first book people think about is James A. Michener's *Hawaii* (Fawcett Crest, 1974). This epic novel manages to put the island's history into chronological order, but remember, it is still fiction, and very sanitized fiction, too. For a more contemporary look at life in Hawaii today, one of the best novels is *Shark Dialogues,* by Kiana Davenport (Plume, 1995). The novel tells the story of Pono, the larger-than-life matriarch, and her four daughters of mixed races. Davenport skillfully weaves legends and myths of Hawaii into the "real life" reality that Pono and her family face in the complex Hawaii of today. Lois-Ann Yamanaka uses a very "local" voice and stark depictions of life in the islands in her fabulous novels *Wild Meat and the Bully Burgers* (Farrar, Straus, Giroux, 1996), *Blu's Hanging* (Avon, 1997), and *Heads by Harry* (Avon, 1999). A great read is *Honolulu Stories, Two Centuries of Writing,* Edited by Gavan Daws and Bennett Hymer (Mutual Publishing, 2008), which has hundreds of writers (from Mark Twain to Robert Louis Stevenson to Jack London to James Jones to second-grade school kids) all telling their stories about Hawaii's most famous city.

Nonfiction

Mark Twain's writing on Hawaii in the 1860s offers a wonderful introduction to Hawaii's history. One of his best books is *Mark Twain in Hawaii: Roughing It in the Sandwich Islands* (Mutual Publishing, 1990). A great depiction of the Hawaii of 1889 is *Travels in Hawaii,* by Robert Louis Stevenson (University of Hawaii Press, 1973).

For contemporary voices on Hawaii's unique culture, one of the best books to get is *Voices of Wisdom: Hawaiian Elders Speak,* by M. J. Harden (Aka Press, 1999). Some 24 different *kahuna* (experts) in their fields were interviewed about their talent, skill, or artistic practice. These living treasures talk about how Hawaiians of yesteryear viewed nature, spirituality and healing, preservation and history, dance and music, arts and crafts, canoes, and the next generation.

Native Planters in Old Hawaii: Their Life, Lore, and Environment (Bishop Museum Press, Honolulu, 2004) was originally published in 1972 but is still one of the most important ethnographic works on traditional Hawaiian culture, portraying the lives of the common folk and their relationship with the land before the arrival of Westerners. This revised edition, with a great index that allows you to find anything, is an excellent resource for anyone interested in Hawaii.

The just-released *Honolulu Stories: Two Centuries of Writing,* edited by Gavan Daws and Bennett Hymer (Mutual Publishing, 2008), is a fascinating 1,000-plus-page book filled with the writings of various authors over the past 200 years. More than 350 selections—ranging from short stories, excerpts from novels, and scenes from plays, musicals, and operas to poems, songs, Hawaiian chants, cartoons, slams, and even stand-up comedy routines—are contained in this must-read for anyone interested in Hawaii. The authors range from Hawaiian kings and queens to Hawaiian chefs and commoners, including some well-known writers (translated from seven different languages)—all telling their own stories about Honolulu.

FLORA & FAUNA Because Hawaii is so lush with nature and blessed with plants, animals, and reef fish seen nowhere else on the planet, a few reference books can help you identify what you're looking at and make your trip more interesting. In the botanical world, Angela Kay Kepler's *Hawaiian Heritage Plants* (A Latitude 20 Book, University of Hawaii Press, 1998) is the standard for plant reference. In a series of essays, Kepler weaves culture, history, geography, botany, and even spirituality into her vivid descriptions of plants. You'll never look at plants the same way. There are great color photos and drawings to help you sort through the myriad species. Another great resource is *Tropicals,* by Gordon Courtright (Timber Press, 1988), which is filled with color photos identifying everything from hibiscus and heliconia to trees and palms.

The other necessary reference to have in Hawaii is one that identifies the colorful reef fish you will see snorkeling. The best of the bunch is John E. Randall's *Shore Fishes of Hawaii* (University of Hawaii Press, 1998). Two other books on reef-fish identification, with easy-to-use spiral bindings, are *Hawaiian Reef Fish: The Identification Book,* by Casey Mahaney (Blue Kirio Publishing, 1993), and *Hawaiian Reef Fish,* by Astrid Witte and Casey Mahaney (Island Heritage, 1998).

To learn everything you need to identify Hawaii's unique birds, try H. Douglas Pratt's *A Pocket Guide to Hawaii's Birds* (Mutual Publishing, 1996).

HISTORY There are many great books on Hawaii's history, but one of the best places to start is with the formation of the Hawaiian Islands, vividly described in David E. Eyre's *By Wind, By Wave: An Introduction to Hawaii's Natural History* (Bess Press, 2000). In addition to chronicling the natural history of Hawaii, Eyre describes the complex interrelationships among the plants, animals, ocean, and people. He points out that Hawaii has become the "extinction capital of the world," but rather than dwelling on that fact, he urges readers to do something about it and carefully spells out how.

For a history of "precontact" Hawaii (before Westerners arrived), David Malo's *Hawaiian Antiquities* (Bishop Museum Press, 1976) is the preeminent source. Malo was born around 1793 and wrote about the Hawaiian lifestyle at that time, as well as the beliefs and religion of his people. It's an excellent reference book, but not a fast read. For more readable books on Old Hawaii, try *Stories of Old Hawaii,* by Roy Kakulu Alameida (Bess Press, 1997), on myths and legends; *Hawaiian Folk Tales,* by Thomas G. Thrum (Mutual Publishing, 1998); and

The Legends and Myths of Hawaii, by His Hawaiian Majesty King David Kalakaua (Charles E. Tuttle Company, 1992).

The best story of the 1893 overthrow of the Hawaiian monarchy is told by Queen Liliuokalani, in her book *Hawaii's Story by Hawaii's Queen Liliuokalani* (Mutual Publishing, 1990). When it was written, it was an international plea for justice for her people, but it is a poignant read even today. It's also a must-read for people interested in current events and the recent rally for sovereignty in the 50th state. Two contemporary books on the question of Hawaii's sovereignty are Tom Coffman's *Nation Within: The Story of America's Annexation of the Nation of Hawaii* (Epicenter, 1998) and Thurston Twigg-Smith's *Hawaiian Sovereignty: Do the Facts Matter?* (Goodale, 2000), which explores the opposite view. Twigg-Smith, former publisher of the statewide newspaper *The Honolulu Advertiser,* is the grandson of Lorrin A. Thurston, one of the architects of the 1893 overthrow of the monarchy. His so-called "politically incorrect" views present a different look on this hotly debated topic.

An insightful look at history and its effect on the Hawaiian culture is *Waikiki, A History of Forgetting and Remembering,* by Andrea Feeser (University of Hawaii Press, 2006). A beautiful art book (designed by Gaye Chan), this is not your typical coffee-table book, but a different look at the cultural and environmental history of Waikiki. Using historical texts, photos, government documents, and interviews, this book lays out the story of how Waikiki went from a self-sufficient agricultural area to a tourism mecca, detailing the price that was paid along the way.

FILM

My favorite films made in Hawaii but about other places are:

- ***Donovan's Reef:*** John Ford directed this 1963 John Wayne romantic comedy about two ex-Navy men who remain on a South Seas island (played by Kauai) after World War II. "Guns" Donovan (Wayne) runs the local bar, while Doc Dedham (Jack Warden) has married a local princess. A former shipmate (Lee Marvin) arrives, followed by a high-society Bostonian (Elizabeth Allen).
- ***Islands in the Stream:*** Filmed on Kauai, this 1977 movie tells the story of Ernest Hemingway's last published novel. Set on the island of Bimini in the Caribbean, it is about artist Thomas Hudson's renewed relationship with his three young sons and former wife.
- ***Jurassic Park:*** Filmed on the islands of Kauai and Oahu, Steven Spielberg's 1993 megahit, which was billed as "an adventure 65 million years in the making," is the story of dinosaurs on the loose at the site of the world's only dinosaur farm and theme park, where creatures from the past are produced using harvested DNA.
- ***The Karate Kid, Part II:*** In one of those instances where the sequel is actually better than the original, this 1986 movie takes our hero Daniel LaRusso (Ralph Macchio) and his mentor, Mr. Miyagi (Pat Morita), to Miyagi's homeland, Okinawa, to visit his dying father and confront his old rival. An entire Okinawan village was re-created on Oahu's Windward Coast.
- ***The Lost World: Jurassic Park:*** In Steven Spielberg's 1997 follow-up to *Jurassic Park,* dinosaurs have been bred and then escaped following the abandonment of the project in the first installment. The sequel features much more Hawaiian scenery than the original.
- ***None But the Brave:*** Frank Sinatra directed and starred in this 1965 story of American and Japanese soldiers who, when stranded on a tiny Pacific island during World War II (filmed on Kauai), must make a temporary truce and

cooperate to survive. This was the only film directed by Sinatra.

- ***Raiders of the Lost Ark:*** Filmed on Kauai, Steven Spielberg's 1981 film follows archaeologist Indiana Jones on a search for the Ark of the Covenant, which is also sought by the Nazis under orders from Hitler.
- ***Six Days Seven Nights:*** Ivan Reitman's 1998 adventure-comedy is about a New York magazine editor and a gruff pilot who are forced to put aside their dislike for each other in order to survive after crash-landing on a deserted South Seas island (filmed on Kauai). It stars Harrison Ford and Anne Heche.
- ***South Pacific:*** The 1958 motion-picture adaptation of the Rodgers and Hammerstein musical was filmed on Kauai. The film has an all-star cast, with Rossano Brazzi and Mitzi Gaynor in the lead roles. It was nominated for three Academy Awards but won only for Best Sound.
- ***Waterworld:*** Kevin Costner directed and starred in this 1995 film about a future in which the polar ice caps have melted, leaving most of the world's surface deep beneath the oceans. The survivors live poorly on the water's surface, dreaming of finding "dry land." Some of the water scenes were filmed off Kauai. The final and most beautiful scenes in the movie were filmed in the Waipio Valley on the Big Island.

My favorite films made in Hawaii and about Hawaii are:

- ***Blue Hawaii:*** Chad Gates (Elvis Presley), upon discharge from the Army, returns to Hawaii to enjoy life with his buddies and girlfriend, against the wishes of his parents, who want him to work for the family business. Elvis Presley, Joan Blackman, and Angela Lansbury make this 1961 film a classic, with great music and beautiful Hawaiian scenery from the early 1960s.
- ***50 First Dates:*** This 2004 romantic comedy stars Drew Barrymore and Adam Sandler in a story about a young woman (Barrymore) who has lost her short-term memory in a car accident and who now relives each day as if it were October 13th. She follows the same routine every day, until she meets Henry Roth (Sandler), who falls in love with her and seeks a way to forge a long-term relationship.
- ***From Here to Eternity:*** Fred Zinnemann's 1953 multiple-Oscar winner, set in pre–World War II Hawaii, tells the story of several Army soldiers stationed on Oahu on the eve of Pearl Harbor. The film won Best Picture, Best Supporting Actor (Frank Sinatra), Best Supporting Actress (Donna Reed), and five other awards.
- ***Hawaii:*** George Roy Hill's 1966 adaptation of the James Michener novel features amazing island scenery and stars Julie Andrews, Max von Sydow, and Richard Harris. It is a great introduction to the early history of Hawaii.
- ***Molokai: The Story of Father Damien:*** This 1999 film follows the life of Belgian priest Damien de Veuster from 1872, the year before his arrival in Kalaupapa, through his years ministering to the patients with Hansen's disease at Kalaupapa, until his death at the Molokai settlement in 1889.
- ***Pearl Harbor:*** Michael Bay's 2001 film depicts the time before, during, and after the December 7, 1941, Japanese attack (with the best re-creation of the Pearl Harbor attack ever put on film) and tells the story of two best friends and the woman they both love.
- ***Picture Bride:*** Japanese director Kayo Hatta presents this 1995 film about a Japanese woman who travels to Hawaii to marry a man that she has never met, but only seen through photos and letters. She soon discovers that he is twice her age and that much turmoil awaits

her in her new home. Beautifully filmed on the North Shore of Oahu and the Hamakua Coast of the Big Island, with a special appearance by Toshiro Mifune.

- *Tora! Tora! Tora!:* This 1970 film tells the story of the Japanese attack on Pearl Harbor as seen from both the American and the Japanese perspectives.

MUSIC

Hawaiian music ranges from traditional ancient chants and hula to slack-key guitar, to contemporary rock and a new genre, Jawaiian, a cross of reggae, Jamaican, and Hawaiian. To listen to Hawaiian music, check out Hawaiian 105 (www.hawaiian105.com). Below are my picks for Hawaiian music.

- ***Best of the Gabby Band,*** by Gabby Pahinui (traditional Hawaiian)
- ***Gently Weeps,*** by Jake Shimabukuro (contemporary Hawaiian)
- ***Hapa,*** by Hapa (contemporary Hawaiian)
- ***Hawaiian Blossom,*** by Raiatea Helm (traditional Hawaiian)
- ***Hawaiian Tradition,*** by Amy Hanaiali'i Gilliom (traditional Hawaiian)
- ***Honolulu City Lights,*** by Keola & Kapono Beamer (contemporary Hawaiian)
- ***Legends of Hawaiian Slack Key Guitar,*** by various artists (a collection of slack-key guitar music and a 2007 Grammy winner)
- ***Masters of Hawaiian Slack Key, Vol. 1,*** by various artists (a collection of slack-key guitar music and a 2006 Grammy winner)
- ***Na Leo Hawaii,*** by the Master Chanters of Hawaii (chanting)
- ***Na Pua O Hawaii,*** by Makaha Sons (contemporary Hawaiian)
- ***Wonderful World,*** by Israel Kamakawiwo'ole (contemporary Hawaiian)

3

Planning Your Trip to Kauai

Kauai has so many places to explore, things to do, sights to see—where do you start? That's where I come in. In the pages that follow, I've compiled everything you need to know to plan your ideal trip to Kauai: information on airlines, seasons, a calendar of events, how to make camping reservations, and much more (even how to tie the knot).

If you are thinking about seeing another island in addition to Kauai, I strongly recommend that you **limit your island-hopping to one island per week.** If you decide to go to more than one island in a week, be warned: You could spend much of your precious vacation time in airports, waiting to board flights and for your luggage to arrive, and checking in and out of hotels. Not much fun!

My second tip is to **fly directly to Kauai;** doing so can save you a 2-hour layover in Honolulu and another plane ride. So let's get on with the process of planning your trip. Searching out the best deals and planning your dream vacation to Hawaii should be half the fun.

For additional help in planning your trip and for more on-the-ground resources in Kauai, please turn to chapter 11.

1 WHEN TO GO

Most visitors don't come to Kauai when the weather's best in the islands; rather, they come when it's at its worst everywhere else. Thus, the **high season**—when prices are up and resorts are booked to capacity—generally runs mid-December through March or mid-April. The last 2 weeks of December in particular are the prime time for travel to Kauai; if you're planning a holiday trip, make your reservations as early as possible, count on holiday crowds, and expect to pay top dollar for accommodations, car rentals, and airfare. Whale-watching season begins in January and continues through the rest of winter, sometimes lasting into May.

The **off seasons,** when the best bargain rates are available, are spring (mid-Apr to mid-June) and fall (Sept to mid-Dec)—a paradox, since these are the best seasons in terms of reliably great weather. If you're looking to save money, or if you just want to avoid the crowds, this is the time to visit. Hotel rates tend to be significantly lower during these off seasons. Airfares also tend to be lower—again, sometimes substantially—and good packages and special deals are often available.

Note: If you plan to come to Kauai between the last week in April and the first week in May, be sure to book your accommodations, interisland air reservations, and car rental in advance. In Japan, the last week of April is called **Golden Week** because three Japanese holidays take place one after the other; the islands are especially busy with Japanese tourists during this time.

Tips What to Pack

Kauai is very informal: You'll get by with shorts, T-shirts, and sneakers at most attractions and restaurants; a casual sundress or a polo shirt and khakis is fine even in the most expensive places. Don't forget a long-sleeved coverup (to throw on at the beach when you've had enough sun for the day), rubber water shoes or flip-flops, and hiking shoes and several pairs of good socks if you plan to do any hiking. You might also want to bring binoculars for whale-watching.

Be sure to bring **sun protection:** sunglasses, strong sunscreen, a light hat (like a baseball cap or a sun visor), and a canteen or water bottle if you'll be hiking—you'll easily dehydrate on the trail in the tropic heat. Experts recommend carrying 2 liters of water per person per day on any hike. Campers should bring water purification tablets or devices. Also see "Staying Healthy," later in this chapter.

Don't bother overstuffing your suitcase with 2 whole weeks' worth of shorts and T-shirts: Kauai has **laundry facilities** everywhere. If your accommodations don't have a washer/dryer or laundry service (most do), there will most likely be a laundry nearby. The only exception to this is Kokee Park, so do a load of laundry before you arrive.

One last thing: **It really can get cold on Kauai,** especially if you are staying in Kokee. It's always a good idea to bring long pants and a windbreaker, sweater, or light jacket. And be sure to bring along rain gear if you'll be in Kauai from November to March.

Due to the large number of families traveling in **summer** (June–Aug), you won't get the fantastic bargains of spring and fall. However, you'll still do much better on packages, airfare, and accommodations than you will in the winter months.

THE WEATHER

Because Kauai lies at the edge of the tropical zone, it technically has only two seasons, both of them warm. The dry season corresponds to summer, and the rainy season generally runs during the winter from November to March. It rains every day somewhere in the islands at any time of the year, but the rainy season can cause "gray" weather and spoil your tanning opportunities. Fortunately, it seldom rains for more than 3 days straight, and rainy days often just consist of a mix of clouds and sun, with very brief showers.

The **year-round temperature** usually varies no more than 15°, from about 70° to 85°F (21°–29°C), but it depends on where you are. Kauai is like a ship in that it has leeward and windward sides. The **leeward** sides (the west and south) are usually hot and dry, whereas the **windward** sides (east and north) are generally cooler and moist. If you want arid, sunbaked, desertlike weather, go leeward. If you want lush, often wet, junglelike weather, go windward. Your best bet for total year-round sun is the Poipu coast.

Kauai is also full of **microclimates,** thanks to its interior valleys, coastal plains, and mountain peaks. If you travel into the mountains, it can change from summer to winter in a matter of hours, because it's cooler the higher up you go. In other words, if the weather doesn't suit you, go to the other side of the island—or head into the hills.

That Long Flight to Hawaii: How to Stay Comfortable

The plane ride probably will not be the most fun part of your trip to Hawaii. Long flights can be trying; stuffy air and cramped seats can make you feel as if you're being sent parcel post in a small box. But with a little advance planning, you can make an otherwise unpleasant experience almost bearable.

- Your choice of airline and airplane will definitely affect your legroom. Find more details at www.seatguru.com, which has extensive details about almost every seat on six major U.S. airlines.
- Emergency exit seats and bulkhead seats typically have the most legroom. Emergency exit seats are usually held back to be assigned the day of a flight (to ensure that the seat is filled by someone able-bodied); it's worth getting to the ticket counter early to snag one of these spots for a long flight. Many passengers find that bulkhead seating (the row facing the wall at the front of the cabin) offers more legroom, but keep in mind that bulkheads are where airlines often put baby bassinets, so you may be sitting next to an infant.
- To have two seats for yourself in a three-seat row, try for an aisle seat in a center section toward the back of coach. If you're traveling with a companion, book an aisle and a window seat. Middle seats are usually booked last, so chances are good you'll end up with three seats to yourselves. And in the event that a third passenger is assigned the middle seat, he or she will probably be more than happy to trade for a window or an aisle.
- To sleep, avoid the last row of any section or a row in front of an emergency exit, as these seats are the least likely to recline. Avoid seats near highly trafficked toilet areas. Avoid seats in the back of many jets—these can be narrower than those in the rest of coach class. You also may want to reserve a window seat so that you can rest your head and avoid being bumped in the aisle.
- Get up, walk around, and stretch every 60 to 90 minutes to keep your blood flowing. This helps avoid **deep vein thrombosis,** or "economy-class syndrome," a potentially deadly condition that can be caused by sitting in cramped conditions for too long. Other preventative measures include drinking lots of water and avoiding alcohol (see next bullet).
- Drink water before, during, and after your flight to combat the lack of humidity in airplane cabins—which can be drier than the Sahara. Bring a big bottle of water (1.5 liter) on board. Avoid alcohol, which will dehydrate you.
- If you're flying with kids, don't forget to carry on toys, books, pacifiers, and chewing gum to help them relieve ear pressure buildup during ascent and descent. Let each child pack his or her own backpack with favorite toys.

Average temperature and rainy days for each month in Lihue:

Month	High	Low	Water Temp	Average Rainy Days
January	81F/27C	70F/21C	75F/24C	15
February	78F/26C	65F/18C	74F/23C	13
March	78F/26C	66 F/19C	74 F/23C	17
April	79F/26C	68F/20C	75F/24C	17
May	81F/27C	70F/21C	76F/24C	16
June	83F/28C	72F/22C	77F/25C	16
July	84F/29C	73F/23C	78F/26C	19
August	85F/29C	74F/23C	79F/261C	18
September	85F/29C	73F/23C	80 F/27C	16
October	83F/28C	72 F/22C	79 F/26C	18
November	81F/27C	70 F/21C	77F/25C	18
December	79F/26C	67F/20C	76F/24C	17

Average temperature and rainy days for each month in Hanalei:

Month	High	Low	Water Temp	Average Rainy Days
January	79F/26C	61F/17C	75F/24C	7.5
February	80F/27C	61F/17C	74F/23C	5
March	80F/27C	62F/17C	74F/23C	6.2
April	82F/28C	63F/17C	75F/24C	3.3
May	84F/29C	65F/18C	76F/24C	2.7
June	86F/30C	66F/19C	77F/25C	1.7
July	88F/31C	66F/19C	78F/26C	7.5
August	88F/31C	67F/20C	79F/26C	2.2
September	87F/31C	68F/20C	80F/27C	2.5
October	86F/30C	67F/20C	79F/26C	3.3
November	83F/28C	65F/18C	77F/25C	3.6
December	80F/27C	62F/17C	76F/24C	6.8

HOLIDAYS

When Hawaii observes holidays, especially those over a long weekend, travel between the islands increases, interisland airline seats are fully booked, rental cars are at a premium, and hotels and restaurants are busier than usual.

Federal, state, and county government offices are closed on all federal holidays: January 1 (New Year's Day); third Monday in January (Martin Luther King, Jr., Day); third Monday in February (Presidents' Day, Washington's Birthday); last Monday in May (Memorial Day); July 4 (Independence Day); first Monday in September (Labor Day); second Monday in October (Columbus Day); November 11 (Veterans Day); fourth Thursday in November (Thanksgiving Day); and December 25 (Christmas).

Tips No Smoking in Hawaii

Well, not *totally* no smoking, but Hawaii has one of the toughest laws against smoking in the U.S. It's against the law to smoke in public buildings, including airports, shopping malls, grocery stores, retail shops, buses, movie theaters, banks, convention facilities, and all government buildings and facilities. There is no smoking in restaurants, bars, or nightclubs. Most bed-and-breakfasts prohibit smoking indoors, and more and more hotels and resorts are becoming smoke-free even in public areas. Also, there is no smoking within 20 feet of a doorway, window, or ventilation intake (so no hanging around outside a bar to smoke—you must go 20 ft. away). Even some beaches have no-smoking policies (and at those that do allow smoking, you'd better pick up your butts and not use the sand as your own private ashtray—or else face stiff fines). Breathing fresh, clear air is "in," while smoking in Hawaii is "out."

State and county offices also are closed on local holidays, including Prince Kuhio Day (Mar 26), honoring the birthday of Hawaii's first delegate to the U.S. Congress; King Kamehameha Day (June 11), a statewide holiday commemorating Kamehameha the Great, who united the islands and ruled from 1795 to 1819; and Admission Day (third Fri in Aug), which honors Hawaii's admission as the 50th state in the United States on August 21, 1959.

Other special days celebrated by many people in Hawaii but that do not involve the closing of federal, state, or county offices are Chinese New Year (Jan or Feb), Girls' Day (Mar 3), Buddha's Birthday (Apr 8), Father Damien's Day (Apr 15), Boys' Day (May 5), Samoan Flag Day (Aug), Aloha Festivals (Sept or Oct), and Pearl Harbor Day (Dec 7).

KAUAI CALENDAR OF EVENTS

As with any schedule of upcoming events, the following information is subject to change; always confirm details and dates before you plan your schedule around an event.

For an exhaustive list of events beyond those listed here, check http://events.frommers.com, where you'll find a searchable, up-to-the-minute roster of what's happening in cities all over the world.

January

Kauaian Days, several locations. "Celebrating our Unity, While Honoring our Diversity" is the theme of this weeklong festival at various locations around the island. Included in the events are entertainment, Hawaiian games for children, sporting events, workshops, dinners, and cultural festivities. Call ✆ **808/338-0111.** Mid-January.

Annual Burns Supper, Waimea. This is a birthday celebration of Scotland's most acclaimed poet, Robert Burns, on the grounds of Waimea Plantation Cottages. The Burns Supper celebrates this special man with food, Burns's poetry, and music. A fabulous dinner under the palms follows the pipes and drums. Call ✆ **808/652-0616.** Late January or early February at the Waimea Plantation Cottages.

February

4th Annual All Angels Jazz Festival, Lihue. Stop by for some jazz at St. Michael and All Angels Church, 4363 Umi St., Lihue. Call ✆ **808/245-3796.** Early Feb.

Waimea Town Celebration, Waimea. This annual party on Kauai's west side celebrates the Hawaiian and multiethnic history of the town where Captain Cook first landed. This is the island's biggest 2-day event, drawing some 10,000 people. Top Hawaiian entertainers, sporting events, rodeo, and lots of food are on tap during the weekend celebration. Call ✆ **808/337-1005;** Weekend after Presidents' Day Weekend.

Captain Cook Fun Run, Waimea. The 2-, 5-, and 10K runs, with a starting time of 7am, go through the old plantation town of Waimea. Call ✆ **808/338-1332.** End of February.

Kilohana Long-Distance Canoe Race, Waimea. Traditional Hawaiian Outrigger Canoe Racing along the Waimea shoreline is the first event of the Kauai canoe-racing season. Starting times for the races Saturday morning are 8am for single person canoes, 9am for women, and 10:30am for men. The finish is around noon. Call ✆ **808/338-1332.** End of February.

March

Note: **Daylight saving time** begins on the second Sunday in March on the Mainland but **not** in Hawaii. Be sure to adjust the time. Starting at 2am, Hawaii is 3 hours behind Pacific Time and 6 hours behind the East Coast (when it's 6pm in New York it's only noon in Hawaii).

Prince Kuhio Celebration of the Arts, Lawai. Celebrate the birth of Jonah Kuhio Kalanianaole, who was born on March 26, 1871, and elected to Congress in 1902. Kauai, his birthplace, starts the celebration at the memorial at Prince Kuhio Park in Lawai, and continues it with daylong festivities. Call ✆ **808/651-6966** for details.

4th Annual Kauai Orchid and Art Festival, Hanapepe. Come and see the exotic displays of tropical orchids at the Garden Island Orchid Society's Spring Fantasy Orchid Show and view Kauai's top artists' work. Popular contemporary Hawaiian music will be offered along with workshops on various art activities. Downtown Hanapepe, late March. Call ✆ **808/335-5944.**

April

Annual Royal Paina, Lihue. The Kauai Historical Society presents its annual celebration of Hawaii's multiethnic heritage, with local entertainment and a great meal at the Kauai Marriott Resort and Beach Club. Call ✆ **808/245-3373.** End of April.

May

Kauai Museum Lei Day Celebrations, Lihue. May Day is Lei Day in Hawaii, celebrated with lei-making contests, pageantry, arts, and crafts. Call ✆ **808/245-6931** for Kauai events.

Annual Visitor Industry Charity Walk, Lihue. Hawaii's largest single-day fundraiser, which takes place across the state, consists of a 3¼-mile fun walk (with some ambitious runners at the front of the pack). Beginning at the Kukui Grove Pavilion, the walk raises money for local charities. Call ✆ **808/923-0404** or visit www.charitywalk.org. Third Saturday in May.

Outrigger Canoe Season, several locations. From May to September, nearly every weekend, canoe paddlers across the state participate in outrigger canoe races. Call ✆ **808/261-6615,** or go to www.y2kanu.com for this year's schedule of events.

June

Annual Taste of Hawaii, Kapaa. The Rotary Club of Kapaa holds its "Ultimate

Sunday Brunch" at Smith's Tropical Paradise, 45971 Kuhio Hwy., Kapaa, where some 60 different chefs will show their culinary skills. Live music all day. Generally, it's the first Sunday in June. Call ✆ **808/783-1407.**

Obon Days & Festival, Koloa. This cultural festival honors the dead (see "Honoring the Dead: Obon Festival," below). Koloa Jodo Mission, 3480 Waikomo Rd., Koloa. Early June. Call ✆ **808/742-6735.**

King Kamehameha Celebration Ho'olaule'a, several locations. Daylong festivities in Lihue feature entertainment, arts and crafts, and food. Call ✆ **808/586-0333;** www.hawaii.gov/dags/king_kamehameha_commission. Mid-June.

Garden Isle Artisan Faire, Lihue. Come browse through the array of handicrafts, products, and art by Kauai's artists in Lihue. There's Hawaiian music all day, and plenty of food to buy. Call ✆ **808/586-0333.** Mid-June.

Kauai Concert Association's 3rd Annual Red Clay Jazz Festival, Lihue. This day-long music extravaganza features local, state, and nationally known jazz artists, plus food and beverages at the Performing Arts Center of Kauai Community College, 3-1901 Kaumualii Hwy., Lihue. Late June. Call ✆ **808/245-7464.**

Annual Hula Exhibition, Lihue. Na Hula O Kaohikukapulani presents an evening of chants, music, and hula at the Kauai War Memorial Convention Hall. The date varies; call ✆ **808/335-6466** for information.

Banana Poka Roundup, Kokee State Park. This forest education fair features music, workshops, crafts, children's activities, and exhibits on ridding Kauai's native forests of this invasive weed. Kokee State Park, Mile Marker 15, Kokee Rd., Kehaha. Late June. Call ✆ **808/335-9975.**

July

21st Annual Concert in the Sky. Fourth of July fundraiser for Kauai Hospice at the Vidinha Stadium, Lihue. Concert and fireworks. For more information, call ✆ **808/245-7277.**

Kekaha Town 4th of July Celebration. Kekaha. Family activities with crafts, food booths, cultural displays, entertainment, and music. Faye Ballpark, Kekaha. Call ✆ **808/346-2342.**

Annual Family Ocean Fair, Kilauea National Wildlife Refuge. Daylong festivities include live entertainment, lectures, games, food, and demonstrations at the Kilauea National Wildlife Refuge. Free admission. Call ✆ **808/246-2860.** Mid-July.

Koloa Plantation Days. Koloa and Poipu. This is a weeklong tribute to Kauai's plantation heritage, with events like the Sunset Ho'olaule'a, Paniolo Rodeo, Plantation Tennis Tournament, Hapa Road Walk, Hawaiian Olympics, Golf Putting Tournament, Craft Faire, ethnic cooking demonstrations, and a parade and festival in Koloa with entertainment, food, and crafts. Mid-July. Various locations around Koloa and Poipu. Call ✆ **808/652-3217.**

Obon Dance and Festival, Waimea, Kapaa, Hanapepe, and Lihue. This traditional Japanese cultural festival honors the dead (see "Honoring the Dead: Obon Festival," above). West Kauai Hongwanji, 4675 Menehune Rd., Waimea, ✆ **808/338-1537;** Kapaa Jodo Mission, 4524 Hauaala Rd., Kapaa, ✆ **808/338-1847;** Waimea Higashi Hongwanji Mission, 9554-C Kaumualii Hwy., Waimea, ✆ **808/338-1847;** West Kaukai Hongwanji,1-3860 Kaumualii Hwy., Hanapepe, ✆ **808/338-1537;** Lihue Hongwanji, Lihue, ✆ **808/245-6262.** Late July or early August.

Moments Honoring the Dead: Obon Festival

The Japanese immigrants who came to Kauai brought their cultural Obon Festival, which honors the departed spirits of those who have died. During the summer months, several Buddhist temples have an Obon Festival, which usually includes dancing and food. They welcome visitors to come to the festivals and encourage people to join in the dancing. The festival has its origins in the story of Buddha's disciple, Mokukren, who used his supernatural powers to see how his deceased mother was doing. He saw she was in the Realm of Hungry Ghosts and was suffering. Upset, he went to the Buddha and asked how he could release his mother from this realm. Buddha told him to help the many Buddhist monks who had just completed their summer retreat, on the fifteenth day of the seventh month. The disciple did this and felt his mother's release. He also began to see the true nature of her past unselfishness and the many sacrifices that she had made for him. The disciple, happy because of his mother's release and grateful for his mother's kindness, danced with joy. From this dance of joy comes *Bon Odori* or "Bon Dance", a time in which ancestors and their sacrifices are remembered and appreciated.

Participants in the Obon Festival traditionally wear colorful yukata, or light cotton kimonos. Many Obon celebrations include a huge carnival with rides, games, and summer festival food. The festival ends with Toro Nagashi, or the floating of lanterns. Paper lanterns are illuminated and then floated down rivers symbolically signaling the ancestral spirits' return to the world of the dead. This ceremony usually culminates in a fireworks display.

August

Kauai Music Festival, Lihue. A 4-day celebration of the art of songwriting. Hilton Kauai Beach Resort, 4331 Kauai Beach Dr., Lihue. Late July or early August. © **808/634-6237.**

9th Annual Kauai Polynesian Festival: Heiva I Kauai Ia Orana Tahiti, Kapaa. This 2-day event features the dances of Tahiti, New Zealand, and Samoa in a competition, as well as exhibitions and educational cultural workshops plus local foods, arts, and crafts. Kapaa Beach Park. Early August. Call © **808/822-9447.**

Kauai County Farm Bureau Fair, Lihue. This family-oriented fair, held at the Vidinha Stadium in Lihue, features a petting zoo, a livestock show, floral demonstrations and exhibits, food booths, and arts and crafts, along with amusement park rides. Call © **808/639-8432** or visit www.kauaifarmfair.com. Late August.

September

All Woman's Koloa Rodeo, Poipu. The only all-female rodeo in the state features women competing in roping, barrel racing, pole bending, and goat tying. CJM Country Stables, a mile past the Grand Hyatt Kauai Resort & Spa, Poipu Rd. Call © **808/639-0091.** End of August or early September.

Aloha Festivals, several locations. Parades and other events celebrate Hawaiian culture and friendliness throughout the island. Call ✆ **800/852-7690,** or visit www.alohafestivals.com for a schedule of events.

Kauai Mokihana Festival, several locations. This weeklong festival includes local and ethnic demonstrations, concerts, and competitions, among them a Kauai composers' contest, a hula competition, and a workshop on Kauai's heritage. Call ✆ **808/822-2166.**

October

Annual Coconut Festival, several locations. Where would Hawaii be without coconuts? This annual event highlights the cultural, social, and historical importance of the coconut with unusual coconut foods, coconut crafts, games with coconuts, and contests. Call ✆ **808/651-3273.**

Hawaiiana Festival, Poipu. This 4-day event is centered on teaching the customs, crafts, and culture of Hawaii. Held at the Grand Hyatt Kauai Resort & Spa, it includes entertainment and a luau. For information call ✆ **808/240-6369.**

Eo E Emalani Festival, Kokee State Park. This festival honors Her Majesty Queen Emma, an inveterate gardener and Hawaii's first environmental queen, who made a forest trek to Kokee with 100 friends in 1871. Call ✆ **808/335-9975.**

November

Note: **Daylight saving time** ends on the Mainland, but **not** in Hawaii (which does not go on daylight saving time). Be sure to adjust the time, on the first Sunday in November. Hawaii will be 2 hours behind the Pacific coast and 5 hours behind the Atlantic coast (5pm in New York is noon in Hawaii).

Hawaiian Slack-Key Guitar Festival, Lihue. The best of Hawaii's folk music is performed by the best musicians in Hawaii. The show, held at the Hilton Kauai Beach Resort, is 5 hours long and absolutely free. For more information call ✆ **808/226-2697** or visit www.slackkeyfestival.com. Mid-November.

Hawaii International Film Festival, several locations. This cinema festival with a cross-cultural spin features filmmakers from Asia, the Pacific Islands, and the United States. Call ✆ **808/528-FILM,** or visit www.hiff.org. First 2 weeks in November.

December

Annual Festival of Lights, Lihue. The lighting of the Christmas decorations on the grounds of Kauai's historic county building in Lihue is accompanied by local entertainment, Christmas caroling, and a parade down Rice Street, ending at the county building. Call ✆ **808/828-0014.** First Friday in December.

Holiday Hula Celebration, Lihue. A Hawaiian Christmas performance by Na Hula O Kaohikukapulani includes chants, hula, and Christmas melodies at the Kauai Marriott Resort & Beach Club. Call ✆ **808/335-6466.** Mid to late December.

Waimea Lighted Christmas Parade, Waimea. Old-fashioned Christmas parade through the tiny town of Waimea. Refreshments and entertainment. Kaumualii Hwy., Waimea. Call ✆ **808/337-1005.** Usually a week before Christmas.

New Year's Eve Fireworks, Poipu. Come out for the annual aerial fireworks display at Poipu Beach Park. For more information, e-mail info@poipubeach.org.

2 ENTRY REQUIREMENTS

PASSPORTS

Virtually every air traveler entering the U.S. (including the U.S. state of Hawaii) is required to show a passport. All persons, including U.S. citizens, traveling by air between the United States and Canada, Mexico, Central and South America, the Caribbean, and Bermuda are required to present a valid passport.

VISAS

The U.S. State Department has a **Visa Waiver Program (VWP)** allowing citizens of the following countries to enter the United States without a visa for stays of up to 90 days: Andorra, Australia, Austria, Belgium, Brunei, Denmark, Finland, France, Germany, Iceland, Ireland, Italy, Japan, Liechtenstein, Luxembourg, Monaco, the Netherlands, New Zealand, Norway, Portugal, San Marino, Singapore, Slovenia, Spain, Sweden, Switzerland, and the United Kingdom. Citizens of Czech Republic, Estonia, Hungary, Latvia, Lithuania, Malta, Republic of Korea, and Slovakia are soon to be admitted to the VWP. (***Note:*** This list was accurate at press time; for the most up-to-date list of countries in the VWP, consult http://travel.state.gov/visa.) Even though a visa isn't necessary, in an effort to help U.S. officials check travelers against terror watch lists before they arrive at U.S. borders, visitors from VWP countries must register online through the Electronic System for Travel Authorization (ESTA) before boarding a plane or a boat to the U.S. Travelers will complete an electronic application providing basic personal and travel eligibility information. The Department of Homeland Security recommends filling out the form at least 3 days before traveling. Authorizations will be valid for up to 2 years or until the traveler's passport expires, whichever comes first. Currently, there is no fee for the online application. ***Note:*** Any passport issued on or after October 26, 2006, by a VWP country must be an **e-Passport** for VWP travelers to be eligible to enter the U.S. without a visa. Citizens of these nations also need to present a round-trip air or cruise ticket upon arrival. E-Passports contain computer chips capable of storing biometric information, such as the required digital photograph of the holder. If your passport doesn't have this feature, you can still travel without a visa if it is a valid passport issued before October 26, 2005, and includes a machine-readable zone, or between October 26, 2005, and October 25, 2006, and includes a digital photograph. For more information, go to **http://travel.state.gov/visa**. Canadian citizens may enter the United States without visas; they will need to show passports and proof of residence, however.

Citizens of all other countries must have (1) a valid passport that expires at least 6 months later than the scheduled end of their visit to the U.S., and (2) a tourist visa.

CUSTOMS

What You Can Bring into the U.S.

Every visitor more than 21 years of age may bring in, free of duty, the following: (1) 1 liter of wine or hard liquor; (2) 200 cigarettes, 100 cigars (but not from Cuba), or 3 pounds of smoking tobacco; and (3) $100 worth of gifts. These exemptions are offered to travelers who spend at least 72 hours in the United States and who have not claimed them within the preceding 6 months. It is forbidden to bring into the country almost any meat products (including canned, fresh, and dried meat products such as buillion, soup mixes, and the like). Generally, condiments including vinegars, oils, spices, coffee, tea, and some cheeses and baked goods are permitted. Avoid rice products, as rice can often harbor insects. Bringing fruits and vegetables is not advised, though not prohibited. Customs will allow produce depending on where you got it and where you're going after you arrive in the U.S. International visitors may carry in or out up to $10,000 in U.S. or foreign currency with no formalities; larger sums must be declared to U.S. Customs on entering or leaving, which includes filing form CM 4790. For details regarding U.S. Customs and Border Protection, consult your nearest U.S. embassy or consulate, or **U.S. Customs** (www.customs.gov).

What You Can Take Home from the U.S.

For information on what you're allowed to bring home, contact one of the following agencies:

Canadian Citizens: Canada Border Services Agency (✆ **800/461-9999** in Canada, or 204/983-3500; **www.cbsa-asfc.gc.ca**).

U.K. Citizens: HM Customs & Excise at ✆ **0845/010-9000** (from outside the U.K., 020/8929-0152), or consult their website at **www.hmce.gov.uk**.

Australian Citizens: Australian Customs Service at ✆ **1300/363-263,** or log on to **www.customs.gov.au**.

New Zealand Citizens: New Zealand Customs, The Customhouse, 17–21 Whitmore St., Box 2218, Wellington (✆ **04/473-6099** or 0800/428-786; **www.customs.govt.nz**).

MEDICAL REQUIREMENTS

Unless you're arriving from an area known to be suffering from an epidemic (particularly cholera or yellow fever), inoculations or vaccinations are not required for entry into the United States.

3 GETTING THERE & GETTING AROUND

GETTING TO KAUAI

By Plane

If possible, fly directly to Kauai; doing so can save you a 2-hour layover in Honolulu and another plane ride.

There are no direct international flights into Kauai. You must go through Honolulu to clear Customs and Immigration if you are flying directly from a foreign country. From Honolulu, take an interisland plane to Lihue, Kauai.

Airlines serving Honolulu, Hawaii, from places other than the U.S. mainland include **Air Canada** (✆ **800/776-3000;** www.aircanada.ca); **Air New Zealand** (✆ **0800/737-000** in Auckland, 64-3/379-5200 in Christchurch, 800/926-7255 in the U.S.; www.airnewzealand.com), which runs 40 flights per week between Auckland and Hawaii; **Qantas** (✆ **008/177-767** in Australia, 800/227-4500 in the U.S.; www.qantas.com.au), which flies between Sydney and Honolulu daily (plus additional flights 4 days a week); **Japan Air Lines** (✆ **03/5489-1111** in Tokyo, 800/525-3663 in the U.S.; www.japanair.com); **All Nippon Airways** (ANA; ✆ **03/5489-1212** in Tokyo, 800/235-9262 in the U.S.; www.fly-ana.com); **China Airlines** (✆ **02/715-1212** in Taipei, 800/227-5118 in the U.S.; www.china-airlines.com); **Air Pacific,** serving Fiji, Australia, New Zealand, and the South Pacific (✆ **800/227-4446;** www.airpacific.com); **Korean Airlines** (✆ **02/656-2000** in Seoul, 800/223-1155 on the U.S. east coast, 800/421-8200 on the U.S. west coast, 800/438-5000 from Hawaii; www.koreanair.com); and **Philippine Airlines** (✆ **631/816-6691** in Manila, 800/435-9725 in the U.S.; www.philippineair.com).

Operated by the European Travel Network, **www.discount-tickets.com** is a great online source for regular and discounted airfares to destinations around the world. You can also use this site to compare rates and book accommodations, car rentals, and tours. Click on "Special Offers" for the latest package deals.

Airlines from the U.S. Mainland flying directly into Lihue, Kauai, are: **United Airlines** (✆ **800/225-5825;** www.ual.com), which offers direct service to Kauai, with daily flights from Los Angeles. **American Airlines** (✆ **800/433-7300;** www.aa.com) offers a nonstop, daily flight from Los Angeles. **America West** (✆ **800/327-7810;** www.americawest.com) has direct flights from Phoenix to Lihue. **SunTrips** (✆ **800/SUN-TRIP;** www.suntrips.com) offers a charter from Oakland International Airport (OAK) once a week. **Pleasant Hawaiian Holidays** (✆ **800/742-9244;** www.pleasantholidays.com), one of Hawaii's largest travel companies offering low-cost airfare and package deals, has two weekly nonstop flights from Los Angeles and San Francisco using American Trans Air. All other airlines land in Honolulu, where you'll have to connect to a 30-minute interisland flight to Kauai's Lihue Airport.

There are three interisland carriers: **Hawaiian Airlines** (✆ **800/367-5320,** 808/245-1813, or 808/838-1555; www.hawaiianair.com); **go!** (✆ **888/IFLYGO2;** www.iflygo.com), and Mokulele Airlines (✆ **866/260-7070;** www.mokuleleairlines.com) where there is a flight at least every hour to Lihue.

Arriving at the Airport

Lihue Airport is a couple of miles from downtown Lihue. There is no public transportation, and there are no shuttle vans available at the airport, so you must either rent a car or hire a taxi.

Flying for Less: Tips for Getting the Best Airfare

- Passengers who can book their ticket either **long in advance or at the last minute,** or who **fly midweek** or **at less-trafficked hours** may pay a fraction of the full fare. If your schedule is flexible, say so, and ask if you can secure a cheaper fare by changing your flight plans.
- Search the **Internet** for cheap fares. The most popular online travel agencies are **Travelocity.com** (www.travelocity.co.uk); **Expedia.com** (www.expedia.co.uk and www.expedia.ca); and **Orbitz.com**. In the U.K., go to **Travelsupermarket** (✆ **0845/345-5708;** www.travelsupermarket.com), a flight search engine that offers flight comparisons for the budget airlines whose seats often end up in bucket-shop sales. Other websites for booking airline tickets online include **Cheapflights.com, SmarterTravel.com, Priceline.com,** and **Opodo** (www.opodo.co.uk). Meta search sites (which find and then direct you to airline and hotel websites for booking) include **Sidestep.com** and **Kayak.com**—the latter includes fares for budget carriers like Jet Blue and Spirit as well as the major airlines. **Site59.com** is a great source for last-minute flights and getaways. In addition, most **airlines** offer online-only fares that even their phone agents know nothing about. British travelers should check **Flights International** (✆ **0800/0187050**) for deals on flights all over the world.
- Watch local newspapers for **promotional specials** or **fare wars,** when airlines lower prices on their most popular routes. Also keep an eye on price fluctuations and deals at websites such as **Airfarewatchdog.com** and **Farecast.com**.
- Try to book a ticket **in its country of origin.** If you're planning a one-way flight from Johannesburg to New York, a South Africa–based travel agent will probably have the lowest fares. For foreign travelers on multi-leg trips, book in the country of the first leg; for

Tips: Your Departure: Agricultural Screening at the Airports

All baggage and passengers bound for the mainland must be screened by agricultural officials before boarding. This takes a little time but isn't a problem unless you happen to be carrying a football-size local avocado home to Aunt Emma. Officials will confiscate fresh avocados, bananas, mangoes, and many other kinds of local produce in the name of fruit-fly control. Pineapples, coconuts, and papayas inspected and certified for export; boxed flowers; leis without seeds; and processed foods (macadamia nuts, coffee, jams, dried fruit, and the like) will pass. Call federal agricultural officials (✆ **808/877-8757**) before leaving for the airport if you're not sure about your trophy.

example, book New York–Chicago–Montreal–New York in the U.S.

- **Consolidators,** also known as bucket shops, are wholesale brokers in the airline-ticket game. Consolidators buy deeply discounted tickets ("distressed" inventories of unsold seats) from airlines and sell them to online ticket agencies, travel agents, tour operators, corporations, and, to a lesser degree, the general public. Consolidators advertise in Sunday newspaper travel sections (often in small ads with tiny type), both in the U.S. and the U.K. They can be great sources for cheap international tickets. On the downside, bucket-shop tickets are often rigged with restrictions, such as stiff cancellation penalties (as high as 50%–75% of the ticket price). And keep in mind that most of what you see advertised is of limited availability. Several reliable consolidators are worldwide and available online. **STA Travel** (www.statravel.com) has been the world's leading consolidator for students since purchasing Council Travel, but their fares are competitive for travelers of all ages. **Flights.com** (✆ **800/TRAV-800;** www.flights.com) has excellent fares worldwide, particularly to Europe. They also have "local" websites in 12 countries. **FlyCheap** (✆ **800/FLY-CHEAP;** www.1800flycheap.com) has especially good fares to sunny destinations. **Air Tickets Direct** (✆ **800/778-3447;** www.airticketsdirect.com) is based in Montreal and leverages the currently weak Canadian dollar for low fares; they also book trips to places that U.S. travel agents won't touch, such as Cuba.
- Join **frequent-flier clubs.** Frequent-flier membership doesn't cost a cent, but it does entitle you to free tickets or upgrades when you amass the airline's required number of frequent-flier points. You don't even have to fly to earn points; **frequent-flier credit cards** can earn you thousands of miles for doing your everyday shopping. But keep in mind that award seats are limited, seats on popular routes are hard to snag, and more and more major airlines are cutting their expiration periods for mileage points—so check your airline's frequent-flier program so you don't lose your miles before you use them. ***Inside tip:*** Award seats are offered almost a year in advance, but seats also open up at the last minute, so if your travel plans are flexible, you may strike gold. To play the frequent-flier game to your best advantage, consult the community bulletin boards on **FlyerTalk** (www.flyertalk.com) or go to Randy Petersen's **Inside Flyer** (www.insideflyer.com). Petersen and friends review all the programs in detail and post regular updates on changes in policies and trends.

Tips: Coping with Jet Lag

Jet lag is a pitfall of traveling across time zones. If you're flying north to south and you feel sluggish when you touch down, your symptoms will be caused by dehydration and the general stress of air travel. When you travel east to west, as you do when going to Hawaii, however, your body becomes thoroughly confused about what time it is, and everything from your digestion to your brain gets knocked for a loop. Traveling east, say, from Kauai to Los Angeles, is less difficult on your internal clock than traveling west, say from Atlanta to Hawaii, as most peoples' bodies find it more acceptable to stay up late than to fall asleep early.

Here are some tips for combating jet lag:

- **Reset your watch** to your destination time before you board the plane.
- **Drink lots of water** before, during, and after your flight. Avoid alcohol.
- **Exercise** and **sleep well** for a few days before your trip.
- If you have trouble sleeping on planes, **fly eastward on morning flights.**
- **Daylight** is the key to resetting your body clock. At the website for **Outside In** (www.bodyclock.com), you can get a customized plan of when to seek and avoid light.
- If you need help getting to sleep earlier than you usually would, doctors recommend taking either the hormone **melatonin** or the sleeping pill **Ambien**—but not together. Take 2 to 5 milligrams of melatonin about 2 hours before your planned bedtime.

GETTING AROUND

By Car

You need a car to see and do everything on Kauai. Luckily, driving here is easy. There are only two major highways, each beginning in Lihue. From Lihue Airport, turn right, and you'll be on Kapule Highway (Hwy. 51), which eventually merges into Kuhio Highway (Hwy. 56) a mile down. This road will take you to the Coconut Coast and through the North Shore before it reaches a dead end at Kee Beach, where the Na Pali Coast begins.

If you turn left from Lihue Airport and follow Kapule Highway (Hwy. 51), you'll pass through Lihue and Nawiliwili. Turning on Nawiliwili Road (Hwy. 58) will bring you to its intersection with Kaumualii Highway (Hwy. 50), which will take you to the south and southwest sections of the island. This road doesn't follow the coast, however, so if you're heading to Poipu (and most people are), take Maluhia Road (Hwy. 520) south.

Kaumualii Highway (Hwy. 50) continues all the way to Waimea, where it then dwindles to a secondary road before reaching a dead end at the other end of the Na Pali Coast.

To get to Waimea Canyon, take either Waimea Canyon Road (Hwy. 550), which follows the western rim of the canyon and affords spectacular views, or Kokee Road (Hwy. 55), which goes up through Waimea Canyon to Kokee State Park (4,000 ft. above sea level); the roads join up about halfway.

Car Rentals

Hawaii has some of the lowest car-rental rates in the country. To rent a car in

Tips Traffic Advisory

Believe it or not Kauai has traffic problems. You do NOT want to be on the highways between 7 to 9am and 4 to 6pm, Monday through Friday. Your serene vacation will go out the car window as you sit in bumper-to-bumper traffic. A normal 10- to 15-minute trip from one town to the next can take up to an hour during these times. The problem is that there is only one road that circles the island and connects all the towns. Local people have to get to work, but you are on vacation so plan accordingly. ***Another traffic note:*** Buckle up your seat belt—Hawaii has stiff fines for noncompliance.

Hawaii, you must be at least 25 years of age and have a valid driver's license and credit card.

Most of the major car-rental agencies are represented on Kauai. The rental desks are just across the street from Lihue Airport, but you must go by van to collect your car.

The major rental-car agencies at Lihue Airport include: **Avis** (© **800/321-3712;** www.avis.com), **Budget** (© **800/935-6878;** www.budgetrentacar.com), **Dollar** (© **800/800-4000;** www.dollarcar.com), **Hertz** (© **800/654-3011;** www.hertz.com), **National** (© **800/227-7368;** www.nationalcar.com), and **Thrifty** (© **800/367-2277;** www.thrifty.com).

We do not recommend Alamo, which apparently is not able to process (in a timely manner) the long line of people wanting to rent their cars. Waits of up to 2 hours are not uncommon. Imagine getting off a 5-hour plane ride and having to stand in line for a couple of hours. Save yourself the aggravation, and book another car-rental agency.

Rental cars are usually at a premium and may be sold out on holiday weekends, so be sure to book well ahead.

INSURANCE Hawaii is a no-fault state, which means that if you don't have collision-damage insurance, you are required to pay for all damages before you leave the state, whether or not the accident was your fault. Your personal car insurance may provide rental-car coverage; read your policy or call your insurer before you leave home. Bring your insurance identification card if you decline the optional insurance, which usually costs from $12 to $20 a day. Obtain the name of your company's local claim representative before you go. Some credit card companies also provide collision-damage insurance for their customers; check with yours before you rent.

DRIVING RULES Hawaii state law mandates that all car passengers must wear a **seat belt,** and all infants must be strapped into car seats. The fine is enforced with vigilance, so buckle up—you'll pay a $50 fine if you don't. **Pedestrians** always have the right of way, even if they're not in the crosswalk. You can turn **right on red** from the right lane after a full and complete stop, unless there's a sign forbidding you to do so.

ROAD MAPS The best and most detailed road maps are published by *This Week Magazine,* a free visitor publication. Another good source of maps is *The Ready Mapbook of Kauai,* published by **Odyssey Publishing,** P.O. Box 11173, Hilo, HI 96721 (© **808/935-0092;** www.hawaiimapsource.com). The 67-page book not only has detailed maps of the island, but also lists points of interest, parks, beaches, golf courses, campgrounds, shopping centers, and trails. The book retails for $11.

For island maps, check out the University of Hawaii Press maps. Updated periodically, they include a detailed network of island roads, large scale insets of towns, historical and contemporary points of interest, parks, beaches, and hiking trails. They cost about $3 each, or about $15 for a complete set. If you can't find them in a bookstore near you, contact **University of Hawaii Press,** 2840 Kolowalu St., Honolulu, HI 96822 (✆ **888/847-7737;** www.uhpress.hawaii.edu). For topographic and other maps of the islands, go to the **Hawaii Geographic Society,** 49 S. Hotel St., Honolulu; or contact them at P.O. Box 1698, Honolulu, HI 96806 (✆ **800/538-3950** or 808/538-3952).

Motorcycle Rentals

The best place to find a customized, cherried-out motorcycle is **Kauai Harley Davidson,** located near Nawiliwili Harbor, 3-1866 Kaumualii Hwy, Lihue (✆ **877/212-9253** or 808/241-7020; www.kauaimotorcycle.com), which has Harleys from $139/day.

Other Transportation Options

Kauai Taxi Company (✆ **808/246-9554;** www.kauai.gov) offers taxi, limousine, and airport shuttle service. **Kauai Bus** (✆ **808/241-6417**) operates a fleet of 15 buses that serve the entire island. Taking the bus may be practical for day trips if you know your way around the island, but you can't take anything larger than a shopping bag aboard, and the buses don't stop at any of the resort areas. However, they do serve more than a dozen coastal towns from Kekaha, on the southwest shore, all the way to Hanalei. Buses run more or less hourly from 5:30am to 6pm. The fare ranges from 50¢ for shuttle service to $1.50 for main line service.

4 MONEY & COSTS

Frommer's lists exact prices in the local currency (in Hawaii, it's the U.S. dollar). The currency conversions quoted below were correct at press time. However, rates fluctuate, so before departing consult a currency exchange website such as **www.oanda.com/convert/classic** to check up-to-the-minute rates.

The Value of the U.S. Dollar vs. Other Popular Currencies

US$	Can$	UK£	Euro (€)	Aus$	NZ$
1	C$1.06	£0.63	€0.68	A$1.12	NZ$1.36

ATMS

Hawaii pioneered the use of **ATMs** more than 3 decades ago, and now they're everywhere. You'll find them at most banks, in supermarkets, at Long's Drugs, and in most resorts and shopping centers. **Cirrus** (✆ **800/424-7787;** www.mastercard.com) and **PLUS** (✆ **800/843-7587;** www.visa.com) are the two most popular networks; check the back of your ATM card to see which network your bank belongs to (most banks belong to both these days).

CREDIT CARDS & DEBIT CARDS

Credit cards are the most widely used form of payment in the United States: **Visa** (Barclaycard in Britain), **MasterCard** (EuroCard in Europe, Access in Britain, Chargex in Canada), **American Express, Diners Club,** and **Discover.** They also

Tips Dear Visa: I'm Off to Kapaa, Koloa & Kilauea!

Some credit card companies recommend that you notify them of any impending trip so that they don't become suspicious when the card is used numerous times in an exotic destination and your charges are blocked. Even if you don't call your credit card company in advance, you can always call the card's toll-free emergency number (see "Fast Facts: Kauai" in chapter 11) if a charge is refused—a good reason to carry the phone number with you. But perhaps the most important advice is to carry more than one card on your trip; if one card doesn't work for any number of reasons, you'll have a backup card just in case.

provide a convenient record of all your expenses, and offer relatively good exchange rates. You can withdraw cash advances from your credit cards at banks or ATMs, but high fees make credit-card cash advances a pricey way to get cash.

It's highly recommended that you travel with at least one major credit card. You must have a credit card to rent a car, and hotels and airlines usually require a credit card imprint as a deposit against expenses.

Credit cards are accepted all over the island. They're a safe way to carry money and they provide a convenient record of all your expenses. You can also withdraw cash advances from your credit cards at banks or ATMs, provided you know your PIN (personal identification number). If you've forgotten yours, or didn't even know you had one, call the phone number on the back of your credit card and ask the bank to send it to you. It usually takes 5 to 7 business days, though some banks will provide the number over the phone if you tell them your mother's maiden name or some other personal information. Still, be sure to keep some cash on hand for that rare occasion when a restaurant or small shop doesn't take plastic.

ATM cards with major credit card backing, known as **"debit cards,"** are now a commonly acceptable form of payment in most stores and restaurants. Debit cards draw money directly from your checking account. Some stores enable you to receive cash back on your debit-card purchases as well. The same is true at most U.S. post offices.

TRAVELER'S CHECKS

Traveler's checks are something of an anachronism from the days before the ATM made cash accessible at any time. Traveler's checks used to be the only sound alternative to traveling with dangerously large amounts of cash. They were as reliable as currency but, unlike cash, they could be replaced if lost or stolen.

These days, traveler's checks are less necessary because most cities have 24-hour ATMs that allow you to withdraw small amounts of cash as needed. However, keep in mind that you will likely be charged an ATM withdrawal fee if the bank is not your own, so if you're withdrawing money every day, you might be better off with traveler's checks—provided that you don't mind showing identification every time you want to cash one.

You can get traveler's checks at almost any bank. **American Express** offers denominations of $20, $50, $100, $500, and (for cardholders only) $1,000. You'll pay a service charge ranging from 1% to 4%. You can also get American Express traveler's checks over the phone by calling ✆ **800/221-7282;** Amex gold and platinum cardholders who use this number are exempt from the 1% fee.

What Things Cost in Kauai	US$
Hamburger	$6.00
Movie ticket (adult)	$9.00
Movie ticket (child)	$5.50
Entry to Kauai Museum (adult)	$10.00
Entry to Kauai Museum (child)	$1.00
Fee Kauai Plantation Railway (adult)	$18.00
Fee Kauai Plantation Railway (child)	$14.00
Admission & Tour Allerton Garden (adult)	$45.00
Admission & Tour Allerton Garden (child)	$20.00
20-ounce soft drink at drug or convenience store	$2.50
16-ounce apple juice	$3.50
Cup of coffee	$3.00
Helicopter ride	$197
Moderate 3-course dinner without alcohol	$50
Moderately priced hotel	$125–$175

Visa offers traveler's checks at Citibank locations nationwide, as well as at several other banks. The service charge ranges between 1.5% and 2%; checks come in denominations of $20, $50, $100, $500, and $1,000. Call ✆ **800/732-1322** for information. AAA members can obtain checks without a fee at most AAA offices.

MasterCard also offers traveler's checks. Call ✆ **800/223-9920** for a location near you.

If you choose to carry traveler's checks, be sure to keep a record of their serial numbers separate from your checks in the event that they are stolen or lost. You'll get a refund faster if you know the numbers.

5 HEALTH

STAYING HEALTHY

Hawaii is one of the healthiest states in the union. You do not need any special vaccinations or medications before you come here.

One thing you should know before you arrive is that Hawaii mandates health care insurance for all employees, so most medical facilities (hospitals, doctor's offices, and the like) are used to dealing with insurance companies, HMOs, and such. If you are uninsured, some doctors will not treat you. If you have medical insurance, be sure to bring your insurance card with you.

Pack prescription medications in your carry-on luggage. Carry written prescriptions in generic form, not brand name form, and dispense all prescription medications from their original labeled vials. If you wear contact lenses, pack an extra pair in case you lose one.

COMMON AILMENTS

Below are the types of "critters" we have on land in Kauai and at sea that you might run into and how to handle bites, scratches, and such.

On Land

As in any tropical climate, there are lots of bugs in Kauai. Most of them won't harm you. However, three insects—mosquitoes, centipedes, and scorpions—do sting, and

What to Do If Your Luggage Is Delayed or (Gasp!) Lost

You're standing at the luggage carousel, watching the same baggage go round and round when you realize there are no more bags being unloaded and your bag is not there.

- The first thing is not to panic; most bags are delivered to their destination within 24 to 48 hours. Here are some tips to help you and your bag get reunited as soon as possible.
- **Have your name and destination address both outside and inside your luggage.** At least you'll have a fighting chance of being contacted if your bag is tagged with where your bag is going (not just your home address, but the address of your hotel/condo in Hawaii, with a contact phone number). While you're at it, get rid of all the old airline baggage tags to other destinations.
- **Know where the lost baggage claim counter is for your airline.** While you are waiting for your luggage, make sure you know where you will have to go to file a claim; that way you can be the first in line if your bag did not arrive. If you flew on more than one airline, always go to the last airline you flew on; they are the ones to start processing your claim.
- **To wait or not to wait for the next flight.** The lost luggage claims desk loves to tell people: "Oh, your bag will be in on the next flight." Smile, and politely ask them if they have proof that the bag is in the system and booked on that flight. If they can't guarantee it, you might want to proceed to your destination, rather than wait around the airport in hopes that the suitcase "might" be on the next flight.
- **Before you leave the airport (without your bag),** be sure to get the following: a copy of your lost luggage claim form, the phone number to call to check on your luggage, an estimate on when they will have more information on when your bag will arrive, and what you should do if your bag does not arrive.
- **If your bag is lost,** don't expect the airlines to write you a check for $2,800 on the spot. You will have to make a list of what was in your bags (no exaggerating here—you probably did not have a couple of designer dresses in your bag to Hawaii); be sure to list the cost of the suitcase itself and any money you have had to pay out to replace items in the suitcase. Unfortunately, the airlines will only reimburse you for the depreciated value of your items, *not* the replacement value.

they can cause anything from mild annoyance to severe swelling and pain.

MOSQUITOES These pesky insects aren't native to Hawaii but arrived as larvae stowed away in the water barrels on the ship *Wellington* in 1826. There's not a whole lot you can do about them, except apply repellent or burn mosquito punk or citronella candles to keep them out of your area. If they've bitten you, head to the

Everything You've Always Wanted to Know about Sharks

The Hawaii State Department of Land and Natural Resources has launched a website with more information than you probably wanted to know about sharks: www.hawaiisharks.com. The site has the biology, history, and culture of these carnivores, plus information on safety and data on shark bites in Hawaii.

drugstore for sting-stopping ointments (antihistamine creams like Benadryl or homeopathic creams like Sting Stop or Florasone); they'll ease the itching and swelling. Most bites disappear in anywhere from a few hours to a few days.

CENTIPEDES These segmented insects with a jillion legs come in two varieties: 6- to 8-inch brown ones and the smaller 2- to 3-inch blue guys; both can really pack a wallop with their sting. Centipedes are generally found in damp places, like under wood piles or compost heaps. Wearing closed-toe shoes can help prevent stings if you accidentally unearth a centipede. If you're stung, the reaction can range from something similar to a mild bee sting to severe pain; apply ice at once to prevent swelling. See a doctor if you experience extreme pain, swelling, nausea, or any other severe reaction.

SCORPIONS Rarely seen, scorpions are found in arid, warm regions; their stings can be serious. Campers in dry areas should always check their boots before putting them on, and shake out sleeping bags and bedrolls. Symptoms of a scorpion sting include shortness of breath, hives, swelling, and nausea. In the unlikely event that you're stung, apply diluted household ammonia and cold compresses to the area of the sting, and seek medical attention immediately.

Ocean Safety

Because most people coming to Kauai are unfamiliar with the ocean environment, they're often unaware of the natural hazards it holds. But with just a few precautions, your ocean experience can be a safe and happy one. An excellent book to get is *All Stings Considered: First Aid and Medical Treatment of Hawaii's Marine Injuries* (University of Hawaii Press, 1997), by Craig Thomas (an emergency-medicine doctor) and Susan Scott (a registered nurse). These avid water people have put together the authoritative book on first aid for Hawaii's marine injuries.

SEASICKNESS The waters off Kauai can range from calm as glass to downright frightening (in storm conditions), and they usually fall somewhere in between; in general, expect rougher conditions in winter than in summer.

Some 90% of the population tends toward seasickness. If you've never been out on a boat or if you've gotten seasick in the past, you might want to heed the following suggestions:

- The day before you go out on the boat, avoid alcohol; caffeine; citrus and other acidic juices; and greasy, spicy, or hard-to-digest foods.
- Get a good night's sleep the night before.
- Take or use whatever seasickness prevention works best for you—medication, an acupressure wristband, ginger root tea or capsules, or any combination—*before* you board; once you set sail, it's generally too late.
- Once you're on the water, stay as low and as near the center of the boat as possible. Avoid the fumes (especially if it's a diesel boat); stay out in the fresh air and watch the horizon. Do not read.
- If you start to feel queasy, drink clear fluids like water, and eat something bland, such as a soda cracker.

Tips Don't Get Burned: Smart Tanning Tips

Tanning just ain't what it used to be. Hawaii's Caucasian population has a higher incidence of the deadly skin cancer malignant melanoma than the population anywhere else in the United States. But none of us are safe from the sun's harmful rays: People of all skin types and races can burn when exposed to the sun too long.

To ensure that your vacation won't be ruined by a painful, throbbing sunburn, here are some helpful tips on how to tan safely and painlessly:

- **Wear a strong sunscreen at all times, and use lots of it.** Use a sunscreen with a sun-protection factor (SPF) of 15 or higher; people with a light complexion should use 30. Apply sunscreen as soon as you get out of the shower in the morning, and at least 30 minutes before you're exposed to the sun. No matter what the label says—even if the sunscreen is waterproof—reapply it every 2 hours and immediately after swimming.
- **Read the labels.** To avoid developing allergies to sunscreens, avoid those that contain para-aminobenzoic acid (PABA). Look for a sunscreen with zinc oxide, talc, or titanium dioxide, which reduce the risk of developing skin allergies. For the best protection from UVA rays (which can cause wrinkles and premature aging), check the label for zinc oxide, benzophenone, oxybenzone, sulisobenzone, titanium dioxide, or avobenzone (also known as Parsol 1789).
- **Wear a hat and sunglasses.** And make sure that your sunglasses have UV filters.
- **Avoid being in the sun between 9am and 3pm.** Use extra caution during these peak hours. Remember that a beach umbrella is not protection enough from the sun's harmful UV rays; in fact, with the reflection from the water, the sand, and even the sidewalk, some 85% of the ultraviolet rays are still bombarding you.
- **Protect children from the sun, and keep infants out of the sun altogether.** Infants under 6 months should not be in the sun at all. Older babies need zinc oxide to protect their fragile skin, and children should be slathered with sunscreen every hour. The burns that children get today predict what their future with skin cancer will be tomorrow.

If you start to turn red, **get out of the sun.** Contrary to popular belief, you don't have to turn red to tan; if your skin is red, it's burned—and that's serious. The redness from a burn may not show until 2 to 8 hours after you get out of the sun, and the full force of that burn may not appear for 24 to 36 hours. During that time, you can look forward to pain, itching, and peeling. The best **remedy** for a sunburn is to get out of the sun immediately and stay out of the sun until all the redness is gone. Aloe vera (straight from the plant or from a commercial preparation), cool compresses, cold baths, and anesthetic benzocaine may also help ease the pain of sunburn.

If you've decided to get a head start on your tan by using a self-tanning lotion that dyes your skin a darker shade, remember that this will not protect you from the sun. You'll still need to generously apply sunscreen when you go out.

STINGS The most common stings in Hawaii come from jellyfish, particularly Portuguese man-of-war and box jellyfish. Since the poisons they inject are very different, you need to treat each sting differently.

A bluish-purple floating bubble with a long tail, the **Portuguese man-of-war** causes thousands of stings a year. Stings, although painful and a nuisance, are rarely harmful; fewer than one in a thousand require medical treatment. The best prevention is to watch for these floating bubbles as you snorkel (look for the hanging tentacles below the surface). Get out of the water if anyone near you spots these jellyfish.

Reactions to stings range from mild burning and redness to severe welts and blisters. *All Stings Considered* recommends the following treatment: First, pick off any visible tentacles with a gloved hand, a stick, or anything handy; then rinse the sting with fresh or salt water; and finally apply ice to prevent swelling and to help control pain.

Hawaiian folklore advises using vinegar, meat tenderizer, baking soda, papain, or alcohol, or even urinating on the wound. Studies have shown that these remedies may actually cause further damage. Most Portuguese man-of-war stings will disappear by themselves within 15 to 20 minutes if you do nothing to treat them. Still, be sure to see a doctor if pain persists or if a rash or other symptoms develop.

Box jellyfish, transparent, square-shaped bell jellyfish, are nearly impossible to see in the water. Fortunately, they seem to follow a monthly cycle: 8 to 10 days after the full moon, they appear in the waters on the leeward side of the island and hang around for about 3 days. Also, they seem to sting more in the morning hours, when they're on or near the surface. The best prevention is to get out of the water.

Stings range from no visible marks to red, hivelike welts, blisters, and pain (a burning sensation) lasting from 10 minutes to 8 hours. *All Stings Considered* recommends the following course of treatment: First, pour regular household vinegar on the sting; this may not relieve the pain, but it will stop additional burning. Do not rub the area. Pick off any vinegar-soaked tentacles with a stick. For pain, apply an ice pack. Seek additional medical treatment if you experience shortness of breath, weakness, palpitations, muscle cramps, or any other severe symptoms. Again, ignore any folk remedies. Most box jellyfish stings disappear by themselves without treatment.

PUNCTURES Most sea-related punctures come from stepping on or brushing against the needlelike spines of sea urchins (known locally as *wana*). Be careful when you're in the water; don't put your foot down (even if you have booties or fins on) if you cannot clearly see the bottom. Waves can push you into *wana* in a surge zone in shallow water (the *wana*'s spines can even puncture a wet suit).

A sea urchin sting can result in burning, aching, swelling, and discoloration (black or purple) around the area where the spines have entered your skin. The best thing to do is to pull out any protruding spines. The body will absorb the spines

Tips Enjoying the Ocean & Avoiding Mishaps

The Kauai Visitors Bureau has an excellent website (www.kauaiexplorer.com) to help you enjoy Kauai's beaches and stay safe in the marine environment. The site introduces visitors to the various beaches, points out any hazards, lists surf conditions, states whether the beach has a lifeguard, and includes a map.

within 24 hours to 3 weeks, or the remainder of the spines will work themselves out. Again, contrary to popular wisdom, do not urinate or pour vinegar on the embedded spines—this will not help.

CUTS All cuts obtained in the marine environment must be taken seriously because the high level of bacteria present can quickly cause the cut to become infected. The most common cuts are from **coral.** Contrary to popular belief, coral cannot grow inside your body. However, bacteria can—and very often does—grow inside a cut. The best way to prevent cuts is to wear a wet suit, gloves, and reef shoes. Never, under any circumstances, should you touch a coral head; not only can you get cut, but you can also damage a living organism that took decades to grow.

The symptoms of a coral cut can range from a slight scratch to severe welts and blisters. *All Stings Considered* recommends gently pulling the edges of the skin open and removing any embedded coral or grains of sand with tweezers, or rinsing well with fresh water. Next, scrub the cut well under fresh water. Never use ocean water to clean a cut. If the wound is bleeding, press a clean cloth against it until it stops. If bleeding continues or if the edges of the injury are jagged or gaping, seek medical treatment.

WHAT TO DO IF YOU GET SICK AWAY FROM HOME

In most cases, your existing health plan will provide the coverage you need. But double-check; you may want to buy **travel medical insurance** instead. Bring your insurance ID card with you when you travel.

We list **hospitals** and **emergency numbers** under "Fast Facts: Kauai," in chapter 11.

If you suffer from a chronic illness, consult your doctor before your departure. Pack **prescription medications** in your carry-on luggage, and carry them in their original containers, with pharmacy labels—otherwise they won't make it through airport security. Visitors from outside the U.S. should carry generic names of prescription drugs. For U.S. travelers, most reliable healthcare plans provide coverage if you get sick away from home. Foreign visitors may have to pay all medical costs upfront and be reimbursed later. For information on medical insurance while traveling please visit www.frommers.com/planning.

We list additional **emergency numbers** in the "Fast Facts" p. 231.

6 SAFETY

IT'S THE LAW

NUDITY Going bare in Hawaii is illegal and you can be arrested. No matter what you have heard or read, nudity in Hawaii is against the law.

TRESPASSING Walking across someone's private property to get to the beach is illegal and called trespassing. Yes, Hawaii law guarantees that the beaches in Hawaii are open to the public, but only at designated "beach access" points. Unfortunately there are some guidebooks that recommend trespassing across public property to get to "remote" beaches. Be warned: This is illegal and you could be arrested. All of the beaches we recommend in this book have public beach accesses, which provide safe, legal access to the beach.

SMOKING Hawaii has very strict nonsmoking laws. It's against the law to smoke in public buildings, including airports, shopping malls, grocery stores, retail shops, buses, movie theaters, banks, convention facilities, and all government

Tips A Few Words of Warning about Crime

Although Kauai is generally a safe tourist destination, visitors have been crime victims, so stay alert. The most common crime against tourists is rental-car break-ins. **Never leave any valuables in your car,** not even in your trunk: Thieves can be in and out of your trunk faster than you can open it with your own keys. Be especially leery of high-risk areas, such as beaches, resorts, scenic lookouts, and other visitor attractions. In fact, after you take your suitcases out of the trunk, do not put anything else in it. Buy a fanny pack to carry your keys and wallet when you go to the beach or for a hike. Also, never carry large amounts of cash. Stay in well-lighted areas after dark. Do not display the parking pass from your hotel (look on your windshield, or sometimes the parking attendants attach it to your rearview mirror) when you leave the resort property.

buildings and facilities. There is no smoking in restaurants, bars, and nightclubs. Most bed-and-breakfasts prohibit smoking indoors; more and more hotels and resorts are becoming nonsmoking even in public areas. Also, there is no smoking within 20 feet of a doorway, window, or ventilation intake (no hanging around outside a bar to smoke; you must go 20 ft. away). Even some beaches have nonsmoking policies (and on those that allow smoking, you'd better pick up your butts and not use the sand as your own private ashtray—or face stiff fines). Breathing fresh, clear air is "in" and smoking in Hawaii is "out."

HIKING SAFETY

In addition to taking the appropriate precautions regarding Kauai's bug population (see above), hikers should always let someone know where they're heading, when they're going, and when they plan to return; too many hikers get lost on Kauai because they don't inform others of their basic plans.

Always check weather conditions with the **National Weather Service** (✆ **808/245-6001**) before you go. Hike with a pal, never alone. Wear hiking boots, a sun hat, clothes to protect you from the sun and from getting scratches, and high-SPF sunscreen on all exposed areas of skin. Take water. Stay on the trail. Watch your step. It's easy to slip off precipitous trails and into steep canyons, with often disastrous, even fatal, results. Incapacitated hikers are often plucked to safety by fire and rescue squads, who must use helicopters to gain access to remote sites. Many experienced hikers and boaters today pack a cellular phone in case of emergency; just dial ✆ **911.**

VOG

The volcanic haze dubbed "vog" is caused by gases released when molten lava—from the continuous eruption of the volcano on the flank of Kilauea on the Big Island—pours into the ocean. This hazy air, which looks like urban smog, limits viewing from scenic vistas and wreaks havoc with photographers trying to get clear panoramic shots. Some people claim that long-term exposure to vog has even caused bronchial ailments.

There actually is a vog season in Hawaii: the fall and winter months, when the trade winds that blow the fumes out to sea die down. The vog is felt not only on the Big Island but also as far away as Maui and Oahu. Kauai generally does not experience vog.

FOR TRAVELERS WITH DISABILITIES

Travelers with disabilities are made to feel very welcome in Kauai. Hotels are usually equipped with wheelchair-accessible rooms, and tour companies provide many special services. The **Hawaii Center for Independent Living,** 414 Kauwili St., Suite 102, Honolulu, HI 96817 (✆ **808/522-5400;** fax 808/586-8129; www.hawaii.gov/health), can provide information and send you a copy of the *Aloha Guide to Accessibility* ($15).

MossRehab ResourceNet (www.mossresourcenet.org) is a great source for information, tips, and resources relating to accessible travel. You'll find links to a number of travel agents who specialize in planning trips for travelers with disabilities here and through **Access-Able Travel Source** (✆ **303/232-2979;** www.access-able.com), another excellent online source. You'll also find relay and voice numbers for hotels, airlines, and car-rental companies on Access-Able's user-friendly site, as well as links to accessible accommodations, attractions, transportation, tours, local medical resources, equipment repair, and much more.

For travelers with disabilities who wish to do their own driving, hand-controlled cars can be rented from **Avis** (✆ **800/331-1212;** www.avis.com) and **Hertz** (✆ **800/654-3131;** www.hertz.com). The number of hand-controlled cars in Hawaii is limited, so be sure to book well in advance. For wheelchair-accessible vans, contact **Accessible Vans of Hawaii,** 186 Mehani Circle, Kihei (✆ **800/303-3750** or 808/879-5521; fax 808/879-0640; www.accessiblevans.com). Kauai recognizes other states' windshield placards indicating that the driver of the car is disabled, so be sure to bring yours with you.

Vision-impaired travelers who use a Seeing Eye dog can now come to Hawaii without the hassle of quarantine. A recent court decision ruled that visitors with Seeing Eye dogs only need to present documentation that the dog is a trained Seeing Eye dog and has had rabies shots. For more information, contact the **Animal Quarantine Facility** (✆ **808/483-7171;** www.hawaii.gov).

FOR GAY & LESBIAN TRAVELERS

Known for its acceptance of all groups, Hawaii welcomes gays and lesbians just as it does anybody else.

For information on Kauai's gay community and related events, contact the **Bisexual/Transgender/Gay/Lesbian Community Bulletin Board** (✆ **808/823-6248**).

Pacific Ocean Holidays, P.O. Box 88245, Honolulu, HI 96830 (✆ **800/735-6600** or 808/923-2400; www.gayhawaii.com), offers vacation packages that feature gay-owned and gay-friendly lodgings.

If you want help planning your trip, the **International Gay & Lesbian Travel Association (IGLTA;** ✆ **800/448-8550** or 954/776-2626; www.iglta.org) can link you with the appropriate gay-friendly service organization or tour specialist. With around 1,200 members, it offers quarterly newsletters, marketing mailings, and a membership directory that's updated quarterly. Members are kept informed of gay and gay-friendly hoteliers, tour operators, and airline and cruise-line representatives. **GayWired Travel Services (www.gaywired.com)** is another great trip-planning resource; click on "Travel Services."

Out and About (✆ **800/929-2268** or 415/486-2591; www.outandabout.com) offers a monthly newsletter packed with good information on the global gay and lesbian scene. Its website features links to gay and lesbian tour operators and other gay-themed travel links, plus extensive online travel information for subscribers only. Out and About's guidebooks are available at most major bookstores and through www.adlbooks.com.

FOR SENIORS

Discounts for seniors are available at almost all of Kauai's major attractions, and occasionally at hotels and restaurants. Always inquire when you make hotel reservations, and especially when you buy your airline ticket—most major domestic airlines offer senior discounts.

Members of the **AARP** (formerly the American Association of Retired Persons; ✆ **800/424-3410** or 202/434-2277; www.aarp.org) are usually eligible for such discounts; AARP also puts together organized tour packages at moderate rates.

Some great, low-cost trips to Hawaii are offered to people 55 and older through **Elderhostel,** 75 Federal St., Boston, MA 02110 (✆ **617/426-8056;** www.elderhostel.org), a nonprofit group that arranges travel and study programs around the world. You can obtain a complete catalog of offerings by writing to Elderhostel, P.O. Box 1959, Wakefield, MA 01880-5959.

FOR FAMILIES

Kauai is paradise for children: beaches to frolic on, water to splash in, unusual sights to see, and a host of new foods to taste. Be sure to check out "Family-Friendly Hotels" in chapter 5, "Family-Friendly Restaurants" in chapter 6, and "Especially for Kids" in chapter 7.

The larger hotels and resorts have supervised programs for children and can refer you to qualified babysitters. You can also contact **People Attentive to Children (PATCH; ✆ 808/246-0622;** www.patch-hi.org), which will refer you to individuals who have taken their training courses on child care.

Remember that Kauai's sun is probably much stronger than what you're used to at home, so it's important to protect your kids. Keep infants out of the sun; infants under 6 months should not be in the sun at all. Older babies need zinc oxide to protect their fragile skin, and children should be slathered with sunscreen every hour.

Condo rentals are a great option for families; the convenience of having your own kitchen is great for Mom and Dad. See "Types of Accommodations," later in this chapter. Our favorite condo complexes are reviewed throughout that section.

8 GETTING MARRIED ON KAUAI

Whatever your budget, Kauai is a great place for a wedding. Not only does the entire island exude romance and natural beauty, but after the ceremony, you're only a few steps away from the perfect honeymoon. And the members of your wedding party will most likely be delighted, since you've given them the perfect excuse for their own island vacation.

More than 20,000 marriages are performed each year on the islands, and nearly half of the couples married here are from somewhere else. This booming business has spawned dozens of companies that can help you organize a long-distance event and stage an unforgettable wedding, Hawaiian-style or your own style.

The easiest way to plan your wedding is to let someone else handle it at the resort or hotel where you'll be staying. All of the major resorts and hotels (and even most of the small ones) have wedding coordinators, whose job is to make sure that your wedding day is everything you've dreamed about. They can plan everything from a simple (relatively) low-cost wedding to an extravaganza that people will remember and talk about for years. Remember that resorts can be pricey—catering, flowers, musicians, and so on may cost more in a resort than outside a resort, but sometimes you can save money because the resort will not charge a room rental fee if they get to do the catering. Be frank with your wedding coordinator if you want to keep costs down. However, you can also plan your own island wedding, even from afar, and not spend a fortune doing it.

If you want to plan the wedding yourself, helpful tools on the Internet are: the Kauai Visitors Bureau's **Official Kauai Travel Planner** (for a free copy call ✆ **800/262-1400**), a great source of information for weddings, accommodations, and activities; information from **Hawaii Visitors and Conventions Bureau** website, www.gohawaii.com; and the **Kauai Wedding Professional Association** (www.kauaiwedpro.com).

THE PAPERWORK

The state of Hawaii has some very minimal procedures for obtaining a marriage license. The first thing you should do is contact the **Marriage License Office** (✆ **808/241-3498;** www.hawaii.gov/doh, then click on "Getting a Marriage License"). The staff will mail you a brochure, *Getting Married,* and direct you to the marriage licensing agent closest to where you'll be staying on Kauai. The office is open Monday through Friday from 8am to 4pm.

Once on Kauai, the prospective bride and groom must go together to the marriage licensing agent to get a license. A license costs $60 and is good for 30 days; if you don't have the ceremony within the time allotted, you'll have to pay another $60 for another license. The only requirements for a marriage license are that both parties are 15 years of age or older (couples 15–17 years old must have proof of age, written consent of both sets of parents, and the written approval of the judge of the family court) and are not more closely related than first cousins. That's it.

Contrary to some reports from the media, gay couples cannot marry in Hawaii. After a protracted legal battle, and much discussion in the state legislature, in late 1999 the Hawaii Supreme Court ruled that the state will not issue a marriage license to a couple of the same sex.

PLANNING THE WEDDING

DOING IT YOURSELF The marriage licensing agents, which range from the governor's satellite office to private individuals, are usually friendly, helpful people who can steer you to a nondenominational minister or someone who's licensed by the state of Hawaii to perform the ceremony. These marriage performers are great sources of information for budget weddings. They usually know great places to have the ceremony for free or for a nominal fee.

If you don't want to use a wedding planner (see below) but want to make arrangements before you arrive on Kauai, our best advice is to get a copy of the daily newspaper the ***Garden Island,*** 3137 Kuhio Hwy., Lihue, HI 96766 (✆ **808/245-3681;** www.kauaiworld.com). People willing and qualified to conduct weddings advertise in the classifieds. They're great sources of information because they know the best places to have the ceremony and can recommend caterers, florists, and everything else you'll need.

USING A WEDDING PLANNER Wedding planners—many of whom are marriage licensing agents as well—can arrange everything for you, from a small, private, outdoor affair to a full-blown formal ceremony in a tropical setting. They charge anywhere from $450 to a small fortune—it all depends on what you want.

Planners on Kauai include **Coconut Coast Weddings & Honeymoons** (✆ **800/585-5595** or 808/828-0999; www.kauaiwedding.com); **A Simple Marriage** (✆ **808/742-6115;** www.asimplemarriagekauai.com); **A Vow Exchange** (✆ **800/460-3434** or 808/826-1869; www.vowexchange.com);

Island Weddings & Blessings (✆ **800/998-1548** or 808/828-1548; www.weddings-kauai.com); and **Tropical Dream Wedding** (✆ **888/615-5656** or 808/332-5664; www.tropicaldreamwedding.com).

9 SUSTAINABLE TOURISM

If there is one place on the planet that signifies eco-tourism (defined as a place people visit because of the ecology: the ocean, the beach, the mountains, and beauty of the place)—it's Kauai.

In many respects the ancient Hawaiians not only knew about sustainable resources, but also practiced sustainability in their daily lives. They had to! When the ancient Hawaiians occupied the islands they did not have the luxury of "importing" goods from anywhere else. They had the land under their feet and the ocean to gain sustenance from, and those resources had to last not only for their immediate lifetime, but also for the lifetimes of generations to come. So these ancient people lived in harmony with the land and sea and had a complex social structure that managed resources and forbade the taking of various resources during certain times of the year, to allow those resources to replenish themselves.

Now fast forward to the 21st century. Today, we, the current stewards of the islands of Hawaii, are just beginning to appreciate just how wise and advanced the "ancient" Hawaiians were. In some ways, the state of Hawaii has pioneered various ways to protect and save its national resources (for example, Hawaii is second only to California in the number of marine reserves in the National System of Marine Protected Areas), but in other ways, Hawaii falls short of the example set by the ancient Hawaiians.

The State of Hawaii has several excellent stewardship programs to preserve the ocean environment and its resources, ranging from Marine Life Conservation Districts to Fishery Management Areas (where what you can take from the ocean is restricted) to Fishery Replenishment Areas to Estuarine Reserves. On land, there are corresponding programs to protect the environment, from the Soil and Water Conservation District to Watershed Reserves.

In the visitor industry, the majority of hotels have adopted green practices, not only to save the environment, but also to save money. Nearly every hotel in the state will have a card in your room asking you to consider if you really need a new towel or if you can hang it up and use it 1 more day. Various statewide organizations have numerous programs recognizing hotels which are helping the environment, such as the Green Business Awards Program.

Kauai has a number of recycling centers ranging from sites that collect recyclable bottles only to places that take everything. For a list of recycling centers, visit the Hawaii State Department of Health website (http://hi5deposit.com/redcenters.html).

Restaurants across the state are using more local products and produce than ever. Many proudly tell you that all of their products were grown, grazed, or caught within 100 miles of their restaurant. You can support this effort by asking the restaurant which items on their menu are grown or raised on the island, then ordering the local items (for example, drink Kauai coffee, not a coffee from Central America; eat local fish, not imported seafood).

Below are helpful hints travelers to Hawaii might keep in mind during their adventure to the islands, so that their ecological footprint on Hawaii will be minimal.

IN THE OCEAN

- Do not touch anything in the ocean. In fact unless you are standing on the sandy bottom where the waves roll into shore, try not to walk or stand on the ocean floor. The no-touch rule of thumb not only is for your protection (there are plenty of stinging, stabbing things out there that could turn your vacation from fun into a nightmare), but also for the protection of the marine environment. Corals are living things that take years to grow, and a careless brush of your hand or foot could destroy them. Fragile habitats for marine critters can be damaged forever by your footprint.
- Don't feed the fish, or any other marine creature. They have their own food; their natural diet can be irreparably harmed by your good intentions to feed them "people food" or even worse, some "fish food" you have purchased.
- Leave the ocean and beach area cleaner than you found it. If you see trash in the ocean (plastic bag, bottles, and such) remove it. This simple act can save the life of a fish, turtle, marine mammal, or even a seabird; trash kills hundreds of marine inhabitants every year. Same thing is true of the beach—pick up trash, even if it is not your trash.
- The beach is not an ashtray—do not use the sand for your cigarette butts.
- Don't approach turtles or Hawaiian monk seals resting on the shoreline. Both are protected by law—you must stay 100 feet away from these species. The good news is that efforts to protect these animals seem to be working, and their numbers are growing. It's fine to watch and take photos, but stay back (some well-meaning visitors think they are injured and are trying to help, but usually they are just resting).
- If you plan to go fishing, practice catch and release (let the fish live another day). Ask your charter boat captain if they practice catch and release, if they say no, book with someone else.
- If you are environmentally conscious, we do not recommend that you rent jet skies, which have a significant environmental impact.

ON LAND

- Don't litter (this includes throwing a cigarette butt out of your car).
- When hiking, wear comfortable, closed-toed, sturdy shoes with good soles, and scrub them (especially the soles) to get rid of seeds and soil you may have brought with you from home.

Volunteering on Vacation

If you are looking for a different type of experience during your next vacation to Hawaii, you might want to consider becoming a volunteer and leaving the islands a little nicer than when you arrived. People interested in volunteering at beach and ocean clean-ups can contact: **University of Hawaii Sea Grant College Program** at ✆ **808/397-2651 ext. 256** or **Hawaii Wildlife Fund** at ✆ **808/756-1808.** For eco volunteering on land, contact: **Malama Hawaii,** www.malamahawaii.org/get_involved/volunteer.phpwhere (click on the box "volunteer opportunities"), a statewide organization dedicated to *malama* (take care) of the culture and environment of Hawaii. At this site you will find a range of opportunities on various islands from weeding gardens and potting plants in botanical gardens to restoring taro patches to cleaning up mountain streams to bird watching to even hanging out at a beach all day, helping with a reef project.

What is the Carrying Capacity of the Hawaiian Islands?

One of the toughest questions Hawaiians struggle with is what is the carrying capacity of the islands? How much can be developed before Hawaii becomes overbuilt, or unable to support the increased infrastructure and population? How many people can Hawaii hold before the beaches are too crowded, the lifestyle is gone, and the islands have more concrete than open green spaces?

Along those same lines, the people of Hawaii are constantly debating cultural issues vs. social issues. For example, currently laws regarding ancient burial sites can stop, reroute, or delay construction projects ranging from new roads to shopping centers. It's a constant struggle to strike a balance between protecting and preserving the culture and allowing new infrastructure to be developed.

Carry a small day pack with a garbage bag in it and be sure to carry out everything you carried in (including your litter and if you see other garbage on the trail, carry it out too). Stay on the trail. Wandering off a trail is not only dangerous to you (you can get lost or fall off overgrown cliffs, or get injured by stepping into a hidden hole), but you could possibly carry invasive species into our native forests. Do not pick flowers or plants along your hike. Just leave the environment the way you found it.

- Consider carefully what kind of car you rent. You will likely be doing a lot of driving as you explore the island. Unfortunately, hybrids from car rental agencies are not only hard to find, but extremely expensive in Kauai. Car rental agencies do have a variety of cars to rent and you can select a car that gets the best gas mileage. Also ask for a white car, as they use less energy to air condition than a dark-colored car.

HOW TO FIT IN LIKE A LOCAL

Most visitors to Hawaii want to fit in and not stand out as an obvious tourist. The best way to do that is to be friendly and practice the same common courtesy that you do in your own neighborhood. If you smile and are polite to local residents, chances are they will smile back at you. There are a few things you might want to think about:

- Be super polite when driving. People in Hawaii do not use their car horn as a comment on other people's driving. Most Kauai residents use their car horn only as a greeting to a friend.
- Another driving comment—you may be on vacation, but not everyone living here is on vacation so check out your rearview mirror. If you are impeding traffic by driving slowly, pull off the road. If you want to watch the sunset, pull off the road. If you have a long line of cars behind you, pull off the road. Kauai has a lot of one-lane bridges; yield if there's a car on the bridge before you and take turns if there are lines on both sides of the bridge (see "Bridge Etiquette: Showing Aloha on Kauai's One-Lane Bridges," p. 211).
- Be respectful. Just because it's Kauai and warm, does not mean that it is acceptable to wear your swimwear into a restaurant. Ask yourself if you would wear the same outfit at home to your neighborhood restaurant or retail store.
- Remember Kauai is part of the United States, and is in fact a state. A good way to alienate local residents is to say something like "I'm from the States...." Or "Back in the States, we do it this way."

General Resources for Green Travel

In addition to the resources for Hawaii listed above, the following websites provide valuable wide-ranging information on sustainable travel. For a list of even more sustainable resources, as well as tips and explanations on how to travel greener, visit www.frommers.com/planning.

- **Responsible Travel** (www.responsibletravel.com) is a great source of sustainable travel ideas; the site is run by a spokesperson for ethical tourism in the travel industry. **Sustainable Travel International** (www.sustainable travelinternational.org) promotes ethical tourism practices, and manages an extensive directory of sustainable properties and tour operators around the world.
- In the U.K., **Tourism Concern** (www.tourismconcern.org.uk) works to reduce social and environmental problems connected to tourism. The **Association of Independent Tour Operators** (**AITO;** www.aito.co.uk) is a group of specialist operators leading the field in making holidays sustainable.
- In Canada, **www.greenlivingonline.com** offers extensive content on how to travel sustainably, including a travel and transport section and profiles of the best green shops and services in Toronto, Vancouver, and Calgary.
- In Australia, the national body which sets guidelines and standards for ecotourism is **Ecotourism Australia** (www.ecotourism.org.au). **The Green Directory** (www.thegreendirectory.com.au), **Green Pages** (www.thegreen pages.com.au), and **Eco Directory** (www.ecodirectory.com.au) offer sustainable travel tips and directories of green businesses.
- **Carbonfund** (www.carbonfund.org), **TerraPass** (www.terrapass.org), and **Carbon Neutral** (www.carbonneutral.org) provide info on "carbon offsetting," or offsetting the greenhouse gas emitted during flights.
- **Greenhotels** (www.greenhotels.com) recommends green-rated member hotels around the world that fulfill the company's stringent environmental requirements. **Environmentally Friendly Hotels** (www.environmentally friendlyhotels.com) offers more green accommodation ratings. The **Hotel Association of Canada** (www.hacgreenhotels.com) has a Green Key Eco-Rating Program, which audits the environmental performance of Canadian hotels, motels, and resorts.
- **Sustain Lane** (www.sustainlane.com) lists sustainable eating and drinking choices around the U.S.; also visit **www.eatwellguide.org** for tips on eating sustainably in the U.S. and Canada.
- For information on animal-friendly issues throughout the world, visit **Tread Lightly** (www.treadlightly.org). For information about the ethics of swimming with dolphins, visit the **Whale and Dolphin Conservation Society** (www.wdcs.org).
- **Volunteer International** (www.volunteerinternational.org) has a list of questions to help you determine the intentions and the nature of a volunteer program. For general info on volunteer travel, visit **www.volunteer abroad.org** and **www.idealist.org**.

HAWAIIAN CULTURE

One of Hawaii's most cherished resources is the Hawaiian culture, which is flourishing more than ever today. The Hawaiian language is making a huge comeback; all children in Hawaii (not just native Hawaiians) can attend classes from kindergarten through college taught in the Hawaiian language. These Hawaiian immersion schools are part of the public school system.

If you want to support the Hawaii culture, plan to attend cultural events (see the Calendar of Events, p. 42) like Hawaiian music and dance performances. Search out locally owned establishments (look for our recommendations in this book). Attempt to buy souvenirs made in Hawaii by local residents (we have recommendations in the shopping chapter).

If you visit a cultural site, like an ancient *heiau* (temple), the protocol calls for reverence. Be as respectful as you would be at a cathedral or church. Never climb or sit on rock walls at a *heiau*. Never take anything from a *heiau*, even rocks, and never pick flowers there. You may see offerings of flowers or fruit; do not disturb them.

10 THE ACTIVE VACATION PLANNER

If you want nothing more on your vacation than a fabulous beach and a perfectly mixed mai tai, you're in luck—Kauai has some of the most spectacular beaches (not to mention the best mai tais) in the world. But Kauai's wealth of natural wonders is hard to resist; the year-round tropical climate and spectacular scenery tend to inspire even the most committed desk jockeys and couch potatoes to get outside and explore.

If you have your own snorkel gear or other watersports equipment, bring it. If you can't, don't fret; everything you'll need is available for rent. We list all kinds of places to rent or buy gear in chapter 7.

SETTING OUT ON YOUR OWN VS. USING AN OUTFITTER

There are two ways to go: Plan all the details before you go and schlep your gear 2,500 miles across the Pacific, or go with an outfitter or a guide and let them worry about the details.

Experienced outdoor enthusiasts can follow their noses to coastal campgrounds or even trek into the rainforest on their own, but it's often preferable to go with a local guide who is familiar with the conditions at both sea level and the summit, knows the land and its flora and fauna in detail, and has all the gear you'll need. It's also good to go with a guide if time is an issue. If you really want to see native birds, for instance, an experienced guide will take you directly to the best areas for sightings. And many forests and valleys in the interiors of the islands are either on private property or in wilderness preserves that are accessible only on guided tours. If you go with a guide, plan on spending at least $100 a day per person; we recommend the best local outfitters and tour-guide operators in chapter 7.

But if you have the time, already own the gear, and love doing the research and planning, try exploring on your own. Chapter 7 discusses the best spots to set out for on your own, from the best offshore snorkel and dive spots to great daylong hikes, as well as the federal, state, and county agencies that can help you with hikes on public property; we also list references for spotting birds, plants, and sea life. We recommend that you always use the resources available and inquire about weather, trail, or surf conditions; water

Tips Safety Tips

Be sure to see "Safety," earlier in this chapter, before setting out on any adventure; it includes useful information on hiking, camping, and ocean safety. Even if you just plan to lie on the beach, check out "Don't Get Burned: Smart Tanning Tips" on p. 58, to learn how to protect yourself against the sun's harmful rays.

When planning sunset activities, be aware that Hawaii, like other places close to the Equator, has a very short (5–10 min.) twilight period after the sun sets. After that, it's dark. If you hike out to watch the sunset, be sure you can make it back quickly, or take a flashlight.

availability; and other conditions before you take off on your adventure.

For hikers, a great alternative to hiring a private guide is taking one of the guided hikes offered by the Kauai chapter of the **Sierra Club,** P.O. Box 3412, Lihue, HI 96766 (© **808/246-8748;** www.hi.sierraclub.org/kauai/outings/index.html). The club offers guided hikes on preserves and at special places during the year, as well as 1- to 7-day work trips to restore habitats and trails and root out invasive plants like banana poka, New Zealand flax, nonnative gorse, and wild ginger. This might not sound like a dream vacation to everyone, but it's a chance to see the "real" Kauai—including wilderness areas that are usually off-limits.

The Sierra Club offers four to seven hikes a month on Kauai. Hikes are led by certified Sierra Club volunteers and are classified as easy, moderate, or strenuous. These half-day or all-day affairs cost $1 for Sierra Club members, $5 for nonmembers. (Bring exact change.) For a copy of the newsletter, which lists all outings and trail repair work, send $2 to the address above.

USING ACTIVITIES DESKS TO BOOK YOUR ISLAND FUN

If you're interested in an activity that requires an outfitter or a guide, such as horseback riding, whale-watching, or sportfishing, consider booking through a discount activities center or activities desk. These agents—who act as a clearinghouse for activities, just as a consolidator functions as a discount clearinghouse for airline tickets—can often get you a better price than you'd get by booking an activity directly with the outfitter yourself.

Discount activities centers will, in effect, split their commission with you, giving themselves a smaller commission to get your business—and passing on, on average, a 10% discount to you. In addition to saving you money, good activities centers should be able to help you find, say, the snorkel cruise that's right for you, or the luau that's most suitable for both you *and* the kids.

But it's in the activity agent's best interest to sign you up with outfitters from which they earn the most commission, and some agents have no qualms about booking you into any old activity if it means an extra buck for them. If an agent tries to push a particular outfitter or activity too hard, be skeptical. Conversely, they'll try to steer you away from outfitters that don't offer big commissions. Another important word of warning: Be careful to avoid those activities centers offering discounts as fronts for timeshare sales presentations. Using a free snorkel cruise or luau tickets as bait, they'll suck you into a 90-minute presentation—and try to get you to buy into a Kauai timeshare in the process. Not only will they try to sell you a big white elephant you never wanted in

Value: Fun for Less: Don't Leave Home Without a Gold Card

Almost any activity you can think of, from submarine rides to Polynesian luau, can be purchased at a discount by using the **Activities and Attractions Association of Hawaii Gold Card,** 355 Hukilike St., no. 202, Kahului, HI 96732 (© **800/398-9698** or 808/871-7947; fax 808/877-3104; www.hawaiifun.org). The Gold Card, accepted by members on every island, including Kauai, offers a discount of 10% to 25% off activities and meals for up to four people; it's good for a year from the purchase date and costs $30.

You can save big bucks with the Gold Card. For example, if you have your heart set on taking a helicopter ride with Blue Hawaiian Helicopters, that goes for $226, you'll pay only $188 with your Gold Card, saving you nearly $38 per person—$152 in savings for a family of four. With just one activity alone, you've gotten the cost of the card back in savings. And there are hundreds of activities to choose from: air tours, attractions, bicycling tours, dinner cruises, fishing, guided tours, helicopter tours, horseback riding, kayaking, luau, snorkeling, rafting, sailing, scuba diving, submarine rides, and more. It even gets you discounts on rental cars, restaurants, and golf!

Here's how it works: You contact the Activities and Attractions Association via mail, e-mail, fax, phone, or Internet (see above). They issue you the card, good for discounts for 1 year after the date you purchase it. You contact the activity (restaurant, rental car, and so on) directly, give them your Gold Card number, and get discounts ranging from 10% to 25%.

the first place, but—since their business is timeshares, not activities—they also won't be as interested, or as knowledgeable, about which activities might be right for you. These shady deals seem to be particularly rampant on Kauai. Just do yourself a favor and avoid them altogether.

OUTDOOR ETIQUETTE

Carry out what you carry in. Find a trash container for all your litter (including cigarette butts). Litterbugs anger the gods.

Observe *kapu* (taboo) and NO TRESPASSING signs. Don't climb on ancient Hawaiian *heiau* (temple) walls or carry home rocks, all of which belong to the Hawaiian volcano goddess, Pele. Some say it's just a silly superstition, but each year the national and state park services get boxes of lava rocks in the mail, sent back to Hawaii by visitors who have experienced unusually bad luck after taking forbidden souvenirs home.

11 MONEY-SAVING PACKAGE DEALS

Booking an all-inclusive travel package that includes some combination of airfare, accommodations, rental car, meals, airport and baggage transfers, and sightseeing can be the most cost-effective way to travel to Kauai.

Package tours are not the same as escorted tours. They are simply a way to buy airfare and accommodations (and sometimes extras like sightseeing tours and rental cars) at the same time. When you're visiting Hawaii, a package can be a smart way to go. You can sometimes save so much money by buying all the pieces of your trip through a packager that your transpacific airfare ends up, in effect, being free. That's because packages are sold in bulk to tour operators, who then resell them to the public at a cost that drastically undercuts standard rates.

Packages, however, vary widely. Some offer a better class of hotels than others. Some offer the same hotels for lower prices. With some packagers, your choice of accommodations and travel days may be limited. Which package is right for you depends entirely on what you want.

Start out by **reading this guide.** Do a little homework, and read up on Kauai so that you can be a smart consumer. Compare the rack rates that we've published to the discounted rates being offered by the packagers to see what kinds of deals they're offering: Are you actually being offered a substantial savings, or have they just gussied up the rack rates to make their offer *sound* like a deal? If you're offered a stay in a hotel we haven't recommended, do more research to learn about it, especially if the franchise isn't a reliable one. It's not a deal if you end up at a dump.

Be sure to **read the fine print.** Make sure you know *exactly* what's included in the price you're being quoted, and what's not. Are hotel taxes and airport transfers included, or will you have to pay extra? Before you commit to a package, make sure you know how much flexibility you have, say, if your kid gets sick or your boss suddenly asks you to adjust your vacation schedule. Some packagers require ironclad commitments, while others will go with the flow, charging only minimal fees for changes or cancellations.

The best place to start looking for a package deal is the travel section of your local Sunday newspaper. Also check the ads in the back of such national travel magazines as *Arthur Frommer's Budget Travel* and *Travel Holiday.* **Liberty Travel** (✆ **888/271-1584;** ww2.libertytravel.com), for instance, one of the biggest packagers in the Northeast, usually boasts a full-page ad in Sunday newspapers. **American Express Travel** (✆ **800/AXP-6898;** www.americanexpress.com/travel) can also book you a well-priced Hawaiian vacation; it advertises in many Sunday newspaper travel sections.

Other reliable packagers include the airlines themselves, which often package their flights with accommodations. Among the airlines offering good-value package deals to Hawaii are **American Airlines FlyAway Vacations** (✆ **800/321-2121;** www.aavacations.com), **Continental Airlines Vacations** (✆ **800/634-5555** or 800/301-3800; www.covacations.com), **Delta Dream Vacations** (✆ **800/872-7786;** www.deltavacations.com), and **United Vacations** (✆ **800/328-6877;** www.unitedvacations.com). If you're traveling to the islands from Canada, ask your travel agent about package deals through **Air Canada Vacations** (✆ **800/776-3000;** www.aircanadavacations.com).

Excellent deals, like a rental car and 6 nights in a Kauai condo starting at $460 per person (based on double occupancy), can be found at **More Hawaii For Less** (✆ **800/967-6687;** www.hawaii4less.com), a California-based company that specializes in air/condominium packages at unbelievable prices.

GREAT DEALS AT HAWAII'S TOP HOTEL CHAIN

The **Outrigger Hotel and Resorts** chain (✆ **866/956-4262;** outrigger.com) has hotels and condos on Kauai. They range dramatically in price and style, from the elegant Outrigger Waipoli Beach Resort & Spa to the moderate Outrigger at Lae nani. There are plenty of package deals available, including family plans, discounted senior rates, and room and car package deals.

12 STAYING CONNECTED

TELEPHONES

Generally, hotel surcharges on long-distance and local calls are astronomical, so you're better off using your **cellphone** or a **public pay telephone.** Many convenience groceries and packaging services sell **prepaid calling cards** in denominations up to $50; for international visitors these can be the least expensive way to call home. Many public pay phones at airports now accept American Express, MasterCard, and Visa credit cards. **Local calls** made from pay phones in most locales cost 50¢ (no pennies, please).

Most long-distance and international calls can be dialed directly from any phone. **For calls within the United States and to Canada,** dial 1 followed by the area code and the seven-digit number. **For other international calls,** dial 011 followed by the country code, city code, and the number you are calling.

Calls to area codes **800, 888, 877,** and **866** are toll-free. However, calls to area codes **700** and **900** (chat lines, bulletin boards, "dating" services, and so on) can be very expensive—usually a charge of 95¢ to $3 or more per minute, and they sometimes have minimum charges that can run as high as $15 or more.

For **reversed-charge or collect calls,** and for person-to-person calls, dial the number 0 then the area code and number; an operator will come on the line, and you should specify whether you are calling collect, person-to-person, or both. If your operator-assisted call is international, ask for the overseas operator.

For **local directory assistance** ("information"), dial 411; for long-distance information, dial 1, then the appropriate area code and 555-1212.

CELLPHONES

Just because your cellphone works at home doesn't mean it'll work in Kauai (thanks to our nation's fragmented cellphone system). Take a look at your wireless company's coverage map on its website before heading out—T-Mobile, Sprint, and Nextel are particularly weak in Kauai's rural areas. If you need to stay in touch at a destination where you know your phone won't work, **rent** a phone that does from **InTouch USA** (✆ **800/872-7626;** www.intouchglobal.com) or a rental car location, but be aware that you'll pay $1 a minute or more for airtime.

If you're not from the U.S., you'll be appalled at the poor reach of our **GSM (Global System for Mobile Communications) wireless network,** which is used by much of the rest of the world. Your phone will probably work in most major U.S. cities; it definitely won't work in many rural areas. To see where GSM phones work in the U.S., check out www.t-mobile.com/coverage/national_popup.asp. And you may or may not be able to send SMS (text messaging) home.

VOICE-OVER INTERNET PROTOCOL (VOIP)

If you have Web access while traveling, you might consider a broadband-based telephone service (in technical terms, **Voice-over Internet Protocol,** or **VoIP**) such as Skype (www.skype.com) or Vonage (www.vonage.com), which allows you to make free international calls if you use their services from your laptop or in a

The Welcoming Lei

Nothing makes you feel more welcome than a lei. The tropical beauty of the delicate garland, the deliciously sweet fragrance of the blossoms, the sensual way the flowers curl softly around your neck—there's no doubt about it: Getting lei'd in Hawaii is a sensuous experience.

Leis are much more than just a decorative necklace of flowers; they're also one of the nicest ways to say hello, goodbye, congratulations, I salute you, my sympathies are with you, or I love you. The custom of giving leis can be traced back to Hawaii's very roots: According to chants, the first lei was given by Hiiaka, the sister of the volcano goddess, Pele, who presented Pele with a lei of lehua blossoms on a beach in Puna.

During ancient times, leis given to *alii* (royalty) were accompanied by a bow, since it was *kapu* (forbidden) for a commoner to raise his arms higher than the king's head. The presentation of a kiss with a lei didn't come about until World War II; it's generally attributed to an entertainer who kissed an officer on a dare, then quickly presented him with her lei, saying it was an old Hawaiian custom. It wasn't then, but it sure caught on fast.

Lei-making is a tropical art form. All leis are fashioned by hand in a variety of traditional patterns; some are sewn of hundreds of tiny blooms or shells, or bits of ferns and leaves. Some are twisted, some braided, some strung. Every island has its own special flower lei. On Oahu, the choice is *ilima,* a small orange flower. Big Islanders prefer the *lehua,* a large, delicate red puff. Maui likes the *lokelani,* a small rose. On Kauai, it's the *mokihana,* a fragrant green vine and berry. Molokai prefers the *kukui,* the white blossom of a candlenut tree. Lanai's lei is made of *kaunaoa,* a bright yellow moss, while Niihau uses its abundant seashells to make leis that were once prized by royalty and are now worth a small fortune.

Leis are available at the Lihue Airport, from florists, and even at supermarkets.

Leis are the perfect symbol for Hawaii: They're given in the moment, their fragrance and beauty are enjoyed in the moment, but when they fade, their spirit of aloha lives on. Welcome to the islands!

cybercafe. The people you're calling must also use the service for it to work; check the sites for details.

INTERNET ACCESS AWAY FROM HOME

Travelers have any number of ways to check e-mail and access the Internet on the road. Of course, using your own laptop—or a PDA (personal digital assistant) or electronic organizer with a modem—gives you the most flexibility. But even if you don't have a computer, you can still access your e-mail and your office computer from cybercafes.

Without Your Own Computer

It's hard nowadays to find a city that *doesn't* have a few cybercafes, and Kauai is no exception. Although there's no definitive directory for cybercafes—these are independent businesses, after all—a good place to start is **www.cybercaptive.com**.

You can get Web access at the following places, prices range from a low of $2.50 for 15 minutes to a high of $7.50 for 15 minutes.

In Poipu, the Business Center at the **Grand Hyatt Kauai** (✆ **808/742-1234**) charges $7.50 for 15 minutes; in Waimea, **Na Pali Explorer,** 9935 Kaumualii Hwy. (✆ **808/338-9999**), charges 25¢ a minute or $6 an hour.

In Kapaa, try **Business Support Services,** 4-1191 Kuhio Hwy. (✆ **808/822-5504**), which charges $2.50 every 15 minutes.

In Hanalei, try **Bali Hai Photo,** 5-5190 Kuhio Hwy. (✆ **808/826-9181**), $3 for 20 minutes.

Aside from formal cybercafes, all **public libraries** on Kauai offer free access if you have a library card, which you can purchase for a $10 fee. For the location of the nearest library, call the Lihue library at ✆ **808/241-3222.** All hotels on Kauai have **in-room dataports** and **business centers,** but the charges can be exorbitant.

To retrieve your e-mail, ask your **Internet Service Provider (ISP)** if it has a Web-based interface tied to your existing e-mail account. If your ISP doesn't have such an interface, you can use the free **mail2web** service (www.mail2web.com) to view (but not reply to) your home e-mail. For more flexibility, you may want to open a free, Web-based e-mail account with **Yahoo! Mail** (mail.yahoo.com). (Microsoft's Hotmail is another popular option, but Hotmail has severe spam problems.) Your home ISP may be able to forward your e-mail to the Web-based account automatically.

With Your Own Computer

Major ISPs have **local access numbers** allowing you to go online by simply placing a local call in Kauai. Check your ISP's website or call its toll-free number and ask how you can use your current account away from home, and how much it will cost.

Wherever you go, bring a **connection kit** of the right power, as well as phone adapters, a spare phone cord, and a spare Ethernet network cable.

All hotels on Kauai (and even some of the B&Bs) offer dataports for laptop modems, and a few have high-speed Internet access using an Ethernet network cable. You'll have to bring your own cables either way, so **call your hotel in advance** to find out what the options are.

13 TIPS ON ACCOMMODATIONS

Kauai offers a tremendous variety of accommodations, from ritzy resorts to simple bed-and-breakfasts. Before you book a room, read this section to find out what each option typically offers. We've included tips on how to get the best rates.

TYPES OF ACCOMMODATIONS

HOTELS In Hawaii, the term *hotel* can indicate a wide range of options, from accommodations with few or no on-site amenities to those with enough extras to qualify as resorts. Generally, a hotel offers daily maid service and has a restaurant, on-site laundry facilities, a pool, and a sundries/convenience-type shop (as opposed to the shopping arcades that most resorts have). Top hotels also provide activities desks, concierge service, business centers, bars and/or lounges, and perhaps a few more shops. The advantages of staying in a hotel are privacy and convenience; the disadvantage is generally noise—due either to thin walls between rooms or to loud music from a lobby lounge late into the night.

RESORTS In Hawaii, a resort offers everything a hotel offers and more. What

Tips What to Do If Your Dream Hotel Turns Out to Be a Nightmare

To avoid any unpleasant surprises, ask lots of questions when you make your reservation. Find out exactly what the accommodations entail, particularly the cost, minimum stay, and included amenities. Ask if there's a penalty fee for leaving early. Read the small print in the contract—especially the part on cancellation fees. Discuss the cancellation policy ahead of time with the B&B, vacation rental, condominium agent, or booking agency so you'll know what your options are if the accommodations don't meet your expectations. Get this in writing so there are no misunderstandings later.

When you arrive, if the room you're given doesn't meet your expectations, notify the front desk, rental agent, or booking agency immediately. Approach the management in a calm, reasonable manner, and suggest a constructive solution (such as moving to another unit). Be reasonable and be willing to compromise. Do not make threats or leave; if you leave, it may be harder to get your deposit returned.

you get varies from property to property, of course, but expect facilities, services, and amenities such as direct beach access, with cabanas and chairs; a pool (often more than one) and a Jacuzzi; a spa and fitness center; restaurants, bars, and lounges; a 24-hour front desk; concierge, valet, and bell services; room service (often round-the-clock); an activities desk; tennis and golf (some of the world's best courses are at Hawaii resorts); ocean activities; a business center; children's programs; and more.

The advantage of staying at a resort is that you have everything you could possibly want in the way of services and things to do; the disadvantage is that the price generally reflects this. Don't be misled by a name—just because a place is called "ABC Resort" doesn't mean it actually *is* a resort. Make sure you're getting what you pay for.

CONDOS The roominess and convenience of a condo—usually a fully equipped multibedroom apartment—make this a great choice for families. Condominium properties in Hawaii are generally several apartments set in either a single high-rise or a cluster of low-rise units. Condos generally have amenities such as some degree of maid service (ranging from daily to weekly; it may or may not be included in your rate, so be sure to ask), a pool, laundry facilities (either in your unit or in a central location), and an on-site front desk or a live-in property manager. The advantages of a condo are privacy, space, and conveniences—which usually include a fully equipped kitchen, a washer and dryer, a private phone, and perhaps your own lanai or balcony. The downsides include the absence of an on-site restaurant and the density of the units. (The condo may be more private than a B&B or hotel but not quite as private as your own cottage, villa, or house.)

Condos vary in price according to size, location, and amenities. Many of them are located on or near the beach, and they tend to be clustered in resort areas. While there are some very high-end condos, most tend to be quite affordable, especially if you're traveling in a group that's large enough to require more than one bedroom.

BED & BREAKFASTS Kauai has a wide variety of places that fall into this category: everything from the traditional B&B—several bedrooms in a home (which may or may not share a bathroom), with breakfast served in the morning—to what is essentially a vacation rental on an owner's property that comes with fixings for you to make your own breakfast. Make sure that the B&B you book matches your own mental picture of it. Would you prefer conversation around a big dining-room table as you eat a hearty breakfast, or just a muffin and juice to enjoy in your own private place? Laundry facilities, televisions, and private phones are not always available at B&Bs. We've reviewed lots of wonderful places in this book. If you have to share a bathroom, we've spelled it out in the reviews; otherwise, you can assume that you will have a private bathroom.

There are a few things you should be aware of before you book your first B&B. You do not have the "run" of the house. Generally there is a guest area, which may have a small refrigerator for the guests' use, places to sit and read, and perhaps a television. You are not renting the house of your hosts. And generally they do not allow cooking (especially in their kitchen).

The lower rate at B&Bs can be attributed to **no daily maid service.** You might have to make your own bed, and unless you are staying 3 or 4 days, your sheets will not be changed.

Due to Kauai County restrictions, most of the B&Bs do not have certified kitchens, so they can only bake, not cook breakfast. Several hosts are very clever and have recipes for "baked French toast" and "baked" eggs, but generally expect a continental breakfast.

The advantages of a traditional B&B are its individual style and congenial atmosphere. B&Bs are great places to meet other visitors, and the host is generally very happy to act as your private concierge, offering tips on where to go and what to do. In addition, B&Bs are usually an affordable way to go (though fancier ones can run $250 or more a night). The disadvantages are lack of privacy, usually a set time for breakfast, few amenities, generally no maid service, and the fact that you'll have to share the quarters beyond your bedroom with others. In addition, B&B owners usually require a minimum stay of 2 or 3 nights, and it's often a drive to the beach.

VACATION RENTALS This is another great choice for families as well as for long-term stays. The term *vacation rental* usually means there will be no one on the property where you're staying. The actual accommodations can range from an apartment in a condominium building to a two-room cottage on the beach to an entire fully equipped house. Generally, vacation rentals are the kinds of places you can settle into for a while: They have kitchen facilities (sometimes a full kitchen; sometimes just a microwave, minifridge, stovetop, and coffeemaker), on-site laundry facilities, and phone; some have such extras as TV, VCR, and stereo. The advantages of a vacation rental are complete privacy, your own kitchen (which can save you money on meals), and lots of conveniences. The disadvantages are the lack of an on-site property manager, no organized ocean activities, and generally no maid service. Often, a minimum stay is required (sometimes as long as a week). If you book a vacation rental, be sure you have a 24-hour contact so that when the toilet won't flush or you can't figure out how to turn on the air-conditioning, you'll have someone to call.

HOME EXCHANGE If you are interested in trading your home on the mainland for someone's home in Hawaii so that you can both have an inexpensive vacation, the best book to read first is *Home Exchange Guide: How to Find Your Free Home Away from Home,* by M. T. Simon and T. T. Baker, published by Poyee Publishing (2901 Clint Moore, no. 265, Boca Raton, FL 33496; ✆ **561/892-0494;** www.poyeen.com). This step-by-step guidebook first helps you determine if home exchange is right for you. It then helps you develop a strategy to get the word out. You'll utilize "surefire ways" to have a successful home exchange on both sides.

BARGAINING ON PRICES

Rates can sometimes be bargained down, but it depends on the place. In general, each type of accommodation allows a different amount of latitude in bargaining on its rack (or published) rates.

The best bargaining can be had at **hotels** and **resorts.** Hotels and resorts regularly pay travel agents as much as 30% of the rate they get for sending clients their way; if business is slow, some hotels might give you the benefit of at least part of this commission if you book directly instead of go through an airline or travel agent. Most also have *kamaaina* or "local" rates for islanders, which they might extend to visitors during slow periods. It never hurts to ask politely for a discounted or local rate; a host of special rates are also available for the military, seniors, members of the travel industry, families, corporate travelers, and long-term stays.

Ask about package deals, which might include a car rental or free breakfast for the same price as a room. Hotels and resorts offer packages for everyone: golfers, tennis players, families, honeymooners, and more. See "Money-Saving Package Deals," earlier in this chapter.

We've found that it's worth the extra few cents to make a local call to the hotel; sometimes the local reservationists know about package deals that the toll-free operators are unaware of.

If all else fails, try to get the hotel or resort to upgrade you to a better room for the same price as a budget room, or get them to waive the parking fee or the extra fees for children. Persistence and polite inquiries can pay off.

It's harder to bargain at **bed-and-breakfasts.** You may be able to bargain down the minimum stay or negotiate a discount if you're staying a week or longer. But generally, a B&B owner has only a few rooms and has already priced the property at a competitive rate, so expect to pay what's asked.

You have somewhat more leeway to negotiate on **vacation rentals** and **condos.** In addition to asking for a discount on multinight stays, also ask whether the condo or vacation rental can throw in a rental car to sweeten the deal; believe it or not, they often will.

Nickel-&-Dime Charges at High-Priced Hotels

Several upscale resorts in Kauai have begun a practice that we find distasteful and dishonest: charging a so-called "resort fee." This daily fee is added on to your bill for such "complimentary" items as a daily newspaper, local phone calls, use of the fitness facilities, and the like. Amenities that the resort has been happily providing free to its guests for years are now tacked on to your bill under the guise of a "fee." In most cases you do not have an option to decline the resort fee—in other words, this is a sneaky way to further increase the prices without telling you. The only way that this obnoxious fee will ever be rescinded is if you, the consumer, complain, and complain loudly.

Hawaii on the Web

Below are some of the best Hawaii-specific websites for planning your trip.

- **Hawaii Visitors & Convention Bureau (HVCB; www.gohawaii.com):** An excellent, all-around guide to activities, tours, lodging, and events, plus a huge section on weddings and honeymoons. But keep in mind that only members of the HVCB are listed.
- **Kauai: Island of Discovery (www.kauaidiscovery.com):** Extensive listings cover activities, events, recreation, attractions, beaches, and much more. The Vacation Directory includes information on golf, fishing, and island tours; some listings include e-mail addresses and links to websites. You'll also find an interactive map of the island with listings organized by region.
- **The Hawaiian Language Web Site (www.olelo.hawaii.edu):** This fabulous site not only has easy lessons on learning the Hawaiian language, but a great cultural calendar, links to other Hawaiian websites, a section on the hula, and lyrics (and translations) to Hawaiian songs.

USING A BOOKING AGENCY VS. DOING IT YOURSELF

Sometimes you can save money by making arrangements yourself—not only can you bargain on the phone, but some accommodations may also be willing to pass on a percentage of the commission they would normally have to pay a travel agent or a booking agency.

However, if you don't have the time or money to call several places to make sure they offer the amenities you'd like and to bargain for a price you're comfortable with, consider using a booking agency. The time the agency spends on your behalf might well be worth any fees you'll have to pay.

The top reservations service in the state is **Hawaii's Best Bed & Breakfasts,** P.O. Box 758, Volcano, HI 96785 (✆ **800/262-9912** or 808/985-7488; fax 808/967-8610; www.bestbnb.com). The fee for this service starts at $20 to book. The staff personally selects the traditional homestays, cottages, and inns, based on each one's hospitality, distinctive charm, and attention to detail.

For vacation rentals, contact **Hawaii Beachfront Vacation Homes** (✆ **808/247-3637** or 808/235-2644; www.hibeach.com). **Hawaii Condo Exchange** (✆ **800/442-0404;** www.hawaiicondo exchange.com) acts as a consolidator for condo and vacation-rental properties.

4

Suggested Kauai Itineraries

Your vacation time is precious, you only have so many days, and you don't want to waste one of them. That's where I come in. Below are several suggestions for things to do and how to organize your time. I've included ideas if you have 1 week or 2, are traveling with kids, or want a more active vacation.

The number-one thing I would suggest is don't max out your days. This is Hawaii; allow some time to do nothing but relax. Remember that you most likely will arrive jet-lagged. Ease into your vacation. Your first day you most likely will be tired—hitting the pillow at 8 or 9pm will sound good. Don't be surprised if you wake up your first morning in Kauai before the sun comes up. Your internal clock is probably still set 2 to 6 hours earlier than Hawaii.

Finally, think of your first trip as a "scouting" trip. Kauai is too beautiful, too sensual, too enticing to see just once in a lifetime. You'll be back. You don't need to see and do everything on this trip. In fact, if you find something in the itinerary below and just fall in love with it, go back again. It's your vacation. I've included general, sample itineraries. If you are a golf fan or a scuba diver, check out chapter 1, "Best of Kauai" (p. 1), to plan your trip around your passion.

One last thing—you will need a car to get around. Kauai does have a local bus system, but it does not go to the resorts, so plan to rent a car. But also plan to get out of the car as much as possible. This is Hawaii; don't just view it from your car window. You have to get out to smell the sweet perfume of plumeria, to feel the warm rain on your face, to hear the sound of the wind through a bamboo forest, and to plunge into the gentle waters of the Pacific.

THE ISLAND IN BRIEF

Kauai's three main resort areas, where nearly all the island's accommodations are located, are all quite different in climate, price, and type of accommodations offered, but the range is wide and wonderful. On the south shore, dry and sunny **Poipu** is anchored by perfect beaches. This is the place to stay if you like the ocean, watersports, and plenty of sunshine. The **Coconut Coast,** on the east coast of Kauai, has the most condos, shops, and traffic—it's where all the action is. Hanalei, up on the **North Shore,** is rainy, lush, and quiet, with spectacular beaches and deep wilderness. Because of its remote location, the North Shore is a great place to get away from it all—but not a great place from which to explore the rest of the island.

Lihue & Environs

Lihue is where most visitors first set foot on the island. This red-dirt farm town, the county seat, was founded by sugar planters and populated by descendants of Filipino and Japanese cane cutters. It's a plain and simple place, with used-car lots and mom-and-pop shops. It's also the source of bargains: inexpensive lodging, great deals on dining, and some terrific shopping buys. One of the island's most beautiful beaches, **Kalapaki Beach** ★★, is just next door at **Nawiliwili,** by the island's main harbor.

The Poipu Resort Area

Poipu Beach ★★★ On Kauai's sun-soaked south shore, this is a pleasant if sleepy resort destination of low-rise hotels set on gold-sand pocket beaches. Well-done, master-planned Poipu is Kauai's most popular resort, with the widest variety of accommodations, from luxury hotels to B&Bs and condos. It offers 36 holes of golf, 38 tennis courts, and outstanding restaurants. This is a great place for watersports, and a good base from which to tour the rest of Kauai. The only drawback is that the North Shore is about 1 to 1½ hours away.

Koloa This tiny old town of gaily painted sugar shacks just inland from Poipu Beach is where the Hawaiian sugar industry was born more than a century and a half ago. The mill is closed, but this showcase plantation town lives on as a tourist attraction, with delightful shops, an old general store, and a vintage Texaco gas station with a 1930s Model A truck in place, just like in the good old days.

Kalaheo/Lawai Just a short 10- to 15-minute drive inland from the beach at Poipu lie the more residential communities of Lawai and Kalaheo. Quiet subdivisions line the streets, restaurants catering to locals dot the area, and life revolves around family and work. Good bargains on B&Bs, and a handful of reasonably priced restaurants, can be found here.

Western Kauai

This region, west of Poipu, is more remote than its eastern neighbor and lacks its terrific beaches. But it's home to one of Hawaii's most spectacular natural wonders, **Waimea Canyon** ★★★ (the "Grand Canyon of the Pacific"); and farther upland and inland, one of its best parks, **Kokee State Park** ★★.

Hanapepe For a quick trip back in time, turn off Highway 50 at Hanapepe, once one of Kauai's biggest towns. Founded by Chinese rice farmers, it's so picturesque that it was used as a backdrop for the miniseries *The Thornbirds.* Hanapepe makes a good rest stop on the way to or from Waimea Canyon. It has galleries selling antiques as well as local art and crafts, including Georgio's surfboard art and coconut-grams. It's also home to one of the best restaurants on Kauai, the **Hanapepe Café** (p. 146). Nearby, at **Salt Pond Beach Park** ★ (p. 168), Hawaiians have dried a reddish sea salt in shallow, red-clay pans since the 17th century. This is a great place to swim, snorkel, and maybe even observe an ancient industry still in practice.

Waimea This little coastal town, the original capital of Kauai, seems to have quit the march of time. Dogs sleep in the street while old pickups rust in front yards. The ambience is definitely laid-back. A stay in Waimea is peaceful and quiet (especially at the Waimea Plantation Cottages on the beach), but the remote location means this isn't the best base if you want to explore the other regions of Kauai, such as the North Shore, without a lot of driving.

On his search for the Northwest Passage in 1778, British explorer Capt. James Cook dropped anchor at Waimea and discovered a sleepy village of grass shacks. In 1815, the Russians arrived and built a fort here (now a national historic landmark), but they didn't last long: A scoundrel named George Anton Scheffer tried to claim Kauai for Russia, but he was exposed as an impostor and expelled by Kauai's high-ranking *alii,* Kaumualii.

Niihau: The Forbidden Island

Just 17 miles across the Kaulakahi Channel from Kauai lies the arid island of Niihau, "The Forbidden Island." Visitors are not allowed on this privately owned island, which is a working cattle and sheep ranch with about 200 residents living in the single town of Puuwai.

However, you can spend a couple of hours on the beach in Niihau. **Niihau Helicopter,** the only helicopter company to offer tours of Niihau, has half-day tours, which include a helicopter ride to Niihau, an aerial tour over the island, and landing on the island at a beach. For more information, see p. 208.

Niihau's history of being forbidden dates back to 1864 when, after an unusually wet winter that turned the dry scrubland of the small island (18×6 miles) into green pasture, Eliza Sinclair, a Scottish widow, decided to buy Niihau and move her family here. King Kamehameha IV agreed to sell the island for $10,000. The next year, normal weather returned, and the green pastures withered into sparse semi-desert vegetation.

Today, Sinclair's great-great-grandson, Bruce Robinson, continues to run the ranching operation and fiercely protects the privacy of the island residents. From the outside, life on Niihau has not changed much in 140 years: There's no running water, indoor plumbing, or electrically generated power. The Hawaiian language is still spoken. Most of the men work for the ranch when there is work, and fish and hunt where there is no work. The women specialize in gathering and stringing *pupu Niihau,* prized, tiny white seashells (found only on this island), into Niihau's famous leis, which fetch prices in the thousands of dollars.

Today, even Waimea's historic relics are spare and simple: a statue of Cook alongside a bas-relief of his ships, the rubble foundation of the Russian fort, and the remains of an ancient aqueduct unlike any other in the Pacific. Except for an overabundance of churches for a town this size, there's no sign that Waimea was selected as the first landing site of missionaries in 1820.

The Coconut Coast

The eastern shore of Kauai north of Lihue is a jumble of commerce and condos strung along the coast road named for Prince Kuhio, with several small beaches beyond. Almost anything you need, and a lot of stuff you can live without, can be found along this coast, which is known for its hundreds of coconut trees waving in the breeze. It's popular with budget travelers because of the myriad B&Bs and affordable hotels and condos to choose from, and it offers great restaurants and the island's major shopping areas.

Kapaa ★ The center of commerce on the east coast and the capital of the Coconut Coast condo-and-hotel district, this restored plantation town looks just like an antique. False-fronted wooden stores line both sides of the highway; it looks as though they've been here forever—until you notice the fresh paint and new roofs and realize that everything has been rebuilt since Hurricane Iniki smacked the town flat in 1992. Kapaa has made an amazing comeback without losing its funky charm.

The North Shore

Kauai's North Shore may be the most beautiful place in Hawaii. Exotic seabirds, a half-moon bay, jagged peaks soaring into the clouds, and a mighty wilderness lie around the bend from the Coconut Coast, just beyond a series of one-lane bridges traversing the tail ends of waterfalls. There's only one road in and out, and only two towns, Hanalei and Kilauea—the former by the sea, the latter on a lighthouse cliff that's home to a bird preserve. Sun seekers may fret about all the rainy days, but Princeville Resort offers elegant shelter and two golf courses where you can play through rainbows.

Kilauea ★ This village is home to an antique lighthouse, tropical-fruit stands, little stone houses, and Kilauea Point National Wildlife Refuge, a wonderful seabird preserve. The rolling hills and sea cliffs are hideaways for the rich and famous, including Bette Midler and Sylvester Stallone. The village itself has its charms: The 1892 Kong Lung Company, Kauai's oldest general store, sells antiques, art, and crafts; and you can order a jazzy Billie Holiday Pizza to go at Kilauea Bakery and Pau Hana Pizza.

Anini Beach ★ This little-known residential district on a 2-mile reef (the biggest on Kauai) offers the safest swimming and snorkeling on the island. A great beach park is open to campers and day-trippers, and there's a boat ramp where locals launch sampans to fish for tuna. On Sunday, there's polo in the park and the sizzle of barbecue on the green. Several residents host guests in nearby B&Bs.

Princeville ★ Princeville Resort is Kauai's biggest project (and, some argue, a little out of place on Kauai's wild North Shore). This 11,000-acre development sits on a high plain overlooking Hanalei Bay, and includes a luxury Sheraton hotel, 10 condo complexes, new timeshare units around two championship golf courses, cliff-side access to pocket beaches, and one B&B right on the golf course.

Hanalei ★★★ Picture-postcard Hanalei is the laid-back center of North Shore life and an escapist's dream; it's also the gateway to the wild Na Pali Coast. Hanalei is the last great place on Kauai yet to face the developer's blade of progress. At **Hanalei Bay,** sloops anchor and surfers play year-round. The 2-mile-long crescent beach, the biggest indentation on Kauai's coast, is ideal for kids in summer, when the wild surf turns placid. Hanalei retains the essence of its original sleepy, end-of-the-road charm. On either side of two-lane Kuhio Highway, you'll find just enough shops and restaurants to sustain you for a week's visit—unless you're a hiker, surfer, or sailor, or have some other preoccupation that just might keep you here the rest of your life.

Haena ★★ Emerald-green Haena isn't a town or a beach; it's an ancient Hawaiian district, a place of exceptional natural beauty, and the gateway to the Na Pali Coast. It's the perfect tropical escape, and everybody knows it: old house foundations and temples, now covered by jungle, lie in the shadow of new million-dollar homes of movie stars and musicians like Jeff Bridges and Graham Nash. This idyllic, 4-mile coast has lagoons, bays, great beaches, spectacular snorkeling, a botanical garden, and the only North Shore resort that's right on the sand, the Hanalei Colony Resort.

The Na Pali Coast ★★★

The road comes to an end, and now it begins: the Hawaii you've been dreaming about. Kauai's Na Pali Coast (*na pali* means "the cliffs") is a place of extreme beauty and Hawaii's last true wilderness. Its majestic splendor will forever remain unspoiled because no road will ever traverse it. You can enter this state park only on foot or by sea. Serious hikers—and we mean very serious—tackle the ancient 11-mile-long trail down the forbidding coast to Kalalau Valley (see "Hiking & Camping," in chapter 7). The lone, thin trail that creases these cliffs isn't for the faint of heart or anyone afraid of heights. Those of us who aren't up to it can explore the wild coast in an inflatable rubber Zodiac, a billowing sailboat, a high-powered catamaran, or a hovering helicopter, which takes you for the ride of your life.

1 ONE WEEK ON KAUAI

I've outlined the highlights for those who just have 7 days and want to see everything. It's a jampacked 7-day, 6-night itinerary; however, you might want to skip a few suggestions and just veg out on the beach, or substitute your own interests such as sailing, scuba diving, or golf.

Day ❶: Arrive in Kauai; Head for the Beach ★★

After you get off the plane, head for the beach closest to your accommodations. Lather up in sunscreen, take sunglasses and a hat, and plop down on the soft sand of the beach. Enjoy a Hawaiian dinner at one of the **luau** offered (see chapter 6) to get into the spirit of your Hawaiian vacation. Don't be surprised if you find yourself nodding off at 8 or 9pm.

Day ❷: See a Bird's-Eye View of Kauai from a Helicopter ★★★

Since you're probably on mainland time and will be wide awake before the break of dawn, either plan an early morning **helicopter tour** (p. 205) of the island to get your bearings, or get up and watch the sunrise from the east shore. If it's not raining, head out to Hanalei Beach to watch the sun make its appearance in the east at 5:30am in summer and 6:30am in winter. Then head into Hanalei for an early breakfast at **Hanalei Wake-up Café** (p. 159).

With the whole day ahead of you, after breakfast drive out to the end of the road at **Kee Beach** (p. 170). Here you can either hike a couple of miles along the **Na Pali Coast** (p. 189) and back (make sure you have good hiking shoes, water, snacks, and sunscreen); or you can venture down the highway to **Tunnels Beach** (p. 170) for an early morning snorkel. After a couple of hours at the beach, continue on to the **Limahuli Garden of the National Tropical Botanical Garden** (p. 213) and step into Eden.

By now you should be hungry. Head back to Hanalei and order takeout at the **Hanalei Gourmet** (p. 158) and head down to Hanalei Beach for a picnic lunch. After lunch, you might want to try kayaking. **Kayak Kauai** (p. 173) in Hanalei has both guided tours as well as kayak rentals so you can explore by water.

If kayaking is not your preferred activity, then wander through the shops at Hanalei, get a shave ice, and take in the slow pace of life on the North Shore.

Finish the day with a *pau hana*–time (quit-work time) cocktail at **Tahiti Nui** (p. 228), then enjoy a relaxing dinner in Hanalei at **Postcards Café** (p. 159).

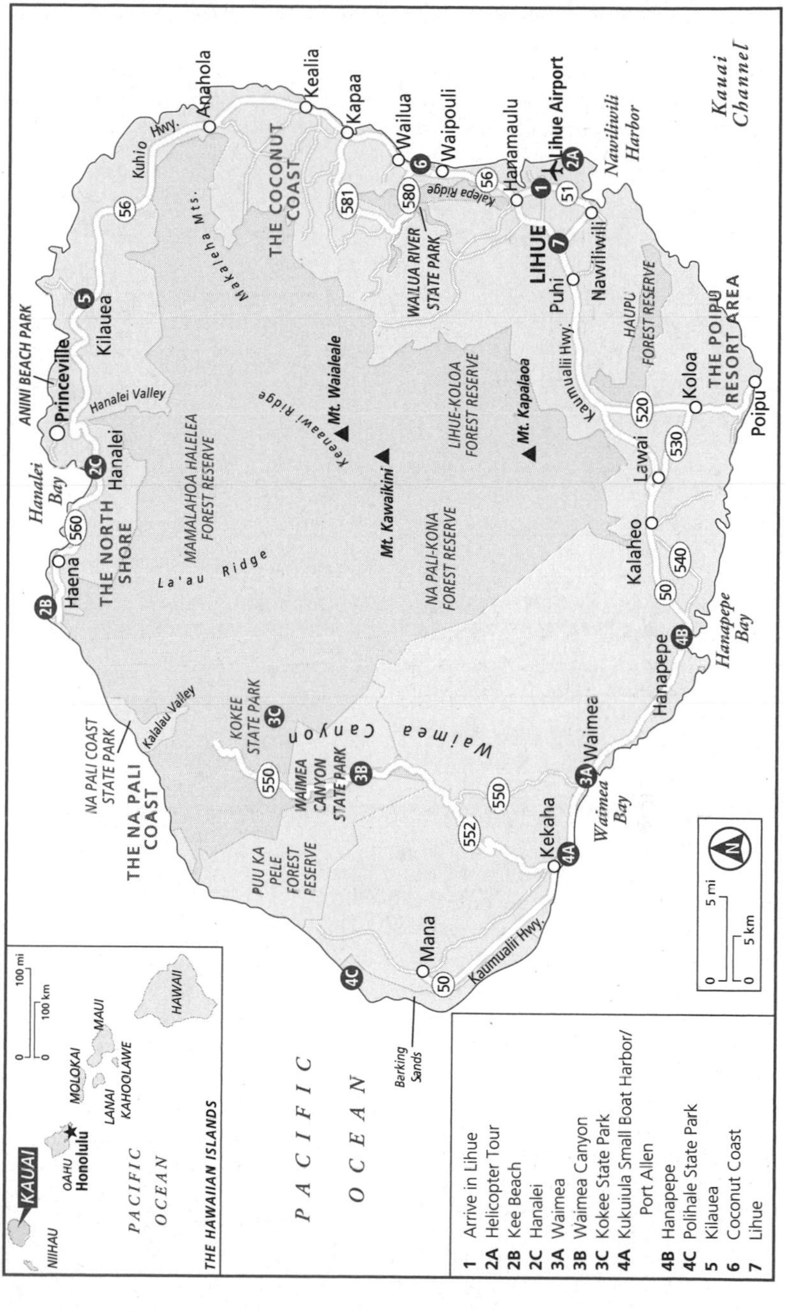
1 Arrive in Lihue
2A Helicopter Tour
2B Kee Beach
2C Hanalei
3A Waimea
3B Waimea Canyon
3C Kokee State Park
4A Kukuiula Small Boat Harbor/ Port Allen
4B Hanapepe
4C Polihale State Park
5 Kilauea
6 Coconut Coast
7 Lihue
THE HAWAIIAN ISLANDS
KAUAI
NIIHAU
OAHU
Honolulu
MOLOKAI
LANAI
KAHOOLAWE
MAUI
HAWAII
PACIFIC OCEAN
0 100 mi
0 100 km
PACIFIC OCEAN
Barking Sands
Mana
Kaumualii Hwy.
Kekaha
Waimea Bay
Waimea
Hanapepe
Hanapepe Bay
Kalaheo
Lawai
Koloa
Poipu
THE POIPU RESORT AREA
HAUPU FOREST RESERVE
Nawiliwili
Puhi
LIHUE
Lihue Airport
Nawiliwili Harbor
Kauai Channel
Hanamaulu
Kalepa Ridge
Waipouli
Wailua
Kapaa
Kealia
Anahola
Kuhio Hwy.
THE COCONUT COAST
WAILUA RIVER STATE PARK
Makaleha Mts.
Kilauea
Princeville
ANINI BEACH PARK
Hanalei Valley
Hanalei
Hanalei Bay
Haena
THE NORTH SHORE
MAMALAHOA HALELEA FOREST RESERVE
La'au Ridge
Keenaawi Ridge
Mt. Waialeale
Mt. Kawaikini
Mt. Kapalaoa
LIHUE-KOLOA FOREST RESERVE
NA PALI-KONA FOREST RESERVE
Kalalau Valley
NA PALI COAST STATE PARK
THE NA PALI COAST
KOKEE STATE PARK
Waimea Canyon
WAIMEA CANYON STATE PARK
PUU KA PELE FOREST PESERVE
0 5 mi
0 5 km
N

Day 3: Hike Through Kauai's Grand Canyon ★★

Head out west, up to **Waimea Canyon** (p. 204) and **Kokee State Park** (p. 205). Have warm clothes, as it can get cold at 4,000 feet, and be prepared for rain. Get an early start and have breakfast or coffee at the **Kalaheo Coffee Co. & Cafe** (p. 151). Stop in Waimea town to explore the **Russian Fort Elizabeth State Historical Park** (p. 204) and the **Menehune Ditch** (p. 203), then plan to spend most of the morning (before the clouds roll in) hiking the various trails in the **Waimea Canyon** area (see p. 204 for hikes). Then travel another 16 miles and a few thousand feet up the road to Kokee. Stop for lunch at the **Kokee Lodge** (p. 116), open from 9am to 3pm. Check in at the **Kokee Natural History Museum** (p. 205) to learn about the forests and surrounding area, locate good hiking trails, and pick up a couple of trail maps. In the afternoon, wander around the park, and stay for sunset. If it's Friday night, eat at the **Hanapepe Café** (p. 146; they only serve dinner on Friday); if it's not, go Italian at **Pomodoro** (p. 144) in Kalaheo.

Day 4: Winging It on the Water ★

After a day in the mountains, it's time to head to the beach again. If you like sailing and snorkeling, book a **sail/snorkel tour** out of the Kukuiula Small Boat Harbor or Port Allen (see "Boating," in chapter 7) for the trip of a lifetime—exploring the **Na Pali Coast.**

If you pass on sailing, wander into the old plantation town of **Hanapepe** (p. 221) and browse at the unique shops. Continue west to Kauai's biggest beach at **Polihale State Park** (p. 168). Spend the day here, and be sure to check out the "barking" sands at **Barking Sands Beach** (p. 168). Enjoy the sunset; then head over to **The Beach House** (p. 138) for a fabulous dinner.

Day 5: Explore Kilauea ★

Your beach quotient should be filled by now, so spend the day in the **Kilauea** (p. 83) area exploring gardens and the **Kilauea Point National Wildlife Refuge** (p. 196). First, call **Na Aina Kai Botanical Gardens** (p. 213) to make sure they are open, and book a tour. This incredible, magical garden is for people who shudder at the thought of seeing a botanical garden: The whimsical magic of the place will win over even the most stubborn. Build up an appetite for lunch by checking out the very unusual shops at Kong Kung in Kilauea. Pick up a delicious picnic lunch at **Kilauea Fish Market** (p. 160). Then head down the road to the **Kilauea Point National Wildlife Refuge** (see "Birding," on p. 196), a 200-acre habitat for Hawaii's ocean birds. Eat your picnic on the coast, join a guided hike, or just wander through the fairyland of the wilderness area. Have dinner at the wonderful **Lighthouse Bistro Kilauea** (p. 154).

Day 6: Casting About on the Coconut Coast ★

For those who just can't get enough beach time, make your way to **Wailua Beach** (p. 168) on the **Coconut Coast.** This beach, which features Hawaiian historical and cultural sites, is also a great place to just sit under a palm tree and figure out how you can move here permanently. For those non-beach people, you can visit the great shopping along the coast, or head inland and see the sacred Hindu temple, **San Marga Iraivan Temple** (p. 209). Eat lunch in Kapaa at **Mermaids Cafe** (p. 152). In the afternoon, consider either hiking up **Sleeping Giant Mountain** (p. 210), bicycling along the shoreline, or renting a kayak from **Kauai Water Ski & Surf** (p. 223). By dinnertime, you'll be hungry; head for **Caffè Coco** (p. 148).

Day 7: Getting the Most Out of Your Last Day

If this is your last day, spend it in the **Lihue** (p. 198) area. It's close to the airport and there are plenty of things to do. You might want to step back in history and visit the **Kauai Museum** (p. 198) in Lihue or take a train ride at **Kilohana** (p. 200) in Puhi. Or drive up to the **Wailua Falls** (p. 202), just outside of town. Shoppers may like wandering around the old town of Lihue. Die-hard beachgoers can head to **Kalapaki Beach** (p. 161) for their last few hours of sun. If you are in a casual mode, get some burgers for the beach at **Kalapaki Beach Hut** (p. 137). If you are in the mood for a more filling meal—and you know that it won't get served by the airline—stop at **Duke's Canoe Club** (p. 150) for your last meal on the island.

2 TWO WEEKS ON KAUAI

Two weeks on Kauai is perfect. It allows you to see everything at a much slower pace with plenty of relaxation and lazy beach days. I'd suggest adding lots of naps, vegging out on the beach, and stopping to smell all the exotic flowers.

Day ❶: Arrive in Kauai; Go Directly to the Beach ★★

After you get off the plane, head for the beach closest to your accommodations. Don't forget the sunscreen, sunglasses, and a hat before you leave your hotel. Just as we recommended in the itinerary for 1 week, you might consider a Hawaiian dinner at one of the **luau** offered (see chapter 6) to get into the spirit of your Hawaiian vacation. Plan on an early bedtime; you'll be pooped.

Day ❷: See Kauai from the Sky in a Helicopter ★★★

With the time difference between Kauai and the mainland, most likely you will be wide-awake before the break of dawn. We suggest you book an early morning **helicopter tour** (p. 205) of the island to get your bearings. The reason you want to book a tour early in your stay is that if weather conditions cancel your flight, you still have plenty of days remaining to rebook a flight. If your flight is canceled, you might as well get up early and watch the sunrise. After your helicopter ride out of Lihue, grab your snorkel gear and head for **Poipu Beach** (p. 164) to see what the fish are up to. Terrific lunches can be had at **Brennecke's Beach Broiler** (p. 141), just across the beach from the park. As the sun sets, stop by the **Beach House** (p. 138) for divine *pupu* (appetizers) and a liquid libation. Then head to **Roy's Poipu Bar & Grill** in the Poipu Shopping Center (p. 140) for a fabulous dinner.

Day ❸: Dive into the Ocean at the North Shore ★★★

With the whole day ahead of you, take a post-breakfast drive out to the end of the road at **Kee Beach** (p. 170). If you get up early, have breakfast at the **Hanalei Wake-up Café** (p. 159). Head out to the end of the road, park, and hike a couple of miles along the **Na Pali Coast** (p. 189) and back (make sure you have good hiking shoes, water, snacks, and sunscreen); or you can venture down the highway to **Tunnels Beach** (p. 170) for an early morning snorkel. After a couple of hours at the beach, continue on to the **Limahuli Garden of the National Tropical Botanical Garden** (p. 213) and step into Eden.

By now you should be hungry. Head back to Hanalei and grab a bite at the **Hanalei Gourmet** (p. 158); take it down to the beach for a picnic lunch. After lunch, wander through the shops at Hanalei, get a shave ice, and take in the slow pace of life on the North Shore. Finish the day with a *pau hana*–time (quit-work time) cocktail at **Tahiti Nui** (p. 228), then enjoy a relaxing dinner at either **Bar Acuda** in Hanalei (p. 154) or in Haena at **Mediterranean Gourmet** at the Hanalei Bay Colony Resort (p. 158).

Day ❹: Hike Through Kauai's Grand Canyon ★★

Head out west, up to **Waimea Canyon** (p. 204). Have warm clothes and be prepared for rain. Get an early start and have breakfast or coffee at the **Kalaheo Coffee Co. & Cafe** (p. 151), where you can pick up a picnic lunch. Stop in Waimea town to explore the **Russian Fort Elizabeth State Historical Park** (p. 204) and the **Menehune Ditch** (p. 203), then plan to spend most of the day hiking the various trails in the Waimea Canyon area (see p. 182 for hikes). All that hiking will work up an appetite, so for dinner go Italian at **Pomodoro** (p. 144) in Kalaheo.

Day ❺: Spend a Day in the Clouds at Kokee ★★★

If you aren't too sore from hiking in Waimea Canyon, head back up the mountain another 16 miles up the hill from the Waimea Canyon, where at 4,000 feet lies the **Kokee State Park** (p. 205). Stop for lunch at the **Kokee Lodge** (p. 116), open from 9am to 3pm. Check in at the **Kokee Natural History Museum** (p. 205) to learn about the forests and surrounding area, locate good hiking trails, and pick up a couple of trail maps. In the afternoon, wander around the park, and stay for sunset. If it's Friday night, plan dinner at the **Hanapepe Café** (p. 146); if it's not, **Toi's Thai Kitchen,** in Eleele (p. 147), has terrific and affordable Thai cuisine; or, **Keoki's Paradise,** in Poipu (p. 142) offers great seafood and steaks in a tropical jungle decor.

Day ❻: Out on the Water ★

After a couple of days in the mountains, it's time to head to the beach again. If you are coming from the North Shore or from the Coconut Coast, stop for a yummy breakfast at the **Tip Top Café/Bakery** (p. 137), in Lihue. If you like sailing and snorkeling, book a **sail/snorkel tour** out of the Kukuiula Small Boat Harbor or Port Allen (see "Boating," in chapter 7) for the trip of a lifetime—exploring the **Na Pali Coast.**

If you pass on sailing, wander into the old plantation town of **Hanapepe** (p. 221) and browse at the unique shops. Continue west to Kauai's biggest beach at **Polihale State Park** (p. 168). Spend the day here, and be sure to checkout the "barking" sands at **Barking Sands Beach** (p. 168). Enjoy the sunset; then head over to **Tidepool Restaurant** (p. 141) at the Grand Hyatt in Poipu for dinner on the water.

Day ❼: Explore Kilauea ★

Your beach quotient should be filled by now, so spend the day in the **Kilauea** (p. 83) area exploring gardens and the **Kilauea Point National Wildlife Refuge** (p. 196). First, call **Na Aina Kai Botanical Gardens** (p. 213) to make sure they are open, and book a tour. This incredible, magical garden is for people who shudder at the thought of seeing a botanical garden: The whimsical magic of the place will win over even the most stubborn. Build up an appetite for lunch by checking out the very unusual shops at Kong Kung in Kilauea. Pick up a delicious picnic lunch at **Kilauea Fish Market** (p. 160). Then head down the road to the **Kilauea Point National Wildlife Refuge** (see "Birding" on p. 196), a 200-acre habitat for Hawaii's ocean birds. Eat your picnic on the coast, join a guided hike, or just wander through the fairyland of the wilderness area. Have dinner at the wonderful **Lighthouse Bistro Kilauea** (p. 154).

Day ❽: Cruise the Coconut Coast ★

For those who just can't get enough beach time, make your way to **Wailua Beach** (p. 168) on the **Coconut Coast.** This beach, which features Hawaiian historical and cultural sites, is also a great place to just sit under a palm tree and figure out

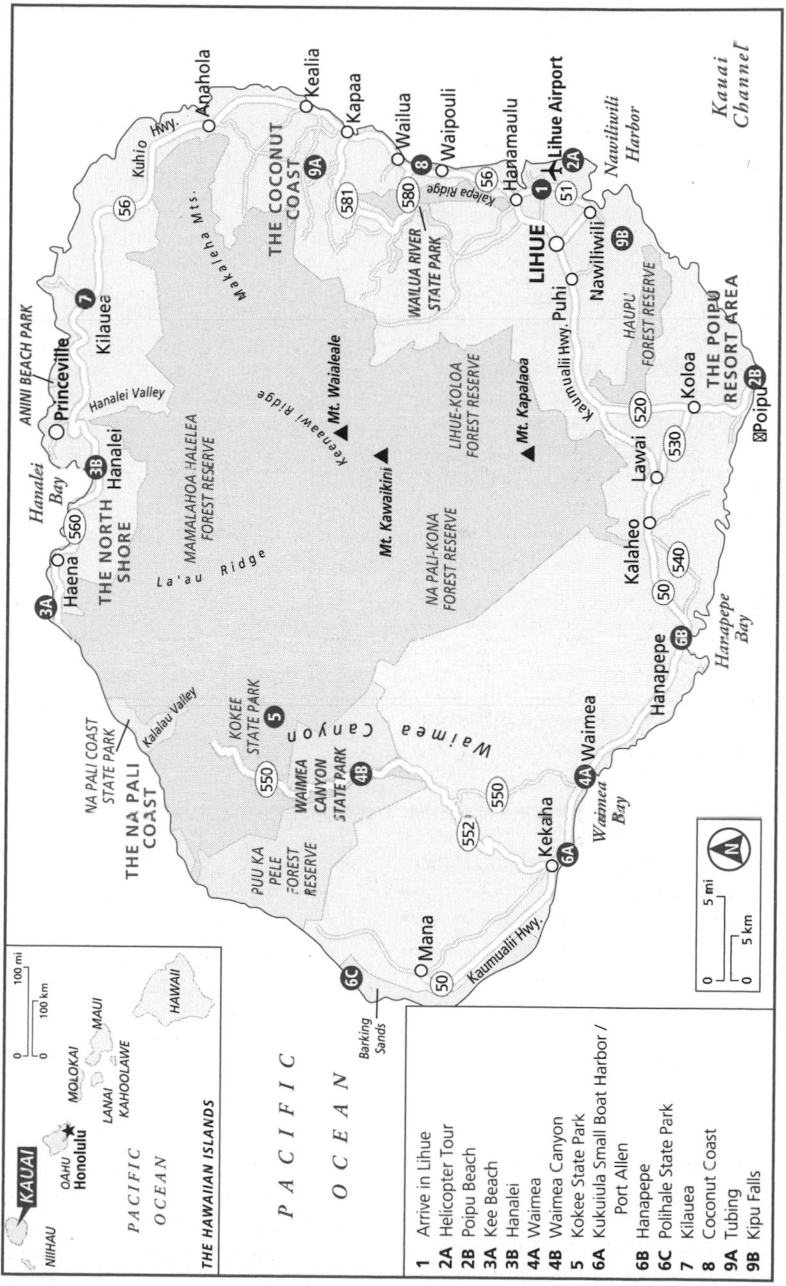
THE HAWAIIAN ISLANDS
NIIHAU
KAUAI
OAHU
Honolulu
MOLOKAI
LANAI
KAHOOLAWE
MAUI
HAWAII
PACIFIC OCEAN
0 100 mi
0 100 km
PACIFIC OCEAN
Barking Sands
Mana
Kaumualii Hwy.
Kekaha
Waimea
Waimea Bay
Hanapepe
Hanapepe Bay
Kalaheo
Lawai
Koloa
Poipu
THE POIPU RESORT AREA
HAUPU FOREST RESERVE
Nawiliwili
Nawiliwili Harbor
Puhi
LIHUE
Lihue Airport
Hanamaulu
Kalepa Ridge
Waipouli
Wailua
WAILUA RIVER STATE PARK
Kapaa
Kealia
Anahola
Kuhio Hwy.
THE COCONUT COAST
Makaleha Mts.
Kilauea
Princeville
ANINI BEACH PARK
Hanalei Valley
Hanalei
Hanalei Bay
Haena
THE NORTH SHORE
MAMALAHOA HALELEA FOREST RESERVE
La'au Ridge
Keenaawi Ridge
Mt. Waialeale
Mt. Kawaikini
Mt. Kapalaoa
LIHUE-KOLOA FOREST RESERVE
NA PALI-KONA FOREST RESERVE
Kalalau Valley
NA PALI COAST STATE PARK
THE NA PALI COAST
KOKEE STATE PARK
Waimea Canyon
WAIMEA CANYON STATE PARK
PUU KA PELE FOREST RESERVE
Kauai Channel
0 5 mi
0 5 km
N
1 Arrive in Lihue
2A Helicopter Tour
2B Poipu Beach
3A Kee Beach
3B Hanalei
4A Waimea
4B Waimea Canyon
5 Kokee State Park
6A Kukuiula Small Boat Harbor / Port Allen
6B Hanapepe
6C Polihale State Park
7 Kilauea
8 Coconut Coast
9A Tubing
9B Kipu Falls

how you can move here permanently. For those non-beach people, you can visit **Kauai's Children's Discovery Museum** (p. 176) in Kapaa, and then either explore the great shopping along the coast, or head inland and see the sacred Hindu temple, **San Marga Iraivan Temple** (p. 209). Eat lunch in Kapaa at **Mermaids Cafe** (p. 152). In the afternoon, consider either hiking up **Sleeping Giant Mountain** (p. 210), bicycling along the shoreline, or renting a kayak from **Kauai Water Ski and Surf** (p. 223). By dinnertime, you'll be hungry; head for **Caffè Coco** (p. 148).

Day ❾: A Day of Adventure ★

Try something you have never done before. Sign up for a **Tubing Adventure** with **Kauai Backcountry Adventures** (p. 177), for a chance to float down the former sugar-cane irrigation flumes. Or sail through the air on the new **Zipline** adventure; we recommend **Outfitters Kauai's Kipu Falls Zipline Trek** (p. 180) for an adrenaline rush that you won't soon forget. Plan a quiet afternoon at the beach to relax after your big adventure of the day.

Day ❿: See Kauai from a Different Perspective

See Kauai from the ocean by joining a **kayak tour** (p. 173), where you will skim over the ocean's (or a river's) surface coming eyeball-to-eyeball with turtles, flying fish, and other marine creatures. In the afternoon, book a **horseback riding tour** and see Kauai from a different vantage point. There are a variety of different types of tours (p. 196), from riding along secluded beaches to trekking back to hidden waterfalls. Plan a quiet dinner and an early bedtime.

Day ⓫: Get Pampered—A Day at the Spa

Plan an entire day at a **spa.** In chapter 1, we recommend several top spas (p. 15), which will soothe your aching muscles from your days of adventure. Try something new—maybe a traditional Hawaiian lomilomi massage or an ayurvedic massage (once given only to royalty for rejuvenation). Do nothing but lie around and relax. Order room service or get takeout for dinner.

Day ⓬: Back to the Beach

Polish up your tan at the beach (my list of favorites is in chapter 7). Even if it is raining on one side of the island, frequently you can drive to the other side and it will be bright sunshine. Get a tropical-flavored shave ice (p. 147) and enjoy a taste of the islands.

Day ⓭: Shop 'Til You Drop

Get out the list of people you must buy gifts for and then turn to chapter 9, **"Shopping,"** for my list of great places to shop, great buys, and ideas on what to take home.

Day ⓮: Getting the Most Out of Your Last Day

If this is your last day, spend it in the **Lihue** (p. 198) area. It's close to the airport, and there are plenty of things to do. You might want to step back in history and visit the **Kauai Museum** (p. 198) in Lihue or **Kilohana** (p. 200) in Puhi. Or drive up to the **Wailua Falls** (p. 202), just outside of town. Shoppers may like wandering around the old town of Lihue. Die-hard beachgoers can head to **Kalapaki Beach** (p. 161) for their last few hours of sun. If you are in a casual mode, get some burgers for the beach at **Kalapaki Beach Hut** (p. 137).

3 KAUAI FOR FAMILIES

Your itinerary is going to depend on the ages of your kids. The number-one rule is don't plan too much; especially with young children, who will be fighting jet lag, trying to get adjusted to a new bed (and most likely new food), and may be very hyped up and excited

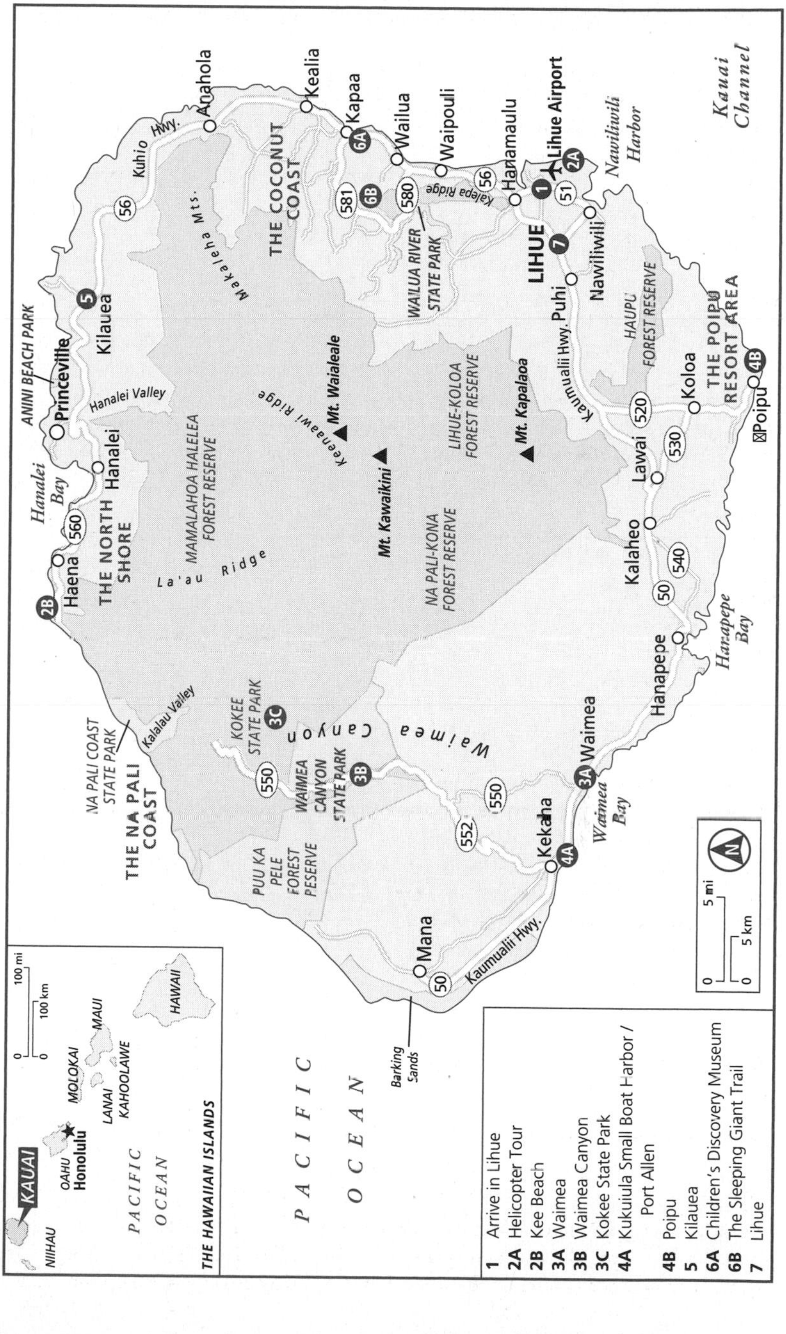
1 Arrive in Lihue
2A Helicopter Tour
2B Kee Beach
3A Waimea
3B Waimea Canyon
3C Kokee State Park
4A Kukuiula Small Boat Harbor / Port Allen
4B Poipu
5 Kilauea
6A Children's Discovery Museum
6B The Sleeping Giant Trail
7 Lihue
THE HAWAIIAN ISLANDS
NIIHAU
KAUAI
OAHU
Honolulu
MOLOKAI
LANAI
KAHOOLAWE
MAUI
HAWAII
PACIFIC OCEAN
0 100 mi
0 100 km
PACIFIC OCEAN
Barking Sands
Mana
Kaumualii Hwy.
Kekaha
Waimea Bay
Waimea
Hanapepe
Hanapepe Bay
Kalaheo
Lawai
Koloa
Poipu
THE POIPU RESORT AREA
HAUPU FOREST RESERVE
Nawiliwili
Puhi
LIHUE
Lihue Airport
Hanamaulu
Nawiliwili Harbor
Kauai Channel
Kalepa Ridge
Waipouli
Wailua
WAILUA RIVER STATE PARK
Kapaa
Kealia
THE COCONUT COAST
Anahola
Kuhio Hwy.
Makaleha Mts.
Kilauea
Princeville
ANINI BEACH PARK
Hanalei Valley
Hanalei
Hanalei Bay
THE NORTH SHORE
Haena
MAMALAHOA HALELEA FOREST RESERVE
La'au Ridge
Keenaawi Ridge
Mt. Waialeale
Mt. Kawaikini
Mt. Kapalaoa
LIHUE-KOLOA FOREST RESERVE
NA PALI-KONA FOREST RESERVE
Kalalau Valley
NA PALI COAST STATE PARK
THE NA PALI COAST
KOKEE STATE PARK
Waimea Canyon
WAIMEA CANYON STATE PARK
PUU KA PELE FOREST RESERVE
Kaumualii Hwy.
0 5 mi
0 5 km
N

to the point of exhaustion. The 7-day itinerary below is a guide to various activities. Pick and choose the ones everyone in your family will enjoy.

Day ❶: Arrive in Kauai; Settle in, and Head for the Swimming Pool ★★

Even kids suffer from jet lag and need to reset their internal clock. So expose the family to sunlight as soon as you arrive; even an hour or so will help them adjust to the time difference. If you have young kids who are not used to the waves, you might consider taking them to the swimming pool at your accommodations. They'll be happy playing in the water, and you won't have to introduce them to ocean safety after that long plane ride. Plan an early dinner with food your kids are used to; if you're in Poipu take them to **Brennecke's Beach Broiler** (p. 141). On the Coconut Coast, try **Bubba Burgers** (p. 152).

Day ❷: Up, Up, and Away in a Helicopter ★★★

Since you're probably on mainland time, the kids will be wide-awake while it's still dark out. If the kids are old enough (8 years or more), plan an early morning **helicopter tour** (p. 205) so they can see the island from the air. Or if it's not raining, head out to Hanalei Beach to watch the sun make its appearance in the east, at 5:30am in summer, and 6:30am in winter. Then head into Hanalei for an early breakfast at **Hanalei Wake-up Café** (p. 159).

Since you are already at the North Shore, plan a day at the beach with the kids. Gear up with snorkel equipment, lots of floating equipment, and plenty of sunscreen, and plan to spend the morning at **Kee Beach** (p. 170). When the kids start to complain about being hungry, head back to Hanalei and grab a bite at **Tropical Taco** (p. 160); take it down to Hanalei Beach for a picnic lunch.

The kids may be passed out after lunch and all that sunshine. Head back to your hotel (and grab a quick nap yourself). Plan another early dinner.

Day ❸: Wow—Kauai's Own Grand Canyon ★★

If the kids are 8 or older, head out west, up to **Waimea Canyon** (p. 204) and **Kokee State Park** (p. 205). Have warm clothes along, as it can get cold at 4,000 feet, and be prepared for rain. Get an early start and have breakfast at the **Kalaheo Coffee Co. & Café** (p. 151). Stop in Waimea town to explore the **Russian Fort Elizabeth State Historical Park** (p. 204) and the **Menehune Ditch** (p. 203), then plan to spend most of the morning (before the clouds roll in) either hiking the various trails in the Waimea Canyon area (see p. 182 for hikes) or at least pulling over in the scenic look out areas and viewing the canyon. Then travel another 16 miles and a few thousand feet up the road to Kokee. Stop for lunch at the **Kokee Lodge** (p. 116), open from 9am to 3pm. Check in at the **Kokee Natural History Museum** (p. 205) to learn about the forests and surrounding area, locate good hiking trails, and pick up a couple of trail maps. In the afternoon, wander around the park, and stay for sunset. Stop for dinner at the **Brick Oven Pizza** (p. 144) in Kalaheo.

Day ❹: Sailing or Swimming in the Ocean ★

Head for the ocean. If you think the tykes will like sailing and snorkeling, book a **sail/snorkel tour** out of the Kukuiula Small Boat Harbor or Port Allen (see "Boating," in chapter 7) for the trip of a lifetime—exploring the **Na Pali Coast.**

If your clan is not the boating type, drive west to Kauai's **Poipu Beach Park** (p. 164). Spend the day here. Plan on dinner at **Poipu Beach Broiler** (p. 143), where the kids' menu has all their favorites.

Day ❺: Explore a Magical Garden ★

Take a day off the water, call **Na Aina Kai Botanical Gardens** (p. 213) to make sure they are open, and book a tour. If you have tiny tots, they will love the children's play area. This incredible, magical garden is for people who shudder at the thought of seeing a botanical garden: The whimsical magic of the place will win over even the most stubborn. Drop by **Kilauea Fish Market** (p. 160) to get a picnic lunch to eat down the road at the **Kilauea Point National Wildlife Refuge** (see "Birding" on p. 196), a 200-acre habitat for Hawaii's ocean birds. Eat your picnic on the coast, join a guided hike, or just wander through the fairyland of the wilderness area. Have dinner at the wonderful **Lighthouse Bistro Kilauea** (p. 154).

Day ❻: Discover a Museum or Walk on a Sleeping Giant ★

You can visit **Kauai's Children's Discovery Museum** (p. 176) in Kapaa—where the kids can have the time of their lives playing with virtual reality television, playing Hawaiian musical instruments, or hiding out in a "magical" treehouse. Eat lunch just outside of Kapaa at **Duane's Ono-Char Burger,** in Anahola (p. 154). In the afternoon, if your kids are teenagers, hike up **Sleeping Giant Mountain** (p. 210). If they are very young, head for Lydgate State Park, where one of the best kid's playgrounds on the island is located. By dinnertime, you'll be hungry; try the **Ono Family Restaurant** (p. 153), in Kapaa.

Day ❼: Getting the Most Out of Your Last Day

If this is your last day, spend it in the **Lihue** (p. 198) area. It's close to the airport and there are plenty of things to do. Take the family to the **Kauai Museum** (p. 198) in Lihue or take the train ride at **Kilohana** (p. 200) in Puhi. Die-hard beachgoers can head to **Kalapaki Beach** (p. 161) for their last few hours of sun. Get some burgers for the beach at **Kalapaki Beach Hut** (p. 137). Start planning your next trip to Kauai.

4 KAUAI FOR THE ADVENTUROUS

Are you one of those people who hates the thought of lying around at the beach, doing nothing? Is your idea of the perfect vacation to be up, active, and trying new adventures? Then Kauai is the place for you. Our suggested itinerary below covers all the basic things to see on Kauai, with added adventures that active people like you love.

Day ❶: Arrive in Kauai; Head for the Beach ★★

I can't say this too often: To readjust your internal clock, get outside and get some sunshine (don't forget the sunscreen). I'd suggest going to the closest beach to your hotel (see my picks in chapter 7). Start your adventure by dining on ethnic cuisine that you have never tried; check out our restaurant picks in chapter 6.

Day ❷: Fly Through the Sky and Swim Through the Water ★★★

One of the best adventures on Kauai is a **helicopter tour** (p. 205) of the island. You most likely will still be on mainland time, so book an early flight (you'll be up long before the sun rises anyway). Plan a day snorkeling for your first adventure. Get snorkel equipment through **Snorkel Bob's** (p. 171). If it is summer, and the weather is good, go to the North Shore. In fact, take an island tour and drive all the way to the end of the road at **Kee Beach** (p. 170). If you are up for it, hike a couple of miles along the **Na Pali Coast** (p. 189) and back (make sure you have good hiking shoes, water, snacks, and sunscreen); or jump into that cool blue water and check out the marine life.

If it is winter, and the waves are up on the North Shore, head south for **Poipu Beach** (p. 164). Snorkel in the morning and then take an easy hike to **Makawehi Point** (p. 180).

Day ❸: Hiking Through a Canyon and Up in the Clouds ★★

Head out west, up to **Waimea Canyon** (p. 204) and **Kokee State Park** (p. 205). Bring warm clothes along, as it can get cold at 4,000 feet, and be prepared for rain. Get an early start and have breakfast or coffee at the **Kalaheo Coffee Co. & Café** (p. 151). Stop in Waimea town to explore the **Russian Fort Elizabeth State Historical Park** (p. 204) and the **Menehune Ditch** (p. 203), then plan to spend most of the morning (before the clouds roll in) hiking the various trails in the Waimea Canyon area (see p. 182 for hikes). Then travel another 16 miles and a few thousand feet up the road to Kokee. Stop for lunch at the **Kokee Lodge** (p. 116), open from 9am to 3pm. Check in at the **Kokee Natural History Museum** (p. 205) to learn about the forests and surrounding area, locate good hiking trails, and pick up a couple of trail maps. In the afternoon, wander around the park, and stay for sunset. If it's Friday night, eat at the **Hanapepe Café** (p. 146); if it's not, go Italian at **Pomodoro** (p. 144) in Kalaheo.

Day ❹: Cruising the Na Pali Coast ★★

See a side of Kauai that you can only see from the water. Book a **sail/snorkel tour** out of the Kukuiula Small Boat Harbor or Port Allen (see "Boating," in chapter 7) for the trip of a lifetime—exploring the **Na Pali Coast.**

Day ❺: Tubing Through the Water, Zipping Through the Air ★

Try something you have never done before. Sign up for a **Tubing Adventure** with **Kauai Backcountry Adventures** (p. 177), for a chance to float down the former sugar cane irrigation flumes. Or do something zippy like the new **Zipline** adventure; we recommend **Outfitters Kauai's Kipu Falls Zipline Trek** (p. 180) for an adrenaline rush that you won't forget. Plan a quiet afternoon at the beach to relax after your big adventure for the day.

Day ❻: Glide Through the Water, and Gallop to Secluded Waterfalls

See Kauai from the ocean by joining a **kayak tour** with Kayak Kauai in Hanalei or Outfitters Kauai in Poipu (p. 173), where you will skim over the ocean's (or a river's) surface coming eyeball-to-eyeball with turtles, flying fish, and other marine creatures. In the afternoon, book a **horseback riding tour** with Princeville Ranch Stables near Hanalei or CJM Country Stables in Koloa (p. 196) and see Kauai from the vantage point of sitting on a horse. There are a variety of different types of tours, from riding along secluded beaches to trekking back to hidden waterfalls. Plan a quiet dinner and an early bedtime.

Day ❼: Relax on Your Last Day

Plan your last day at a **spa.** In chapter 1, we recommend several top spas that will soothe your aching muscles from your days of adventure (my favorite is the ANARA spa at the Grand Hyatt in Koloa). Try something new; perhaps a traditional Hawaiian lomilomi massage or an ayurvedic massage (once given only to royalty for rejuvenation). Relax, and start planning your next trip to Kauai.

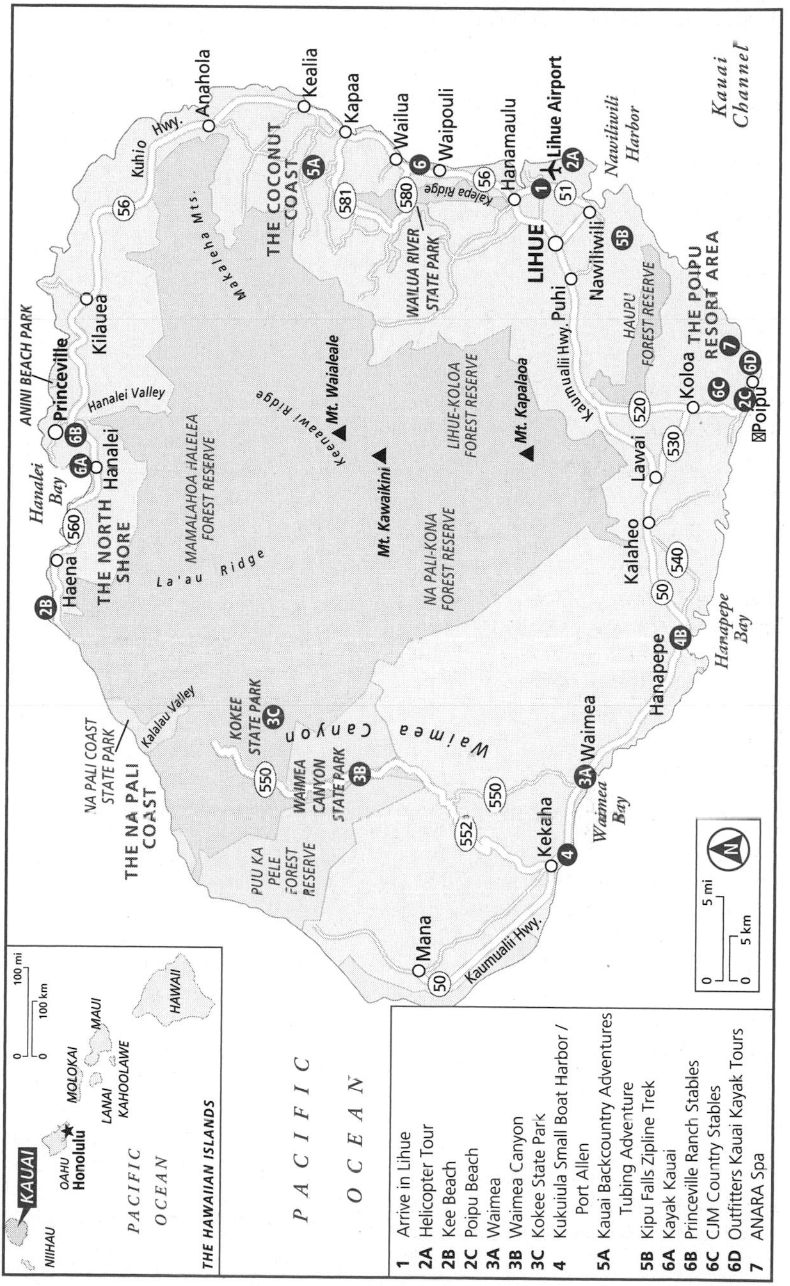
THE HAWAIIAN ISLANDS
NIIHAU
KAUAI
OAHU
Honolulu
MOLOKAI
LANAI
KAHOOLAWE
MAUI
HAWAII
PACIFIC OCEAN
0 100 mi
0 100 km
PACIFIC OCEAN
1 Arrive in Lihue
2A Helicopter Tour
2B Kee Beach
2C Poipu Beach
3A Waimea
3B Waimea Canyon
3C Kokee State Park
4 Kukuiula Small Boat Harbor / Port Allen
5A Kauai Backcountry Adventures Tubing Adventure
5B Kipu Falls Zipline Trek
6A Kayak Kauai
6B Princeville Ranch Stables
6C CJM Country Stables
6D Outfitters Kauai Kayak Tours
7 ANARA Spa
0 5 mi
0 5 km
THE NA PALI COAST
NA PALI COAST STATE PARK
Kalalau Valley
PUU KA PELE FOREST RESERVE
WAIMEA CANYON STATE PARK
KOKEE STATE PARK
Waimea Canyon
Mana
Kekaha
Kaumualii Hwy.
Waimea
Waimea Bay
Hanapepe
Hanapepe Bay
Kalaheo
Lawai
Koloa
Poipu
THE POIPU RESORT AREA
HAUPU FOREST RESERVE
Nawiliwili
Nawiliwili Harbor
Puhi
LIHUE
Lihue Airport
Hanamaulu
Kalepa Ridge
WAILUA RIVER STATE PARK
Wailua
Waipouli
Kapaa
Kealia
THE COCONUT COAST
Anahola
Kuhio Hwy.
Kauai Channel
Makaleha Mts.
Mt. Waialeale
Kawaikini Ridge
Mt. Kawaikini
Mt. Kapalaoa
LIHUE-KOLOA FOREST RESERVE
NA PALI-KONA FOREST RESERVE
MAMALAHOA HALELEA FOREST RESERVE
La'au Ridge
THE NORTH SHORE
Haena
Hanalei
Hanalei Bay
Princeville
ANINI BEACH PARK
Hanalei Valley
Kilauea

5

Where to Stay

Kauai has accommodations to fit every taste and budget, from luxury oceanfront suites to quaint bed-and-breakfast units to reasonably priced condos that will sleep a family of four without requiring that you take out a second mortgage.

Remember to consider *when* you will be traveling to the islands. The high season, during which rooms are always booked and rates are at the top end, runs from mid-December to March. A second high season, when rates are high but reservations are somewhat easier to get, is summer (June–Sept). The low seasons, with fewer tourists and cheaper rates, are April to June and September to mid-December.

Important note: Before you book, be sure to read "The Island in Brief" in chapter 2, which will help you choose your ideal location (you don't want to be stuck with long drives every day), as well as "Tips on Accommodations," also in chapter 2. Also check out the accommodations "bests" in chapter 1 for a quick look at our favorites.

Taxes of 11.42% are added to all hotel bills. Parking is free unless otherwise noted.

1 LIHUE & ENVIRONS

If you need to stay overnight near the airport, try the **Garden Island Inn** (see below).

VERY EXPENSIVE

Kauai Marriott Resort & Beach Club ★★ Kids The pluses to this luxury resort are its oceanfront location on Kalapaki Beach (one of the best in Kauai), several enormous swimming pools combined into an awesome "water playground," a terrific kids' program, and a central islandwide location (about an hour's drive to Hanalei and the North Shore in one direction, and about an hour's drive to the Waimea Canyon in the other direction). The minus: The location—Lihue Airport is only a mile away—allows for easy arrival and departure, but it also means you can hear the takeoff and landing of every jet. Fortunately, most air traffic stops by 9pm, but it begins again bright and early in the morning.

Once upon a time, this was a glitzy megaresort (the Westin Kauai) with ostentatious fantasy architecture, but then a hurricane (and new owners) toned it down. The result is grand enough to be memorable, but it's now grounded in reality—it looks like a Hawaiian hotel rather than a European palace. Water is everywhere throughout the resort: lagoons, waterfalls, fountains, a 5-acre circular swimming pool (some 26,000 sq. ft., the largest on the island), and a terrific stretch of beach. The lagoons are home to six islands that serve as an exotic minizoo, which still lends an air of fantasy to the place and, along with the enormous pool and children's program, makes the resort popular with families.

It's a little pricey for Lihue, but affordable compared with nearby Poipu Resort. Guest rooms are comfortable, with fabulous views of gold-sand Kalapaki Beach, verdant gardens, and palm trees; a recent refurbishment has them all looking brand-new.

There are also timeshare units in this resort.

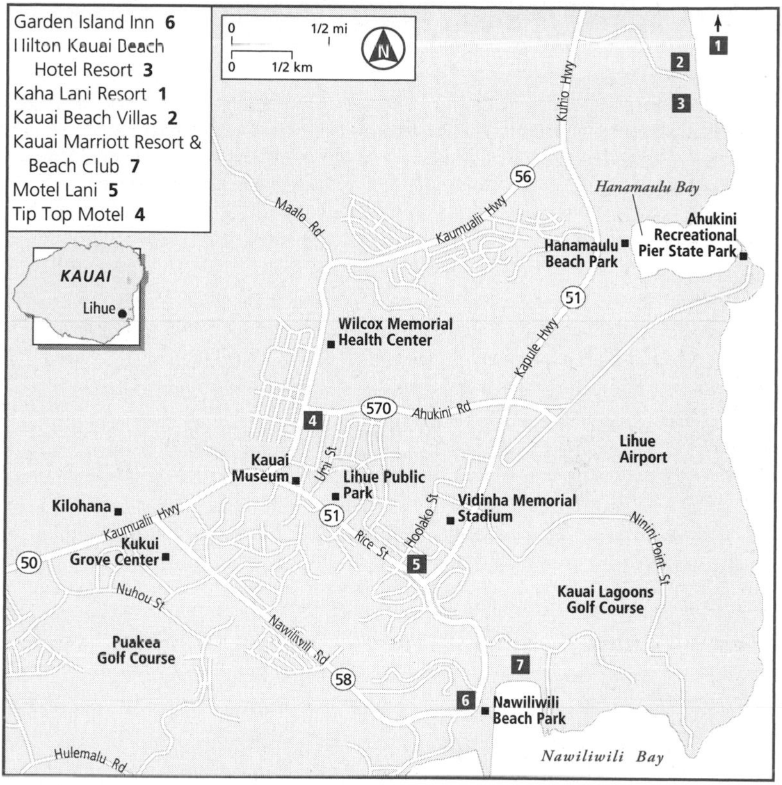

Kalapaki Beach, Lihue, HI 96766. ✆ **800/220-2925** or 808/245-5050. Fax 808/246-5148. www.marriott.com/lihhi. 356 units. $279–$429 double; from $694 suite. Vacation Package Deals include deluxe accommodations and a choice of car or daily breakfast for 2 starting at $309. Extra person $40. AE, DC, DISC, MC, V. Valet parking $14, self-parking $11. **Amenities:** 4 restaurants (including Duke's Kauai, p. 136), 2 bars; free airport shuttle; babysitting; children's program; concierge; 36-hole Jack Nicklaus golf course; state-of-the-art fitness center; 5 hot tubs; the largest pool on the island; room service; 8 tennis courts; watersports equipment rentals. *In room:* A/C, TV/VCR, fridge, hair dryer, Wi-Fi ($13/day).

EXPENSIVE

Hilton Kauai Beach Hotel Resort I would give this oceanfront property a multistar rating if not for a couple of very serious problems: the windy conditions and the lack of safe swimming on the beautiful white-sand beach. Formerly the Radisson Kauai, this property went through a $7-million renovation in 2006 to convert it to a condo-hotel (which means that while the hotel will continue to operate as a full-service resort for visitors, a portion of the rooms in the hotel will be available for private ownership). Then, the Hilton took over the management of the property and spent another $17 million to renovate and add such amenities as a business center, an executive-club floor, Hilton's

Kids Family-Friendly Hotels

Grand Hyatt Kauai Resort & Spa (p. 101) It's the collection of swimming pools here—freshwater and salt, with slides, waterfalls, and secret lagoons—that makes this oceanfront Hyatt a real kids' paradise. Camp Hyatt (ages 3–12) offers arts and crafts, scavenger hunts, and other special activities for $80 for a full day (9am–4pm), including lunch and activities. It's $60 for a half-day with lunch, and $50 for a half-day without lunch. Plus, the Hyatt is one of the few hotels to offer "camp" in the evening; it's $80 for a full evening (4-10pm) including dinner, $60 for up to 3 hours with dinner, or $50 for up to 3 hours without dinner. Babysitting and activities on weekend evenings give Mom and Dad some time alone.

Hanalei Colony Resort (p. 128) These spacious two-bedroom condos come equipped with full kitchens. Management has badminton and croquet sets on hand for the whole family, as well as toys, puzzles, and games for the kids.

Kalaheo Inn (p. 114) Families on a budget will love this wallet-friendly motel. One-bedroom apartments start at $103, 2-bedrooms at $133, and 3-bedrooms at $183, all with kitchenettes. What a deal! Located in the town of Kalaheo, a 12-minute drive from world-famous Poipu Beach, a 5-minute drive from the Kukuiolono Golf Course, and within walking distance of shops and restaurants. Hosts Chet and Tish Hunt love families and have a storeroom full of games to keep the kids entertained. Plus, they happily hand out complimentary beach towels, beach toys, and even golf clubs to guests (to use at the nearby course). This is a must-stay for vacationers on a budget.

Kauai Marriott Resort & Beach Club (p. 96) This place has Hawaii's largest pool (26,000 sq. ft.), in addition to a new kids' pool—but that's just the beginning. Water runs everywhere throughout the resort: lagoons, waterfalls,

bedding and bath items, and an expanded fitness center. The 25-acre beachfront property, located 4 miles north of Lihue, commands a 3-mile stretch of the beach, next door to a top-ranked municipal golf course. There is a complimentary airport shuttle. The rooms have all been renovated and updated with plush new carpeting, a Balinese-style wood entry door, marble bathroom and floors, top-of-the-line bedding, and high-speed wireless Internet service. The Hilton also added a new quartzite stone decking at the resort's four-pool complex, a 12-foot waterfall cascading into the main pool, a flume and lava-tube waterslide at the sand-bottom pool, and a whirlpool spa in a stone grotto surrounded by ferns and a waterfall. The entire property is nonsmoking; the only places you can light up are on the oceanside luau lawn and in the parking lot. The location is good, about equidistant from both north- and south-shore activities, and also close to the Wailua River and its kayaking, water-skiing, river tours, historical sites, and waterfalls. There is one policy that they instituted a few years ago that I find beneath the dignity of a Hilton: Guests must sign for a beach towel and if you don't return it by 10pm, you will be charged $15 (per day) for your towel. Since a majority of the guests are families, this fountains, a 5-acre circular swimming pool (the largest on the island), and a terrific stretch of beach, Nawiliwili Harbor, Kauai's port of call. As we went to press, the informal Kalapaki Kids program (ages 5–12) had been discontinued, but there was talk of starting up again in 2010. The program offers activities ranging from boogie boarding to treasure hunting.

Kiahuna Plantation Resort (p. 105) As we went to press, and the visitor industry was flagging, these condominium units feature a children's program (next door at the Sheraton Kauai) during the summer months. The activities for children 5 to 12 include everything from lagoon fishing to arts and crafts and cost $70 with lunch for a full day (9am–4pm) or $55 for a half-day with lunch. Plus they will take potty-trained 3- and 4-year-olds for a half-day.

Sheraton Kauai Resort (p. 102) With the recent decline in visitors to Kauai, the kids program here was restricted to Monday through Friday and offers camp-type activities like bamboo pole fishing, lei making, hula lessons, and tide-pool explorations from 9am to 4pm for $65 with lunch (or half-days for $50 with lunch) for Sheraton guests (for non-guests the program costs $75 for a full day, or $60 for a half-day, both including lunch).

Waimea Plantation Cottages (p. 116) Among groves of towering coco palms are these clusters of meticulously restored plantation cottages that offer families the opportunity to relax off the beaten track. Some people may find Waimea a little too out-of-the-way (it's a 1½-hr. drive to the North Shore), but it is close to Waimea Canyon and Kokee State Park. The re-created village allows kids plenty of room to wander and play away from traffic and crowds. There are also tennis courts and a pool.

policy has really created havoc—on my last trip, numerous guests told me they have a hard time just keeping track of their kids' sandals, let alone where the kids may have left the beach towel. I hope the Hilton will amend this not-so-family-friendly policy.

4331 Kauai Beach Dr., Lihue, HI 96766. ✆ **800/HILTONS** or 808/245-1955. Fax 808/246-9085. www.hilton.com. 350 units. $160–$249 double; from $600 suite. Daily $13 resort fee for nightly sunset cocktail party and Polynesian dance show, use of the fitness center, coffee/tea service (6–7am), in-room coffee and tea service, local calls, in-room wireless Internet access, shuttle service to airport, and parking. Numerous packages available, including car rentals, senior rates, and more. AE, DC, DISC, MC, V. **Amenities:** Restaurant, bar; free airport shuttle; babysitting; concierge; fitness center; 4 outdoor pools; spa; tennis courts; watersports equipment rentals. *In room:* A/C, TV, fridge, hair dryer, Wi-Fi.

Kaha Lani Resort (Finds) Located on the outskirts of Lihue, almost to the Coconut Coast, this 75-unit condominium project, set back from the ocean by a wide, grassy lawn, overlooks miles of white sandy beaches. It's a quiet location but not perfect. Conditions can be fair for swimming, but a good percentage of the time it's just too windy and turbulent. The property does have a heated swimming pool, plus barbecue areas, tennis courts, and a putting green. If you are looking for a peaceful, restful vacation this could work for you. The property is bordered by a golf course on one side and the ocean on the other. The units are older, most of them recently renovated, with full kitchens, ceiling fans, and great ocean views from the big lanais. I'd recommend getting an "ocean view" unit with a perfectly fabulous view of the blue Pacific, instead of an "oceanfront" unit; these units are away from the pool and more private, but they're close to the sewerage treatment plant and occasionally you can get a whiff of what goes on there.

4460 Nehe Rd., Lihue, HI 96766. ✆ **800/367-5004** or 808/822-9331. Fax 808/822-2828. www.castleresorts.com. 75 units (40 in rental pool). $235–$320 1-bedroom; $295–$415 2-bedroom; $385–$485 3-bedroom. Check Internet specials, which start at $149. AE, DC, DISC, MC, V. **Amenities:** 3 barbecue areas; heated outdoor pool; putting green; and tennis court. *In room:* TV, hair dryer, full kitchen, Wi-Fi access available in some units and in office.

MODERATE

Kauai Beach Villas These beachfront condos are a good option for families and others seeking more space and privacy than they'd get elsewhere in Lihue. You get all the space of a condo, plus access to the amenities next door at the Hilton (see above) where there is a spa, restaurant, and so forth. The only drawback is the unsafe swimming conditions on the beautiful but windy white-sand beach. The buildings were painted and upgraded (new barbecues areas) a couple of years ago. All units are outfitted with tropical decor and bamboo-style furniture, a fully equipped kitchen, a washer/dryer, and a lanai big enough for two lounge chairs, a table, and four chairs. The two-bedroom units have lanais off each bedroom, too. Although the units are individually owned and decorated, the website has photos of each unit so you can see the exact unit you are renting. The immaculately landscaped grounds contain pools, tennis courts, barbecue areas, and a volleyball court. The Wailua Municipal golf course is next door.

4330 Kauai Beach Dr., Lihue, HI 96766. Reservations c/o Kauai Vacation Rentals, 3-3311 Kuhio Hwy., Lihue. ✆ **800/367-5025** or 808/245-8841. Fax 808/246-1161. www.kauaivacationrentals.com. 150 units. $135–$200 1-bedroom for 4; $119–$275 2-bedroom for 6. 3- to 7-night minimum. Cleaning fee $110–$170. MC, V. **Amenities:** Access to nearby health club; hot tub; outdoor pool; tennis courts. *In room:* A/C (in bedrooms), TV/VCR, hair dryer, Internet access (in some units), kitchen, washer/dryer.

INEXPENSIVE

Garden Island Inn ★ (Finds) This bargain-hunter's delight is located 2 miles from the airport, 1 mile from Lihue, and within walking distance of shops, restaurants, and a beach just across the street. The spacious rooms are decorated with island-style furniture, bright prints, original artwork on the walls, and fresh tropical flowers (grown right on the grounds). Each unit has a hand-painted entry door of an island plant (palm trees, orchids, and so on) and contains a fridge, microwave, wet bar, TV, coffeemaker, and ocean view; some have private lanais, and the suites have sitting areas. The grounds are filled with flowers and banana and papaya trees (and you're welcome to help yourself to the fruit at the front desk). This is the kind of place where old-fashioned aloha is still practiced. The staff offers friendly service, lots of advice on activities (and even uses their connections to get you discounts), and even complimentary use of beach gear, golf clubs (a course is nearby, as are tennis courts), barbecue grills, and coolers. Guests are encouraged to stop by the office for cookies and coffee and to "talk story." If they are booked, ask about their two-bedroom condo nearby for $180 to $220 per night. The only caveat is that it is located on a fairly busy road, which can be canceled out with the use of earplugs at night.

3445 Wilcox Rd. (across the street from Kalapaki Beach, near Nawiliwili Harbor), Lihue, HI 96766. ✆ **800/648-0154** or 808/245-7227. Fax 808/245-7603. www.gardenislandinn.com. 21 units, private bathrooms have shower only. $99–$180 double. Extra person $10. AE, DISC, MC, V. **Amenities:** Complimentary watersports equipment. *In room:* A/C, TV.

SUPER-CHEAP SLEEPS

Motel Lani (Value) For a no-frills budget bed and shower, this place will do the job. You won't find a little basket of toiletries in the bathroom or a mint on your pillow, but you will get a clean, basic room (no TV) for as little as $62 for 1 night, or only $50 per night if you stay 2 nights or more. This small, concrete-block motel mainly serves interisland travelers and a few visitors on a budget. The location, on a busy street right in the heart of Lihue, isn't bad—the airport is just a 5-minute drive away, making this a good rest stop if you have an early-morning flight—but the beach is a significant schlep away.

P.O. Box 1836 (4240 Rice St.), Lihue, HI 96766. ✆ **808/245-2965.** 6 units (with shower only). $62 double. No credit cards. *In room:* A/C, fridge.

Tip Top Motel (Value) The Tip Top is an institution on Kauai. Their motto, "Over 75 years of service on the island of Kauai," lets you know they've been around a while. The two-story concrete tile building, with a cafe on the first floor, provides very basic accommodations: twin beds (with solid, hard mattresses), shower, air-conditioning unit in the window, and a dresser. Don't look for expensive carpeting here—just institutional linoleum tile. Guests are usually interisland business travelers who like the convenience of the central Lihue location, just 5 minutes from the airport.

3173 Akahi St., Lihue, HI 96766. ✆ **808/245-2333.** Fax 808/246-8988. 34 units (with shower only). $73 double. MC, V. From the airport, follow Ahukini Rd.; turn left on Akahi St. **Amenities:** Coffee shop. *In room:* A/C, TV, no phone.

2 THE POIPU RESORT AREA

VERY EXPENSIVE

Grand Hyatt Kauai Resort & Spa ★★★ (Kids) It's hard to believe that this luxury hotel (one of Hawaii's best) could get grander, but multimillion-dollar renovations have taken the level of casual elegance to a new level. This is one of Hawaii's best luxury hotels and one of the top-ranked tropical resorts in *Condé Nast Traveler*'s annual readers' poll. The four-story resort, built into the oceanside bluffs, spreads over 50 acres that overlook Shipwreck Beach (which is too rough for most swimmers) at the end of the road in Poipu. The $250-million Hyatt uses the Island architecture of the mid-1920s to recapture the Old Hawaii of the Matson Line steamship era.

The airy atmosphere takes you back to the days of a grand plantation overlooking the sea. This is a comfortable, unostentatious place where you can bring the kids and Grandma. The rooms are large (nearly 600 sq. ft.) and elegantly outfitted. All have marble bathrooms and spacious private lanais; most have ocean views. Club floors have their own concierge and a lounge serving continental breakfast, drinks, and snacks. The hotel is next door to the Robert Trent Jones, Jr.–designed Poipu Golf Course. If you stay here, don't leave without a treatment from the **ANARA Spa,** the best spa on Kauai. (Also check out the large selection of classes—some of them free—at the fitness center.) There may be 23 Grand Hyatt hotels on the planet, but frankly, I can't image any of them better than this.

The collection of swimming pools here—freshwater and salt, with slides, waterfalls, and secret lagoons—makes this oceanfront Hyatt a real kids' paradise. The Camp Hyatt children's program offers arts and crafts, scavenger hunts, and other special activities. Plus, the Hyatt is one of the few hotels to offer "camp" in the evening, from 4 to 10pm.

1571 Poipu Rd., Koloa, HI 96756. ✆ **800/55-HYATT** or 808/742-1234. Fax 808/742-1557. www.kauai.hyatt.com. 602 units. $432–$600 double; from $546 Grand Club; from $1,630 suite. Packages available (as we went to press the lowest Internet rate was $306). Extra person $50. Children 17 and under stay free in parent's room. Resort fee of $18 a day for local and toll-free calls, self-parking, daily local newspaper, 1 hr. at the tennis court free, fitness access to the ANARA Spa and to classes, and 10% off various shops on property. AE, DC, MC, V. Valet parking $10. **Amenities:** 6 restaurants (including Dondero's, p. 138, and Tidepool, p. 141), 6 bars (the partially open-air Stevenson's Library has mellow jazz Thurs–Sat nights); babysitting; bike rental; extensive Camp Hyatt kids' program; concierge; concierge-level rooms; one of the best fitness centers on the island; 3 hot tubs; an elaborate freshwater fantasy pool complex, plus 2 more pools and 5 acres of saltwater swimming lagoons w/islands and a man-made beach; room service; a 25,000-sq.-ft. ANARA Spa w/lava-rock shower gardens, a 10-headed Swedish shower, and indoor and outdoor treatment rooms; 4 tennis courts; and watersports equipment rentals. *In room:* A/C, TV/DVD, hair dryer, Wi-Fi ($15/day).

Ko'a Kea Hotel & Resort ★★★ Just opened in 2009 is this oasis—a small boutique hotel on one of the most beautiful stretches of beach in Poipu, with luxurious accommodations and first-class amenities (including an espresso maker in your room). In the footprints of the former Poipu Beach Hotel (which was destroyed by Hurricane Iniki in 1992), the 121-room hotel offers a central location in Poipu for dining, shopping, and activities, but the truth is that you will feel so relaxed on the manicured grounds and so happy with the beach out front, you won't want to leave. And, really there's no reason to: between the culinary creations at the Resort's dining room, Red Salt (see p. 140), the on-property spa, and the beckoning waves at the beach, you could happily spend your Kauai vacation here just relaxing. The rooms feature everything from a flatscreen TV to iPod docking station.

2251 Poipu Rd., Poipu, HI 96756. ✆ **877/806-2288** or 808/828-8888. Fax 808/332-5316. www.koakea.com. 121 units. $446–$725. Suites from $1,625. See website for deals, as we went to press garden rooms started at $299. Extra person $50, children 18 and under stay free in parent's room. Resort fee $16/day for valet-only parking, use of Internet and the fitness center. AE, DC, DISC, MC, V. **Amenities:** Restaurant (Red Salt, p. 140) and lounge; small fitness center; nearby golf courses; pool with whirlpool; small spa. *In room:* A/C, TV/DVD/CD, fridge, iPod docking station, hair dryer, Internet access.

Sheraton Kauai Resort ★★ Kids For the money, this modern Sheraton (since 1997) has the feeling of Old Hawaii with a dynamite location on one of Kauai's best beaches. It features buildings on both the ocean side and the mountain side of the road. You have a choice of three buildings: one nestled in tropical gardens with koi-filled ponds; one facing the palm-fringed, white-sand beach (my favorite); and one looking across green grass to the ocean, with great sunset views. The rooms overlook either the tropical gardens or the rolling surf. The rooms and public area were all recently updated (to the tune of $14 million): 32" Flatscreen TVs have been added, new tropical furniture and drapes now adorn the rooms. The resort offers such programs asoceanfront luau twice a week, educational lectures on the Hawaii monk seal (a frequent visitor to the white-sand beach in front of the property), and every Wednesday night, Sheraton guests can enjoy a "Movie Under the Stars"—relax on the grassy lawn and watch a recent box office hit on a 30-foot screen.

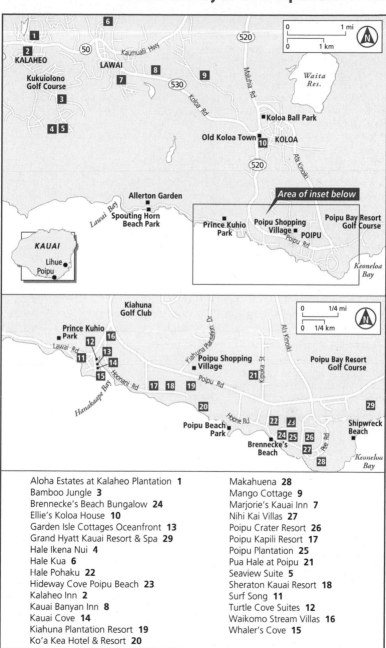

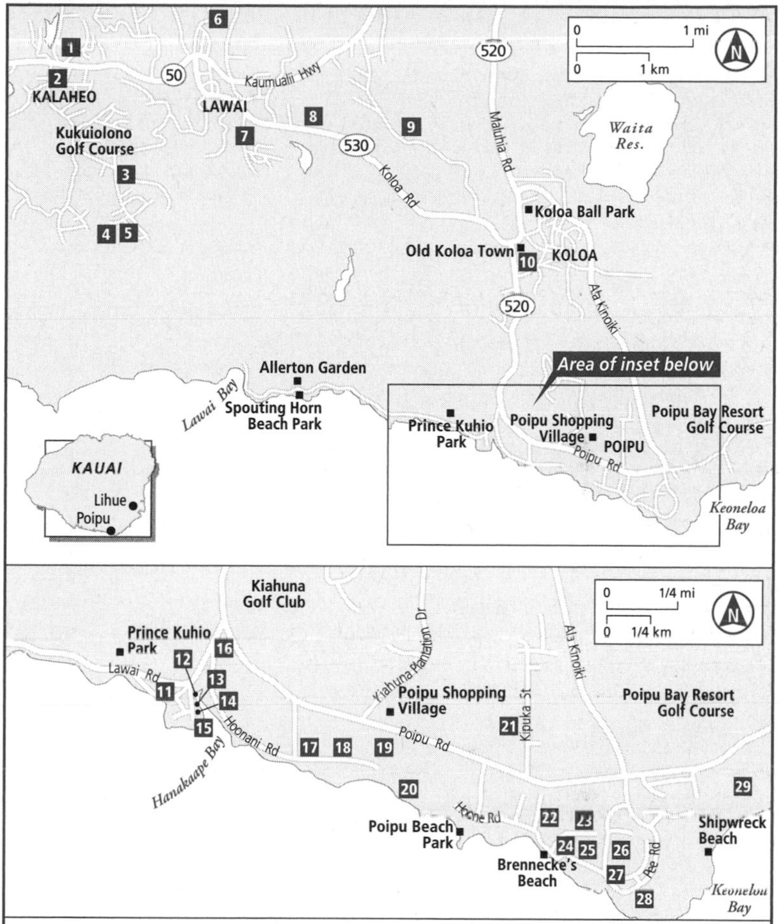

Aloha Estates at Kalaheo Plantation **1**
Bamboo Jungle **3**
Brennecke's Beach Bungalow **24**
Ellie's Koloa House **10**
Garden Isle Cottages Oceanfront **13**
Grand Hyatt Kauai Resort & Spa **29**
Hale Ikena Nui **4**
Hale Kua **6**
Hale Pohaku **22**
Hideway Cove Poipu Beach **23**
Kalaheo Inn **2**
Kauai Banyan Inn **8**
Kauai Cove **14**
Kiahuna Plantation Resort **19**
Ko'a Kea Hotel & Resort **20**
Makahuena **28**
Mango Cottage **9**
Marjorie's Kauai Inn **7**
Nihi Kai Villas **27**
Poipu Crater Resort **26**
Poipu Kapili Resort **17**
Poipu Plantation **25**
Pua Hale at Poipu **21**
Seaview Suite **5**
Sheraton Kauai Resort **18**
Surf Song **11**
Turtle Cove Suites **12**
Waikomo Stream Villas **16**
Whaler's Cove **15**

Construction in Poipu

There is major construction going on in the **Poipu Resort** area. If you are headed that way, be warned that the number of condominium and hotel rooms currently under construction (and not counting the ones still in the planning process) will increase the number of visitor accommodations in Poipu by 25%.

The good news is that Kauai County has very strict guidelines for noise and dust abatement, which is vigorously enforced. Just be aware that you will be facing traffic delays, construction noise, and the general problems caused by a lot of construction work in a small area.

Current construction will add 227,000 square feet of retail space, 423 condominium units, and 190 lots for single family homes to the area.

In the permit process, with no definite construction timetable yet, are plans for another 824 condominium units, 75,000 square feet of retail space, and an 11,000-square-foot spa and fitness center.

As we went to press, the projects currently under construction in Poipu are:

- **Koloa Landing,** 2251 Kapili Rd: 232 condominium units, scheduled for completion in 2010.
- **Kukuiulu Development,** between Poipu and Lawai Valley: A master-planned resort community on 1,010 acres, including a boutique hotel with 31 cottage units, a resort spa, a 75,000-square-foot commercial village, an 18-hole golf course, and condominiums and homes. Roadways are currently under construction, scheduled to be finished in 2010.
- **Kukui'ula Village Shopping Center,** off Ala Kalanikaumaka (the new western bypass road): A 90,000-square-foot replica of an old sugar plantation town with plantation-style architecture which will house 45 restaurants, specialty shops, and offices including Merriman's Kaua`i, Quiksilver, The Josselin Restaurant, Palm Palm, Bubba Burgers Hawaii, Bungalow 9, and Lappert's Hawaii. The opening is now estimated to be late 2009 or early 2010.

The bar is fabulous. Even if you don't stay here, come by to order a cocktail and an appetizer, and take in the view and the Hawaiian music. A golf course is nearby. ***Families, take note:*** Kids eat free with a paying adult at the Shell Restaurant, at both breakfast and dinner.

2440 Hoonani Rd., Koloa, HI 96756. ✆ **866/716-8109** or 808/742-1661. Fax 808/742-9777. www.starwoodhotels.com/hawaii. 413 units. $475–$820 double (maximum 4 in room); from $850 suite for 4. (Starwood members get 35% off rack rates.) Extra person $60. Daily $18 resort fee for sunset mai tai punch hour (Sun, Mon, Wed & Fri) w/torch-lighting ceremony, self-parking, Internet access, guest library w/daily newspapers, computers in the lobby w/Internet access, and use of fitness center and tennis courts. AE, DC, DISC, MC, V. Valet parking $8. **Amenities:** 3 restaurants, extraordinary bar; babysitting; children's program; concierge; fitness room facing the ocean (one of the most scenic places to work out on Kauai); 2 outdoor pools (1 w/water playground, 1 for children) and hot tub; small massage-and-skin-care center; room service; 3 tennis courts (2 night-lit); and watersports equipment rentals, *In room:* A/C, TV, hair dryer, Wi-Fi.

- **Pili Mai at Poipu,** off Kiahuna Plantation Drive: 191 condo units. Infrastructure has been completed; more construction depends on the sales of the units.
- **Poipu Aina Estates,** 2800 Ala Kinoki: Infrastructure for the 17-lot agricultural subdivision is complete.
- **Poipu Beach Estates,** Poipu Road at the roundabout: Landscaping for the 106-lot subdivision is completed.
- **Poipu Shopping Village Phase II,** Poipu Road: Construction of an additional 62,000 square feet of retail space is expected to be complete by the end of 2010.
- **Village at Poipu Phase I,** Poipu Road: A 50-lot, single-family subdivision.
- **Wainani at Kiahuna,** Kiahuna Plantation Drive: This subdivision of 70 single-family homes is under construction.

Projects still in the county planning and permit process are:

- **Kiahuna Poipu Golf Resort,** adjacent to Kiahuna Golf Course, off Kiahuna Plantation Drive: 280 condominium units and 2 single-family homes.
- **Koloa Creekside Estate,** Weliweli-Waikomo Road: A 9.38-acre condominium development.
- **Koloa Marketplace,** Koloa and Maluhia roads: Plans for the 75,000-square-foot retail space are in the final stages of the permit process.
- **Poipu Spa and Fitness Center,** Poipu Road, fronting the Kiahuna Tennis and Swim Club: Plans are underway for an 11,000-square-foot spa and fitness center.
- **Royal Palms at Poipu Beach,** Kiahuna Plantation Drive: This 164-condo unit project is in the permit process.

For more information, contact the **Poipu Beach Resort Association,** ✆ **888/744-0888** or www.poipubeach.org.

EXPENSIVE

Kiahuna Plantation Resort ★★ Kids One of the best condominium developments in the Poipu area, this complex consists of several plantation-style buildings, loaded with Hawaiian style and sprinkled on a 35-acre garden setting with lagoons, lawns, and a gold-sand beach at reasonable prices for the Poipu resort area. Golf, shopping, and restaurants are within easy walking distance. Two different management companies handle the rental pool: Outrigger oversees about two-thirds of the units, Castle the remaining third. (I have found Outrigger to have the superior units and to be very responsive to the guests.) All condo units are spacious, with full kitchens, daily maid service, and lanais. Kiahuna offers an activities program for children 5 to 12 during spring break, summer, and winter for $70 for a full day and $55 for a half-day, both include lunch. The Kiahuna Swim and Tennis Club (with the Casa Blanca at Kiahuna restaurant) is just across the street, and a championship golf course is nearby.

2253 Poipu Rd., Koloa, HI 96756. 333 units. Under 2 different management groups: Outrigger, ✆ **800/ OUTRIGGER** or 808/742-6411. Fax 808/742-1698. www.outrigger.com. $195–$365 1-bedroom apt. (sleeps up to 4); $288–$550 2-bedroom apt. (sleeps up to 6). Packages available, including 5th night free, car packages, senior rates, and more. AE, DC, DISC, MC, V. Castle Resorts & Hotels, ✆ **800/367-5004** or 808/742-2200. Fax 800/477-2329 or 808/742-1047. $165–$229 1-bedroom apt.; $433–$1,050 2-bedroom apt. Ask about packages like 5th night free or free car. AE, DC, DISC, MC, V. **Amenities:** Restaurant (see review of Plantation Gardens on p. 140), bar; barbecue areas; children's program; outdoor pool; tennis courts; watersports equipment rentals. *In room:* TV/VCR, hair dryer, kitchen.

Whaler's Cove ★★ If money is not a worry and you want something really special right on the water, you can't go wrong with these ultraluxury units. In 2009, the management just completed renovating six of the 39 units with stainless steel appliances, granite counter tops, tile floors, and large 2-person showers. The other units will undergo the same renovations in 2010. From the koa door at the entry to the ocean view from the master bedroom, this is first class all the way. The two-bedroom, two-and-a-half bathroom units are in a town house with a two-story configuration, plenty of space (1,400sq. ft.), and plenty of privacy for two couples. These units have it all: a huge deck overlooking the Pacific, top-of-the-line appliances in the kitchen, washer/dryers in the units, and an entertainment center. The property itself features an oceanside infinity pool, a whirlpool, and a barbecue area. Other amenities include an orchid garden, full concierge, and easy access to Koloa Landing (an outcrop of lava where the river and ocean meet, which is great for snorkeling and good for turtle spotting).

2640 Puuholo Rd. Reservations: The Parrish Collection, 3176 Poipu Rd., Koloa, HI 96756. ✆ **800/325-5701** or 808/742-2000. Fax 808/742-9093. www.parrishkauai.com. 39 units. $345–$469 2-bedroom, 2 ½-bathroom. Ask for Frommer's special discount. DC, DISC, MC, V. **Amenities:** Barbecue area; concierge; outdoor pool and whirlpool. *In room:* TV/VCR, hair dryer, kitchen.

MODERATE

Garden Isle Cottages Oceanfront (Finds) The site is spectacular: a 13-foot cliff overlooking historic Koloa Landing and an ocean inlet (where you can see turtles swimming). Nestled in a tropical garden setting, these one-bedroom apartments have an island feel, with rattan furniture, batiks, and original art on the walls—and great views. (Some of the artwork is by owner Robert Flynn, whose work is also on display at the Honolulu International Airport.) All units, so large that they can easily sleep four, feature full kitchens and spacious lanais. This is a quiet, peaceful place to stay in the heart of the Poipu area, within walking distance of beaches, golf, tennis, shopping, and restaurants.

2666 Puuholo Rd. (overlooking Waikomo Stream), Koloa, HI 96756. ✆ **800/742-6711** or 808/742-6717. www.oceancottages.com. 2 units. High season $240 1-bedroom; low season $216 1-bedroom, plus cleaning fee of $55. Extra person $10. No credit cards. *In room:* TV, kitchen.

Hideaway Cove Poipu Beach ★★ (Value) These gorgeous condominium units in a plantation setting are just a short walk to a white sandy beach, and are located next door to an excellent restaurant. The difference between this property and the dozens of others in Poipu is in the details. Amenities are top-drawer, and no expense was spared in the interior decorations. Units have hardwood floors, comfy furniture, roomy beds (either four-poster beds or wood sleigh designs), spacious living areas, kitchenettes with quality appliances and granite countertops, and big outdoor lanais (with top-of-the-line stainless steel grills). You get all of this in a lush, landscaped tropical jungle at affordable prices. Owner Herb Lee is always on hand to guide you to Kauai's best spots. A few of the units have Jacuzzi tubs, so ask when you book.

Value The King of Condos

One of the easiest ways to find lodging in the Poipu Beach area is to contact **The Parrish Collection** (formerly Grantham Resorts), 3176 Poipu Rd., Koloa, HI 96756 (✆ **800/325-5701** or 808/742-2000; fax 808/742-9093; www.parrishkauai.com), which handles more than 100 "handpicked" rental units for 12 different condo developments, plus dozens of vacation homes, ranging from quaint cottages to elite resort homes. The Parrish Collection has high standards for their rental units and offers extremely fair prices. If the properties are not maintained to their standards, they have no problem taking the units (and, in one case, an entire condominium project) out of their selected rentals. The condos start at $159 for a spacious two-bedroom, garden-view unit in low season, and vacation cottages start at $250 and go up to $4,885 for exquisite multimillion-dollar ocean estates. There's a 5-night minimum for condos and a 7-night minimum for homes.

If you're staying on Kauai for 5 days, ask The Parrish Collection about the **"Frommer's Preferred Guest Discount."** You'll get a large one- or two-bedroom condo, well-equipped (full kitchen, washer/dryer, wet bar, TV/DVD, phone, and most units have high-speed Internet), starting as low as $109 a night for one-bedrooms and $151 for two-bedrooms with garden views, or $180 a night for oceanview condos (see the reviews for Nihi Kai Villas, Poipu Crater Resort, and Waikomo Stream Villas, below). There's not a better deal on Kauai. Kudos to The Parrish Collection for these fabulous vacation bargains.

2307 Nalo Rd. Reservations: P.O. Box 1113, Koloa, HI 96756. ✆ **866/849-2426** or 808/635-8785. www.hideawaycove.com. 7 units. $185–$205 studio double; $220–$265 1-bedroom double; $275–$310 2-bedroom for 4; $395–$450 3-bedroom for 4; from $670 5-bedroom (discount for 7 nights or more). Cleaning fee $90–$335. Extra person $20. 2-night minimum. AE, DISC, MC, V. **Amenities:** Restaurant and bar next door; free beach toys and bicycles. *In room:* TV/VCR/DVD, hair dryer, kitchen, Wi-Fi.

Makahuena ★ Finds The pluses at these very luxurious condos include moderately priced two-bedroom oceanfront and oceanview units, an oceanfront pool, hydro-spa, complimentary tennis courts, a private lava-rock barbecue area, and some of the most dramatic ocean vistas in Poipu. The units have vaulted ceilings and fully equipped kitchens, with top-of-the-line appliances. The only minus we can find here is no maid service. Swimming is just a few blocks away, along the coast, at Poipu Beach.

1661 Pe'e Rd., Poipu. Reservations: The Parrish Collection, 3176 Poipu Rd., Suite 1, Koloa, HI 96756. ✆ **800/325-5701** or 808/742-2000. Fax 808/742-9093. www.parrishkauai.com. 78 units. $195 $290 2-bedroom/2-bathroom. Ask for Frommer's Special Discount. 5-night minimum. DC, DISC, MC, V. **Amenities:** Outdoor pool; barbecue area. *In room:* TV/VCR, hair dryer, kitchen, Wi-Fi.

Poipu Kapili Resort ★★ This quiet, upscale oceanfront cluster of condos is outstanding in every area. We like the home-away-from-home comforts and special touches: a video and book library, a spacious pool, several barbecues, tennis courts lit for night play, and an herb garden. (You're welcome to take samples if you're cooking.) A golf course is also nearby. The apartments are large (1-bedroom/2-bathroom units are 1,150

What's the Story on "Cleaning Fees?"

Several bed-and-breakfasts and some condo units have instituted yet another fee (an add-on fee, similar to the "resort fee" that hotels charge) called a "cleaning fee." Personally, I hate this. Why not just incorporate all costs into the room rate? I think "cleaning fees" is a chintzy way to look "affordable" but then add yet another cost on to your unit. (Travelers: Be sure to read the fine print; if you are getting a unit for $135 a night plus an $80 cleaning fee for a 2-night minimum—you really are buying a $175-a-night unit.) I have gotten numerous cards, letters, and e-mails from guests complaining about these "cleaning fees," all saying they feel slightly cheated by this additional cost. *B&B and condo owners:* Take note that it is better to have one rate (including cleaning fees and all other costs) than to have unhappy guests.

sq. ft.; 2-bedroom/3-bathroom units are 1,820 sq. ft.) and have fully equipped kitchens, tropical furnishings, ceiling fans, and private lanais. The oceanfront two-story town houses are our favorites because they catch the trade winds. The two-bedroom units also have washer/dryers. (Common laundry facilities are available on the property as well.) Although the Pacific is right outside your window, the nearest sandy beach is a block away (which can be a blessing because it means more privacy).

2221 Kapili Rd., Koloa, HI 96756. ✆ **800/443-7714** or 808/742-6449. Fax 808/742-9162. www.poipukapili.com. 60 units. $250–$400 1-bedroom apt. (sleeps up to 4); $395–$600 2-bedroom apt. (up to 6). Discounts for longer stays; package rates available; 7th night free May 1–Dec 20. Rates include Fri continental breakfast by the pool. MC, V. **Amenities:** Barbecue area; oceanside pool; night-lit championship tennis courts. *In room:* TV/VCR, hair dryer (on request), kitchen, Wi-Fi.

Turtle Cove Suites ★★ Value What makes this property so incredible is not only the fabulous location (overlooking the stream and ocean) but also the great eye of the interior designer. It also helps that owner Joe Sylvester and his wife previously owned a furniture and fine arts store from which they could choose the "perfect" items for their four units. Our favorite unit, located on a quiet street, away from the crowds, is the 1,100-square-foot oceanfront suite with a full kitchen and private hot tub, original art on the walls, and a zillion little touches that make this place seem more like a home than a vacation rental. All units (even the $170 one) come with lanais and use of the swimming pool and hot tub; they feature top-of-the-line materials like slate from India, four-poster beds, and marble bathrooms. At these prices, the units are a deal. Book in advance.

P.O. Box 1899, Poipu Beach, HI 96756. ✆ **866/294-2733.** www.kauaibeachrentals.com. 4 units. $170–$265, plus cleaning fees of $85. 5-night minimum (negotiable). AE, DC, DISC, MC, V. **Amenities:** Outside pool and hot tub. *In room:* TV/DVD, fridge, Wi-Fi. Some units have complete kitchens; some have kitchenettes.

INEXPENSIVE

Brennecke's Beach Bungalow ★ Finds Attention honeymooners (or honeymooner wannabes): This is your place. It's so close to Poipu Beach that you can see it from your private lanai (about a 45-second walk from the front door to the waves). Tucked into a large two-story house is this private-entrance studio decorated with bamboo floors, maple cabinets, and lots of Hawaiian decor. This studio also has a small kitchenette (microwave, toaster oven, blender, coffeemaker, and fridge), cozy sitting area, and a big, comfortable bed. Outdoors there's a beach shower, barbecue area, and big, green lawn. Restaurants, dining, tennis, and golf are just minutes away. Book this baby!

2233 Nalu Rd., Poipu Beach, Kauai, Hawaii 96756. ✆ **888/393-4646** or 808/742-1116. Fax 808/246-2505. www.poipubeachbungalow.com. 1 studio. $150–$175, plus a cleaning fee of $115. 7-night minimum. No credit cards. **Amenities:** Barbecue area; golf nearby; tennis courts nearby. *In room:* TV/DVD/VCR/CD, fridge, hair dryer, free Wi-Fi.

Ellie's Koloa House (Kids) (Finds) For years Ellie ran the popular Koloa Landing Cottages, then in 2007, she sold that business and renovated an old plantation house in the heart of Koloa. This two-bedroom/two-bathroom home, surrounded by tropical gardens, is for the traveler who wants a "real" Hawaii experience living in a residential area. Ellie has a terrific eye for color and design, and has taken this plain-Jane house and converted it into a whimsical tropical cottage—perfect for a family. Entry is through a plant-filled, outdoor lanai, where you will likely spend lots of time—just like Hawaii residents. The house (with full kitchen) has antique furniture recovered in old Hawaiian-print fabric, with paddle fans to keep the house cool, TV, washer and dryer, barbecue, and everything you can think of to make your vacation. Just a mile and a half to the beach and walking distance to Koloa town's shops and restaurants.

5335 Malino Rd., Koloa, HI 96756. ✆ **800/779-8773** or 808/635-0054. www.koloavacationrental.com. 1 house. $125 for 4. 2-night minimum. No credit cards. **Amenities:** Barbecue. *In room:* TV, fridge, Internet, kitchen.

Hale Pohaku ★ (Finds) This half-acre tropical compound can be either a great bargain for independent travelers or a terrific find for a big, big family. Just 30 seconds from Poipu Beach, this four-house complex was purchased and renovated in 2005, and consists of a five-bedroom manager's house, two restored plantation-era two-bedroom cottages, and a third two-bedroom cottage built in the same plantation style. You can rent everything from a studio to the entire lot (sleeps 22). Each unit features a fully equipped kitchen, washer/dryer, private barbecue area, hardwood floors, and outdoor beach shower. This gated compound has a swimming pool, extra amenities for kids (highchairs, and so forth), and plenty of beach toys (boogie boards, snorkeling equipment, and such). Golf, tennis, restaurants, and shopping are close by.

2231 Pane Rd., Koloa, HI 96756. ✆ **866/742-6462** or 808/742-6462. www.vacationrental-kauai.com. 5 units. $135 studio double; $275 2-bedroom cottage double; $625 5-bedroom house, plus cleaning fee $80–$250. 2-night minimum. AE, DISC, MC, V. **Amenities:** Pool; golf nearby; tennis courts nearby. *In room:* TV/VCR, barbecue area, hair dryer, kitchen, Wi-Fi.

Kauai Banyan Inn ★ (Finds) On a hilltop, overlooking an acre of landscaped property, a stream, and, of course, an old banyan tree, is this country inn, with five rooms and a darling cozy cottage next door. Centered around a courtyard with a burbling fountain, this is a place of peace and quiet, great for relaxing and resting. The owner, Lorna, has a daughter who is a licensed massage therapist and can give you an in-room massage to relieve jet lag and built-up tension. Each room is good sized with hardwood floors, comfy beds, and either a kitchenette (a ¾-size fridge, microwave, two-burner stove, and coffeemaker) or a complete kitchen. All the rooms have terrific pastoral views of the rolling countryside, lanais, separate private bathrooms, and private entrances. There's a barbecue area outside. Not appropriate for kids under 10.

3528-B Mana Hema Place, Lawai, HI 96765. ✆ **888/786-3855.** www.kauaibanyan.com. 6 units. $130–$150 (plus cleaning fee of $45). 3-night minimum. MC, V. **Amenities:** Barbecue area; hot tub; beach equipment. *In room:* TV/DVD, hair dryer, kitchen or kitchenette, Wi-Fi.

Kauai Cove ★ Value These immaculate cottages, located just 300 feet from Koloa Landing, next to Waikomo Stream, are the perfect private getaway. Each studio has a full kitchen, private lanai (with barbecue grill), and big bamboo four-poster bed. The cozy rooms feature beautiful hardwood floors, tropical decor, and cathedral ceilings. Kauai Cove is within walking distance of sandy beaches, great restaurants, and shopping, yet it's far enough off the beaten path that privacy and quiet are assured.

2672 Puuholo Rd., Poipu, HI 96756. ✆ **800/624-9945** or 808/742-2562. www.kauaicove.com. 3 units. $99–$175 double ($50–$85 cleaning fee). 3-night minimum. DISC, MC, V. *In room:* A/C, TV/CD, barbecue, kitchen.

Mango Cottage ★ Value A path cutting through lush tropical foliage leads you to this free-standing cottage in the rolling hills outside of Koloa. A skylight in the 550-square-foot bungalow illuminates the full kitchen and living room area. The separate bedroom has a king-size bed with adjoining bathroom. White tile creates clean lines throughout, and there is a queen-size sofa bed in the living room for additional guests. Owner George Coates spent years in the hotel industry and his experience shows in attention to detail and anticipation of his guests' needs. It's very private, very peaceful, but just 15 minutes to Poipu Beach, restaurants, shopping, golf, and tennis.

4333 Naulu, Koloa, HI 96756. ✆ **808/742-1216.** Fax 808/742-7344. www.hawaiian.net/~quaylo/bnb.htm. 1 cottage. $130 double. 3-night minimum. No credit cards. *In room:* TV, kitchen, no phone.

Marjorie's Kauai Inn ★★ This quiet property, perched on the side of a hill, is just 10 minutes from Poipu Beach and 5 minutes from Old Koloa Town. From its large lanai it offers stunning views over rolling pastures and the Lawai Valley. Every unit has a kitchenette with dining table, ceiling fan, and lanai. The new Sunset View unit has a separate sitting area and a futon sofa for extra guests. On the hillside is a huge, 50-foot swimming pool, perfect for lap swimming. New owners Mike and Alexis have kept former owner Marjorie Ketcher's motto "do one fun thing a day," and have a treasure-trove of beach toys (from snorkel gear to kayaks to bicycles and even bike racks for cars) to help you live up to the motto. The well-traveled owners (who have owned bed-and-breakfasts for 20-plus years) have spruced up the property, redecorated the rooms with contemporary tropical decor (and added flatscreen TVs), and made this wonderful inn even more fabulous. Every room is beautiful, but my favorite is the Sunset View Room with its own hot tub outside and a view that will linger in your memory forever. ***Note:*** The inn is not appropriate for families with young children.

P.O. Box 866 (off Hailima Rd., adjacent to the National Tropical Botanical Garden), Lawai, HI 96765. ✆ **800/717-8838** or 808/332-8838. www.marjorieskauaiinn.com. 3 units. $130–$175 double. Rates include continental breakfast. Extra person $20. 3-night minimum. Credit cards through Pay Pal. **Amenities:** Barbecue; pool; 2 whirlpool spas; complimentary beach toys. *In room:* A/C in 2 rooms, TV, hair dryer, kitchenette, Wi-Fi.

Nihi Kai Villas ★ Value One of the best values in the Poipu Beach area. If you stay 5 nights, the rate for these large, well-equipped, two-bedroom, two-bathroom units starts at an unbelievable $159 a night (for four, which works out to just $40 per person). You may not get new carpeting, new furniture, new drapes, or a prime beachfront location, but you *do* get a clean, well-cared-for unit just 200 yards from the beach with full kitchen, washer/dryer, and TV/VCR, all at an unbeatable price. The property is a 2-minute walk from world-famous Brennecke's Beach (great for bodysurfing) and a block from Poipu Beach Park. On-site amenities include an oceanfront swimming pool, tennis and paddle courts, and a barbecue and picnic area. Within a 5-minute drive are two great golf courses, several restaurants, and loads of shopping.

Moa Better: Chickens & Roosters

One of the first things that visitors notice about Kauai is there seems to be an unusually large number of *moa* (wild chickens). Kauai has always had a history of having more than its fair share of chickens and roosters running about, but after Hurricane Iniki picked up and scattered the fowl all over the island in 1992, they have been populating at a prodigious rate. Generally, having a few chickens scratching around in the dirt is quaint and downright picturesque. However, the "dark side" of the chicken population explosion is the increase in the number of roosters. In fact, a new industry has cropped up: Rooster Eradicators. Resorts hire these eradicators to remove the roosters from the well-manicured grounds because the large number of these male birds has led to, well, a sort of crowing contest. Generally roosters will crow as the sun comes up. But on Kauai, with the population increase, the roosters crow all day long and throughout the night in some places. Just be warned that part of the "charm" of Kauai is the rooster population, and you might want to consider bringing earplugs.

1870 Hoone Rd. Reservations: c/o The Parrish Collection, 3176 Poipu Rd., Suite 1, Koloa, HI 96756. ✆ **800/325-5701** or 808/742-2000. Fax 808/742-9093. www.parrishkauai.com. 70 units. Regular rates: $145–$244 1-bedroom double; $159–$380 2-bedroom for 4; $300–$469 3-bedroom/2-bathroom oceanfront for 6 (5-night minimum). Ask about Frommer's "Special Discount" (5-night minimum). DC, DISC, MC, V. From Poipu Rd., turn toward the ocean on Hoowili Rd., then left on Hoone Rd.; Nihi Kai Villas is just past Nalo Rd. on Hoone Rd. **Amenities:** Concierge; hot tub; outdoor pool; nearby golf course; tennis courts. *In room:* TV/VCR, kitchen, Internet.

Poipu Crater Resort (Value) Attention, travelers on a budget: Two-bedroom garden-view units for just $119 a night in low season ($60 a couple!) is a deal you can't pass up. This resort consists of 15 duplexes in a tropical garden setting. Each unit is about 1,500 square feet with living area, kitchen, large lanai, bathroom, and guest bedroom downstairs, and master bedroom and bathroom upstairs. Each has a full kitchen (with microwave), as well as a washer/dryer and VCR. The complex has a swimming pool, tennis and paddle ball courts, sauna, Ping-Pong tables, and barbecues. Poipu Beach is about a 10-minute walk away, and the entire Poipu Beach resort area (offering everything from restaurants to golf courses) is within a 5-minute drive. The only caveats are no maid service and no air-conditioning.

2330 Hoohu Rd., Poipu. Reservations: c/o The Parrish Collection, 3176 Poipu Rd., Suite 1, Koloa, HI 96756. ✆ **800/325-5701** or 808/742-2000. Fax 808/742-9093. www.parrishkauai.com. 30 units. $119–$205 2-bedroom garden view (5-night minimum); ask about Frommer's "Special Discount" (5-night minimum). DC, DISC, MC, V. From Poipu Rd., turn toward the ocean on Hoowili Rd., then left on Hoone Rd.; continue on Hoone Rd., past the bends, where the road is now called Pee Rd; turn left off Pee Rd. onto Hoohu Rd. **Amenities:** Barbecue area; nearby golf course; outdoor pool; tennis courts. *In room:* TV/VCR, CD, kitchen, washer/dryer.

Poipu Plantation (Value) Budget vacationers looking for an old-fashioned bed-and-breakfast (with real breakfast, not food items in your refrigerator)—here's your place. This tropical property has three bed-and-breakfast rooms in the main house and separate apartment vacation rentals on the same property. The large rooms in the house are reminiscent of the old plantation days, with shining wooden floors, huge bathrooms, and lots of privacy. Breakfast is served in the dining room; you're also welcome to take yours out on the lanai. The impeccably decorated one- and two-bedroom apartments are huge and come with big lanais, spacious living rooms, large separate bedrooms (with shoji doors), full kitchens, and big bathrooms. Gleaming hardwood floors, air-conditioning, and ocean views add to the value. The location also offers value, in the heart of Poipu, within walking distance of beach and water activities, golfing, tennis, shops, and restaurants.

1792 Pee Rd., Koloa, HI 96756. ✆ **800/634-0263** or 808/742-6757. Fax 808/742-8681. www.poipubeach.com. 3 units, 9 apts. $145–$220 double (including continental breakfast); $135–$175 1-bedroom; $175–$210 2-bedroom for 4. Extra person $20. 3-night minimum (some units have a 5-night minimum). MC, V. From Poipu Rd., turn toward the ocean onto Pee Rd. **Amenities:** Hot tub. *In room:* A/C, TV/VCR, kitchen (in apartment units).

Pua Hale at Poipu ★ *Finds* Created by an artist and designed by an engineer, Pua Hale is a large (850 sq.ft.) cottage on a quiet dead-end street, just 2 blocks from Poipu Beach. Artist/photographer Carol Ann Davis and her husband, engineer Walter Briant, took an empty space in their yard and created an open, airy cottage with an Asian-influenced interior. The cottage is surrounded by a high fence to ensure privacy; entrance is through a rustic wooden gate draped with colorful bougainvillea. Sliding glass doors run nearly the entire length of the cottage, bringing the outside in. The open-beam ceiling and white-tile floors add to the overall feeling of lightness, and the wood trim, rattan furniture, and colorful throw rugs add to the island vibe. The large main room has a complete kitchen at one end, and living and dining areas (with a queen-size sofa bed) at the other. The bathroom has a wonderful tiled Japanese *furo* (sunken tub) for soaking as well as a shower. A real bonus is the intimate, curved lanai overlooking Japanese gardens blooming with ginger, heliconia, and plumeria. Other pluses include a barbecue, a stereo, and laundry facilities. Walk to Poipu beaches, shopping, and restaurants.

2381 Kipuka St., Koloa, HI 96756. ✆ **800/745-7414** or 808/742-1700. Fax 808/742-7392. www.kauai-puahale.com. 1 cottage. $145 double, plus a $75 cleaning fee. Extra person $12. 4-night minimum. MC, V. From Poipu Rd., turn left on Kipuka St. (just past shopping center). No children under 8. **Amenities:** Barbecue. *In room:* A/C, TV/VCR, CD, kitchen.

Surf Song *Value* Located in a quiet residential neighborhood among million-dollar oceanfront homes, these three studios and one apartment unit offer excellent value for your vacation dollar. Each unit has a private lanai, queen-size bed, and sleeper sofa. (Some even have ocean views.) The studios have kitchenettes with microwave, coffeemaker, small refrigerator, and other appliances; the apartment has a full kitchen. All units face a courtyard, landscaped with tropical flowers, with a picnic table and barbecue. The Surf Song is walking distance to the beach, and a 2-minute drive to restaurants and shops in the Poipu Resort area. A couple of years ago, the entire complex was repainted and redecorated.

5135 Ho'ona Rd., Poipu Beach, HI 96756. ✆ **877/373-2331** or 808/742-2331. Fax 808/826-6033. www.surfsong.com. 4 units. $85–$145 double. Cleaning fee $60–$75. Extra person $25. AE, DISC, MC, V. 3-night minimum. *In room:* TV, kitchenette or kitchen.

Waikomo Stream Villas ★ *Value* Another great deal from The Parrish Collection (see box on p. 107): The 800- to 900-square-foot, one-bedroom apartments comfortably sleep four and start at $115 a night; larger two-bedroom units that sleep six start at $159 a night. Tucked into a lush tropical garden setting, the spacious, well-decorated units have everything you could possibly need on your vacation: full kitchen, VCR, washer/dryer, and private lanai. The complex—which has both adults' and children's pools, tennis courts, and a barbecue area—is adjacent to the Kiahuna Golf Club and just a 5-minute walk from restaurants, shopping, and Poipu's beaches and golf courses. The only

Tips: B&B Etiquette

In Hawaii, it is traditional and customary to remove your shoes before entering anyone's home. The same is true for most bed-and-breakfast facilities. Most hosts post signs or will politely ask you to remove your shoes before entering the B&B. Not only does this keep the B&B clean, but you'll be amazed how relaxed you feel walking around barefoot. If this custom is unpleasant to you, a B&B may not be for you. Consider a condo or hotel, where no one will be particular about your shoes.

If you have never stayed at a B&B before, here are a few other hints: Generally the host lives on property and their part of the house is off-limits to guests. (You do not have the run of the house.) Most likely there will be a common area that you can use. Don't expect daily maid service. Your host may tidy up but will not do complete maid service. Also don't expect amenities like little bottles of shampoo and conditioner; this is a B&B, not a resort. Remember that you are sharing your accommodations with other guests; be considerate (that is, quiet) when you come in late at night.

There is a strict no smoking law in Hawaii: no smoking in hotels, restaurants, bars, and public buildings. Most bed-and-breakfast units, condos, and vacation rentals also do not allow smoking. If this matters to you, be sure to check the policy of your accommodations before you book.

caveat is that there is lots of construction going on in this area. Call Parrish for updates; they'll give you the honest scoop (and sometimes discounts to compensate for nearby construction).

2721 Poipu Rd. (just after entry to Poipu, on ocean side of Poipu Rd.), Poipu, HI 96741. Reservations: c/o Parrish Collection, 3176 Poipu Rd., Suite 1, Koloa, HI 96756. ✆ **800/325-5701** or 808/742-2000. Fax 808/742-9093. www.parrishkauai.com. 60 units. $105–$199 1 bedroom for 4, $135–$239 2-bedroom for 6 (5-night minimum). Ask about Frommer's "Special Discount." DC, DISC, MC, V. **Amenities:** Concierge; 2 outdoor pools (1 for children, 1 for adults) with whirlpool spas; complimentary tennis courts. *In room:* TV/VCR, kitchen, Wi-Fi.

ELSEWHERE ON THE SOUTH COAST

Further inland and about 10 to 15 minutes from Poipu Beach, the towns of Kaleheo and Lawai offer very affordable accommodations.

Moderate

Bamboo Jungle ★ (Finds) New owners Lucy and Terry Ryan recently took over this property, consisting of a jungle of verdant plants, a quaint gazebo, an 82-foot lap pool, and an impeccably decorated old plantation-era house. They are making much-needed repairs and renovations to the rooms, each of which has a private entrance and French doors opening onto a private lanai with an ocean view. The netting over the beds creates a romantic mood and serves a functional purpose (it keeps Hawaii's insects on their side of the sleeping quarters). Accommodations range from a single room with deck to a studio with minikitchen. There are no phones in the units, but you can use the house phone. Breakfast is served in the "great room" inside the house and is a full breakfast (frittata, waffles, French toast, pancakes, and the like). Golf and tennis courts are nearby; in-room massage can be arranged. Note that there is no air-conditioning, which 350 days of the year is fine, but on the few days the trade winds stop blowing, it's not so great.

3829 Waha Rd. Reservations: P.O. Box 737, Kalaheo, HI 96741. ✆ **808/332-5515.** www.kauai-bedandbreakfast.com. 3 units. $140–$180 double. 3-night minimum rooms, 5-night minimum suite, cleaning $35–$45. MC, V. From Hwy. 50, turn left at the traffic light onto Papalina Rd., then right on Waha Rd. **Amenities:** Outdoor pool; hot tub. *In room:* TV, kitchenette (in 1 room), no phone, free Wi-Fi.

Inexpensive

Hale Ikena Nui (Value) One of the best deals in this area. Patti Pantone opened this 1,000-square-foot, self-contained guest suite on the first floor of her home in 1995, had instant success, and still is charging only $95 a night. It has a private entrance, a full-size kitchen (with dishwasher), and large dining room and living room areas (and recently the entire place was re-tiled). With a queen-size bed and a queen-size sofa bed, the unit easily sleeps four. Outside on the private lanai are a gas barbecue and all the beach and picnic equipment you could possibly need. Throw in a full-size washer/dryer, and you can see why this place is so popular. In 1996 Patti also opened a room upstairs in her house for people looking for less space and a smaller bite out of their budget. The room has a huge walk-in closet, plus gives you run of the house, including the gourmet kitchen, all for just $75. Guests are greeted by "Bear," her tiny Pomeranian/poodle who is happy to act as your dog-away-from-home.

3957 Ulualii St. (P.O. Box 171), Kalaheo, HI 96741. ✆ **800/550-0778** or 808/332-9005. Fax 808/332-0911. www.kauaivacationhome.com. 2 units. $75 double (includes continental breakfast); $95 double apt. Extra person $15. 3-night minimum for apt. only. MC, V. At the 11-mile marker on Hwy. 50, turn down Papalina Rd. toward the ocean; continue for 1¼ miles; turn right on Waha Rd., then left on Ulualii St. *In room:* TV, kitchen.

Hale Kua ★ (Value) This is for people who love the beach—at a distance—and who want to sleep in the quiet and cool climate of the hills of Lawai Valley, away from the madding crowds. If you want to stay in a forest, wake up to the sound of birds singing, and see incredible sunsets each night, one of these five units in three different houses may be for you. Hale Kua features a two-story house with a complete three-bedroom home unit with a big kitchen, wraparound dining bar, walk-in closets, washer/dryer, and a view of the bucolic rolling hills. Downstairs are two separate one-bedroom units with a full kitchen, wraparound lanai, washer/dryer, and birds serenading you all day long. Next door, on hosts Bill and Cathy Cowern's 8-acre tree farm, are a one-bedroom separate cottage and a studio apartment in their large home. The beach is just a 10-minute drive down the hill. If you are looking for privacy and all the comforts of a honeymoon or family accommodations, you won't find anything better at this price.

4896-E Kua Rd., Lawai, HI 96765. ✆ **800/440-4353** or 808/332-8570. www.halekua.com. 5 units. $120 1-bedroom apt. for 2; $130 1-bedroom cottage for 2; $145 3-bedroom unit for 4. No credit cards. **Amenities:** Barbecue areas. *In room:* TV/VCR/DVD, kitchen, Wi-Fi.

Kalaheo Inn ★ (Kids) (Value) What a deal! Located in the town of Kalaheo, a 12-minute drive from Poipu Beach, a 5-minute drive from the Kukuiolono Golf Course, and within walking distance of shops and restaurants, the inn is a comfortable 1940s motel totally remodeled in 1999 and converted into apartment units with kitchens. In 2005, owners Chet and Tish Hunt replaced the beds with Simmons "Heavenly" mattresses, put hair dryers in the bathrooms and new refrigerators in all the rooms, and gave the place a polishing. The Hunts couldn't be friendlier, handing out complimentary beach towels, beach toys, games for the kids, and even golf clubs to guests (links are nearby). They love families and have a storeroom full of games to keep the kids entertained. This is a must-stay for vacationers on a budget.

4444 Papalina Rd. (just behind the Kalaheo Steakhouse), Koloa, HI 96756. ✆ **888/332-6023** or 808/332-6023. Fax 808/332-5242. www.kalaheoinn.com. 15 units. $83 double studio; $93–$103 1-bedroom; $133 2-bedroom; $183 3-bedroom with full kitchen. MC, V. **Amenities:** Complimentary Internet access, watersports equipment. *In room:* TV, hair dryer, kitchen or kitchenette, no phone.

Super-Cheap Sleeps

Aloha Estates at Kalaheo Plantation (Value) This is a love story. Part one: A Japanese visitor, LeeAnn, meets stained-glass artist James Hargraves while on vacation on Oahu. They fall in love and marry. Part two: While visiting Kauai, they discover a 1924 plantation house and fall in love with it. They carefully restore the old house and fill it with 1920s and 1930s furniture and fabrics, and James's stained-glass work. Their single unit, a bargain at $65, has two full-size beds, a kitchenette, a private entrance, a stereo and VCR, and private lanai. Part three: Guests arrive and fall in love with this grand old house themselves . . . and everyone lives happily ever after (at least while they're on Kauai!). Epilogue: They just celebrated their 15th anniversary.

4579 Puuwai Rd. (P.O. Box 872), Kalaheo, HI 96741. ✆/fax **808/332-7812.** 1 unit. $65 double. Extra person $10. 2-night minimum. No credit cards. Turn off Hwy. 50 toward the mountain onto Puuwai Rd. at Steve's Mini Mart, then turn right immediately again to stay on Puuwai Rd. *In room:* TV/VCR, kitchenette.

Seaview Suite (Value) Even if you are on a really tight budget, you can still stay in the popular south shore area. Located in a private home in a residential area about a 15-minute drive from the beach is this budget place with two small but affordable rooms. The Seaview Suite, a large studio with separate bedroom area hidden behind sliding shoji doors, contains a full kitchen, big bathroom, walk-in closet, and private lanai with barbecue. Downstairs, owner Monica has added a tiny "ti suite" for those on a very strict budget. The small one-room unit has a tiny kitchenette (microwave, full-size refrigerator), a king-size bed, and just enough room for a small sitting area with TV. Great for the frugal crowd that plans to come home only to sleep. Monica has lots of beach paraphernalia she's happy to loan out and her husband recently added a washer/dryer laundry area just for the two units.

3913 Ulualii St., Kalaheo, HI 96741. ✆/fax **808/332-9744.** www.seakauai.com. 2 units. $75 small studio; $95 larger studio. $10 extra person. 3-night minimum. Credit cards through Pay Pal. **Amenities:** Complimentary watersports equipment. *In room:* TV/VCR, Internet, full kitchen in 1 unit, kitchenette in other.

3 WESTERN KAUAI

Inn Waimea (Finds) The former residence of a church pastor (good karma!), converted into a four-suite inn, this quaint two-story inn occupies an ideal location in Waimea. It is 1 block from the ocean, 1 block from "downtown," and walking distance to restaurants and shops. Each of the suites is uniquely decorated and has a special feature; for example, one room has a Jacuzzi for two, another room has an ADA-compliant shower. All of the rooms have private phones (free local phone calls), bathroom, coffeemaker, refrigerator, cable TV, ceiling fans, even free high-speed Internet. The same company also has one- and two-bedroom cottages available in the Waimea area. If you plan to visit the North Shore, this is not a good location, as you will be on the road doing quite a bit of driving.

 4469 Halepule Rd., Waimea, HI 96796. ✆ **808/338-0031.** Fax 808/338-1814. www.innwaimea.com. $110–$145 double rooms; $150 double cottages. 3-night minimum for cottages. Extra person $25. AE, MC, V. **Amenities:** Barbecue. *In room:* TV, fridge, free Wi-Fi. *Cottages:* TV, kitchen.

Kokee Lodge (Value) This is an excellent choice, especially if you want to do some hiking in Waimea Canyon and Kokee State Park. There are two types of cabins here: The older ones have dormitory-style sleeping arrangements (and resemble a youth hostel), while the new ones have two separate bedrooms each. Both styles sleep six and come with cooking utensils, bedding, and linens. We recommend the newer units, which have wood floors, cedar walls, and more modern kitchen facilities (some are wheelchair-accessible as well). There are no phones or TVs in the units, but there is a pay phone at the general store. You can purchase firewood for the cabin stove at Kokee Lodge, where a restaurant is open for continental breakfast and lunch every day. The lodge also has a cocktail lounge, a general store, and a gift shop. ***Warning for light sleepers:*** This area is home to lots of roosters that crow at dawn's first light.

P.O. Box 819, Waimea, HI 96796. ✆ **808/335-6061.** 12 units. $93 double the first night, $73 for nights 2–5. Cleaning fee $20. Extra person $5. 5-night maximum. AE, DC, DISC, MC, V. *In room:* Kitchen, no phone.

Waimea Plantation Cottages ★ (Kids) This beachfront vacation retreat is like no other in the islands: Among groves of towering coco palms sit clusters of restored sugar-plantation cottages dating from the 1880s to the 1930s and bearing the names of their original plantation-worker dwellers. The lovely cottages have been transformed into cozy, comfortable guest units with period rattan and wicker furniture and fabrics from the 1930s, sugar's heyday on Kauai. Each has a furnished lanai and a fully equipped modern kitchen and bathroom; some units are oceanfront. Facilities include an oceanfront pool, tennis courts, and laundry. The seclusion of the retreat makes it a nice place for kids to wander and explore away from traffic. They've added a spa on property, which is perfect to get massages as you relax in this tranquil setting. The only downsides: the black-sand beach, which is lovely but not conducive to swimming (the water is often murky at the Waimea River mouth); and the location at the foot of Waimea Canyon Drive—its remoteness can be very appealing, but the North Shore is 1½ hours away. Golf courses and tennis courts, however, are much closer.

9400 Kaumualii Hwy., Waimea, HI 96796. ✆ **866/774-2924** (Aston Hotels and Resorts) or 808/338-1625. Fax 808/338-2338. www.waimea-plantation.com. 48 units. $197–$367 1-bedroom double; $253–$434 2-bedroom (sleeps up to 4); $299–$332 3-bedroom (up to 5); $536 4-bedroom (up to 8); $615 5-bedroom (up to 10). Children under 18 stay free in parent's room. AE, DC, DISC, MC, V. **Amenities:** Restaurant (Waimea Brewing Company, p. 146), bar; large outdoor pool; Wi-Fi. *In room:* TV, kitchen.

4 THE COCONUT COAST

This is the land of B&Bs and inexpensive vacation rentals. In addition to those reviewed below, we recommend **Opaeka'a Falls Hale** (✆ **888/822-9956;** www.opaekaafallskauai.ws), which has two exquisite units with pool and hot tub for $110 to $130 (plus a $50 cleaning charge).

EXPENSIVE

Aston Kauai Beach at Makaiwa ★ One of the best things about this resort is the convenient location: close to shopping and visitor attractions along the Coconut Coast,

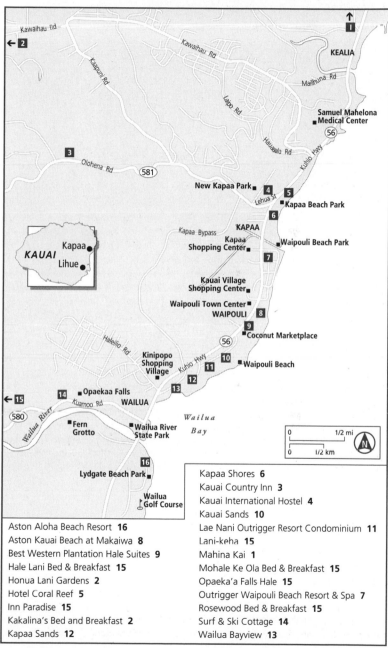

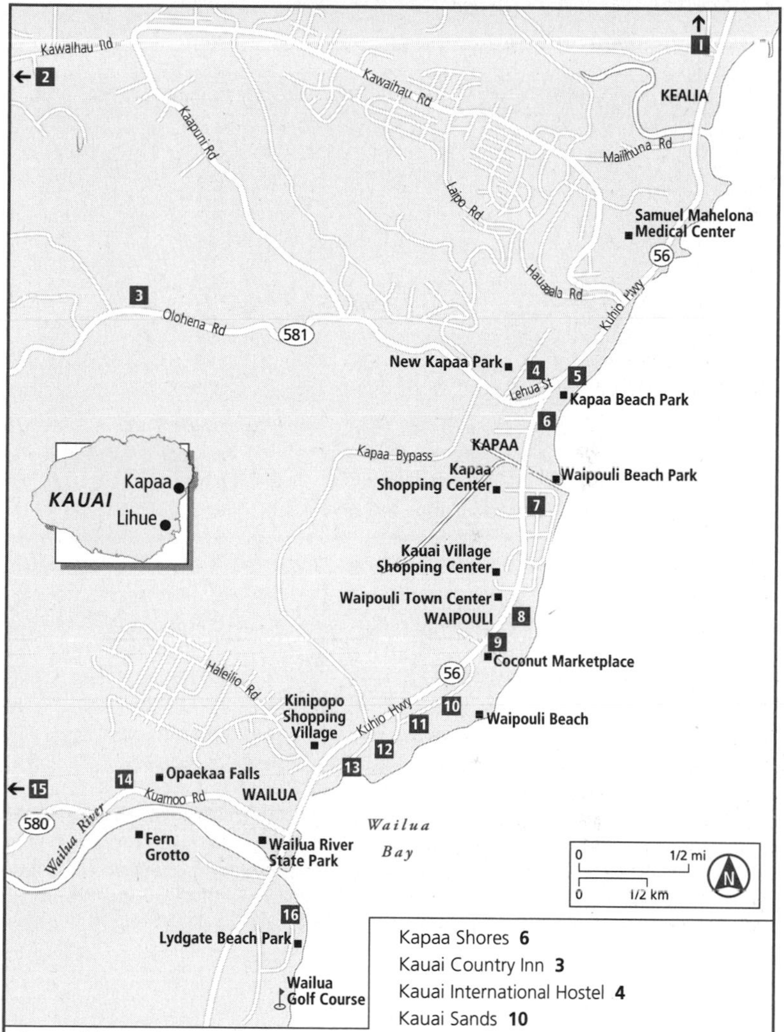

Aston Aloha Beach Resort **16**
Aston Kauai Beach at Makaiwa **8**
Best Western Plantation Hale Suites **9**
Hale Lani Bed & Breakfast **15**
Honua Lani Gardens **2**
Hotel Coral Reef **5**
Inn Paradise **15**
Kakalina's Bed and Breakfast **2**
Kapaa Sands **12**
Kapaa Shores **6**
Kauai Country Inn **3**
Kauai International Hostel **4**
Kauai Sands **10**
Lae Nani Outrigger Resort Condominium **11**
Lani-keha **15**
Mahina Kai **1**
Mohale Ke Ola Bed & Breakfast **15**
Opaeka'a Falls Hale **15**
Outrigger Waipouli Beach Resort & Spa **7**
Rosewood Bed & Breakfast **15**
Surf & Ski Cottage **14**
Wailua Bayview **13**

A Rose by Any Other Name: Timeshares

Timeshares are very big on Kauai, only no one will say that dreaded word. It conjures up slick salesmen from the 1970s hustling people on the beach with promises of nearly free vacations in Hawaii if you just sign on the dotted line. Timeshares denote a condominium project that sells the same unit to several owners, who are allotted a "time" when they can visit the unit. Today, timeshare projects have gone upscale in Hawaii; major resorts like Marriott, Westin, Hilton, and Shell are now building mega-resorts with top-notch units, all furnished with the same top-drawer furniture and equipped with the best electronics and kitchen equipment. But they never, *never,* call them timeshares. The new, politically correct term is "vacation ownership"—but the idea is the same: Several owners have a share in the unit and are allotted a certain amount of time every year (from a week to a month) to stay in the unit. These respectable management companies make sure that the unit is well-maintained and even rent out the units if none of the owners wishes to stay there. Sometimes you can get "deals" at the various "vacation ownerships" because, quite frankly, they are trying to get you to buy the place (or at least a share in the unit). So guests are offered everything from a free snorkeling trip to a free vacation in Hawaii, if you are willing to sit through a sales pitch. All this is great, as long as you know what you are getting into. The so-called "45-minute" pitch may last all morning, and the sales pressure may not be your idea of a tranquil vacation. So buyer beware; even in paradise there are no free lunches (or breakfasts, or snorkeling trips).

and also centrally positioned on the island for easy access to the North Shore and the Poipu Beach area on the south shore. Located just 10 minutes from Lihue Airport, in the town of Waipouli, this 311-room resort was totally refurbished in 2005 when Courtyard by Marriott rebranded the old Kauai Coconut Beach Resort. In 2006, ResortQuest took over the property, which sits on 11 acres, nestled between a coconut grove and a white-sand beach, and renovated the open-air lobby (complete with stained-glass artwork depicting a sailing canoe, plus a two-story mural chronicling Kauai's sailing history and a 20th-century replica of a Hawaiian voyaging canoe), upgrading the landscaping and restaurant. In 2009, Aston Hotels & Resorts took over the property management. The resort features a large swimming pool with hot tub, day spa, business center, fitness center, tennis courts, jogging paths, lounge (with nightly entertainment), and expanded restaurant. The large guest rooms were gutted and redecorated with a Hawaiian theme, and include such amenities as hardwood furniture and a 27-inch television.

650 Aleka Loop, Kapaa, HI 96746. ✆ **877/997-6667** or 808/924-2924. Fax 808/822-0035. www.resortquesthawaii.com. 311 units. $115–$375 double; suites from $380. Extra person $30. Children 17 and under stay free in parent's room. Daily resort fee $12 for: parking, Wi-Fi, and local phone calls. AE, DC, DISC, MC, V. **Amenities:** Full-service restaurant, bar; outdoor pool; golf nearby; tennis nearby; hot tub; room service; jogging path. *In room:* A/C, TV/VCR, fridge, hair dryer, Wi-Fi.

Lae Nani Outrigger Resort Condominium ★ The Lae Nani ("beautiful promontory point") offers a quiet, relaxing setting right on the beach, next door to restaurants and bars. On the point is the Kukui Heiau, where an ancient temple once stood. The one- and two-bedroom units are roomy with large living rooms, separate dining rooms, complete kitchens, and generous lanais. The two-bedroom/two-bathroom units can easily fit a family of six. Maid service is provided daily. Extras include a swimming pool, lava-rock-protected swimming area, barbecue facilities, tennis courts, and self-service laundry facilities. Next door is the Coconut Marketplace, with shops, restaurants, and nightlife; a golf course is nearby. This is a totally nonsmoking property; no smoking is allow anywhere on the property. The only caveat I found is that the units are individually owned (and decorated); however, the website does not show the individual units, so what you see on the website may not be what you get.

410 Papaloa Rd., Kapaa, HI 96746. ✆ **800/OUTRIGGER** or 808/822-4938. Fax 808/822-1022. www.outrigger.com. 54 units. $159–$375 1-bedroom for 4; $169–$445 2-bedroom for 6. Rollaway bed/crib $20. AE, DC, DISC, MC, V. **Amenities:** Oceanfront outdoor pool; complimentary tennis courts. *In room:* TV, kitchen.

Outrigger Waipouli Beach Resort & Spa ★★★ **Kids** The lap of luxury, this $200-million condominium project on 13 acres (between the historic towns of Wailua and Kapaa) is located right on the beach within walking distance to restaurants, shops, and recreational activities. The resort, which opened in 2007, features six hotel rooms, and 190 high-end condo units (153 two-bedroom/three-bathroom units and 37 one-bedroom/two-bathroom units), of which 130 units are in the rental pool (75% are the two-bedroom units). Each unit is furnished with top-of-the-line materials like granite countertops; stainless steel appliances by Sub-Zero, Wolf, and Fisher/Paykel; double dishwasher; full-size Whirlpool washer/dryer; whirlpool bathtub in the master bathroom; and 37-inch flatscreen TV in the living room and both bedrooms. The two-bedroom units are 1,300 square feet with floor-to-ceiling windows and two lanais.

The resort features a long list of amenities like complimentary Wi-Fi, a 4,000-square-foot Aveda spa, a fitness center, and a 300,000-gallon heated saltwater fantasy pool, with flowing river, garden, dual serpentine waterslides, sand-bottom children's pool, and three sand-bottom whirlpool tubs. Plus the entire property, all the guest rooms and the common areas are nonsmoking.

Location, across the street from the Kauai Village Shopping Center and the Waipouli Town Center, means guests are within walking distance of restaurants and shops and, more importantly, just across the street from a Safeway grocery store and a Longs Drug Store and pharmacy.

4-820 Kuhio Hwy., Kapaa, HI 96746. ✆ **800/OUTRIGGER** or 808/823-1401. Fax 808/823-8301. www.outrigger.com. 196 units. $215–$245 hotel double; $295–$439 1-bed/2-bathroom for 4; $339–$609 2-bed/3-bathroom for 6. 2-night minimum. AE, DC, DISC, MC, V. **Amenities:** 2 restaurants, bar; fitness center; nearby golf course; huge oceanside outdoor pool; spa; nearby tennis courts; and 3 outdoor whirlpools. *In room:* A/C, TV/DVD, full kitchen (not in hotel rooms), hair dryer, Wi-Fi.

MODERATE

Aston Aloha Beach Resort ★ **Kids** New ownership and management of this 10-acre property, located next door to a 57-acre beach park and playground on one side and a very sacred historical Hawaiian site on the other side, has brought back the feeling of Old Hawaii at this moderately priced resort. After a $10-million renovation, the entire property is rich in Hawaiian culture from the historical presentation given by the general manager himself to the decor of the rooms to the full-time *kupuna* (senior cultural expert) who gives classes to the guests in Hawaiian arts and crafts. Every room was renovated in 2006 with new carpet and furniture, oversize Balinese mahogany doors, upgraded bathrooms, and Hawaiian-style quilts on the beds. The result is a family-friendly choice located right next door to Lydgate Beach Park (with Kamalani Playground for the kids) and convenient to nearby golf. Restaurants and shopping are within minutes of the resort along the Coconut Coast.

3–5920 Kuhio Hwy., Kapaa, HI 96746. © **877/997-6667** or 808/823-6000. Fax 808/823-6666. www.abrkauai.com. 216 units. $120–$250 double; $160–$315 suites; $191–$340 1-bedroom cottages. Extra person $30. Rollaway beds/cribs $30. Children 18 and under stay free in parent's room. Check the Internet for specials. AE, DC, DISC, MC, V. **Amenities:** Restaurant, bar; small fitness room; 2 outdoor pools with whirlpool spas; complimentary tennis court. *In room:* A/C, TV, fridge, hair dryer.

Best Western Plantation Hale Suites (Kids) These one-bedroom condos, all with the same standard decor, offer guests moderately priced accommodations with kitchen facilities in the heart of the Coconut Marketplace, and a central location from which to tour the island. Built in 1972, this property, featuring a row of 10 (two-story) buildings, has been well-maintained and features three swimming pools, two whirlpools, plenty of barbecue areas, a putting green, and a shuffleboard court. The rooms are spotlessly clean and have full kitchens (fridge, microwave, four-burner stove/oven, and cooking utensils) and complimentary high-speed wireless Internet access. At these prices you may be able to afford to stay a couple extra days.

484 Kuhio Hwy., Kapaa, HI 96746. © **800/775-4253** or 808/822-4941. Fax 808/882-5599. www.Plantation-Hale.com. 145 units. $104–$144 for 4. AE, MC, V. **Amenities:** Barbecue areas; golf and tennis nearby; 3 outdoor pools with 2 whirlpools; shuffleboard. *In room*: A/C, TV, full kitchen, hair dryer, Wi-Fi.

Mahina Kai (Finds) Mahina Kai ("moon over the water") is a traditional Japanese villa (complete with teahouse next door) on two landscaped acres just across the road from one of the most picturesque white-sand beaches on Kauai. The property is unique, but in the past few years the rates have continued to creep up to the point that I think it is way, way, way too expensive. Three rooms in the main house come complete with shoji screen doors, private bathrooms and lanais, use of the gorgeous living room (with fish-pond, vintage Hawaiian furniture, and views of Japanese gardens and Aliomanu Beach), and shared kitchenette. Although this place is undeniably unique, the rooms are tiny and sparsely furnished (no TVs or phones), and the walls are paper-thin. Also available are a large one-bedroom suite with private entrance, and a separate cottage (with kitchenette) next to the saltwater pool. Landscaped into the gardens are a lagoon-style pool and a hot tub. Sitting in the hot tub, listening to the surf across the street, and watching the stars move slowly across the sky, you're pretty darn close to heaven on Earth. When Mahina Kai opened in 1985, it was exclusively a gay B&B; although still gay-owned, everyone with the aloha spirit is welcome.

4933 Aliomanu Rd. (off Kuhio Hwy. at mile marker 14). P.O. Box 699, Anahola, HI 96703. © **800/337-1134** or 808/822-9451. www.mahinakai.com. 5 units. $225–$375 double. Rates include continental breakfast. 3-night minimum. AE, MC, V. **Amenities:** Saltwater lagoonlike swimming pool; hot tub. *In room:* No phone.

INEXPENSIVE

Hale Lani Bed & Breakfast ★★ (Value) This terrific find offers great value for visitors looking for a stay in a quiet residential area but only a 10-minute drive to the beach, shopping, and dining. The four units (two cottages with their own private hot tubs and two units in the main house) all have private entrances, patio, full kitchens, comfy pillow-top queen-size beds, TV/DVD and stereo, plus complimentary breakfast (hot breakfast, fruit, juice) waiting for you outside your unit (pick it up when you want) every morning, setting this B&B apart from the rest. The units are exquisitely decorated in tropical colors and furniture. The host, Ruth, couldn't be nicer or more accommodating.

283 Aina Lani Place, Kapaa, HI 96746. ✆ **877/423-6434** or 808/823-6434. www.halelani.com. 4 units. $125–$185 double. Rates include continental breakfast. 3-night minimum. AE, DC, DISC, MC, V. **Amenities:** Barbecue area; complimentary snorkel equipment; boogie boards; fins; beach chairs; beach towels. *In room:* TV/VCR/DVD, fridge, hair dryer, hot tub (only in 2 units), Wi-Fi.

Honua Lani Gardens ★ Honeymooners: Picture your own private cabin away from the crowds, nestled in a tropical garden on a hill overlooking rolling hills and the ocean in the distance. Honua Lani (Gardens of Heaven on Earth) has a very cute honeymoon cottage (one bedroom with full kitchen and a loft and bed upstairs) and a 600-square-foot apartment with small kitchenette in the owner's redwood and cedar home (but with your own private entrance). You are welcome to pick fruit and vegetables from the lush property. All the comforts you can imagine just a 5-minute drive from the beach, shops, and restaurants.

6204 Helena Lane, Kapaa, HI 96746. ✆ **877/240-6151** or 808/822-4982. www.honualani.com. 2 units. $131 cottage double; $109 apartment double. Extra person $15. Cleaning $80. 5-night minimum. No credit cards. **Amenities:** Barbecue; sauna. *In room*: A/C, TV/VCR, kitchen, Wi-Fi.

Hotel Coral Reef (Value) This is your chance to stay right on the beach, in a hotel, at modest prices. This small, older hotel faces a grassy lawn, coconut trees, and a white-sand beach. Don't expect the Hyatt, but at these prices and this location it's a great way for frugal travelers to enjoy the beach. It offers economical rooms and friendly service in an ideal location, within walking distance of shops, restaurants, golf, and tennis, and just 50 yards away from good swimming and snorkeling. There's even an 8-mile bike path that starts right on the grounds. A new owner is in the process of renovating the old hotel, bringing it up to the 21st century in both decor and amenities in the rooms (flatscreen TVs, DVDs, and so forth). Of the two wings in the hotel, we prefer the oceanfront one that has big rooms that overlook the beach through sliding-glass lanai doors. Each two-room unit has a separate bedroom and a living room with a sofa bed—perfect for families. Also added are a new fitness center, plus sauna. Coffee and pastries are served in the lobby in the morning.

1516 Kuhio Hwy. (at the northern end of Kapaa, between mile markers 8 and 9), Kapaa, HI 96746. ✆ **800/843-4659** or 808/822-4481. Fax 808/822-7705. www.hotelcoralreefresort.com. 21 units. $110–$245 double. Extra person $25. Children 12 and under stay free in parent's room. AE, DC, MC, V. **Amenities:** Exercise room. *In room:* A/C, TV, fridge.

Inn Paradise (Finds) Out in the country, about a 10- to 15-minute drive from the beach, Inn Paradise is a plantation-style building with a wraparound lanai that houses three guest units on 3½ landscaped acres. The units range from the one-room "Prince," with a tiny kitchenette tucked away in a closet; to the large, two-bedroom "King," which has a full kitchen. Carefully decorated rooms with sparkling tile floors and a quiet, relaxing ambience come together to make this property a good budget choice. Plus, every guest gets a "welcome basket" with all the makings for your first day's breakfast. The large deck overlooks the flower-filled grounds and a valley dotted with fruit trees beyond. A bonus is the hot tub for soaking after a long day of sightseeing.

6381 Makana Rd., Kapaa, HI 96746. ✆ **808/822-2542.** www.innparadisekauai.com. 3 units. $85–$120 double. Rates include welcome basket with fruit, juice, cereal, and bread or muffins. Extra person $15. 2- to 3-night minimum (depending on the unit). AE, DISC, MC, V. **Amenities:** Free use of beach toys; hot tub. *In room:* TV, kitchenette.

Kakalina's Bed and Breakfast *(Finds)* Nestled in the foothills of Mount Waialeale, about a 10- to 15-minute drive from the beach, is this 3-acre flower farm and bed-and-breakfast. You can just imagine the view: flowers, flowers, and more flowers. Just wandering around the grounds is like being in a botanical garden. The most popular unit is Hale Akahi, a two-room unit located beneath Kathy and Bob Offley's round home, on the ground floor. You enter through an enclosed wooden porch, which has a spectacular view of the verdant valley; the apartment is decorated in white wicker furniture with brilliant tropical flowers splashing color throughout. The views are breathtaking and the king-size bed is comfortable, but the draw here is the bathroom: A huge, blue-tiled tub, big enough to soak in and surrounded by green plants, makes this unit one of a kind. Also on the property, in a separate house, is Hale Elua, with a full kitchen, and a breakfast nook with a view of the flower gardens, a mountain lake, and the ocean in the distance; a queen-size futon can accommodate extra guests.

6781 Kawaihau Rd., Kapaa, HI 96746. ✆ **800/662-4330** or 808/822-2328. Fax 808/823-6833. www.kakalina.com. 4 units. $85–$175 double, plus a $40 cleaning fee. Rates include continental breakfast in 2 units. Extra person $15. 2-night minimum. MC, V. Turn left off Kuhio Hwy. (Hwy. 56) onto Kawaihau Rd. and go 4½ miles. **Amenities:** Complimentary use of beach toys. *In room:* TV/VCR, hair dryer, kitchen, no phone.

Kapaa Sands ★ *(Finds)* This boutique establishment (just 24 units) offers older (built in 1973), compact condo units right on the ocean, enveloped in lush, tropical vegetation, with all the comforts of home at bargain prices. Each unit is individually decorated by its owners, but they are all comfortable (some studio units have pull-down beds to take advantage of the living space) and have everything you need for a vacation. The bathrooms tend to be tiny, but the kitchens are roomy enough. Ask for a unit on the ocean; they cost a bit more but are worth it. On-site amenities include a freshwater swimming pool, laundry facilities, maid service, and a very friendly staff happy to advise on where to eat and what to do. There is no air-conditioning in the units, as the tropical breeze generally keeps the units cool. The pool area has high-speed wireless Internet access but not the rooms.

380 Papaloa Rd., Kapaa, 96746. ✆ **800/222-4901** or 808/822-4901. Fax 808/822-1556. www.kapaasands.com. 24 units. $120–$150 studio double, cleaning $75; $170–$205 2-bedroom units for 4, cleaning $125. Extra person $10. 3-night minimum Apr 16–Dec 14; 7-night minimum Dec 15–Apr 15. MC, V. **Amenities:** Barbecue area; swimming pool; Wi-Fi on the grounds. *In room:* TV, kitchen.

Kapaa Shores These apartments are located right on the beach in the heart of Kapaa. Even the budget units have partial views of the ocean, but oceanfront units are available for a bit more money. The one-bedrooms can comfortably sleep four, while the two-bedrooms can sleep as many as six (the sofa in each unit pulls out into a queen-size bed). All units are in excellent shape and come with fully equipped modern kitchens and large lanais where you can enjoy a sunrise breakfast or sunset cocktails.

900 Kuhio Hwy. (between mile markers 7 and 8). Reservations c/o Garden Island Properties, 4–928 Kuhio Hwy., Kapaa, HI 96746. ✆ **800/801-0378** or 808/822-4871. Fax 808/822-7984. www.kauaiproperties.com. 84 units. $150–$165 1-bedroom; $160–$175 2-bedroom. Cleaning $98–$115. Reservation fee $40. 7-night minimum Dec 15–Jan 5. AE, MC, V. **Amenities:** Outdoor pool with hot tub whirlpool; complimentary tennis courts. *In room:* TV/VCR or TV/DVD, Internet in some rooms, kitchen.

Kauai Country Inn ★★ *(Finds)* Run to the phone right now and book this place! Mike and Martina Hough, refugees from the fast life of running an international advertising agency in Los Angeles, have taken their considerable creative talents and produced a slice of paradise on 2 acres nestled in the rolling hills behind Kapaa. Each of the four suites in this old-fashioned inn is uniquely decorated in Hawaiian Art Deco, complete with hardwood floors, private bathrooms, kitchen or kitchenette, complimentary laundry, your own Mac with Wi-Fi connection, and lots of little amenities that will make you break out into laughter at the Hough's sense of humor. Everything is top drawer, from the "rain" shower head in the bathroom to the subzero refrigerator. They recently added a two-bedroom country cottage for families with young children. The grounds are immaculate, and you can pick as much organic fruit as you want from the abundance of mango, guava, lilikoi, star fruit, oranges, and lemons. Beatles fans take note: Mike has been collecting memorabilia for decades and has the only private Beatles Museum in the state (including a Mini Cooper S car owned by Brian Epstein, the Beatles manager; original paintings by John Lennon; and a host of books, records, movies, tapes, T-shirts, and other interesting and unusual rare items). And for those missing the family pooch, Annie, the staff golden retriever, personally greets each guest like her long-lost friend.

6440 Olohena Rd., Kapaa, HI 96746. ✆ **808/821-0207.** www.kauaicountryinn.com. 4 units. $129–$179 1- and 2-bedroom suites double; $249 3-bedroom, 2-bathroom cottage for 6. $30 extra person in suites. 4-night minimum suites and cottage. Discount car rentals available. AE, MC, V. **Amenities:** Barbecue facilities; complimentary use of beach toys; hot tub; kayak rentals available. *In room:* TV/VCR/DVD, computer, hair dryer, kitchen or kitchenette, Wi-Fi.

Kauai Sands *Value* These modest motel-style accommodations will do just fine for budget travelers who want a basic, clean room with a central location. Right on the ocean, next door to the Coconut Marketplace, the Kauai Sands is located near tennis courts and a golf course. The small rooms have simple furniture (two doubles or twin beds), ceiling fans, tiny TV sets, desks/chairs, and small refrigerators; most have tiny lanais.

420 Papaloa Rd., Kapaa, HI 96746. ✆ **800/560-5553** or 808/822-4951. Fax 808/882-0978. www.kauaisandshotel.com. 200 units. $78–$108 double. Extra person $20. Children 12 and under stay free in parent's room. MC, V. **Amenities:** Nearby golf and tennis; small exercise room; 2 small outdoor pools. *In room:* A/C, TV, fridge, kitchenette (some units).

Mohala Ke Ola Bed & Breakfast Looking for a healthy, relaxing, rejuvenating vacation at frugal prices? Here's the place. Acupuncturist and massage therapist Ed Stumpf hosts this three-room B&B in a luxurious house with spectacular views of waterfalls and mountains in the residential area of Kapaa. He offers his services of various healing techniques that include acupuncture and Hawaiian lomilomi massage. The rooms are all light and airy with private bathrooms. Complimentary breakfast (pastry, fruit, cereal, coffee, tea, and juice), a big swimming pool, and a hot tub are the extras that make this place well worth the money.

5663 Ohelo Rd., Kapaa, HI 96746. ✆ **888/GO-KAUAI** or 808/823-6398. Fax 808/823-6398. www.waterfallbnb.com. 3 rooms. $115–$140 double. Rates include continental breakfast. Extra person $25. 3-night minimum. Credit cards through Pay Pal. **Amenities:** Pool with hot tub. *In room:* A/C (1 room), TV/VCR/DVD, shared use of kitchen, Wi-Fi.

Rosewood Bed & Breakfast ★ *Finds* This lovingly restored century-old plantation home, set amid tropical flowers, lily ponds, and waterfalls, has accommodations to suit everyone. There's a Laura Ashley–style room in the main house (with a sleigh bed, Jacuzzi bathtub, and heated floor for cool mornings) along with three private cottages: one a miniature of the main house, with oak floors and the same Laura Ashley decor; another is a little grass shack set in a tropical garden, with an authentic thatched roof and an outside shower. There's also a bunkhouse with three separate small rooms with a shared shower and toilet. Hostess Rosemary Smith also has a list of other properties she manages. ***Note:*** Smoking is not permitted on the property.

 872 Kamalu Rd., Kapaa, HI 96746. ✆ **808/822-5216.** Fax 808/822-5478. www.rosewoodkauai.com. 7 units, 3 with shared bathroom. $95 double in main house (includes continental breakfast); $50–$60 double in bunkhouse; $135 1-bedroom cottage double (sleeps up to 4); $145 2-bedroom cottage (up to 4); $175 3-bedroom home (up to 6). Extra person $15. 3-night minimum. Cleaning fee $25–$200. No credit cards. From Kuhio Hwy. (Hwy. 56), turn left at the light at Coco Palms onto Hwy. 580 (Kuamoo Rd.); go 3 miles; turn right at junction of Hwy. 581 (Kamalu Rd.); go 1 mile and look for the yellow house on the right with the long picket fence in front. *In room:* No phone. *In cottages:* TV, computer w/Internet access, hair dryer, kitchen, no phone. *In bunkhouse:* Kitchenette, no phone.

Wailua Bayview ★ (Value) Located right on the ocean, these spacious one-bedroom apartments offer excellent value. All units have ceiling fans, full kitchens (including microwave and dishwasher), washer/dryers, and large lanais. Some have air-conditioning as well. The bedrooms are roomy, and the sofa bed in the living room allows you to sleep up to four. Several of the units were renovated in 1998 with new carpet and reupholstered furniture. Some of the $163 garden units are close to the road and can be noisy; ask for one with air-conditioning, which generally drowns out the street sounds. The oceanview units are more expensive but still a great deal. On-site facilities include a pool and barbecue area. Restaurants, bars, shopping, golf, and tennis are nearby.

320 Papaloa Rd., Kapaa, HI 96746. ✆ **800/882-9007.** www.wailuabay.com. 45 units. $163–$175 double. Cleaning fee $95. 7-night minimum. Dec. 21-Jan. 3, check for 7th night free promotion. Discount car rentals available. AE, DISC, MC, V. **Amenities:** Barbecue area; small outdoor pool. *In room:* A/C (most units), TV/VCR, Internet access, kitchen.

SUPER-CHEAP SLEEPS

Kauai International Hostel (Value) Located in the heart of Kapaa, a block from the beach, this hostel provides clean rooms in a friendly atmosphere. Guests are generally European backpackers. The low-rise buildings feature a very clean kitchen and laundry facilities, a TV, a pool table, and a barbecue area; just 1 block from the highway, it's within walking distance of shops and restaurants. In addition to the bunk-bed dorm rooms, there are private rooms for two (with shared bathrooms). There's also a women-only bunk-bed room.

4532 Lehua St. (off Kuhio Hwy.), Kapaa, HI 96746. ✆ **808/823-6142.** www.kauaiinternationalhostel.com. 32 bunk beds, 6 private rooms (shared bathrooms with showers only). $25 dorm single; $60–$75 private double. AE, MC, V. **Amenities:** Community-shared kitchen; community TV; pay phone; Internet $3 per 30 minutes. *In room:* No phone.

Lani-keha ★ (Finds) Step back in time to the 1940s, when old Hawaiian families lived in open, airy, rambling homes on large plots of land lush with fruit trees and sweet-smelling flowers. This gracious age is still alive and well in Lani-keha, a *kamaaina* (old-timer) home with an open living/game/writing/dining room, with oversize picture windows to take in the views, and bedrooms with private bathrooms. The house is elegant yet casual, with old-style rattan furniture—practicality and comfort outweigh design aesthetics. The large communal kitchen has everything a cook could want, even a dishwasher. All the guests share the TV/VCR and single phone in the living area.

848 Kamalu Rd. (Hwy. 581), Kapaa, HI 96746. ✆ **800/821-4898** or 808/822-1605. Fax 808/822-2429. www.lanikeha.com. 3 units. $65–$80 double. Rates include continental breakfast. Extra person $15. 3-night minimum. No credit cards. From Kuhio Hwy. (Hwy. 56), turn left at the stoplight at Coco Palms onto Hwy. 580 (Kuamoo Rd.); go 3 miles; turn right at Hwy. 581 (Kamalu Rd.) and go 1 mile. **Amenities:** Free Internet access. *In room:* No phone.

Surf & Ski Cottage ★ (Value) Even if you aren't a kayaking/water-skiing/watersports enthusiast, this is a fantastic place to stay. Right on the Wailua River, surrounded by fruit trees and tropical plants, Surf & Ski Cottage is an adorable 22-square-foot, self-contained guesthouse. Essentially one large room (with a separate bathroom), the open, airy, high-ceilinged cottage has a complete kitchen, a TV, and a queen-size bed. Located close to the old Coco Palms Resort, the cottage is within walking distance of Kapaa's shops, restaurants, and beaches. Kenny and Kathy Terheggen, the owners of Kauai Water Ski & Surf (who also live on the property), are a wealth of information on nearly everything to do on Kauai. If you plan to play in the water, this is the place to stay—cottage guests get a 20% discount on all outdoor equipment rentals and activities at Kauai Water Ski & Surf Co. (including water-skiing, kayaking, and surfing lessons, plus boogie board and snorkel rentals, and much more), which could really save you a lot of dough.

Ohana St. (in Wailua River Lots), off Hwy. 580 (Kuamoo Rd.), Kapaa. Reservations: c/o Kauai Water Ski & Surf Co., 4-356 Kuhio Hwy., Kapaa, HI 96746. ✆ **808/822-3574.** Fax 808/822-3574. surfski@aloha.net. 1 cottage (with shower only). $75 double. 4-night minimum. DISC, MC, V. *In room:* TV, fridge, hair dryer, kitchenette.

5 THE NORTH SHORE

Rosemary Smith, of **Rosewood Kauai** (✆ **808/822-5216;** www.rosewoodkauai.com), has a range of properties from country homes and cottages to fabulous beach homes and affordable condos. Also try **Hanalei North Shore Properties** (✆ **800/488-3336** or 808/826-9622; fax 808/826-1188; www.kauai-vacation-rentals.com), which handles all kinds of weekly rentals—from beachfront cottages and condos to romantic hideaways and ranch houses—along the North Shore. Renting a home is a great way to enjoy the area's awesome nature, especially for those who like to avoid resorts and fend for themselves. Shopping, restaurants, and nightlife are abundant in nearby Hanalei.

VERY EXPENSIVE

St. Regis Resort Princeville ★★★ Kids As we went to press, this jewel in the Sheraton crown was set to reopen. Formerly the Princeville Resort, the property was a palace full of marble and chandeliers, but after the multi-million dollar massive interior renovation, it has been reborn as a luxurious reflection of the island (rather than a European castle). With the new opening comes four new restaurants, a new spa, and St. Regis butler service for the suites. The location still enjoys one of the world's finest settings, between Hanalei Bay and Kauai's steepled mountains. Nearby are outstanding surfing and windsurfing areas, as well as a wonderful reef for snorkeling. The panoramic view from the lobby has to be the most dramatic vista from any hotel in the state.

The footprint of the building remains the same: stepping down a cliff, with the entrance on the 9th floor, and you take elevators down to your room and the beach. Each opulent room has such extras as a door chime, dimmer switches, bedside control panels, a safe, original oil paintings, an oversize bathtub, and a "magic" bathroom window: a liquid-crystal shower window that you can switch in an instant from clear to opaque. There are no lanais, but oversize windows allow you to admire the awesome view from your bed.

In addition to a great children's program, this property has oodles of activities not only for children but also for teens and even activities for the entire family, from horseback riding to adventures exploring the island. The hotel grounds are a fantasy land, with a huge swimming pool next to a sandy beach.

Other great amenities here: twice-daily fresh towels, daily newspaper, complimentary resort shuttle, comprehensive Hawaiiana program, riding stables, in-house cinema, arts program (from photography to painting), and a wealth of outdoor activities. Golfers may choose from two courses, both designed by Robert Trent Jones, Jr.; and an on-property spa. Next door are golf and tennis courts.

P.O. Box 3069 (5520 Kahaku Rd.), Princeville, HI 96722-3069. ✆ **800/826-4400** or 808/826-9644. Fax 808/826-1166. www.princevillehotelhawaii.com. 252 units. $800–$1100 double; from $1,575 suite. Extra person $135. Children under 18 stay free in parent's room. AE, DC, DISC, MC, V. Parking $20. **Amenities:** 3 restaurants, 3 bars; babysitting; bike rental; children's program; concierge; outstanding golf on 2 courses; huge oceanside outdoor pool with outdoor whirlpools; room service; 25 tennis courts; watersports equipment rentals. *In room:* A/C, TV/VCR/CD player, fridge, hair dryer, Wi-Fi.

EXPENSIVE

Hanalei Bay Resort & Suites (Overrated) This 22-acre resort is just up the street from ritzy Princeville Resort (see above), overlooking the fabled Bali Hai cliffs and Hanalei Bay. It has the same majestic view, and until recently was a deal. But on our last visit here we were bitterly disappointed in the level of upkeep, the musty smell in our unit, general maintenance and repair work that needed to be done to the entire property, weeds in the once pristine landscape, and so forth. New management claims they are aware of the problems and are diligently working to make the necessary repairs and bring this once fabulous resort back to its former high standards. I'm keeping my fingers crossed that they will follow through because I have always loved staying here: Guests can choose from units ranging from a hotel room to a studio or one-bedroom suite (with kitchenette). The units all stair-step down the hill to a gold-sand, palm-fringed beach. Shuttle service is available for those who may have problems walking on the steep hillside. Travelers should be aware that this property offers timeshares (see the box "A Rose by Any Other Name: Timeshares" on p. 118).

P.O. Box 220 (5380 Honoiki St.), Princeville, HI 96722. ✆ **800/827-4427** or 808/826-6522. Fax 808/826-6680. www.hanaleibayresort.com. (Managed by Celebrity Resorts). 236 units. $140–$175 double; $106 studio with kitchenette (up to 4); $217–$242 1-bedroom apt (up to 4). AE, DC, DISC, MC, V. **Amenities:** Concierge; 2 inviting outdoor freshwater pools with whirlpool spas; Princeville Resort's top-ranked golf courses; 8 tennis courts, pro shop, and tennis school. *In room:* A/C, TV, hair dryer, kitchenette, Wi-Fi.

The Palmwood ★★ (Finds) This is a unique property with a tranquil setting (atop a hill on a 4-acre estate), fabulous views (360-degree panorama of the rolling hills of Moloa'a Valley and out to the ocean), and unbelievably beautiful rooms and surrounding landscaping. Eddi Henry has traveled the globe picking up decorating and landscaping ideas, and along with her husband, Steven, has turned this property into a comfortable, calming retreat in the midst of paradise. From the stone entryway to the leather/palm-wood chairs (so comfortable you will be hard-pressed to leave them) to the sound of water falling—this tiny, 2-unit inn is the lap of luxury. The amenities include flatscreen TVs, double doors leading to a large lanai, a hot tub and Japanese Zen gardens outside, a barbecue area, and a full breakfast (such as crab cakes with mango and banana bread). Relax in the free-form hammock—you may find it hard to tear yourself away and explore the rest of the island. It's pricey, but worth every penny. Not appropriate for children.

6867 Koolau Rd., Kilauea, HI 96754. ✆ **562/688-3433.** www.thepalmwood.com. 2 units. $325–$350 double. 3-night minimum. AE, DISC, MC, V. **Amenities:** Barbecue. *In room*: Flatscreen TV/DVD, fridge, Internet, hot tub.

MODERATE

Aloha Sunrise Inn/Aloha Sunset Inn ★★ (Finds) Hidden on the North Shore are these two unique cottages nestled on a quiet 7-acre farm with horses, fruit trees, native

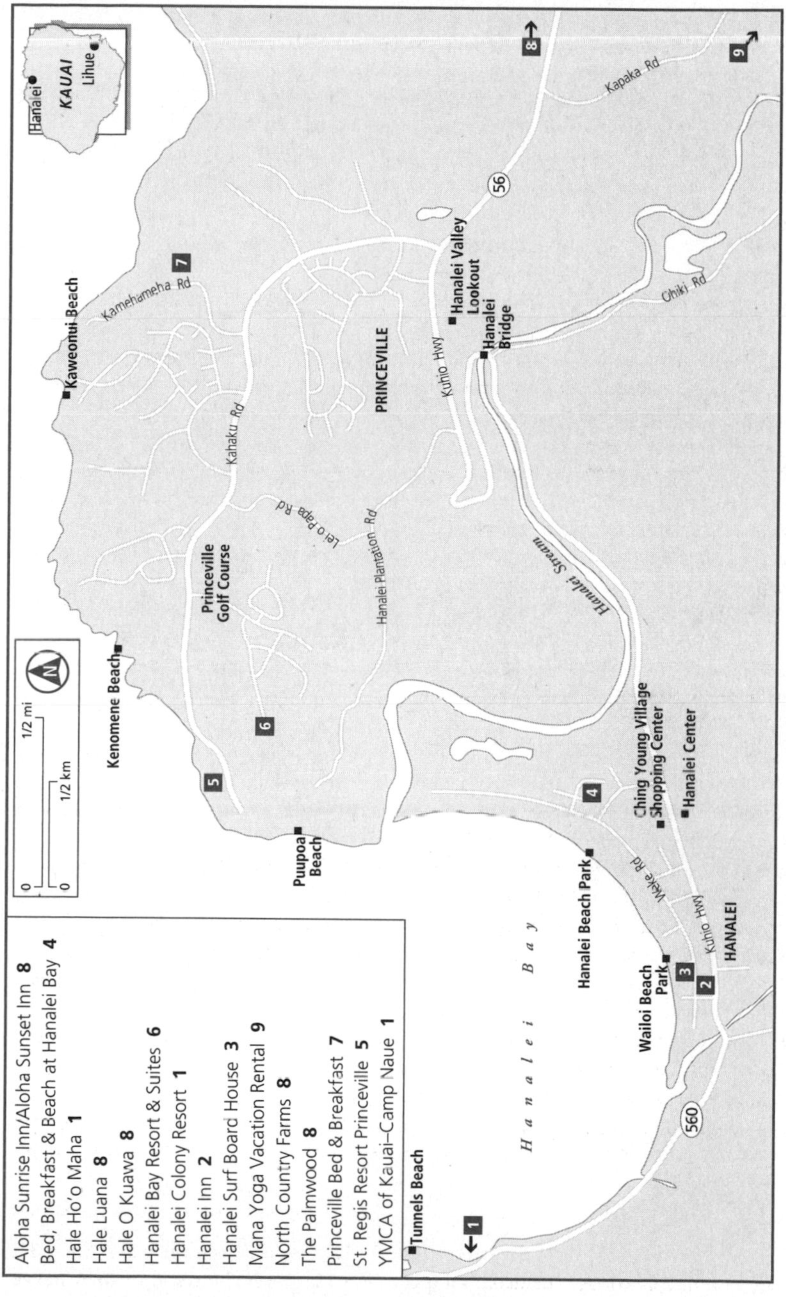
Aloha Sunrise Inn/Aloha Sunset Inn 8
Bed, Breakfast & Beach at Hanalei Bay 4
Hale Ho'o Maha 1
Hale Luana 8
Hale O Kuawa 8
Hanalei Bay Resort & Suites 6
Hanalei Colony Resort 1
Hanalei Inn 2
Hanalei Surf Board House 3
Mana Yoga Vacation Rental 9
North Country Farms 8
The Palmwood 8
Princeville Bed & Breakfast 7
St. Regis Resort Princeville 5
YMCA of Kauai–Camp Naue 1
Hanalei
KAUAI
Lihue
0
1/2 mi
0
1/2 km
N
Kaweonui Beach
Kamehameha Rd
Kahaku Rd
PRINCEVILLE
Princeville Golf Course
Lei o Papa Rd
Hanalei Plantation Rd
Kuhio Hwy
Hanalei Valley Lookout
Hanalei Bridge
56
Kapaka Rd
Ohiki Rd
Hanalei Stream
Kenomene Beach
Puupoa Beach
Hanalei Beach Park
Ching Young Village Shopping Center
Hanalei Center
Weke Rd
Kuhio Hwy
HANALEI
Wailoi Beach Park
Hanalei Bay
560
Tunnels Beach

gardens, flowers, and organic vegetables (you are welcome to pick dinner). We highly recommend both of these darling bungalows. Each is fully furnished with hardwood floors, top-of-the-line bedding, tropical island–style decor, complete kitchen, washer/dryer, and everything you can think of to make your stay heavenly (from a great selection of movies to an excellent CD library). It's close to activities, restaurants, and shopping, yet far enough away to have the peace and quiet of the Hawaii of yesteryear. Hosts Allan and Catherine Rietow, who have lived their entire lives in the islands, can help you plan your stay and give you money-saving tips, and they even hand out complimentary masks, snorkels, boogie boards, and other beach items while pointing you to their favorite beaches. Not appropriate for children.

P.O. Box 79, Kilauea, HI 96754. ✆ **888/828-1008** or 808/828-1100. Fax 808/828-2199. www.kauaisunrise.com. 2 units. $185 double, plus a 1-time $95 cleaning fee. 3-night minimum. (***Note:*** check Internet for deals.) No credit cards. **Amenities:** Washer/dryer. *In room:* TV (satellite dish), fridge,high-speed wireless Internet access, hair dryer, kitchen.

Hale Ho'o Maha *Finds* If you are looking for a moderately priced bed-and-breakfast on the North Shore, check out this property. For years, Kirby Guyer and her husband, Toby, ran a spacious four-bedroom, three-bathroom home on 5 acres. Then in 2006 they finished their own custom-designed B&B located on the North Shore in the Hanalei area known as Wainiha. Overlooking the mountains, waterfalls, and pristine Wainiha Bay, the Hawaiian antiques–filled home is just 110 steps to the beach (and a 10-min. drive to golf courses, shops, restaurants, and two riding stables). This spacious five-bedroom/five-bathroom home features an elevator (something you don't often see on Kauai). Guests are welcome to use the gourmet kitchen, gas barbecue, washer/dryer, refrigerator with ice maker/water, and TV/VCR/DVD in the "great room." Plus there is complimentary use of the laundry facilities. Use of the boogie boards and snorkel equipment, beach chairs, towels, and coolers is all complimentary. Each of the four guest suites is named for a tropical fruit. All have hardwood floors, large closets, cable TV/DVD, ceiling and auxiliary fans, a telephone, and Wi-Fi. We recommend the Pineapple Room, with its 7-foot round bed (with custom-quilted pineapple spread and matching handmade area rug). This is a true bed-and-breakfast with real breakfasts, ranging from macadamia-nut waffles to pancakes and plenty of sausage or bacon to go with them, plus all the fresh island fruit and homemade granola you can eat. The best part is your hosts, Kirby and Toby, who know Kauai inside and out and can point you in the right direction on what to do, where to go, and how to save money.

7083 Alamihi Rd., Hanalei. Reservation: P.O. Box 82, Hanalei, HI 96714. ✆ **800/851-0291** or 808/826-7083. Fax 808/826-7084. www.aloha.net/~hoomaha. 4 units. $150 double. Rates include full breakfast. DC, MC, V. **Amenities:** TV/VCR/DVD in great room; use of full kitchen and outdoor barbecue; complimentary use of water toys. *In room:* TV/DVD, hair dryer, Wi-Fi.

Hanalei Colony Resort ★★ *Kids* Picture this: a perfect white-sand beach just steps from your door, with lush tropical gardens, jagged mountain peaks, and fertile jungle serving as your backdrop. Welcome to Haena, Kauai's northernmost town and gateway to the famous Na Pali Coast, with miles of hiking trails, fabulous sunset views, and great beaches. This 5-acre resort is the place to stay if you're looking to experience the magic of the enchanting North Shore. The units are unbelievably spacious—six people could sleep here comfortably—making them great for families. Each has a private lanai (the less-expensive budget units face the garden), a full kitchen, a dining area, a living room, and ceiling fans (the area is blessed with cooling trade winds, so air-conditioning isn't necessary). The atmosphere is quiet and relaxing: no TVs, stereos, or phones. The property has a large pool, laundry facilities, and a barbecue and picnic area. Guests have access to complimentary beach mats and towels, a lending library, and children's toys, puzzles, and games (plus badminton and croquet for the entire family). A full spa and an award-winning restaurant (with free Wi-Fi) are located next door.

P.O. Box 206 (5–7130 Kuhio Hwy.), Hanalei, HI 96714. ✆ **800/628-3004** or 808/826-6235. Fax 808/826-9893. www.hcr.com. 48 units. $240–$420 2-bedroom apt for 4. Check for discounts and 7th-night free promotions. Rates include continental breakfast once a week. Extra person $15. AE, MC, V. **Amenities:** Outdoor pool; hot tub. *In room:* kitchen, no phone.

Hanalei Surf Board House ★★ Finds Just a block from the beach, these two incredibly decorated studio units are a steal at $195 (book well in advance). Host Simon Potts is a former record company executive from England who claims he's retired to Hawaii, but he's the hardest working retired guy I have ever met. One studio is filled with whimsical "cowgirl" decor, and the other in pure Elvis Presley memorabilia. Both units have kitchenettes, comfy beds, water purification systems, 300-channel televisions, free high-speed wireless Internet access, Bose CD players, DVDs, iPod docks, barbecues, and backyard lanais. The whole property is "fenced" with old surfboards that Potts collected from locals. But the best reason to stay here (besides the 2-minute walk to either the beach or downtown Hanalei) is Simon himself; his stories about the record industry will keep you howling with laughter for hours.

5459 Weke Rd., Hanalei, HI 96714. ✆ **808/826-9825.** www.hanaleisurfboardhouse.com. 2 units. $195 double, plus $65 cleaning fee. 3-night minimum. Extra person $60. No credit cards. **Amenities:** Barbecue area. *In room:* TV, DVD, CD, kitchenette, Wi-Fi.

INEXPENSIVE

Bed, Breakfast & Beach at Hanalei Bay Finds On a quiet street in a residential area just 150 yards from Hanalei Bay lies one of the few bed-and-breakfasts in Hanalei. The three guest rooms in Carolyn Barnes's three-story house range from a 700-square-foot suite with a 360-degree view to a miniapartment on the ground floor with a kitchenette and an outdoor shower. The location couldn't be better (some guests don't even bother to rent a car). It's a 4-minute walk to Hanalei Bay's 2-mile-long beach, and a 10-minute walk to the shops and restaurants of Hanalei. For families, Carolyn also has a cozy two-bedroom, one-bathroom house a couple of blocks away.

5095 Piikoa St. Reservations: P.O. Box 748, Hanalei, HI 96714. ✆ **808/826-6111.** www.bestofhawaii.com/hanalei. 4 units. $120–$170 double room (includes continental breakfast); extra person $15. $1,175 a week for cottage (for 2); extra person $150 a week. 2- to 3-night minimum for rooms; 7-night minimum in cottage. No credit cards. *In room:* TV, phone in cottage only.

Hale Luana Finds Located in the rolling hills of Kilauea is this 5-acre property, with two B&B rooms available inside an architect-designed home, as well as a five-bedroom vacation rental. The light and airy rooms have several great conveniences like a microwave, refrigerator, coffeemaker, huge TV/VCR, and ocean views. Breakfast (banana/macadamia nut pancakes, tarragon baked eggs, or pecan waffles) is served outside on the lanai overlooking the 50-foot-long swimming pool. Tropical foliage landscapes the area around the home as well as acres of the working fruit farm (avocado, banana, papaya, and grapefruit). Guests are welcome to the plentiful supply of beach toys (snorkel, masks, fins, boogie boards). Also on the property is a five-bedroom vacation rental, which sleeps 14 for $2,800 a week plus a $250 cleaning fee.

4680 Kapuna Rd., Kilauea, HI 96754. ✆ **808/828-6784.** Fax 808/828-1564. www.haleluana.com. 2 rooms. $135 double, includes breakfast. 3-night minimum. MC, V. **Amenities:** Barbecue; complimentary beach toys; outdoor pool. *In room:* TV/VCR, fridge, hair dryer, Wi-Fi.

Hale O Kuawa ★ Finds Tucked away in the town of Kilauea, looking out on a tropical landscape is this 650-square-foot, one-bedroom apartment in the lower level of a family home. A private entrance looks out on the bamboo and exotic plants and view of the Kilauea River Valley. The large living room, with rattan furniture, has huge windows that bring the outdoor inside, and the comfy bedroom and kitchenette (fridge, two-burner stove, microwave, and everything else you need to cook a meal) make this a very complete accommodation for your stay. Host Conrad Schmidt is a contractor and has made the unit soundproof, so you feel like you have your own private oasis. Barbecue and laundry facilities make the price of this retreat a fabulous deal.

4327 Kuke St. Reservation: P.O. Box 48, Kilauea, HI 96754. ✆ **866/864-3788** or 808/828-2092. www.Vacation.KauaiStyle.com. 1 unit. $110 double. 3-night minimum. No credit cards. **Amenities:** Barbecue; use of beach gear. *In room:* TV/DVD, CD, hair dryer, kitchenette.

Hanalei Inn The Hanalei Inn offers compact, frugal accommodations in this very "high-end" neighborhood. Located on the sometimes noisy main highway, the "inn" is a series of very basic rooms (which were recently upgraded with air-conditioning, new paint, tiny new decks, and flatscreen HD TVs). If the rooms were under $100, we would highly recommend them, but the $149 price tag is high for the very plain and utilitarian accommodations you get: small studios with a bed, small kitchens, tiny bathroom, small table with a couple of chairs, and TV—period. You can do better for this rate. The rooms are clean, and generally serve backpackers who want clean, affordable accommodations for a couple of nights. For those on a shoestring budget looking for stripped down lodging, the Hanalei Inn has a few rooms that offer bed and bathroom only (no cooking facilities); they are even tinier than the already small units and at $139 a night, not exactly a bargain. No maid service. It's within walking distance to shops and restaurants, 2 miles to Hanalei Beach.

5-5468 Kuhio Hwy., Hanalei 96714. ✆ **808/826-9333.** www.hanaleiinn.com. 5 units. $149 studio with kitchen; $139 bed and bathroom only. MC, V. **Amenities:** Barbecue; pay phone. *In room:* A/C, TV, kitchenette, no phone.

Mana Yoga Vacation Rental ★ Finds About a 10-minute drive to the beach in the rolling hills of the Princeville Ranch agricultural area, this thriving yoga studio and accommodations hosted by Michaelle Edwards is for those looking to study yoga and stay in a peaceful country environment. Located downstairs from her family home, the units include an 800-square-foot, two-bedroom apartment and a separate smaller studio. Both have private entrances, their own kitchens, bathrooms, and outside lanais. The views are of the verdant hills surrounding the farm. The amenities range from pillow-top mattresses to complimentary Wi-Fi. Guests are welcome to pick the fruit and vegetables in season on the 5-acre farm. Most guests stay here to study with Michaelle, who has developed the unique YogAlign method, a pain-free way of stretching.

3212 Ahonui Place. Reservations: P.O. Box 681, Hanalei, HI 96714. ✆ **808/826-9230.** http://www.kauainorthshorevacationrentals.com. 2 units. $100 double studio; $135 double 2-bedroom; plus $35 and $65 cleaning fee, respectively. Extra person $15. 3-night minimum. No credit cards. **Amenities:** Barbecue area; complimentary use of bicycles and beach toys. *In room:* TV/DVD/CD, kitchen, Wi-Fi.

North Country Farms ★ Kids In the rolling green hills outside of Kilauea, on a 4-acre organic vegetable, fruit, and flower farm, Lee Roversi and her family have two private, handcrafted redwood cottages for rent. This restful spot is an excellent choice, both in terms of comfort and value, especially for a family. Each cottage has hardwood floors, a large lanai with garden or orchard views, a compact kitchenette for cooking (Lee stocks fruit, juice, muffins, croissants, fresh eggs, coffee, and tea for breakfast), and a separate bedroom with a beautiful Hawaiian quilt on the queen-size bed. The couch in one living room turns into two separate beds, the other cottage's couch turns into a queen-sized bed plus a futon, so the cottages can easily sleep four to six. (Children are welcome.) Outside, each has a shower for washing off sand from the beach. The only thing the cottage lacks is a TV, but since it's so close to beaches, hiking, shopping, and restaurants, you're likely to find yourself too tired at the end of the day to watch the tube anyway.

Kahlili Makai St. (P.O. Box 723, off Kuhio Hwy. at mile marker 22), Kilauea, HI 96754. ✆ **808/828-1513.** Fax 808/828-0805. www.northcountryfarms.com. 2 cottages. $150 double. Rate includes fixings for breakfast, plus fruits and veggies from organic farm. Extra person $10. Children under 18 stay free in parent's room. No credit cards. *In room: Hair dryer,* kitchen.

Princeville Bed & Breakfast **Finds** Golfers take note: This large home, which looks like something out of *Architectural Digest,* fronts 480 feet of the fairway and the 6th hole of the Makai Golf Course at Princeville. In addition to discounts on greens fees at both the Prince and the Makai courses, the former Hale 'Aha ("House of Gathering") offers luxury accommodations in a beautiful Princeville setting, where every detail is thought out: No guest rooms have adjoining walls, thereby ensuring all their visitors peace and privacy. The four rooms range from the well-priced Bali Hai Room, with an ocean view, a private entrance, and a refrigerator; to the Penthouse Suite, where you can splurge in the 1,000-square-foot suite with a whirlpool tub in the bathroom, a private lanai, and 360-degree panoramic views of the golf course, mountains, and ocean. All units get complimentary breakfast, consisting of pancakes or an egg casserole with plenty of fruit, coffee, tea, and pastries. Not appropriate for children.

3875 Kamehameha Dr. (the 3rd street on the right past the entrance to Princeville), P.O. Box 3370, Prince ville, HI 96722. ✆ **800/826-6733** or 808/826-6733. Fax 808/826-9052. www.kauai-bandb.com. 4 units. $135–$145 double; $205–$300 suite. Rates include full breakfast. 3-night minimum. MC, V. *In room:* A/C, TV/DVD, hair dryer, kitchenette (in suite), hair dryer, Wi-Fi.

SUPER-CHEAP SLEEPS

YMCA of Kauai–Camp Naue **Value** Attention, campers, hikers, and backpackers: This is the ideal spot to stay before or after conquering the Na Pali Trail, or if you just want to spend a few days lounging on fabulous Haena Beach. This Y campsite sits right on the ocean, on 4 grassy acres ringed with ironwood and kamani trees and bordered by a sandy beach that offers excellent swimming and snorkeling in the summer (the ocean here turns really rough in the winter). Camp Naue has two bunkhouses overlooking the beach; each has four rooms with 10 to 12 beds. The facilities are coed, with separate bathrooms for men and women. There's no bedding here, so bring your sleeping bag and towels. Large groups frequently book the camp, but if there's room, the Y will squeeze you into the bunkhouse or offer tent space. Also on the grounds are a beachfront pavilion, and a campfire area with picnic tables. You can pick up basic supplies in Haena, but it's best to stock up on groceries and other necessities in Lihue or Hanalei. Remember, this is the Y, not the Ritz: They only have one employee who handles all the bookings, plus everything else related to the Y activities. The best way to find out if they have space available is to call a few months before your trip (*do not* e-mail, *do not* send a letter, keep calling as they cannot return long distance calls). They will let you know if there is space in the campsite or if the bunkhouse will be available.

YMCA, P.O. Box 1786, Lihue, HI 96766. ✆ **808/246-9090.** On Kuhio Hwy., 4 miles west of Hanalei and 2 miles from the end of the road, Haena. 50 bunk beds (with shared bathroom), 1 cabin, tent camping. $15 per bunk; $15 tent camping. No credit cards.

6

Where to Dine

Dining in Kauai is an activity unto itself. Dining is not just eating (although you will find scrumptious meals created from locally grown, raised, or caught products) but an entire feast for the senses.

Dining on Kauai begins with views and decor. Resort areas will feast your eyes with romantic settings and panoramic ocean views. In Poipu, the Beach House and the restaurants at the Grand Hyatt Kauai Resort and Spa offer spectacular settings right on the beach that will linger in your memory long after you return home. In Hanalei, the restaurants at Princeville Resort look out onto an awe-inspiring vista of Hanalei Bay with cloud-shrouded, majestic peaks in the background.

Next on Kauai's sensuous dining experiences are the enticing aromas, especially at ethnic restaurants. Even if the cuisine is unfamiliar to you, your taste buds will be standing up to applaud at just the wonderful scents wafting out from the kitchen. Kauai offers a rainbow of different ethnic cuisines, from Asian and Polynesian to Mexican/Central American, European, and eclectic mixes.

Dining also means soothing sounds, from the strumming of a ukulele to the gentle rhythm of tumbling waves in the sand. In our reviews we note which restaurants feature live music, which is so important not only to the digestion, but also to the relaxing atmosphere that seems to calm the soul and makes the entire dining experience a banquet for the senses.

Best of all, dining on Kauai is a divine experience in tasting. Taste the familiar, the new, the exotic, and even the adventurous. I urge you to try at least one restaurant featuring cuisine you are totally unfamiliar with. Who knows, you may become enamored with it.

Don't pass up the small mom-and-pop places, the takeouts, the hole-in-the-wall eateries; some very fine food at very budget-pleasing prices comes out of these tiny places.

On your jaunt across the island, you'll find affordable choices in every town, from hamburger joints to *saimin* stands (selling noodles in broth topped with scrambled eggs, onions, and sometimes pork) to busy neighborhood diners. As long as you don't expect filet mignon on a fish-and-chips budget, it shouldn't be difficult to please both your palate and your pocketbook. But if you're looking for lobster, rack of lamb, or risotto to write home about, you'll find those pleasures, too.

For condo dwellers preparing your own meals, chapter 9 features a variety of markets and shops around Kauai—including some wonderful green markets and fruit stands—where you can pick up the island's best foodstuffs.

Restaurants listed in this chapter do not require reservations unless otherwise noted.

1 LIHUE & ENVIRONS

You'll find the restaurants in this section on the "Where to Dine in Lihue" map on p. 133.

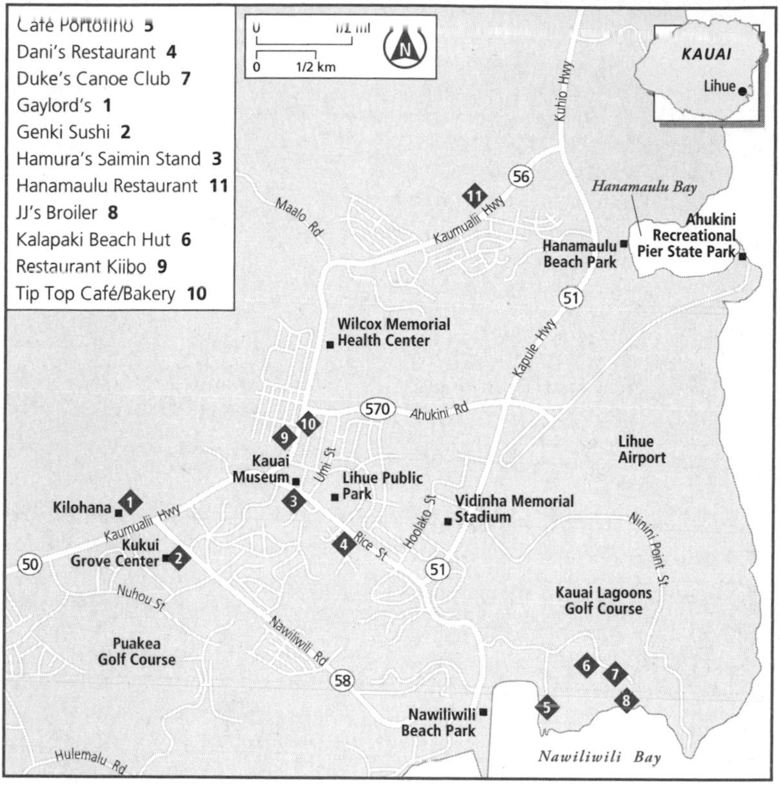

EXPENSIVE

Gaylord's ★★ CONTINENTAL/PACIFIC RIM One of Kauai's most splendid examples of *kamaaina* architecture, Gaylord's is the anchor of a 1930s plantation manager's estate on a 1,700-acre sugar plantation. You'll enter a complex of shops, galleries, and a living room of Hawaiian artifacts and period furniture. The private dining room has a lavish table, always elegantly set as if Queen Liliuokalani were expected at any minute; another room accommodates private parties. The main dining room, which winds around a flagstone courtyard overlooking rolling lawns and purple mountains, serves American classics (New York strip steak, rack of lamb, prime rib) along with pasta, fresh seafood, and lavish desserts. The ambience, historic surroundings, and soothing views from the terrace make Gaylord's a special spot for lunch—salads, soups, fresh fish, Oliver Shagnasty's signature baby back ribs, burgers, sandwiches, and lighter fare predominate. Daily specials include international dishes such as kalua pork and Mexican fajitas, and fresh island fish in various cross-cultural preparations.

At Kilohana, 3-2087 Kaumualii Hwy., Lihue. ✆ **808/245-9593.** www.gaylordskauai.com. Reservations recommended. Main courses $9–$14 lunch, $19–$42 dinner, Sunday brunch $25. AE, DC, DISC, MC, V. Mon–Sat 11am–2pm; daily 5:30–9pm; Sun 7:45am–2:30pm (brunch).

Plate Lunch Palaces

If you haven't yet come face-to-face with the local phenomenon called *plate lunch,* Kauai is a good place to start. Like saimin, the plate lunch is more than a gastronomic experience—it's part of the local culture. Lihue is peppered with affordable plate-lunch counters that serve this basic dish: two scoops of rice, potato or macaroni salad, and a beef, chicken, fish, or pork entree—all on a single plate. Although heavy gravies are usually de rigueur, some of the less traditional purveyors have streamlined their offerings to include healthier touches, such as lean grilled fresh fish. Pork cutlets and chicken or beef soaked in teriyaki sauce, however, remain staples, as does the breaded and crisply fried method called *katsu,* as in chicken katsu. Most of the time, *fried* is the operative word; that's why it's best to be ravenously hungry when you approach a plate lunch, or it can overpower you. At its best, a plate lunch can be a marvel of flavors, a saving grace after a long hike; at its worst, it's a plate-size grease bomb.

The following are the best plate-lunch counters on Kauai. How fortunate that each is in a different part of the island!

The **Koloa Fish Market** ★, 5482 Koloa Rd. (✆ **808/742-6199**), is in southern Kauai on Koloa's main street. A tiny corner stand with plate lunches, prepared foods, and two stools on a closet-size veranda, it sells excellent fresh fish poke, Hawaiian-food specials, and seared ahi to go. It's gourmet fare masquerading as takeout. Daily specials may include sautéed ahi or fresh opakapaka with capers, one of life's consummate pleasures. For a picnic or outing on the south shore, this is a good place to start.

On the Hanamaulu side of Lihue, across the street from Wal-Mart, look for the prim, gray building that reads **Fish Express** ★, 3343 Kuhio Hwy. (✆ **808/245-9918**). It's astonishing what you'll find here for the price of a movie: Cajun-st[illegible]d ahi with guava basil, fresh fish grilled in a passion-orange-tarragon sa[illegible]h fish tacos in garlic and herbs, and many other delectables, all serve[illegible]h rice, salad, and vegetables. The Hawaiian plate lunch (laulau or kalua [illegible] lomi salmon, ahi poke, rice, or poi) is a top seller, as are the several variet[illegible]f smoked fish, everything from ahi to swordfish. The owners mari-nate [illegible]sh in soy sauce, sugar, ginger, and garlic (no preservatives) and

JJ's Broiler ★ AMERICAN Famous for its Slavonic steak (tenderloin in butter, wine, and garlic), JJ's is a lively spot on Kalapaki Bay with open-air dining and a menu that covers more than the usual surf and turf. We have found the service to be both laudable and lamentable, but the quality of the food is consistent. The coconut shrimp and Manila clams are big sellers, and the scallops Florentine are an imaginative twist on seafood. Lunchtime appetizers range from potato skins to calamari rings. The high ceilings, two-story dining, Kenwood Cup posters, and nautically designed rooms are enhanced by stellar views of the bay.

3416 Rice St., Nawiliwili. ✆ **808/246-4422.** www.jjsbroiler.com. Reservations recommended for dinner. Lunch sandwiches $12–$16; dinner main courses $25–$33. DISC, MC, V. Daily 11am–10pm.

smoke it with kiawe wood. The fresh fish specials, at $8.95, come in six preparations and are flavored to perfection. At the chilled counter you can choose freshly sliced sashimi and many styles of poke, from scallop, ahi, and octopus to exotic marinated crab. This is a potluck bonanza that engages even newcomers, who point and order while regulars pick up sweeping assortments of seafood appetizers on large platters. They're all fresh and at good prices, especially for Friday-afternoon *pau hana* (after-work) parties.

In east Kauai's Kapaa town, the indispensable **Pono Market,** 4–1300 Kuhio Hwy. (✆ **808/822-4581**), has similarly enticing counters of sashimi, poke, Hawaiian food, sushi, and a diverse assortment of takeout fare. It's known for its flaky *manju* (sweet potato and other fillings in baked crust), apple turnovers, sandwiches, excellent boiled peanuts, pork and chicken laulau, and plate lunches—shoyu chicken, sweet-and-sour spareribs, pineapple-glazed chicken, teriyaki fish, and so on. The potato-macaroni salad (regulars buy it by the pound for barbecues and potlucks) and roast pork are top sellers. Pono Market is as good as they come. If they're available, pick up some Taro Ko taro chips; they're made in Hanapepe, hard to find, and definitely worth hand-carrying home.

At **Mark's Place,** 1610 Haleukana St. in Puhi Industrial Park (✆ **808/245-2722**), just southwest of Lihue, island standards (Korean-style chicken, teriyaki beef, beef stew, chicken katsu) come with brown rice (or white) and salad for $6.75 or $7.75. The selection, which changes daily, always includes two salad and three entree choices as well as hot sandwiches (chicken, beef, and hamburgers) and the ever-popular bentos. Mark's is a takeout and catering operation, so don't expect table seating.

Lihue, the island's county and business seat, is full of ethnic eateries serving inexpensive plate lunches. **Po's Kitchen,** 4100 Rice St. (✆ **808/246-8617**), offers Japanese specials: cone sushi, chicken katsu, teriyaki beef plates, and bentos. One block away, **Garden Island BBQ,** 4252-A Rice St. (✆ **808/245-8868**), is the place for Chinese plate lunches and local staples such as barbecued or lemon chicken and teriyaki steak, as well as soups and tofu dishes.

MODERATE

Café Portofino ★★ ITALIAN For a romantic dinner with a harpist playing softly in the background, this candlelit restaurant offers authentic Italian cuisine at reasonable prices in a relaxing atmosphere. Owner Giuseppe Avocadi personally greets every guest and then checks again when you leave to make sure that your dining experience was impeccable. The menu lists appetizers ranging from ahi (or beef) carpaccio to the house special antipasto (with five different daily choices). But it's the pasta that will bring you back here a second time: These homemade dishes are so light you'd swear you could keep on eating all night. There's a dozen different dishes to choose from, plus the chef usually has a few new creations to make your decision all the harder. Also on the menu are fresh fish, a variety of chicken dishes, veal and beef dishes (from the traditional *osso buco* to scaloppini a la Marsala to chicken cacciatore), and a few items for vegetarians. Live music is featured every night.

3481 Hoolaulea St., Nawiliwili. ✆ **808/245-2121.** www.cafeportofino.com. Reservations recommended. Main courses $20–$40. MC, V. Daily 5–9:30pm.

Duke's ★ STEAK/SEAFOOD It's hard to go wrong at Duke's. Part of a highly successful restaurant chain (including Duke's Canoe Club in Waikiki and three similar restaurants on Maui), this oceanfront oasis is the hippest spot in town, with a winning combination of great view, affordable menu, attractive salad bar, popular music, and a very happy happy hour. The noontime bestseller is stir-fried cashew chicken, but the fresh mahimahi sandwich and the grilled chicken quesadilla are front-runners, too. The inexpensive fish tacos are a major attraction. The five or six varieties of fresh catch each night are a highlight and a great value. Hawaiian musicians serenade diners nightly, while downstairs in the Barefoot Bar traditional and contemporary Hawaiian music adds to the cheerful atmosphere. On Tropical Friday, tropical drinks go for under $6 from 4 to 6pm, and live music stirs up the joint.

In the Kauai Marriott Resort & Beach Club, 3610 Rice St., Nawiliwili. ✆ **808/246-9599.** www.dukeskauai.com. Reservations recommended for dinner. Main courses $8–$12 lunch, $19–$29 dinner. "Taco Tuesdays" 4–6pm, with $2.50 fish tacos and $3.25 draft beer. AE, DISC, MC, V. Barefoot Bar daily 11am–11pm; main dining room daily 5–10pm.

INEXPENSIVE

Dani's Restaurant AMERICAN/HAWAIIAN Always packed for breakfast, Dani's is the pancake palace of Lihue. Varieties include banana, pineapple, papaya, and buttermilk, plus such options as sweet-bread French toast and kalua-pig omelets. Regulars know that fried rice is offered on Thursday only and that the papaya hot cakes are always a deal. At lunch, Hawaiian specials—laulau, kalua pig, lomi salmon, and beef stew in various combinations—dominate the otherwise standard American menu of fried foods and sandwiches. Generally the restaurant is full of local residents, so smile and introduce yourself and tell 'em how much you are enjoying Kauai.

4201 Rice St., Lihue. ✆ **808/245-4991.** Main courses $4.50–$8 breakfast, $7.50–$8.50 lunch. MC, V. Mon–Fri 5am–1pm; Sat 5–11am.

Genki Sushi SUSHI This affordable chain is a great place to take the family: The sushi is inexpensive, and it's fun to select as it circulates the counter on a conveyor belt. Prices are based on the color of the plate containing the sushi: Gold plates (which have items like tamago, a green salad, miso soup, and tofu) are $1.55; green (ahi poke, spicy tuna, mochi ice cream) $2.30; red (hamachi, ahi, ebi sushi) $2.90; silver (dragon roll) $3.95; and black (ahi sashimi, ikura, rainbow roll) $4.95. The sushi is continually made fresh and added to the conveyor belt.

Kukui Grove Shopping Center, 3-2600 Kaumualii Hwy., Lihue. ✆ **808/632-2450.** Sushi plates $1.55–$4.95. MC, V. Sun–Thurs 11am–9pm; Fri–Sat 11am–10pm.

Hamura's Saimin Stand ★ (Finds) SAIMIN If there were a saimin hall of fame, Hamura's would be in it. It's a cultural experience, a renowned saimin stand where fans line up to take their places over steaming bowls of this island specialty at a few U-shaped counters that haven't changed in decades. The saimin and teriyaki barbecue sticks attract an all-day, late-night, pre- and post-movie crowd. The noodles come heaped with vegetables, wontons, hard-boiled eggs, sweetened pork, vegetables, and condiments. We love the casualness of Hamura's and the simple pleasures it consistently delivers.

2956 Kress St., Lihue. ✆ **808/245-3271.** Most items less than $9. No credit cards. Mon–Thurs 10am–10pm; Fri–Sat 10am–midnight; Sun 10am–9pm.

Hanamaulu Restaurant Kids CHINESE/JAPANESE/SUSHI When passing this restaurant, you'd never know that serene Japanese gardens with stone pathways and tatami-floored teahouses are hidden within. You can dine at the sushi bar, American style, or in the teahouse for lunch or dinner (the teahouse requires reservations). At lunch enter a world of chop suey, wontons, teriyaki chicken, and sukiyaki (less verve than value), with many other choices in budget-friendly Japanese and Chinese plate lunches. Special Japanese and Chinese menus can be planned ahead for groups of up to 60 people, who can dine at low tables on tatami floors in a Japanese-garden setting. Old-timers love this place, and those who came here in diapers now stop in for after-golf pupu and beer.

3-4291 Kuhio Hwy., Hanamaulu. ✆ **808/245-2511.** Reservations recommended. Main courses $6–$15. MC, V. Tues–Fri 10am–1pm; Tues–Sun 5–8:30pm.

Kalapaki Beach Hut Kids AMERICAN Tricky to find, but what a savings for your wallet! (***Hint:*** Look for an anchor chain in front of a blue building.) Opened in 1990 by Steve and Sharon Gerald as Kalapaki Beach Burgers, the tiny eatery started adding more items and then evolved into serving breakfast. This "hut" has window service, a few tables downstairs, and more tables upstairs (with an ocean view out the screen windows). The basic fare is served on paper plates with plastic cutlery at cheap, cheap prices. Breakfasts are hearty omelets, pancakes, and numerous egg dishes. Lunches are heavy on the hamburgers (prepared 10 different ways), lots of sandwiches, a few healthy salads, and fish and chips. Kids get their own menu in a smaller portion size. This casual restaurant welcomes people in their bathing suits and slippers.

3474 Rice St., Nawiliwili. ✆ **808/246-6330.** Breakfast $4.50–$8.50; lunch $5–$9. MC, V. Daily 7am–8pm.

Restaurant Kiibo Finds JAPANESE Neither a sleek sushi bar nor a plate-lunch canteen, Kiibo is a neighborhood staple with inexpensive, unpretentious, tasty, home-style Japanese food served in a pleasant room accented with Japanese folk art. You can dine on sushi, ramen, sukiyaki, tempura, teriyaki, or the steamed egg-rice-vegetable marvel called *oyako donburi.* There are satisfying, affordable lunch specials and teishoku specials of mackerel, salmon, soup, dessert, and condiments.

2991 Umi St., Lihue. ✆ **808/245-2650.** Main courses $8–$19. No credit cards. Mon–Fri 11am–1:30pm; Mon–Sat 5:30–9pm.

Tip Top Café/Bakery Kids LOCAL This small cafe/bakery (also the lobby for the Tip Top Motel) has been serving local customers since 1916. The best deal is their breakfast: Most items are $7 or under, and their macadamia pancakes are known throughout Kauai. Lunch ranges from pork chops to teriyaki chicken, but their specialty is oxtail soup. For a real treat, stop by the bakery (where you pay your bill) and take something home (we recommend the freshly baked *malasadas*).

3173 Akahi St., Lihue. ✆ **808/245-2333.** Breakfast items under $7; lunch entrees $3.50–$11. MC, V. Bakery daily 6:30am–3pm, Café Tues–Sun 6:30am–1:45pm.

2 THE POIPU RESORT AREA

EXPENSIVE

The Beach House ★★★ HAWAII REGIONAL This is the place to go for a "splurge" meal: Celebrate a birthday, anniversary, or any excuse for a romantic dinner on the beach with delicious food. The Beach House remains the south shore's premier spot for sunset drinks, appetizers, and dinner—a treat for all the senses. The oceanfront room is large, accented with oversize sliding-glass doors, with old Hawaii Regional favorites on the menu. Come for cocktails or early dinner, when you can still see the sunset and perhaps a turtle or two bobbing in the waves. Menus change daily and include Kauai asparagus salad, seared macadamia-nut-crusted mahimahi with miso sauce, sea scallops with lemon grass and kaffir lime, and the Beach House crab cake with mint sambal butter sauce and grilled tomato compote. Desserts shine, too, like the molten chocolate desire—a hot chocolate tart—and the mango crème brûlée.

5022 Lawai Rd., Poipu. ✆ **808/742-1424.** www.the-beach-house.com. Reservations recommended. Main courses $20–$40. AE, DC, MC, V. Daily 5:30–10pm (winter), 6:30–10pm (summer).

Casa di Amici ★★ ITALIAN/INTERNATIONAL New Chef Ray Dikilato (a former sous chef here for years) has taken over this wonderful Italian bistro and kept the atmosphere and yummy cuisine the same in this free-standing wood-and-stone building in Poipu. At night the fairy lights, high ceilings, beveled glass, and a generous open deck make dining among palms and heliotropes very romantic. (There's live classical music Sat evenings 6:30–9:30pm on the baby grand piano.) It's worth seeking out: It's the third left turn past Brennecke's Beach, not more than 2 minutes from Poipu Beach Park, in an enclave of condos and vacation rentals.

The memorable Italian food has strong Mediterranean and cross-cultural influences. You'll find organic greens from Kilauea, several risotto choices (quattro formaggio and Thai beef are outstanding), black tiger prawns in orange saffron lobster sauce, and surprises, such as Thai lobster bisque and pork loin saltimbocca. Among the nearly two dozen pasta selections is a classic fettuccine Alfredo for which Casa di Amici is deservedly famous. The set menu is Italian, but the specials showcase international influences, such as soy-sauce reductions, *furikake* (seaweed sprinkle), and assertive touches of jalapeño tequila aioli on salmon and grilled tiger prawns. This is flamboyant, joyful Italian fare. Plus you can order either light- or regular-size entrees, a policy I love.

2301 Nalo Rd., Poipu. ✆ **808/742-1555.** www.casadiamici.com. Reservations recommended. Main courses $22–$23 light size, $26–$35 regular size. DC, MC, V. Daily 6pm–closing.

Dondero's ★★★ ITALIAN If you are looking for a romantic dinner either under the stars overlooking the ocean or tucked away at an intimate table (surrounded by inlaid marble floors, ornate imported floor tiles, and Franciscan murals), the Grand Hyatt's stellar Italian restaurant is the place for you. You get all this atmosphere at Dondero's, plus the best Italian cuisine on the island, served with efficiency. It's hard to have a bad experience here. My recommendations for a meal to remember: Start with either the fresh mozzarella with tomatoes and basil or the minestrone with oxtail ravioli. Then move on to the ricotta gnocchi with white truffle cream; the *osso buco* with gremolatta; or the roast seabass with fennel, capers, cured olives, and tomato broth. Save room for dessert, especially the crème brûlée with fresh berries. Dinners are pricey but worth every penny.

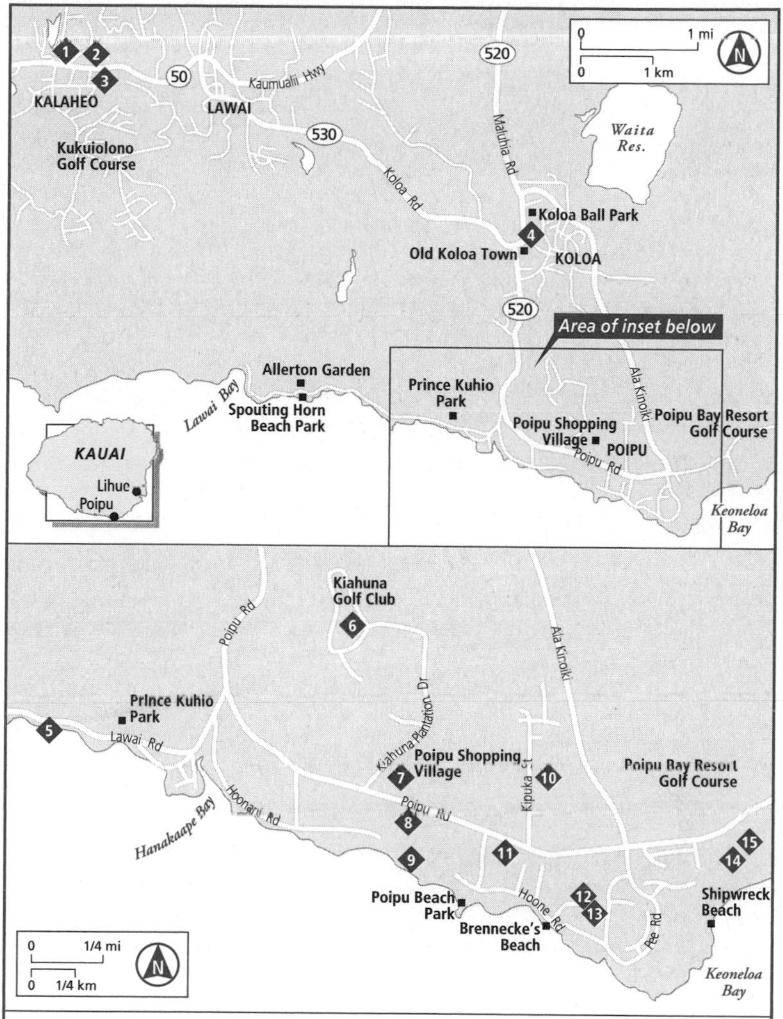

The Beach House 5
Brennecke's Beach Broiler 12
Brick Oven Pizza 1
Casa Blanca at Kiahuna 10
Casa di Amici 13
Dondero's 14
Joe's on the Green 6
Kalaheo Café & Coffee Co. 2
Keoki's Paradise 7
Plantation Gardens Restaurant 8
Poipu Beach Broiler 11
Pomodoro 3
Red Salt 9
Roy's Poipu Bar & Grill 7
Tidepool Restaurant 14
Tomkats Grille 4
Yum Cha 15

At the Grand Hyatt Kauai Resort & Spa, 1571 Poipu Rd., Koloa. ✆ **808/742-1234.** www.kauai.hyatt.com. Reservations are a must. Main courses $11–$51. AE, DC, DISC, MC, V. Daily 6–10pm.

Plantation Gardens Restaurant HAWAII REGIONAL I was very disappointed when I last ate here: It's still a mix of irresistible garden ambience and a well-executed menu fashioned around fresh local ingredients, but the portions are small, everything is a la carte, and the prices are high (pupu selections in the $9–$22 range, salads $9–$11, and entrees $19–$31). The seaweed, fish, and shellfish are from local waters, and many of the fruits, herbs, and vegetables are grown on the resort premises. The historic architecture includes a generous veranda, koa trim and Brazilian cherry floors, and gracious details of a 1930s estate that belonged to the manager of Hawaii's first sugar plantation. A sprawling horticultural marvel, the property includes koi ponds, coconut and kou trees, orchids, bromeliads, and a cactus and succulent garden.

At the Kiahuna Plantation Resort, 2253 Poipu Rd., Koloa. ✆ **808/742-2121.** www.pgrestaurant.com. Reservations recommended. Main courses $19–$31. AE, DC, MC, V. Daily 5:30–9pm (open at 5pm for pupu and cocktails).

Red Salt HAWAII REGIONAL The just-opened Ko'a Kea Resort (which replaced the old Poipu Beach Hotel) features this airy dining room with large windows overlooking the swimming pool and the beach beyond. The dinner menu has several preparations for Hawaii's fresh fish (like vanilla-seared mahi, grilled ono with a buerre blanc sauce, and seven-spiced ahi with a cilantro risotto) plus rack of lamb, New York strip steak, and even marinated grilled tofu with coconut crème fraîche, for the vegetarians.

Ko'a Kea Hotel, 2251 Poipu Rd., Koloa, 96756. ✆ **808/332-5316.** www.koakea.com. Main course $24–$44. AE, DC, DISC, MC, V. Daily 6:30–11am and 6–10pm.

Roy's Poipu Bar & Grill ★★★ EURO-ASIAN This is a loud, lively room with ceiling fans, marble tables, works by local artists, and a menu tailor-made for foodies. The signature touches of Roy Yamaguchi (of Roy's restaurants in Oahu, Big Island, Maui, Tokyo, New York, and Guam) are abundantly present: an excellent, progressive, and affordable wine selection; fresh local ingredients prepared with a nod to Europe, Asia, and the Pacific; and service so efficient it can be overbearing. Because appetizers (such as blackened ahi with mustard soy sauce, grilled Szechuan baby back ribs, and crispy crab cakes with butter sauce) are a major part of the menu, you can sample Roy's legendary fare without breaking the bank. The three dozen nightly specials invariably include eight fresh-fish dishes a night, prepared at least five or six different ways.

Moments A Taste of the Islands

Hawaii's Meadow Gold Dairies has a line of rich premium ice cream for true aficionados looking for a melt-in-your-mouth taste of Hawaii. We recommend the Kona coffee, macadamia nut, or honeydew melon. Traditionalists will go for the vanilla, chocolate, Neapolitan, rocky road, or cookies and cream. People who can't make up their minds will love the blended flavors like mint chocolate chip or the espresso fudge pie. Sherbet fans have two flavors to choose from: rainbow rapture or orange. You can find these ice creams in the frozen section of most supermarkets across the island. For more information: www.lanimoo.com.

In Poipu Shopping Village, 2360 Kiahuna Plantation Dr., Poipu. ✆ **808/742-5000.** www.roysrestaurant.com. Reservations highly recommended. Main courses $25–$40. AE, DC, DISC, MC, V. Daily 5:30–9:30pm.

Tidepool Restaurant ★★★ SEAFOOD Here's another ultraromantic restaurant at the Grand Hyatt: A cluster of Polynesian-style thatched bungalows overlook the lagoon in a dreamy, open-aired restaurant with Tiki torches flickering in the moonlight. The atmosphere would be enough to make you book a table, but the cuisine is outstanding, a definite "do not miss." Their specialty is fresh fish, which they prepare in a number of ways (the signature dish is banana and macadamia-nut-crusted mahimahi with grilled shrimp and scallops and lilikoi butter sauce), but they also have juicy steaks and ribs, as well as entrees for vegetarians. Service is quick and efficient. Book early, and ask for a table overlooking the water.

Grand Hyatt Kauai Resort and Spa, 1571 Poipu Rd., Poipu. ✆ **808/742-1234.** www.kauai.hyatt.com. Reservations recommended. Main courses $31–$56. AE, DC, DISC, MC, V. Daily 5:30–10pm.

MODERATE

Brennecke's Beach Broiler ★ Kids AMERICAN/SEAFOOD Cheerful petunias in window boxes and second-floor views of Poipu Beach are pleasing touches at this seafood/burger house, a longtime favorite for a couple of decades. The view alone is worth the price of a drink and pupu, but it helps that the best hamburgers on the south shore are served here, as well as excellent vegetarian selections. Quality is consistent in the kiawe-broiled steak, fresh fish, and vegetarian gourmet burger. It's so casual that you can drop in before or after the beach and dine on nachos and peppers, fresh-fish sandwiches, kiawe-broiled fish and kabobs, prime rib, pasta, build-your-own gourmet burgers, and the salad bar. Look for happy-hour specials daily and the Alaskan king crab and prime rib nights.

2100 Hoone Rd. (across from Poipu Beach Park), Poipu. ✆ **808/742-7588.** www.brenneckes.com. Main courses $10–$20 lunch, $12–$40 dinner. AE, DC, DISC, MC, V. Daily 11am–10pm (street-side deli takeout daily 7am–8pm).

Casa Blanca at Kiahuna ★ MEDITERRANEAN This used to be one of my favorite dining places on Kauai; I planned my trips around eating here. But it has just gotten too unreliable in recent years—you can either have the meal of your life here with great service or a total fiasco with bad service to boot. If the owner Elizabeth "Liz" Foley, a culinary genius, who opened this stylish, elegant, open-air restaurant overlooking the manicured grounds at the Kiahuna Swim and Tennis Club, is on property, then you stand a good chance of having great food and good service. When Liz is on-site, she makes sure that every detail is taken care of, from the polished slate floors to the fresh flowers. Unfortunately, if Liz is not at the restaurant, it is not so sterling, and the service and the culinary dishes coming out of the kitchen suffer. Call in advance and ask if Liz is there—if she is, make a reservation; if not, you might want to pass. Lunch is a creative selection of Greek and Mediterranean dishes including brochettes (Moroccan lamb, Algerian chicken skewers, and Moroccan vegetable with couscous), and there is even a kids' menu with such classics as PB&J and grilled cheese. They also have a delicious tapas menu of small items: Spanish shrimp, crostini with olive tapanade, spicy eggplant caponata, and more at Happy Hour. But it's at dinner that Liz's famous culinary talents really stand out, with zarzuela (Spanish stew with lobster, shrimp, mussels, tomato, and saffron), *Tangine al Dajaj* (traditional Moroccan street fare of stewed chicken with olives and spices served over couscous), *agnello* (New Zealand lamb with roasted red potatoes),

Kids Family-Friendly Restaurants

In addition to the plate-lunch eateries, where children are welcome, the following restaurants not only tolerate kids but make them feel right at home:

LIHUE

Hanamaulu Restaurant (3–4291 Kuhio Hwy., Hanamaulu; ✆ **808/245-2511**). Generations of local families have grown up dining at this Japanese/Chinese eatery. You can feed your family for less than $12 each and still leave food on the plate. Stop by for lunch; the kids will get a kick out of dining at low tables on tatami floors in a Japanese-garden setting.

Kalapaki Beach Hut (3474 Rice St., Nawiliwili; ✆ **808/246-6330**). This tiny "hut" is a great place for burgers (prepared 10 different ways). After a day at the beach, heck, you and the kids can show up in your bathing suits and slippers. Burgers for four, plus drinks, will only set you back $20.

Tip Top Café/Bakery (3173 Akahi St., Lihue; ✆ **808/245-2333**). This is a great place to take the entire family to breakfast. Most items are $6 or under, and the kids will love the macadamia-nut pancakes. On the way out, stop by the bakery and get the freshly baked *malasadas.*

POIPU RESORT AREA

Brennecke's Beach Broiler (2100 Hoone Rd., across from Poipu Beach Park; ✆ **808/742-7588**). After a morning at Brennecke's Beach, just walk across the street to this casual eatery and chow down on their famous hamburgers. They also have "kid" items like nachos and peppers, fresh-fish sandwiches, build-your-own gourmet burgers, and desserts. Look for the early dinner (4–6pm) to save even more money.

Poipu Beach Broiler (1941 Poipu Rd., Poipu; ✆ **808/742-6433**). The kids' menu at this steak-and-seafood restaurant features "mac 'n cheese" ($5), chicken nuggets and fries ($7), and the standard grilled cheese sandwich and fries ($6). Come early and take in the sunset.

Brick Oven Pizza (2-2555 Kaumualii Hwy. [Hwy. 50], Kalaheo, inland from Poipu; ✆ **808/332-8561**). Kids and pizza just go together, especially at this

and nightly specials. Whatever you order, do not miss the chocolate mousse with orange for dessert. After the sun has set, it is hard to find the unlit turnoff to the restaurant, but it's worth the search.

2290 Poipu Rd. (in the Kiahuna Swim and Tennis Club), Poipu. ✆ **808/742-2929.** Reservations recommended for dinner. Lunch $6–$14; tapas $6–$12; dinner entrees $14–$38. DISC, MC, V. Daily 11am–3pm and 5–9pm; happy hour 2–6pm.

Keoki's Paradise STEAK/SEAFOOD It's a great place to take the kids; they will love the tropical ambience here. Keoki's Paradise is sprawling and lively and has improved with the years, with lunch favorites that include a fresh-fish sandwich, fresh-fish tacos, Thai shrimp sticks, and chicken Caesar salad—all good and affordable. In the evenings, old-fashioned stone-oven pizzeria featuring more pizza toppings than you can count. There will be something here to please every member of the family, including Mom and Dad when they get the bill. A 15-inch cheese pizza will feed four and costs less than $7 a person.

COCONUT COAST

Bubba Burgers (4-1421 Kuhio Hwy., Kapaa; ✆ **808/823-0069;** also Hanalei Center, Hanalei; ✆ **808/826-7839**). Here at the house of Bubba they dish out humor, great T-shirts, and old-fashioned hamburgers. They also serve up the Slopper (open-faced with chili), the half-pound Big Bubba (three patties), the Hubba Bubba (with rice, hot dog, and chili—a Bubba's plate lunch), chicken burgers, Bubba's famous Budweiser chili, and a daily trio of fresh-fish specials, fish burgers, and fish and chips.

Ono Family Restaurant (4-1292 Kuhio Hwy., Kapaa; ✆ **808/822-1710**). Most items on the breakfast/lunch menu are less than $10, and the portions are huge. (You may want to split an order with the kids, and you'll still walk away full.) Breakfast is a big deal here, with many egg dishes; banana, coconut, and macadamia-nut pancakes; and a few dozen other choices. The lunch menu lets you choose from fish, veggie, steak, tuna, and turkey sandwiches. Burgers with various toppings highlight the menu.

Duane's Ono-Char Burger (on Kuhio Hwy., Anahola; ✆ **808/822-9181**). If you're on your way to or from the beaches on the North Shore and the kids are starvin', stop at this hamburger stand for Duane's huge selection of burgers: teriyaki, mushroom, cheddar, barbecue, and the Special, with grilled onions, sprouts, and two cheeses. (Even Boca burgers are offered for vegetarians.) These one-of-a-kind burgers will set you back $4.40 to $7.25, with plenty of money left over for the marionberry ice-cream shake.

NORTH SHORE

Tropical Taco (Hale Lea Building, 5-5088 Kuhio Hwy., Hanalei; ✆ **808/827-TACO;** www.tropicaltaco.com). Kids will love the assortment of tacos and burritos at this counter service restaurant, and you'll love the prices.

regulars tout the fresh fish crusted in lemon grass, basil, and bread crumbs. When it's time for dessert, the original Hula pie from Kimo's in Lahaina is an ever-sinful winner. The cafe in the bar area serves lighter fare and features live Hawaiian music Sunday, Monday, and Wednesday through Friday nights.

In Poipu Shopping Village, 2360 Kiahuna Plantation Dr., Poipu. ✆ **808/742-7534.** Reservations recommended. Main courses $8.50–$15 lunch, $18–$35 dinner. AE, DC, DISC, MC, V. Daily 5–9:30pm in the main dining room; cafe menu daily 11am–11pm.

Poipu Beach Broiler Kids STEAK/SEAFOOD Located in the former House of Seafood, this new casual eatery has a relaxing atmosphere, like an old beach house. We love their large appetizer menu. In fact, we recommend that you drop by at sunset, have a drink, and chow down on the great variety of pupu—like vegetable summer rolls, sea scallops, seared ahi sashimi, or tender calamari. You can easily make a meal of these appetizers. Dinner entrees include fresh fish, prime rib, grilled sirloin, and baby back ribs. There's also a menu for the kids.

1941 Poipu Rd., Poipu. ✆ **808/742-6433.** Dinner $13–$28. AE, DC, DISC, MC. V. Daily 2–9pm. (Bar serves burgers and sandwiches 2–5pm; dining room opens at 5pm.)

Pomodoro ★ ITALIAN Pomodoro is the Italian magnet of the west side, a small, casual, and intimate second-floor dining room with a bar, potted plants, soft lighting, and pleasing Italian music. It's a warm, welcoming place where Hawaiian hospitality meets European flavors: homemade garlic focaccia, chicken saltimbocca, and homemade pastas (cannelloni, manicotti, and excellent lasagna, the house specialty). Whether you order the veal, chicken, scampi, calamari, or very fresh organic green salads, you'll appreciate the wonderful home-style flavor and the polite, efficient servers.

In Rainbow Plaza, Kaumualii Hwy. (Hwy. 50), Kalaheo (inland from Poipu). ✆ **808/332-5945.** Reservations recommended. Main courses $16–$27. MC, V. Mon–Sat 5:30–9:30pm.

Tomkats Grille AMERICAN/GRILL ***Warning:*** If you are on a low-fat or low-carb diet, this is not the place for you. Fried appetizers, inexpensive New York steak, rotisserie chicken, seafood salad with fresh catch, and sandwiches and burgers are among the offerings at the Grille, in a serene garden setting in Old Koloa Town. Old-fashioned brews are big here—everything from local micro brews to Guinness Stout plus two dozen others, all the better to wash down the kalua pork quesadillas or the seared poke.

5404 Koloa Rd., Old Koloa Town. ✆ **808/742-8887.** Main courses $9–$24. AE, DC, DISC, MC, V. Daily 10:30am–10pm; happy hour daily 3–6pm; bar daily until midnight.

Yum Cha ASIAN Located in the Poipu Bay Golf Course Clubhouse, Yum Cha (which means "drink tea") offers families a range of Asian dishes at fairly reasonable prices. Small plate appetizers range from chilled summer rolls ($10) to vegetable tempura ($11) to a grilled chicken satay ($9). My faves were the soups: tom yum (a small bowl is $10) and the yellow coconut curry ($9 for a small bowl). Entrees seem to cover the map of Asia from Korean beef short ribs ($25) to Mandarin chicken ($17) to stir-fried udon noodles ($11). Don't forget to drink tea; they specialize in a great selection of Chinese loose teas. Pick the jasmine lovers' ball tea, a great fragrance of orange lily and jasmine.

Poipu Bay Golf Course, 1571 Poipu Rd., Poipu. ✆ **808/742-1515.** Main courses $11–$25. MC, V. Tues–Sat 5:30–9:30pm.

INEXPENSIVE

Brick Oven Pizza (Kids) PIZZA A Kalaheo fixture for nearly 25 years, Brick Oven Pizza is the quintessential mom-and-pop business. This is the real thing! The pizza is cooked directly on the brick hearth, brushed with garlic butter, and topped with cheeses and long-simmering sauces. You have a choice of whole-wheat or white crust, plus many toppings: house-made Italian sausage, Portuguese sausage, bay shrimp, anchovies, smoked ham, vegetarian combos, and more. The result: very popular pizza. I recommend topping your pie with fresh garlic and enjoying it with an ice-cold beer. The seafood-style pizza-bread sandwiches are big at lunch, and the "super pizza" with everything on it—that's *amore.*

2-2555 Kaumualii Hwy. (Hwy. 50), Kalaheo (inland from Poipu). ✆ **808/332-8561.** Sandwiches less than $9; pizzas $12–$35. AE, MC, V. Mon. 4–10pm; Tues–Sun 11am–10pm.

Buffet

Where's All the Bottom Fish on the Menu?

What happened to the signature Hawaii bottom fish on the menus in Kauai's restaurants? The state and federal governments have instituted closures for fishing of Hawaii's popular bottom fish (opakapaka, hapuupuu, onaga, lehi, ehu, kalekale, and gindai) during several months (May–Sept, as we went to press, but the ban may be extended) to revive the depleting stocks of these very yummy fish, which are the star "signature" items of numerous restaurants around the state. If you see one of these fish on the menu during the months of May to September, it may not be fresh, or it may have been caught in waters elsewhere in the Pacific but not Hawaii.

Joe's on the Green ★ Finds AMERICAN Psst! We'll let you in on a secret. This "hidden" eatery is mainly known to local residents, who flock here for breakfast or for lunch after a round of golf. They don't want the secret to get out because then their local hangout will be flooded with tourists. This is the place to go for breakfast; not only do you have a great setting—outdoors overlooking the golf course—but the menu has everything from fluffy pancakes (banana-macadamia nut are the best) to biscuits 'n' gravy to healthy tofu scramble. And if you go before 8:30am, you can get the early bird special for $7. Lunch is popular because of a range of sandwiches (from fresh fish to Joe's Mama Burger to "a dog named Joe," which is a quarter-pounder with sauerkraut and Cleveland stadium mustard), salads (build your own), and desserts. (Do not pass up the large, warm, chocolate-chip cookie.)

2545 Kiahuna Plantation Dr., at the Kiahuna Golf Club Clubhouse, Poipu. ✆ **808/742-9696.** www.ygli.bluedomino.com. Breakfast $6.75–$13; lunch $7.75–$13. MC, V. Daily 7am–2:30pm and happy hour 3–5:30pm.

Kalaheo Café & Coffee Co. COFFEEHOUSE/CAFE John Ferguson has long been one of my favorite Kauai chefs, and his cafe is a coffee lover's fantasy: Kauai Estate Peaberry, Kona dark roast, Guatemalan French roast, Colombian, Costa Rican, Sumatran, and African coffees—you can visit the world on a coffee bean! The coffeehouse also serves masterful breakfasts: Bonzo Breakfast Burritos (sautéed ham, peppers, mushrooms, onions, and olives scrambled with cheese and served with salsa and sour cream); veggie omelets with sun-dried tomatoes and mushrooms; and bagels. At lunch the fabulous grilled turkey burgers (heaped with grilled onions and mushrooms on a sourdough bun) are the headliner on a list of winners that also includes fresh-from-the-garden salads and a tasty, inexpensive soup that changes daily. The cinnamon "knuckles" (baked fresh daily), fresh apple pie, and carrot cake are more reasons to stop by. And, finally, by popular demand, they are serving dinner (Wed–Sat only): from pasta primavera (vegetarian $16, fresh fish $22, chicken $21) and homemade turkey meatloaf ($18) to a bourbon-orange-glazed half chicken ($16), a fresh fish seafood wrap ($23), and a grilled NY sirloin steak ($27).

2–2560 Kaumualii Hwy. (Hwy. 50), Kalaheo (across the street from Brick Oven Pizza). ✆ **808/332-5858.** Breakfast $5–$13; lunch $6.50–$14; dinner entrees $16–$28. MC, V. Mon–Sat 6:30am–2:30pm; Sun 6:30am–2pm; Wed–Sat 5:30–10pm.

* Coconut cake

3 WESTERN KAUAI

MODERATE

Hanapepe Café ★★ GOURMET VEGETARIAN/ITALIAN The food here is so delicious that you cannot believe it's vegetarian. They have introduced fish to the menu, added dinners on Friday nights with live entertainment, and added a bakery (open Mon–Fri) with wonderful baked goods and quiche. It's packed at lunchtime, when people come for the several varieties of veggie burger. They have elevated this modest staple to gourmet status: You can top yours with sautéed mushrooms, grilled onions, pesto, fresh-grated Parmesan, and other choices. Other lunch notables: fresh red-skinned home fries, a heroic grilled vegetable sandwich, and whole roasted garlic heads. Friday night's dinner menu changes every week, but Italian and fresh seafood specialties shine: fresh spinach salad; lasagna quattro formaggio with spinach, mushrooms, and four cheeses; crepes; and the nightly special with the cafe's famous marinara sauce—terrific choices all. There's no liquor license, so if you want wine, bring your own ($5 corkage fee).

3830 Hanapepe Rd., Hanapepe. ✆ **808/335-5011.** Reservations recommended for dinner. Main courses $7–$15 lunch, $24–$30 dinner. DISC, MC, V. Mon–Thurs 7am–3pm. Dinner Fri 5–9pm.

Waimea Brewing Company ECLECTIC This popular brewery in the Waimea Plantation Cottages is a welcome addition to the dry west side, serving pub fare with a multiethnic twist. "Small plates" for grazing are composed of ale-steamed shrimp, taro-leaf-and-goat-cheese dip with warm pita bread, or seafood chowder. "Big plates" come with steak with wasabi mashed potatoes, kalbi short ribs, or kalua pork. In between are soups, salads, and sandwiches, including fresh catch. The beer is brewed on the premises. It's a pleasant stop, one of the top two places in Waimea for dinner.

In Waimea Plantation Cottages, 9400 Kaumualii Hwy., Waimea. ✆ **808/338-9733.** Main courses $10–$30. AE, DISC, MC, V. Daily 11:30am–8:30pm.

Wrangler's Steakhouse STEAK Good service and pleasant veranda seating are among the pluses of this family-run operation. Western touches abound: a wagon in the loft, log-framed booths with gas lanterns, and *lauhala paniolo* hats in the made-in-Hawaii gift shop. A combination of cowboy, plantation, and island traditions, Wrangler's serves lots of steak—big, hand-selected cuts—and adds some island touches, from vegetable tempura to grilled steak to ahi with penne pasta. Families like Wrangler's because its multicourse dinners won't break the bank.

9852 Kaumualii Hwy., Waimea. ✆ **808/338-1218.** Lunch $9.50–$19; dinner main courses $17–$45. AE, DISC, MC, V. Mon–Fri 11am–8:30pm; Sat 5–9pm.

INEXPENSIVE

Grinds Café AMERICAN Grinds, which sits right along the highway, is a great place to get a takeout lunch on the way to or from the beach. They serve tasty sandwiches and pizza for lunch and have a range of reasonably priced dinners ranging from mahimahi ($12) to barbecue chicken ($11). I suggest takeout—the last time I stopped in not only was the place packed, but when the table was available, it was "cleaned" with a dirty cloth that belonged in the garbage. We opted to take our meal in takeout containers.

4469 Waialo Rd., Eleele. ✆ **808/335-6027.** Burgers and sandwiches $7.50–$9.50; main courses $7–$13. AE, DISC, MC, V. Daily 6am–9pm.

Icy-Cold Dessert

Maybe it's because Hawaii can be hot. Maybe it's because it's just downright refreshing and delicious. But there's nothing quite like enjoying some Hawaiian shave ice under the tropical sun—don't leave Kauai until you've tried it. The mainland has "snow cones," which are made from crushed ice with sweet flavorings poured over the top. Shave ice (not "shaved" ice) is made by shaving a block of ice with an ultrasharp blade, which results in ice as thin as frozen powder. The shave ice is then saturated with a sweet syrup. (Flavors can range from old-fashioned strawberry to such local treats as *li hing mui.*) You can also ask for shave ice on top of ice cream. (Try it with sweet Japanese azuki beans for a special treat.) Shave ice can be found all over the island, from small, hole-in-the-wall stores to vans alongside the road. A few to look for are: **Shave Ice Paradise,** in the Hanalei Center (✆ **808/826-6659**); **Hawaiian Blizzard,** a small stand in front of Big Save, in the Kapaa Shopping Center, 4-1105 Kuhio Hwy., no phone; and **Halo Halo Shave Ice,** 2956 Kress St., Lihue (✆ **808/245-5094**).

Shrimp Station SHRIMP Looking for a picnic lunch to take up to Waimea Canyon? This roadside eatery is nothing more than a kitchen with a few picnic tables outside, but the shrimp cooking up inside will make up for the lack of ambience. The shrimp is prepared a variety of ways, from shrimp taco to a shrimp burger, but the star attraction is their shrimp plates (choice of garlic, Cajun, Thai, or sweet chile garlic shrimp). If you order takeout, make sure you have plenty of napkins to clean up with after munching these tasty but messy dishes. (They offer a sink with soap for those who eat in.)

9652 Kaumualii Hwy., Waimea. ✆ **808/338-1242.** Shrimp platters $11–$12. MC, V. Daily 11am–5pm.

Toi's Thai Kitchen THAI/AMERICAN A west Kauai staple, Toi's has gained a following for its affordable, authentic Thai food and a casual atmosphere. Tucked into a corner of a small shopping complex (look for the McDonald's on the highway), Toi's serves savory dishes made with fresh herbs and local ingredients, many of them from the owner's garden. Popular items include the house specialty, Toi's Temptation (homegrown herbs, coconut milk, lemon grass, and your choice of seafood, meat, or tofu); vegetable curries; shrimp satay; and ginger-sauce nua (your choice of seafood, meat, or tofu in a fresh ginger stir-fry). Most of the rice, noodle, soup, curry, and main-course selections allow you to choose from pork, chicken, seafood, beef, or vegetarian options. Buttered garlic nua, peanut-rich satays, and stir-fried Basil Delight are among Toi's many tasty preparations. Lunch dishes come with green-papaya salad and a choice of jasmine, sticky, or brown rice; at dinner, they add dessert.

In the Eleele Shopping Center, Eleele. ✆ **808/335-3111.** Main courses $11–$19. AE, MC, V. Tues–Sat 10:30am–2pm and 5:30–9pm.

Wong's Restaurant CHINESE/JAPANESE/DELI/BAKERY "Eat at Wong's, you can't go Wrong," proclaims the menu of this longtime island institution. Wong's has all the bases covered for lunch and dinner: They feature both Japanese and Chinese dishes and have one of the best delis and bakeries (Omoide's Deli and Bakery—great for picking up picnic fixings and sandwiches for the beach). Wong's also has one of the world's best homemade lilikoi (passion fruit) chiffon pies—it's worth the drive just to sample this piece of heaven. Wong's is not known for its ambience; in fact, it looks like a typical Chinese restaurant—one big giant cafeteria-size room. If you go at the wrong time, you'll find it packed with tour-bus crowds. But the portions are huge, the prices right, and the service smiling. No sit down service; counter service and take-out only.

1-3543 Kaumualii Hwy., Hanapepe. ✆ **808/335-5066.** Most items under $10. MC, V. Tues–Sun 9:30am–8:45pm.

4 THE COCONUT COAST

EXPENSIVE

The Bull Shed STEAK/SEAFOOD The informality and oceanfront location are big pluses, but Kauai regulars also tout the steaks and chops—prime rib, Australian rack of lamb, garlic tenderloin—and the fresh catch. The seafood selection includes broiled shrimp, Alaskan king crab, and Parmesan-drenched scallops. Dinner orders include rice and the salad bar. Combination dinners target the ambivalent, with chicken, steak, seafood, and lobster pairings. The salad bar alone is a value, and the entrees are so big they're often shared.

796 Kuhio Hwy., Waipouli. ✆ **808/822-3791.** www.bullshedrestaurant.com. Reservations recommended for parties of 6 or more. Main courses $16–$22 (many items are market price). AE, DC, DISC, MC, V. Daily 5:30–10pm.

MODERATE

Caffè Coco ★★ BISTRO This gets my vote for the most charming ambience on Kauai, with gourmet fare cooked to order, at cafe prices. Food gets a lot of individual attention here. Caffè Coco appears just off the main road at the edge of a cane field in Wailua, its backyard shaded by pomelo, avocado, mango, tangerine, litchi, and banana trees, with a view of the Sleeping Giant Mountain. The trees provide many of the ingredients for the muffins, chutneys, and salsas that Ginger Carlson whips up in her kitchen. Seats are indoors (beyond the black-light art gallery) or on the gravel-floored back courtyard, where Tiki torches flicker at night. From interior design to cooking, this is clearly a showcase for Carlson's creativity. The food is excellent, with vegetarian and other healthful delights such as homemade chai, Greek salad and fish wraps, seared ahi with wasabi cream, and an excellent tofu-and-roast-veggie wrap. Although the regular menu is limited, there are many impressive specials. Service can be, to say the least, laid-back. There's also live music most nights.

4-369 Kuhio Hwy., Wailua. ✆ **808/822-7990.** www.restauranteur.com/caffecoco. Reservations recommended for parties of 4 or more. Main courses $8.50–$14 lunch, $16–$22 dinner; specials usually under $22. AE, DISC, MC, V. Tues–Fri 11am–5pm; Tue–Sun 5–9pm.

Hukilau Lanai STEAK/SEAFOOD The owners of Gaylord's in Kilohana opened this restaurant in the Kauai Coast Resort featuring local products and produce of Kauai; they promise that the dishes "are made from scratch in our kitchen." The menu offers a wide selection of appetizers, from ahi poke nachos to sweet potato ravioli. Entrees include fresh fish, beef, chicken, and pork dishes. Save room for such desserts as banana and chocolate mousse or warm chocolate cake.

Kauai Coast Resort, Kapaa. ✆ **808/822-0600.** Main courses $18–$28. MC, V. Tues–Sun 5–9pm. Live music Tues, Fri, and Sun 6:30–9:30pm.

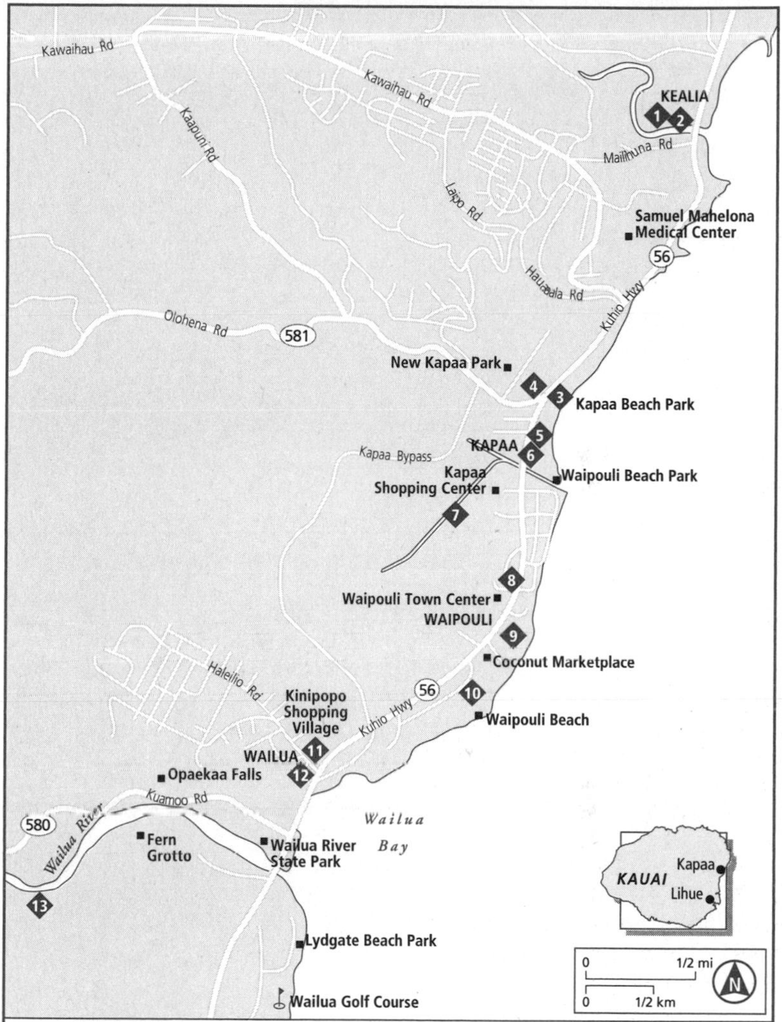

Bubba Burgers **2**
The Bull Shed **9**
Caffè Coco **11**
Hukilau Lanai **10**
The King and I **8**
Kountry Kitchen **1**
Mema **12**
Mermaids Cafe **3**
Norberto's El Cafe **4**
Olympic Café **5**
Ono Family Restaurant **6**
Sukhothai Restaurant **7**
Wailua Marina Restaurant **13**

Vegetarian-Friendly Restaurants

With so much local fresh produce available year-round, Kauai can be a vegetarian's dream. Numerous restaurants cater to vegetarians with several entrees to choose from; in particular, many Asian restaurants offer vegetarian dishes. Below are our veggie-friendly favorites.

LIHUE

Duke's Canoe Club (In the Kauai Marriott Resort & Beach Club, 3610 Rice St., Nawiliwili; ✆ **808/246-9599**). The best deal at this two-story, open-air "happening" eatery is the salad bar, which includes veggies, tofu, and other yummy selections; it's all you can eat for $14.

Gaylord's (At Kilohana, 3–2087 Kaumualii Hwy., Lihue; ✆ **808/245-9593;** www.gaylordskauai.com). Lunch at this elegantly casual restaurant features an array of salads and a divine fettuccini, and for dinner I'd pick the fire-grilled veggies over the fresh pasta.

Kalapaki Beach Hut (3474 Rice St., Nawiliwili; ✆ **808/246-6330**). If you are just looking for a quick breakfast or lunch, this tiny place has waffles for breakfast, veggie burgers for lunch, and lots and lots of salads.

POIPU

The Beach House (5022 Lawai Rd., Poipu; ✆ **808/742-1424**). One of the most romantic places on Kauai, with wraparound views of the Pacific Ocean. Take your sweetheart and dine on pasta or the grilled Portobello mushroom; either sets you back about $20.

Brennecke's Beach Broiler (2100 Hoone Rd., across from Poipu Beach Park; ✆ **808/742-7588;** www.brenneckes.com). Across the street from the Poipu Beach Park, this burger place also features a terrific salad bar, stir-fried veggies, yummy pastas, and veggie burgers, all in the $12 to $32 range.

Casa Blanca at Kiahuna (2290 Poipu Rd., in the Kiahuna Swim and Tennis Club, Poipu; ✆ **808/742-2929**). There are many pastas to choose from at this open-air bistro overlooking the tennis courts, but I'd recommend the vegetarian lasagna (a bargain at $16).

Plantation Gardens Restaurant (In Kiahuna Plantation Resort, 2253 Poipu Rd.; ✆ **808/742-2216**). Dine in a garden on their yummy udon noodles with eggplant, zucchini, and pesto ($19), or you can request a vegetarian stir-fry ($21).

Roy's Poipu Bar & Grill (In Poipu Shopping Village, 2360 Kiahuna Plantation Dr.; ✆ **808/742-5000;** www.roysrestaurant.com). Well-known Hawaii chef, Roy Yamaguchi, has a portobello mushroom dish ($15) that is heavenly. They will

Mema THAI/CHINESE If you're looking for a casual dining experience with something exotic but priced reasonably, this is your place. This family-run restaurant is decorated with a profusion of plants and flowers, and the waitstaff wear traditional Thai costumes. The large menu offers some 50 different appetizers, a range of curries (we recommend the house curry, a Siam-style *panans* curry with lime leaves, lemon grass, and generally feature a couple of vegetarian dishes nightly, or you can request a special vegetarian dish that they will be happy to whip up for you.

Tidepool Restaurant (Grand Hyatt Kauai Resort and Spa, 1571 Poipu Rd., Poipu; ✆ **808/742-1234**). Although this restaurant's specialty is fresh fish, vegetarians can dine in this Polynesian-style thatched bungalow. They generally have vegetarian items on the ever-changing menu. My fave is the teriyaki tofu ($25); it's so yummy, even carnivores order it.

KALAHEO

Kalaheo Coffee Co. & Café (2–2560 Kaumualii Hwy. [Hwy. 50], Kalaheo, across the street from Brick Oven Pizza; ✆ **808/332-5858**). This place is a vegetarian's dream, with many veggie selections for breakfast (veggie tofu), lunch (tofu/eggplant wrap, grilled veggie sandwich, garden burger), and dinner (pasta primavera).

HANAPEPE

Hanapepe Café (3830 Hanapepe Rd., Hanapepe; ✆ **808/335-5011**). This gourmet vegetarian cafe is a feast for non-meat eaters; don't miss their dinners on Friday nights.

COCONUT COAST

Mermaids Café (1384 Kuhio Hwy., Kapaa; ✆ **808/821-2026**). This tiny hole-in-the-wall is loaded with veggie dishes, from the tofu sate plate to the tofu stir-fry to the bean burrito, and prices are very frugal.

KILAUEA

Kilauea Bakery & Pau Hana Pizza (In Kong Lung Center, Kilauea Rd., off Hwy. 56 on the way to the Kilauea Lighthouse, Kilauea; ✆ **808/828-2020**). The vegetarian pizzas here are the best! I'm also partial to their great vegan soups (like the yummy curried carrot soup or the pumpkin soup).

HANALEI

Postcards Cafe (On Kuhio Hwy., at the entrance to Hanalei town; ✆ **808/826-1191**). Vegetarians will love this small, picturesque cafe, with a very veggie-friendly menu. My picks from the changing menu are the sombrero (puff pastry filled with organic cheeses, green chiles, onions, mushrooms, and garlic) or the Shanghai (tofu with veggies and roasted cashews in a tamarind ginger sauce). Save room for the chocolate silk (a chocolate pie in a crust of graham crackers, dried cherries, and crusted cashews)—yum-yum.

coconut milk), and a host of traditional Thai and Chinese specialties. Most of the dishes can be ordered mild, medium, or spicy, with vegetables, tofu, chicken, pork, beef, shrimp, or seafood.

4-369 Kuhio Hwy., Kapaa. ✆ **808/823-0899.** Main Courses $11–$20. MC, V. Mon–Fri 11am–2pm; daily 5–9pm.

Wailua Marina Restaurant AMERICAN This is a strange but charming place, anti-nouvelle to the end. I recommend the open-air seating along the Wailua River to munch on your sandwich (mahimahi is a favorite) and salad. The interior is cavernous, with a high ceiling and stuffed fish adorning the upper walls—bordering on weird, but I love it anyway. The salad bar makes the place friendlier to dieters and vegetarians; otherwise, you'll find the Alaskan king crab legs with filet mignon (or filet paired with lobster tail), stuffed prawns, famous hot lobster salad, steamed mullet, teriyaki spareribs, baked stuffed Island chicken, and some 40 other down-home items heavy on the sauces and gravies. Although the open salad bar is a meal in itself, the more reckless can try the mayo-laden mini–lobster salad appetizer, or the crab-stuffed mushrooms. ***Money-saving tip:*** The early-bird specials (5–6pm) start at $10 for spaghetti dinner and go up to $14 for a mixed plate of shrimp tempura, chicken yakitori, and teriyaki top sirloin.

5971 Kuhio Hwy., Wailua. ✆ **808/822-4311.** Reservations recommended. Lunch $8.75–$27; dinner main courses $16–$45. AE, MC, V. Tues–Sun 10:30am–1:30pm and 5–8pm.

INEXPENSIVE

Bubba Burgers (Kids) AMERICAN At Bubba the burger is king, attitude reigns, and lettuce and tomato cost extra. They dish out humor, great T-shirts, and burgers nonpareil, along with Boca and taro burgers for vegetarians. Grilled fresh-fish sandwiches cater to the sensible, fish and chips to the carefree, and fish burgers to the undecided. But old-fashioned hamburgers are the main attraction. You can order the Slopper (open-faced with chili), the half-pound Big Bubba (three patties), or the Hubba Bubba (with rice, hot dog, and chili—a Bubba's plate lunch), among others. Chicken burgers, Bubba's famous Budweiser chili, and other American standards are also served here. For a burger joint, it's big on fish, too, with a daily trio of fresh-fish specials, fish burgers, and fish and chips.

4-1421 Kuhio Hwy., Kapaa. ✆ **808/823-0069.** All items less than $9. MC, V. Daily 10:30am–9pm.

The King and I THAI This medium-size restaurant, in a small and nondescript roadside complex, serves reasonably priced specials and vegetarian selections, including spring rolls, salads, curries, and stir-fries. The owners grow their own herbs for the menu's savory curries and seasonings. At dinner, the pad thai noodles with shrimp have a special touch and are a popular counterpoint to the red, green, and yellow curries. The vegetarian menu is generous—everything from noodles to spring rolls to curries and eggplant/tofu—but most diners come back for the Evil Jungle Prince: your choice of veggies, chicken, or fish in a sauce of coconut milk, spices, and kaffir-lime leaves.

In Waipouli Plaza, 4-901 Kuhio Hwy., Kapaa. ✆ **808/822-1642.** Reservations recommended. Main courses $10–$14. AE, DC, DISC, MC, V. Daily 4:30–9pm.

Kountry Kitchen AMERICAN Forget counting calories when you sit down to the brawny omelets here. Choose your own fillings from several possibilities, among them kimchi with cream cheese and several vegetable, meat, and cheese combinations. Sandwiches and American dinners (steak, fish, and chicken) are standard coffeehouse fare, but sometimes fresh-fish specials stand out. ***Warning:*** Sit as far away from the grill as possible; the smell of grease travels—and clings to your clothes.

1485 Kuhio Hwy., Kapaa. ✆ **808/822-3511.** Main courses $7.50–$15. MC, V. Daily 6am–1:30pm.

Mermaids Cafe ★ HEALTHFUL/ISLAND STYLE Don't you love these places that use fresh local ingredients, make everything to order, and barely charge anything for all that trouble? A tiny sidewalk cafe with brisk takeout and a handful of tables on Kapaa's main drag, Mermaids takes kaffir lime, lemon grass, local lemons (Meyers when available), and organic herbs, when possible, to make the sauces and beverages to go with its toothsome dishes. Sauces are lively and healthful, such as the peanut satay made with lemon juice instead of fish sauce. It's served in the tofu or chicken satay, chicken coconut curry plate, and chicken satay wrap. The seared ahi wrap is made with the chef's special blend of garlic, jalapeño, lemon grass, kaffir lime, basil, and cilantro, then wrapped in a spinach tortilla—fabulous. The fresh-squeezed lemonade is made daily, and you can choose white or organic brown rice. These special touches elevate the simple classics to dreamy taste sensations. Recently they've added breakfast.

1384 Kuhio Hwy., Kapaa. ✆ **808/821-2026.** Main courses $9–$12. DC, MC, V. Daily 7:30am–8:45pm.

Norberto's El Cafe MEXICAN The lard-free, home-style Mexican fare here includes top-notch chiles rellenos with homemade everything, vegetarian selections by request, and, if you're lucky, fresh-fish enchiladas. All of the sauces are made from scratch, and the salsa comes red-hot with homegrown chile peppers fresh from the chef's garden. Norberto's signature is the spinachy Hawaiian taro-leaf enchiladas, a Mexican version of laulau, served with cheese and taro or with chicken.

4-1373 Kuhio Hwy., Kapaa. ✆ **808/822-3362.** Reservations recommended for parties of 6 or more. Main courses $5.50–$9.45; complete dinners $11–$20. AE, MC, V. Mon–Sat 5–9pm.

Olympic Café AMERICAN It's worth hunting around for this casual second-floor restaurant, which has views of the ocean and historic downtown Kapaa. The breakfasts are huge, lunches filling, and dinners reasonably priced—the Olympic is known for big portions and small prices. Breakfast features a range of espresso drinks, pancakes, omelets, and egg dishes. Lunch includes sandwiches, burgers, salads, and a range of wraps. Dinner includes something for everyone, from burgers to fresh fish and steaks. Stop by for a drink; they have smoothies, juice, Italian sodas, specialty teas, and a menu of specialty coffee drinks.

1354 Kuhio Hwy., Kapaa. ✆ **808/822-5825.** Breakfast under $12; lunch $8–$13; dinner entrees $12–$26. MC, V. Mon–Thurs and Sun 6am–9pm; Fri–Sat 6am–10pm.

Ono Family Restaurant Kids AMERICAN Breakfast is a big deal here, with such dishes as eggs Florentine (two poached eggs, blanched spinach, and hollandaise sauce); eggs Canterbury (much like eggs Benedict, but with more ingredients); and the Garden Patch (a dollop of fried rice topped with fresh steamed vegetables, scrambled eggs, and hollandaise sauce). Steak and eggs; banana, coconut, and macadamia-nut pancakes; and dozens of omelet choices also attract throngs of loyalists. Lunch is no slouch either, with scads of fish, veggie, steak, tuna, and turkey sandwiches to choose from. Ono burgers with various toppings highlight the menu. The gourmet hamburger with fries and soup demands an after-lunch siesta.

1292 Kuhio Hwy., Kapaa. ✆ **808/822-1710.** Most items less than $12. AE, DC, DISC, MC, V. Daily 7am–2pm.

Sukhothai Restaurant THAI/VIETNAMESE/CHINESE Curries, saimin, Chinese soups, satays, Vietnamese pho, and a substantial vegetarian menu are a few of the features of this unobtrusive—but extremely popular—Thai restaurant. Menu items appeal to many tastes and include 85 Vietnamese, Chinese, and Thai choices, along with much-loved curries and the best-selling pad thai noodles. The coconut/lemon grass/kaffir lime soups (eight choices) are the Sukhothai's highlights, along with the red and green curries.

In the Kapaa Shopping Center (next to Kapaa's Big Save Market), 4-1105 Kuhio Hwy., Kapaa. ✆ **808/821-1224.** Main courses $11–$23. AE, DC, DISC, MC, V. Daily 11am–9pm.

EN ROUTE TO THE NORTH SHORE

Duane's Ono-Char Burger Kids HAMBURGER STAND We can't imagine Anahola without this roadside burger stand; it's been serving up hefty, all-beef burgers for generations. (And now they offer Boca burgers for vegetarians.) The teriyaki sauce and blue cheese are only part of the secret of Duane's beefy, smoky, and legendary ono-char burgers served several ways: teriyaki, mushroom, cheddar, barbecue, and the Special, with grilled onions, sprouts, and two cheeses. The broiled fish sandwich (another marvel of the seasoned old grill) and the marionberry ice-cream shake, a three-berry combo, are popular as well.

On Kuhio Hwy., Anahola. ✆ **808/822-9181.** Hamburgers $4.40–$7.25. MC, V. Mon–Sat 10am–6pm; Sun 11am–6pm.

EXPENSIVE

Lighthouse Bistro Kilauea ★ CONTINENTAL/PACIFIC RIM/ITALIAN Even if you're not on your way to the legendary Kilauea Lighthouse, this bistro is so good it's worth a special trip. The charming green-and-white wooden building next to Kong Lung Store has open sides, old-fashioned plantation architecture, open-air seating, trellises, and high ceilings. The ambience is wonderful, with a retro feeling; it's not as polished as Poipu's Plantation Gardens but has its own casual appeal. (I'd describe this as the North Shore version of Casa di Amici in Poipu, p. 138.) The food is excellent, an eclectic selection that highlights local ingredients in everything from fresh-fish tacos and fresh-fish burritos to coconut-crusted pork medallions and three preparations of fresh catch. This is much more elegant than usual lunchtime fare.

In Kong Lung Center, Kilauea Rd. (off Hwy. 56 on the way to the Kilauea Lighthouse), Kilauea. ✆ **808/828-0481.** www.lighthousebistro.com. Reservations recommended for 6 or more. Lunch $5–$14; dinner main courses $19–$34. MC, V. Mon–Sat noon–2pm; daily 5:30–9pm.

MODERATE

Bar Acuda ★★★ TAPAS After launching two successful restaurants in San Francisco (The Slow Club and 42°), chef/owner Jim Moffat up and moved to the tiny town of Hanalei and opened this sleek, romantic restaurant. Candles light the room and exotic mouthwatering aromas waft from the open exhibition kitchen. Bar Acuda specializes in Moffat's favorite tapas dishes from the southern European regions along the 42° latitude (southern France, Italy, Spain, and Portugal). The creative dishes range from onaga en papillote with pineapple, lime, chiles, and vanilla ($27) to lobster- stuffed squid ($14) to a grilled rib-eye steak with shoestring potatoes and salsa verde ($28). There is an excellent wine selection, with some 50 handpicked, estate-bottled wines, mainly from Italy, France, Spain, Oregon, and California (with an emphasis on Rohne-style grapes). Half of the wines are available by the glass.

5-5161 Kuhio Hwy., Hanalei. ✆ **808/826-7081.** www.restaurantbaracuda.com. Tapas $6–$28. MC, V. Tues–Sun 6–9pm.

Bouchons Restaurant and Sushi Bar Hanalei ★ SUSHI/PACIFIC RIM This second-floor oasis has copper tables and a copper topped bar, large picture windows for gazing at the Hanalei waterfalls, and, most importantly, chefs who know their sushi. Traditional sushi, fusion sushi, and hot Pacific American fusion dishes for those who

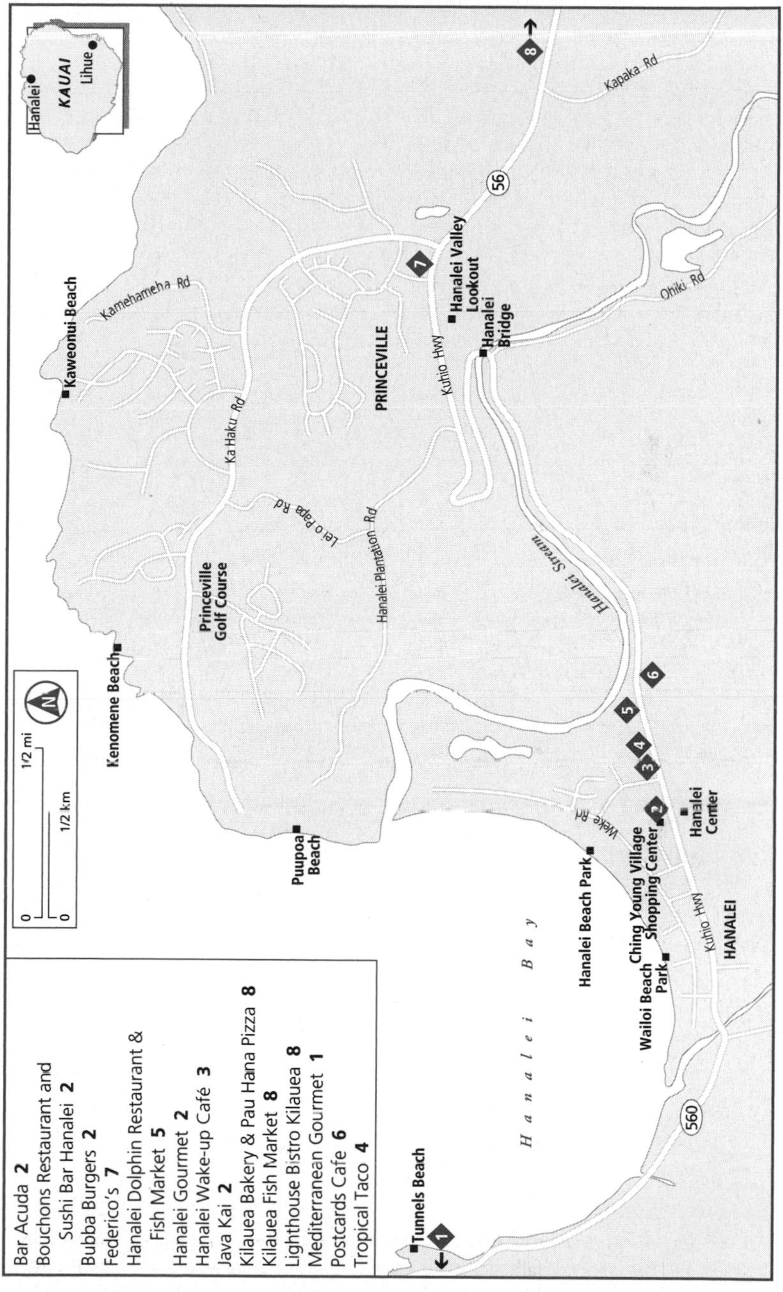
Bar Acuda 2
Bouchons Restaurant and Sushi Bar Hanalei 2
Bubba Burgers 2
Federico's 7
Hanalei Dolphin Restaurant & Fish Market 5
Hanalei Gourmet 2
Hanalei Wake-up Café 3
Java Kai 2
Kilauea Bakery & Pau Hana Pizza 8
Kilauea Fish Market 8
Lighthouse Bistro Kilauea 8
Mediterranean Gourmet 1
Postcards Cafe 6
Tropical Taco 4
0 1/2 mi
0 1/2 km
Hanalei
KAUAI
Lihue
Kaweonui Beach
Kamehameha Rd
Ka Haku Rd
PRINCEVILLE
Hanalei Valley Lookout
Hanalei Bridge
Kuhio Hwy
56
Kapaka Rd
Ohiki Rd
Lei o Papa Rd
Hanalei Plantation Rd
Princeville Golf Course
Hanalei Stream
Kenomene Beach
Puupoa Beach
Weke Rd
Hanalei Beach Park
Ching Young Village Shopping Center
Hanalei Center
Wailoi Beach Park
HANALEI
Hanalei Bay
560
Tunnels Beach

A Hawaiian Feast: The Luau

Originally, an ancient Hawaiian feast was called a *pa'ina* or *'aha'aina,* but in 1856, the *Pacific Commercial Advertiser* (the newspaper of the day) started referring to the feast as a "luau," a name referring to the young taro tops always served at the feast. Try to take in a luau while you're on Kauai. A luau today can range from a backyard affair to a commercial production at a major resort. The best ones are put on by local churches, schools, or hula *halau.* However, most visitors won't have the opportunity to see these truly authentic feasts. Several commercial luau listed below will provide a taste and a feel for them.

Most luau are fixed in price, generally $78 to $99 for adults, less for children. A variety of traditional foods and entertainment is provided. The luau usually begins at sunset and features Polynesian and Hawaiian entertainment, which can range from lavish affairs with flaming knives or torches being juggled, to performances of ancient hula, missionary-era hula, and modern hula, as well as narration of the stories and legends portrayed by the dances. The food always includes imu-roasted kalua pig, lomi salmon, dried fish, poke (raw fish cut into small pieces), poi (made from taro), laulau (meat, fish, and vegetables wrapped in ti leaves), Hawaiian sweet potato, sautéed vegetables, salad, and the ultimate taste treat, a coconut dessert called haupia. Don't worry; if you've never heard of these items (and can't pronounce them either), most luau will also have more common preparations of fish, chicken, and roast beef, as well as easily recognizable salads and standard desserts like cake.

The mainstay of the feast is the imu, a hot earthen pit in which the pig and other items are cooked. The preparations for the feast actually begin in the morning, when the luau master layers hot stones and banana stalks in the pit to get the temperature up to 400°F (204°C). The pig, vegetables, and other items are lowered into the pit and cooked all day. The water in the leaves steams the pig and roasts the meat to a tender texture.

One of the larger commercial luau in the island is **Smith's Tropical Paradise Garden Lu'au,** in the Tropical Paradise Gardens on the Wailua River (✆ **808/821-6895** or 808/821-6896; www.smithskauai.com), every Monday, Wednesday, and

aren't sushi lovers please diners of every stripe. Big hits: the Hanalei, with tempura shrimp, spicy Ebi, avocado, and masago; the Vegas roll, a heroic composition of ahi, hamachi, and avocado, dipped in tempura batter and quickly fried so it's hot on the outside and chilled on the inside; the Rainbow Roll, a super-duper California roll with eight different types of fish; and fresh fish prepared several ways, in fusion flavorings involving mango, garlic, sake, sesame, coconut, passion fruit, and other Pacific Rim ingredients as well as steaks, chicken, and sandwiches. The lunch menu features burgers, salads, sandwiches, and fish tacos. The action fires up Thursday, Friday, Saturday, and Sunday from 7:30pm on, with live music ranging from Hawaiian to blues to jazz to rock 'n' roll.

In Ching Young Village, Hanalei. ✆ **808/826-9701.** www.bouchonshanalei.com. Reservations recommended for parties of 6 or more. Main courses $10–$17 lunch; $10–$30 dinner; sushi rolls $7 and up. MC, V. Daily 11:30am–9:30pm. Live music from 7:30pm on.

Friday at 5pm (during the popular summer months it is 5 days a week Mon–Fri). Luau prices are $78 for adults, $30 for children 7 to 13, and $19 for children 3 to 6; or you can come for just the entertainment at 7:15pm and pay $15 for adults, $7.50 for children under 12.

Recently the **Sheraton Kauai,** Poipu Beach (✆ **808/742-8200;** www.sheraton kauai.com), launched the south shore's only oceanfront luau. The Surf to Sunset Luau is held on Friday, beginning at 5pm with a shell lei greeting and a mai tai. Photos with Poipu Beach serving as the background are offered, and guests can wander among the local artisans who teach lei making, *lauhala* weaving, and coconut frond weaving. After the feast, Pilah's Royal Polynesian Revue begins the entertainment. Cost for adults ranges from $75 for the buffet dinner and entertainment to $99 for premier seating, table service, and professional photos. Cost for children ages 6 to 12 years is $37 to $49.

The luau **Kalamaku,** Kilohana (✆ **808/245-9593;** Tues and Fri) begins at 5:30pm with an imu ceremony where the pig is removed from the pit, followed by a very entertaining performance of the story of how Polynesians came to Hawaii featuring ancient and modern hula performances. The cost is $95 for adults, $65 for teenagers 12 to 18, $45 for children 3 to 12, and free for children 2 and under. The train ride with the luau is an additional $18.

On the south coast, check out **Tihati Production's "Havaiki Nui,"** in the Grand Hyatt Kauai Resort and Spa, 1571 Poipu Rd., Poipu (✆ **800/55-HYATT** or 808/742-1234; www.kauai-hyatt.com), every Sunday and Thursday. They offer an elaborate buffet and a very professional Polynesian show. The cost is $94 for adults, $84 for teens 13 to 20, and $57 for children 6 to 12.

On the North Shore, award-winning Mediterranean Gourmet Restaurant in the Hanalei Colony Resort has the **Ocean Front Luau** (5-7132 Kuhio Hwy, Haena, ✆ **808/826-9875**) with excellent cuisine and wonderful entertainment at very reasonable prices of $69 for adults, $56 for teenagers ages 12 to 17, and $25 for kids ages 3 to 11 (free for children under 3).

Hanalei Dolphin Restaurant & Fish Market SEAFOOD Hidden behind a gallery called Ola's are this fish market and adjoining steak-and-seafood restaurant, on the banks of the Hanalei River. Food is good, but service sometimes can be slow. Particularly inviting are the fresh fish sandwiches, served under umbrellas at river's edge. Most appealing (besides the river view) are the appetizers: artichokes steamed or stuffed with garlic, butter, and cheese; buttery stuffed mushrooms; and seviche fresh from the fish market, with a jaunty dash of green olives. From fresh catch to baked shrimp to Alaskan king crab and chicken marinated in soy sauce, the Dolphin has stayed with the tried-and-true.

5-5016 Kuhio Hwy., Hanalei. ✆ **808/826-6113.** http://www.hanaleidolphin.com. Main courses $18–$36. AE, MC, V. Daily 10:30am–10pm. (Fish market daily 10am–7pm in the winter and until 8pm in the summer.)

Hanalei Gourmet AMERICAN The wood floors, wooden benches, and blackboards of the old Hanalei School, built in 1926, furnish this haven for today's Hanalei hipsters noshing on the Tu Tu Tuna (far-from-prosaic tuna salad with green beans, potatoes, niçoise olives, and hard-boiled eggs); fresh-fish sandwiches; roasted eggplant sandwiches; chicken-salad boats (in papaya or avocado, with macadamia nuts and sans mayonnaise); and other selections. This is an informal cross-cultural tasting, from stir-fried veggies over udon to Oriental ahi-pasta salad to warm artichoke and cheese dip. Big Tim's burger is, unsurprisingly, big, and the sandwiches served on fresh-baked bread represent timeless deli faves, from roast beef and pastrami to smoked turkey and chicken salad. The TV over the bar competes with the breathtaking view of the Hanalei mountains and waterfalls, and the wooden floors keep the noise level high. (The music on the sound system can be almost deafening.) Nightly live music adds to the fun.

In the Old Hanalei Schoolhouse, 5-5161 Kuhio Hwy., Hanalei. ✆ **808/826-2524.** www.hanaleigourmet.com. Main courses $7.50–$27. DC, DISC, MC, V. Daily 8am–10:30pm.

Kilauea Bakery & Pau Hana Pizza ★ PIZZA/BAKERY When owner, baker, and avid diver Tom Pickett spears an ono and smokes it himself, his catch appears on the Billie Holiday pizza, guaranteed to obliterate the blues with its brilliant notes of Swiss chard, roasted onions, Gorgonzola-rosemary sauce, and mozzarella. And the much-loved bakery puts out guava sourdough, coconut cream-filled chocolate éclairs (yum!), blackberry–white chocolate scones, and other fine baked goods. The breads go well with the soups and hot lunch specials, and the pastries with the new full-service espresso bar, which serves not only the best of the bean, but also blended frozen drinks and such up-to-the-minute beverages as iced chai and Mexican chocolate smoothies (with cinnamon). We also love the breakfast Stromboli with eggs, potatoes, and cheese, and the scampi pizza with tiger prawns, roasted garlic, capers, and cheeses. Their latest menu additions are homemade soups, to the tune of four different homemade soups per day, like coconut Thai curry vegetable and rich, cream of porcini mushroom). The Picketts have added a small dining room, a covered area in the courtyard, and the few outdoor picnic tables under umbrellas are as inviting as ever. The macadamia-nut butter cookies and lilikoi-fruit Danishes are sublime.

In Kong Lung Center, Kilauea Rd. (off Hwy. 56 on the way to the Kilauea Lighthouse), Kilauea. ✆ **808/828-2020.** Pizzas $11–$30; sandwiches under $8. MC, V. Daily 6am–9pm.

Mediterranean Gourmet ★★ Finds MIDDLE EASTERN This "hidden" restaurant, located next door to the Hanalei Colony Resort, nearly at the end of the road, was awarded "Best New Restaurant" on Kauai by a local magazine and it is very deserving of the distinction. The oceanfront location is the perfect backdrop for chef/owner Imad Beydoun's Middle Eastern dishes, which he embellishes with an island twist. He married a local Hanalei girl, Yarrow, and the two of them (plus their kids) roll out the best Mediterranean food you will find in Hawaii. People on Kauai have been eating Beydoun's cooking through his packaged products (hummus, baba ghanouj, falafels, and tabbouleh) sold at the local farmer's market. When his family opened the restaurant, they already had a following. The menu has traditional Middle Eastern cuisine (stuffed grape leaves, hand-rolled fatayer, hummus, grilled kafta, Greek salads, and various kabobs) as well as more familiar dishes like chicken quesadillas, rack of lamb, New York strip steak, and fresh fish. Do not leave until you have had Chef Beydoun's homemade baklava and a cup of Turkish coffee. Go on Thursday to catch a belly dancing performance. There's live music Monday through Wednesday, Friday, and Saturday at 6:30pm, and a luau on Tuesday nights at 6pm.

Hanalei Bay Colony Resort, 5-7132 Kuhio Hwy., Hanalei. ✆ **808/826-9875.** Lunch entrees $11–$22; dinner entrees $30–$40. MC, V. Mon–Sat 11am–9pm, Sun 11am–3pm.

Postcards Cafe ★★ GOURMET SEAFOOD/NATURAL FOODS The charming plantation-style building that used to be the Hanalei Museum is now Hanalei's gourmet central. Postcards is known for its use of healthful ingredients, fresh from the island and creatively prepared and presented. It's dinner only at this quaint eatery but a memorable experience. My picks from the changing menu are the wasabi-crusted ahi or the sombrero (puff pastry filled with organic cheeses, green chiles, onions, mushrooms, and garlic) or the Shanghai (tofu with veggies and roasted cashews in a tamarind ginger sauce). Save room for the chocolate silk (a chocolate pie in a crust of graham crackers, dried cherries, and crusted cashews)—yum-yum. In the front yard, an immense, mossy, hollowed-out stone serves as a freestanding lily pond and roadside landmark. Great menu, presentation, and ambience—a winner.

On Kuhio Hwy. (at the entrance to Hanalei town). ✆ **808/826-1191.** Reservations highly recommended for dinner. Main courses $15–$28. AE, DC, DISC, MC, V. Daily 6–9pm.

INEXPENSIVE

Bubba Burgers (Kids) AMERICAN Green picnic tables and umbrellas thatched with coconut leaves stand out against the yellow walls of Bubba's, the burger joint with attitude. The burgers are as flamboyant as the exterior. This North Shore version of the Kapaa fixture (p. 152) has the same menu, same ownership, and same high-quality, all-beef burgers that have made the original such a smashing success.

In Hanalei Center (on the town's main road), Hanalei. ✆ **808/826-7839.** All items less than $9. MC, V. Daily 10:30am–8pm.

Federico's MEXICAN Tucked inside the Food Court at the Princeville Shopping Center is this small cantina featuring natural chicken (no hormones or preservatives), beef (raised in New Zealand), and locally grown, organic avocados and tomatoes. Keeping with the health-conscious theme, they only use trans fat–free cooking oils. There are a few tables, but I recommend ordering a burrito, tostada, or taco and taking your picnic lunch to the beach. Reasonable prices and healthy cuisine.

Princeville Shopping Center, 5-4280 Kuhio Highway, Princeville. ✆ **808/826-7177.** All items under $10. DISC, MC, V. Mon-Sat 10:30am–8pm.

Hanalei Wake-up Café (Finds) BREAKFAST This is where the surfers go to get fueled up for a day on the waves. In fact, breakfast—make that a big, huge, monstrous breakfast—is all they serve in this tiny eatery that truly defines "hole in the wall." Not a lot of atmosphere, not a lot of tables, but cowabunga, dude! The portions are big, the prices small, and the staff surprisingly cheery for 6:30am.

5144 Kuhio Hwy. (at Aku Rd.). ✆ **808/826-5551.** Most items less than $10. No credit cards. Daily 6:30–11am.

Java Kai COFFEEHOUSE Come to this Hanalei Center coffeehouse for a yummy breakfast (I recommend the waffles) or a great lunch (my favorite is the quiche). Of course they also have a great selection of coffee grown in Hawaii and some bakery items.

55183-C Kuhio Hwy., Hanalei. ✆ **808/826-6717.** Most items under $9. MC, V. Daily 6:30am–6pm.

Kilauea Fish Market ★ PLATE LUNCH This is the perfect place to get a picnic takeout lunch or an easy dinner to take back to your condo and eat while you watch the sunset. Coriena Rogers not only has healthy, yummy meals made with just-caught fish, but she also has a deli section with fresh fish for those looking to cook it themselves. Located just off the road to the Kilauea Lighthouse, this tiny hole in the wall has a few tables outside in a garden setting, but generally people pick up and go. Vegetarians will be happy with the daily specials. She has options of brown or white rice and insists on using organic greens in her salads. These are some of the best prices on the North Shore.

4270 Kilauea Lighthouse Rd., Kilauea. ✆ **808/828-6244.** Most items under $15. MC, V. Mon–Sat 11am–8pm.

Tropical Taco ★ Kids MEXICAN For more than a quarter of a century Roger Kennedy has been making tacos and burritos in Hanalei. For years, you could find him working out of his green "taco wagon" parked along the road. But recently Roger has come up in the world; he now has a permanent restaurant (with wood floors and seating along the outside lanai, where you can people-watch) in the Hale Lea Building. He's still serving his tasty assortment of tacos and burritos, plus his signature "fat Jack" (a 10-inch deep-fried tortilla with cheese, beans, and beef or fish). Roger does warn everyone about his tasty treats: "Not to be consumed 1 hour before surfing!" Just as he did with his taco wagon, Roger still offers "anything you want to drink, as long as it's lemonade."

Hale Lea Building, 5-5088 Kuhio Hwy., Hanalei. ✆ **808/827-TACO.** www.tropicaltaco.com. Most items under $9. No credit cards. Mon–Sat 11am–8pm.

7

Fun in the Surf & Sun

This is the part of your vacation you've dreamed about—the sun, the sand, and the surf. In this chapter we'll tell you about the best beaches on Kauai, from where to soak up the rays to where to plunge beneath the waves for a fish-eye-view of the underwater world. Plus, we've scoured the island to find the best ocean activities on the Garden Isle. We'll tell you our favorites and give you a list of the best marine outfitters. Also in this chapter is a range of activities to do on dry land, from hiking and camping to the best golfing on the island.

1 BEACHES

Eons of wind and rain have created this geological masterpiece of an island, with its fabulous beaches. In fact, Kauai, the oldest of the major Hawaiian Islands, has more sand beaches per mile of shoreline than any of the other seven islands. Gorgeous white-sand beaches make up about 50 miles of Kauai's 113 miles of shoreline. That works out to some 44% of the shoreline, far greater than the shoreline percentage of any other island. (Oahu has only half that amount.)

The most popular beaches are on the island's north and south coasts. They can be crowded, especially on weekends. But there are plenty of beaches, white sand, and surf for everyone. Be sure to read "Safety in the Surf" (p. 165) to learn how to avoid potential dangers in Kauai's ocean environment.

Hawaii's beaches belong to the people. All beaches (even those in front of exclusive resorts) are public property, and you are welcome to visit them. Hawaii state law requires that all resorts and hotels offer public right-of-way access (across their private property) to the beach, along with public parking. So just because a beach fronts a hotel doesn't mean that you can't enjoy the water. It does mean that the hotel may restrict certain areas on private property for hotel guests' use only. Generally, hotels welcome nonguests to their facilities. They frown on nonguests using the beach chairs reserved for guests, but if a nonguest has money and wants to rent gear, buy a drink, or eat a sandwich, well, money is money, and they will gladly accept it from anyone. However, that does not mean that you can willy-nilly cross private property to get to a beach. Look for BEACH ACCESS signs; don't trespass.

Note: Despite what you may have heard, nudity is against the law in Hawaii. You can be prosecuted. (Yes, the police do arrest people for being bare on the beach.)

LIHUE

Kalapaki Beach ★

Any town would pay a fortune to have a beach like Kalapaki, one of Kauai's best, in its backyard. But little Lihue turns its back on Kalapaki; there's not even a sign pointing the way through the labyrinth of traffic to this graceful half moon of golden sand at the foot of the Marriott Resort & Beach Club. Fifty yards wide and a quarter mile long, Kalapaki is protected by a jetty, making it very safe for swimmers. The waves are good for surfing when there's a winter swell, and the view from the sand—of the 2,200-foot peaks of the majestic Haupu Ridge that shield Nawiliwili Bay—is awesome. Kalapaki is the best beach not only in Lihue but also on the entire east coast. During certain times of the year there are strong currents and dangerous shorebreaks. From Lihue Airport, turn left onto Kapule Highway (Hwy. 51) to Rice Street; turn left and go to the entrance of the Marriott; pass the hotel's porte-cochere and turn right at the SHORELINE ACCESS sign. Facilities include free parking, restrooms, and showers; food and drink are available nearby at Kalapaki Beach Hut (p. 137). There is no lifeguard.

Ninini Beach

If you are looking for a good snorkeling/swimming beach off the beaten track, this small beach, consisting of two sandy coves separated by lava, is a great place to get away from the crowds. Some local residents call this Running Waters Beach due to the former irrigation runoff when sugar was in production here. Located at the northern end of Nawiliwili Harbor and hidden behind some cliffs, this beach is generally protected from the wind and currents. However, high surf can kick up, and southern storms can charge in suddenly. The small northern sandy cove has good snorkeling and swimming most of the year. Follow the trail down from the dirt road to the beach. Occasionally a few nudists show up here, but remember—nudity is against the law in Hawaii and you can be prosecuted for lewd and lascivious behavior. We prefer the larger beach because of the gentle sandy slope (great for sunbathing) and because the sandy bottom makes for great snorkeling. When the surf does roll in here, the bodysurfers will be in the water. To get here, take Ahukini Road toward the airport; when the road appears to end, veer left (still on Ahukini Rd.) and head for the ocean. When the road meets the ocean, turn right on the dirt road that circumnavigates the airport with the ocean on your left. Travel about 2½ miles on this dirt road to the Nawiliwili Lighthouse. Look for the two trails down to the ocean. Ninini Beach has no facilities and no lifeguard.

Niumalu Beach Park

This is a great place at which to stop in the middle of the day for a picnic. It's located close to Lihue; you can pick up lunch and wander down to this 3-acre quiet area, which has campgrounds. Bordered by Nawiliwili Harbor on one end and the small boat ramp on the other, Niumalu sits next to a very profound archaeological area—the Menehune Fishpond. The pond (also called Alekoko) on the Huleia River was an aquaculture feat built hundreds of years ago. The builders of this 2,700-foot-long stone wall (that cuts off a bend in the river) were believed to be the mythical people who inhabited Kauai before the Polynesians came here (see "Discovering the Legendary 'Little People'" on p. 201). The fishpond is located in the Huleia National Wildlife Refuge, 238 acres of river valley that is a habitat for endangered Hawaiian water birds (ae'o, or Hawaiian stilt; 'alae Ke'oke'o, or Hawaiian coot; 'alae 'ula, or Hawaiian gallinule; and Koloa maoli, or Hawaiian duck). Although you can see the fishpond and the refuge from the road, the area is not open to the public. Various small boats, kayaks, jet skis, windsurfers, and water-skiers use the river. You can spend the day watching them ply their crafts up and down. From Lihue, take Rice Street to Nawiliwili Harbor. Turn left on Niumalu Road and follow it to the beach park. The beach does not have a lifeguard, but it does have picnic tables, showers, and restrooms.

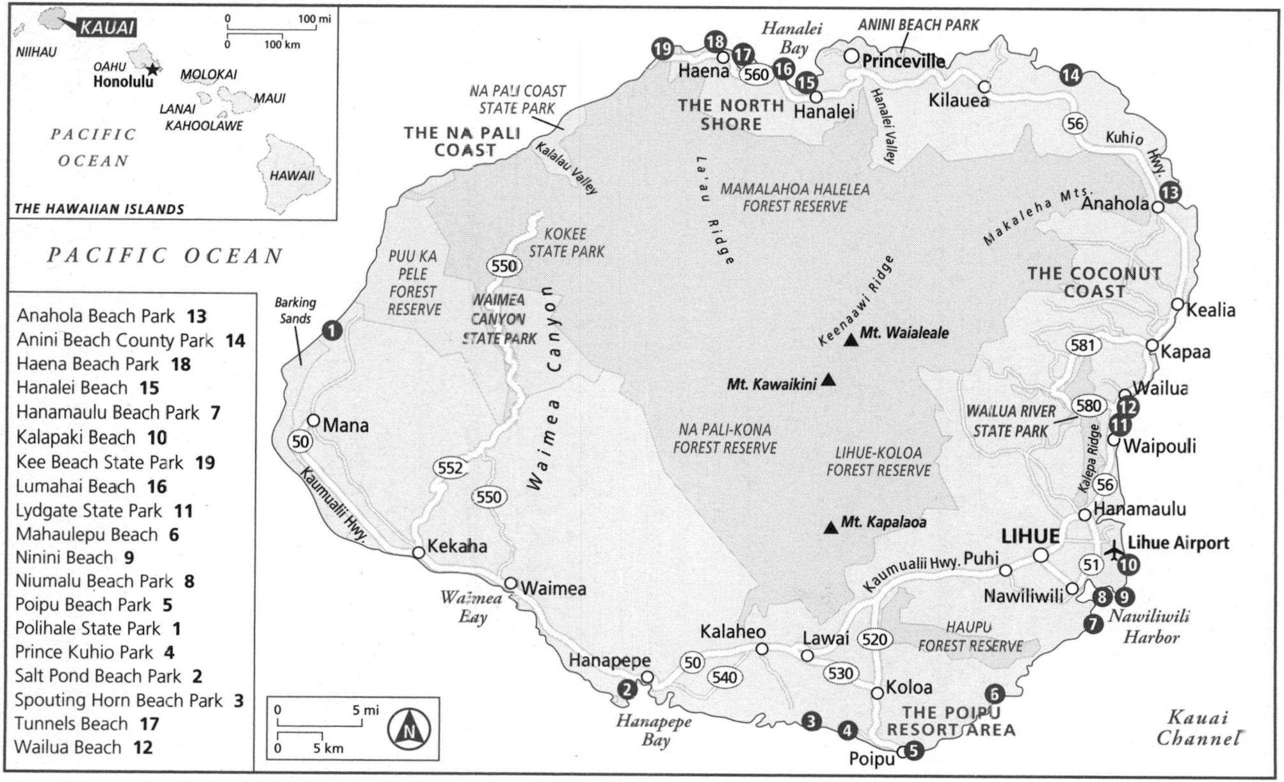
THE HAWAIIAN ISLANDS
KAUAI
NIIHAU
OAHU
Honolulu
MOLOKAI
MAUI
LANAI
KAHOOLAWE
HAWAII
PACIFIC OCEAN
0 100 mi
0 100 km
PACIFIC OCEAN
Anahola Beach Park 13
Anini Beach County Park 14
Haena Beach Park 18
Hanalei Beach 15
Hanamaulu Beach Park 7
Kalapaki Beach 10
Kee Beach State Park 19
Lumahai Beach 16
Lydgate State Park 11
Mahaulepu Beach 6
Ninini Beach 9
Niumalu Beach Park 8
Poipu Beach Park 5
Polihale State Park 1
Prince Kuhio Park 4
Salt Pond Beach Park 2
Spouting Horn Beach Park 3
Tunnels Beach 17
Wailua Beach 12
Barking Sands
Mana
Kaumualii Hwy.
Kekaha
Waimea
Waimea Bay
Hanapepe
Hanapepe Bay
Kalaheo
Lawai
Koloa
Poipu
THE POIPU RESORT AREA
HAUPU FOREST RESERVE
Nawiliwili
Nawiliwili Harbor
Kauai Channel
Puhi
LIHUE
Lihue Airport
Hanamaulu
Kalepa Ridge
Waipouli
Wailua
WAILUA RIVER STATE PARK
Kapaa
Kealia
THE COCONUT COAST
Anahola
Makaleha Mts.
Kuhio Hwy.
Kilauea
Princeville
ANINI BEACH PARK
Hanalei Bay
Hanalei
Hanalei Valley
Haena
THE NORTH SHORE
NA PALI COAST STATE PARK
THE NA PALI COAST
Kalalau Valley
La'au Ridge
MAMALAHOA HALELEA FOREST RESERVE
KOKEE STATE PARK
PUU KA PELE FOREST RESERVE
WAIMEA CANYON STATE PARK
Waimea Canyon
Keenaawi Ridge
Mt. Waialeale
Mt. Kawaikini
Mt. Kapalaoa
NA PALI-KONA FOREST RESERVE
LIHUE-KOLOA FOREST RESERVE
0 5 mi
0 5 km
N

Hawaiian Monk Seals & Turtles: Look, but Don't Get Too Close

If you are lucky, you will get to see one of Hawaii's rare Hawaiian monk seals or endangered Hawaii green sea turtles when they lumber up on a sunny beach. One of the most endangered species on Earth, about 25 seals *(Monachus schauinslandi)* call Kauai home. These 400- to 600-pound seals (stretching out 4–6 ft.) are protected by very strict laws, and it is illegal to get closer than 100 feet from them (or a turtle for that matter). It's understandably exciting when you spot a seal (or turtle), and you'll want to rush up and get a photo. Remember to stay back 100 feet, and do not use your flash when photographing. Be sure to instruct your children to stay back and not throw anything at the seals or turtles. The endangered-species laws are strictly enforced on Kauai, and the fines are very steep. For more information, go to www.kauaimonkseal.com.

Hanamaulu Beach Park

This large bay is not only close to Lihue but is protected from the open ocean. It's a great place to have a picnic. However, it's not a good swimming beach due to the dirt (mainly silt) in the water entering the bay from Hanamaulu stream. The waters outside the bay are cleaner. This area is very popular with scuba divers and with fishermen, who flock here when akule and other migratory fish are schooling in the bay. Camping is allowed in this 6½-acre park; see "Hiking & Camping" (p. 177) for details. From Lihue, take the Kapule Highway (Hwy. 51) north, and turn right on Hehi Road to the beach park. Hanamaulu has no lifeguard, but it does have free parking, restrooms, showers, and a pavilion.

THE POIPU RESORT AREA

Mahaulepu Beach ★★

Mahaulepu is the best-looking unspoiled beach in Kauai and possibly in the whole state. Its 2 miles of reddish-gold, grainy sand line the southeastern shore at the foot of 1,500-foot-high Haupu Ridge, just beyond the Grand Hyatt Kauai Resort & Spa and the McBryde sugar cane fields, which end in sand dunes and a forest of casuarina trees. Almost untouched by modern life, Mahaulepu is a great escape from the real world. It's ideal for beachcombing and shell hunting, but swimming can be risky, except in the reef-sheltered shallows 200 yards west of the sandy parking lot. There's no lifeguard, no facilities—just great natural beauty everywhere you look. (This beach is where George C. Scott portrayed Ernest Hemingway in the movie *Islands in the Stream.*) While you're here, see if you can find the Hawaiian petroglyph of a voyaging canoe carved in the beach rock.

To get here, drive past the Grand Hyatt Kauai Resort & Spa 3 miles east on a red-dirt road, passing the golf course and stables. Turn right at the T-intersection; go 1 mile to the big sand dune, turn left, and drive a half mile to a small lot under the trees.

Poipu Beach Park ★

Big, wide Poipu is actually two beaches in one; it's divided by a sandbar, called a tombolo. On the left, a lava-rock jetty protects a sandy-bottomed pool that's perfect for children; on the right, the open bay attracts swimmers, snorkelers, and surfers. And everyone likes to picnic on the grassy lawn graced by coconut trees. You'll find excellent swimming,

Safety in the Surf

Before you even think about packing your bathing suit, get a copy of the free brochures ***Kauai Beach Guide*** and ***Tips for a Safe Vacation.*** It could save your life. These color brochures explain how to avoid potential dangers in Kauai's ocean environment. The power of the ocean is nothing to fool around with. The surf can increase in size in a short period of time, or an offshore rip current can carry you out to sea. Even a walk alone on the beach without paying attention to the ocean can have potentially dangerous results (like being swept out to sea).

The number-one advice is to swim at beaches where there are lifeguards and to talk to the lifeguards before entering the ocean. The Kauai Beach Guide lists all beaches on Kauai and whether a lifeguard is on duty. It also lists each beach's potential hazards, like strong currents, dangerous shorebreaks, high surf conditions, slippery rocks, sharp coral, sudden drop-offs, and waves on ledges.

In general, the north and west shores are hazardous in winter (Sept–May), with big surf. In summer, the opposite is true, and the big waves occur along the south and east shores. But hazardous conditions can occur on any beach at any time of the year. The brochure stresses the following points:

- **Swim in lifeguard areas** and check with lifeguards on ocean conditions before you go into the water.
- **Watch the ocean at least 20 minutes** before you go in. Lifeguards can show you what potential hazards to look for.
- **Always (always, always, always) swim (or snorkel) with a buddy.**
- **Always keep a close watch over young children.**

You can get these free brochures by contacting the **Kauai Visitors Bureau,** 4334 Rice St., Suite 101, Lihue, HI 96766 (© **808/245-3971**). You'll also find plenty of beach and safety tips at www.kauaiexplorer.com.

small tide pools for exploring, great reefs for snorkeling and diving, good fishing, nice waves for surfers, and a steady wind for windsurfers. Poipu attracts a daily crowd, but the density seldom approaches Waikiki levels except on holidays. Facilities include a lifeguard, restrooms, showers, picnic areas, and free parking in the red-dirt lot. Plus, Brennecke's Beach Broiler (p. 141) is nearby. To get here, turn onto Poipu Beach Road, then turn right at Hoowili Road.

Prince Kuhio Park

This tiny park, across the street from Ho'ai Bay, marks the birthplace of Prince Jonah Kuhio Kalanianaole, who was born March 26 (a state holiday), 1871. Kuhio's mother died shortly after his birth; he was adopted by his mother's sister, Kapiolani, and her husband, Kalakaua. When Kalakaua became king in 1874, Kuhio became prince. However, he did not become king because his aunt, Liliuokalani, ascended to the throne upon Kalakaua's death. In 1893, her reign was overthrown by the U.S. government. However, in 1902 Kuhio was elected as Hawaii's delegate (nonvoting member) to Congress, where

Frommer's Favorite Kauai Experiences

Snorkeling Kee Beach. Rent a mask, fins, and snorkel and enter a magical underwater world. Facedown, you'll float like a leaf on a pond, watching brilliant fish dart here and there in water clear as day; a slow-moving turtle may even stop to check you out. Faceup, you'll contemplate green-velvet cathedral-like cliffs under a blue sky, where long-tailed tropical birds ride the trade winds. See p. 171.

Hiking Waimea Canyon, the Grand Canyon of the Pacific. Ansel Adams would have loved this ageless desert canyon, carved by an ancient river. Sunlight plays against its rustic red cliffs, burnt-orange pinnacles, and blue-green valleys. There's nothing else like it in the islands. See p. 182.

Wandering Around a High Mountain Forest. Kokee State Park, through Waimea Canyon at the end of Highway 550, is a combination rainforest and bog up around 4,000 feet. The park's 45 miles of trails offer everything from casual nature strolls to hardy camping and hiking adventures among the redwoods. See p. 182.

Strolling Through Hawaiian History. Old Waimea Town looks so unassuming that you'd never guess it stood witness to a great many key events in Hawaii's history. This is the place where Capt. James Cook "discovered" the Hawaiian Islands, where Russians once built a fort, and where New England missionaries arrived in 1820 to "save the heathens." A self-guided walking tour is available at **Waimea Public Library,** Kaumualii Highway (✆ **808/338-6848**). See "Waimea Town," in chapter 8.

Taking a Long Walk on a Short (but Historic) Pier. First built in 1910, Hanalei's Pier was once a major shipping port for local farmers. Today, the rebuilt pier makes a great platform for swimming, fishing, and diving. It's at Black Pot Beach where, in the olden days, local families would camp out all summer and always have something cooking in a "black pot" on the shore. Black

he served until his death in 1922. This park is across the street from the ocean, where the rocky drop-off into the water is not very convenient for access (although snorkeling offshore is great). We suggest that you go a bit further east to Keiki (Baby) Beach, a small pocket of sand off Hoona Road, where swimming is generally safe. To get to Prince Kuhio Park, take Poipu Road toward the ocean and veer right at the fork in the road onto Lawai Beach Road. To get to Baby Beach, turn onto Hoona Road.

Spouting Horn Beach Park

According to ancient Hawaiian legend, a *mo'o* (lizard) was returning to Kauai from Niihau, where he had just been to a funeral for his two sisters. With tears streaming down his face, he missed landfall on the south shore and got stuck in the blowhole here, where you can still hear his voice during high surf. One of Hawaii's most famous blowholes,

Pot—and all of Hanalei Beach—is great for swimming, snorkeling, and surfing. See p. 169.

Watching for Whales. Mahaulepu Beach, in the Poipu area, offers excellent land-based viewing conditions for spotting whales that cruise by December through April. See p. 164.

Journeying into Eden. For a glimpse of the spectacularly remote Na Pali Coast, all you need to do is hike the first 2 miles along the well-maintained Kalalau Trail into the first tropical valley, Hanakapiai. Hardier hikers can venture another 2 miles to the Hanakapiai waterfalls and pools. ***Warning:*** Na Pali's natural beauty is so enticing that you may want to keep going—but the trail turns rugged and extremely challenging after the 2-mile mark. Contact the State Division of Parks for a permit if you want to camp along the trail. See "Hiking & Camping," later in this chapter.

Catching a Poipu Wave. Vividly turquoise, curling, and totally tubular; big enough to hang ten yet small enough to bodysurf, the waves at Poipu are endless in their attraction. Grab a boogie board—you can rent one for just dollars a day—or simply jump in and go with the flow. See p. 164.

Watching the Hula. The Coconut Marketplace, on Kuhio Highway (Hwy. 56) between mile markers 6 and 7, hosts free shows every day at 5pm. Arrive early to get a good seat for the hour-long performances of both *kahiko* (ancient) and *auwana* (modern) hula. The real showstoppers are the *keiki* (children) who perform. Don't forget your camera!

Bidding the Sun Aloha. Polihale State Park hugs Kauai's western shore for some 17 miles. It's a great place to bring a picnic dinner, stretch out on the sand, and toast the sun as it sinks into the Pacific, illuminating the island of Niihau in the distance. Queen's Pond has facilities for camping as well as restrooms, showers, picnic tables, and pavilions. See p. 168.

Spouting Horn gets its name from the loud roar created when the surf rushes to the lava shoreline and gets funneled up in the narrow chimney, which then spits out the water. Don't be so distracted by this intense display of Mother Nature that you get too close to the blowhole; not only are the rocks slippery, but people have been killed here when large waves swept them into the ocean or into the blowhole. The main attraction here is the blowhole, as the shoreline is mainly rocks. There is a small sandy beach (most of the year) to the west, which does have good swimming when the waters are calm. However, when the surf comes up, the sandy beach disappears. If you look offshore, you can see several boats bobbing in the water; commercial dive and snorkel tour operators frequently bring their tour groups to this area. Facilities include a paved parking lot, restrooms, and vendors. Take Poipu Road toward the ocean, and veer right at the fork in the road onto Lawai Beach Road. Follow the road for about a couple of miles to the beach park.

Salt Pond Beach Park

Hawaii's only salt ponds still in production are at Salt Pond Beach, just outside Hanapepe. Generations of locals have come here to swim, fish, and collect salt crystals that are dried in sun beds. The tangy salt is used for health purposes and to cure fish and season food. The curved reddish-gold beach lies between two rocky points and features a protected reef, tide pools, and gentle waves. Swimming here is excellent, even for children; this beach is also good for diving, windsurfing, and fishing. Amenities include a lifeguard, showers, restrooms, a camping area, a picnic area, a pavilion, and a parking lot. To get here, take Highway 50 past Hanapepe and turn onto Lokokai Road.

Polihale State Park ★

This mini-Sahara on the western end of the island is Hawaii's biggest beach: 17 miles long and as wide as three football fields. This is a wonderful place to get away from it all, but don't forget your flip-flops—the midday sand is hotter than a lava flow. The golden sands wrap around Kauai's northwestern shore from Kekaha plantation town, just beyond Waimea, to where the ridgebacks of the Na Pali Coast begin. The state park includes ancient Hawaiian *heiau* (temple) and burial sites, a view of the "forbidden" island of Niihau, and the famed **Barking Sands Beach,** where footfalls sound like a barking dog. (Scientists say that the grains of sand are perforated with tiny echo chambers, which emit a "barking" sound when they rub together.) Polihale also takes in the Pacific Missile Range Facility, a U.S. surveillance center that snooped on Russian subs during the Cold War; and Nohili Dune, which is nearly 3 miles long and 100 feet high in some places.

Be careful in winter, when high surf and rip currents make swimming dangerous. The safest place to swim is **Queen's Pond,** a small, shallow, sandy-bottomed inlet protected from waves and shore currents. It has facilities for camping, as well as restrooms, showers, picnic tables, and pavilions. There is no lifeguard. To get here, take Highway 50 past Barking Sands Missile Range and follow the signs through the sugar-cane fields to Polihale. Local kids have been known to burglarize rental cars out here, so don't leave tempting valuables in your car.

THE COCONUT COAST

Lydgate State Park ★

This coastal park has a rock-walled fishpond that blunts the open ocean waves and provides one of the few safe swimming beaches on the Coconut Coast and the best snorkeling on the eastern shore. The 1-acre beach park, near the mouth of the Wailua River, is named for the Rev. J. M. Lydgate (1854–1922), founder and first pastor of Lihue English Union Church, who likely would be shocked by the public display of flesh here. This popular park is a great place for a picnic or for kite flying on the green. It's 5 miles north of Lihue on Kuhio Highway (Hwy. 56); look for the turnoff just before the Kauai Resort Hotel. Facilities include a pavilion, restrooms, outdoor showers, picnic tables, barbecue grills, a lifeguard, and parking.

Wailua Beach

This popular beach includes Wailua River State Park and Wailua Bay. The draw here is the 100-foot-wide beach that runs for about a half mile from the Wailua River to a rocky area north. Surfers love this area for its generally good surfing conditions. However, when the high swells kick up in winter and into spring, the conditions can become dangerous, with strong rip currents, sharp shorebreaks, sudden drop-offs, and high surf. At the Wailea River end of the beach you can see boats being launched into the river for waterskiing, jet skiing, kayaking, and outrigger canoeing. Located where the river meets the ocean is one of the best archaeological sites in the state: a series of Hawaiian *heiau* (temples) and other sacred sites, identified with markers within the state park. Wailua Beach is located just past the intersection of Kuhio Highway (Hwy. 56) and Kuamoo Road (Hwy. 580), across the street from the now-closed Coco Palms Resort. There is a part-time lifeguard, but no public facilities.

Anahola Beach Park

Local residents, who love this park and are here almost every day, say this is the safest year-round swimming beach and great for small children. Tucked behind Kala Point, the narrow park has a shallow offshore reef that protects the sandy shoreline from the area's high surf. Another plus is that board surfing is prohibited in this area. Surfers have to head to the north end of the beach to the sandbar where surfing is allowed. To get here, take Kuhio Highway (Hwy. 56 north) to Anahola. Turn right onto Anahola Road and right on Manai Road. There are no facilities, but there is a part-time lifeguard.

THE NORTH SHORE

Anini Beach County Park ★★

Anini is Kauai's safest beach for swimming and windsurfing. It's also one of the island's most beautiful. It sits on a blue lagoon at the foot of emerald cliffs, looking more like Tahiti than almost any other strand in the islands. This 3-mile-long, gold-sand beach is shielded from the open ocean by the longest, widest fringing reef in Hawaii. With shallow water 4 to 5 feet deep, it's also the very best snorkeling spot on Kauai, even for beginners. On the northwest side, a channel in the reef runs out to the deep blue water with a 60-foot drop that attracts divers. Beachcombers love it, too; seashells, cowries, and sometimes even rare Niihau shells can be found here. Anini has a park, a campground, picnic and barbecue facilities, and a boat-launch ramp; several B&Bs and vacation rentals are nearby. Follow Kuhio Highway (Hwy. 56) to Kilauea; take the second exit, called Kalihiwai Road (the first exit dead-ends at Kalihiwai Beach), and drive a half mile toward the sea; turn left on Anini Beach Road.

Hanalei Beach ★

Gentle waves roll across the face of half-moon Hanalei Bay, running up to the wide, golden sand; sheer volcanic ridges laced by waterfalls rise to 4,000 feet on the other side, 3 miles inland. Is there any beach with a better location? Celebrated in song and hula and featured on travel posters, this beach owes its natural beauty to its age—it's an ancient sunken valley with eroded cliffs. Hanalei Bay indents the coast a full mile inland and runs 2 miles point to point, with coral reefs on either side and a patch of coral in the middle—plus a sunken ship that belonged to a king, so divers love it. Swimming is excellent year-round, especially in summer, when Hanalei Bay becomes a big, placid lake. The aquamarine water is also great for bodyboarding, surfing, fishing, windsurfing, canoe paddling, kayaking, and boating. (There's a boat ramp on the west bank of the Hanalei River.) The area known as **Black Pot,** near the pier, is particularly good for swimming, snorkeling, and surfing. Facilities include a lifeguard, a pavilion, restrooms, picnic tables, and parking. This beach is always packed with both locals and visitors, but you can usually find your own place in the sun by strolling down the shore; the bay is big enough for everyone.

To get here, take Kuhio Highway (Hwy. 56), which becomes Highway 560 after Princeville. In Hanalei town, make a right onto Aku Road just after Tahiti Nui, then turn right again on Weke Road, which dead-ends at the parking lot for the Black Pot section of the beach; the easiest beach access is on your left.

Lumahai Beach

One of the most photographed beaches in Kauai (it's where Mitzi Gaynor "washed that man right out of her hair" in *South Pacific*), this is a great beach for a picnic or for sitting and watching the waves. It is ***not*** a good swimming beach. The scenic beach is almost a mile long and extremely wide; the far eastern end occasionally is calm enough for swimming in the summer, but it can be very, very dangerous during the rest of the year. (The best reason to go to this beach is to picnic, inland, under the trees—chow down on lunch and watch the waves roll in.) ***The reason for caution:*** Unlike other beaches on Kauai, Lumahai has no protective reef offshore, so the open ocean waves come rolling in—full force. The force is so strong that the waves reshape the beach every year, moving the sand from one end to the other. When the surf is up there is a strong rip current and a powerful backwash, along with a dangerous shorebreak. There have been drownings here, so if the surf is up, do not go near the ocean (high surf has swept people out to sea).

Summer is the best time to enjoy this beach. On the eastern side (technically Kahalahala Beach), the surf is only calm enough for swimming on the few days when there are no waves—even small ones. The western end appeals more to body and board surfers. To get here, take Kuhio Highway (Hwy. 560); just after Hanalei, look for the wide turnoff for the scenic lookout, park here, and take the trail from the highway that leads to the beach below. Keep heading east for Kahalahala Beach. There is also a parking area at the western end of the beach, off the highway, just before you get to Lumahai River. Lumahai Beach has no facilities and no lifeguard.

Tunnels Beach & Haena Beach Park ★★

Postcard-perfect, gold-sand Tunnels Beach is one of Hawaii's most beautiful. When the sun sinks into the Pacific along the fabled peaks of Bali Hai, there's no better-looking beach in the islands: You're bathed in golden rays that butter the blue sky, bounce off the steepled ridges, and tint the pale clouds hot pink. Catch the sunset from the pebbly sand beach or while swimming in the emerald-green waters, but do catch it. Tunnels is excellent for swimming almost year-round and is safe for snorkeling because it's protected by a fringed coral reef. (However, the waters can get rough in winter.) The long, curving beach is sheltered by a forest of ironwoods that provides welcome shade from the tropical heat.

Around the corner is grainy-gold-sand Haena Beach Park, which offers excellent swimming in summer and great snorkeling amid clouds of tropical fish. But stay out of the water in winter, when the big waves are dangerous. Haena also has a popular grassy park for camping. Noise-phobes will prefer Tunnels.

Take Kuhio Highway (Hwy. 56), which becomes Highway 560 after Princeville. Tunnels is about 6 miles past Hanalei town, after mile marker 8 on the highway. (Look for the alley with the big wood gate at the end.) Haena is just down the road. Tunnels has no facilities, but Haena has restrooms, outdoor showers, barbecue grills, picnic tables, and free parking (no lifeguard, though).

Kee Beach State Park ★★

Where the road ends on the North Shore, you'll find a dandy little reddish-gold beach almost too beautiful to be real. Don't be surprised if it looks familiar; it was featured in

Moments Stargazing

Any Kauai beach is great for stargazing, almost any night of the year. Once a month, on the Saturday nearest the new moon, when the skies are darkest, the **Kauai Educational Association for the Study of Astronomy** sponsors a star watch at Kaumakani softball field. For information on the next star watch and directions, contact KEASA, P.O. Box 161, Waimea, HI 96796 (✆ **808/332-STAR** [7827]; www.keasa.org).

The Thornbirds. Kee (*kay*-ay) is on a reef-protected cove at the foot of fluted volcanic cliffs. Swimming and snorkeling are safe inside the reef but dangerous outside; those North Shore waves and currents can be killers. This park has restrooms, showers, and parking—but no lifeguard. To get here, take Kuhio Highway (Hwy. 56), which becomes Highway 560 after Princeville; Kee is about 7½ miles past Hanalei.

2 WATERSPORTS

Several outfitters on Kauai offer not only equipment rentals and tours but also expert information on weather forecasts, sea and trail conditions, and other important matters for hikers, kayakers, sailors, and all backcountry adventurers. For watersports questions and equipment rental, contact **Kayak Kauai,** 1 mile past Hanalei Bridge on Highway 560, in Hanalei (✆ **800/437-3507** or 808/826-9844; www.kayakkauai.com), the outfitters' center in Hanalei. They have a private dock (the only one on Kauai) for launching kayaks and canoes. In Kapaa, contact **Kauai Water Ski & Surf Co.,** Kinipopo Shopping Village, 4-356 Kuhio Hwy. (on the ocean side of the highway), Kapaa (✆ **808/822-3574**). In Kapaa and Koloa areas, go with **Snorkel Bob's Kauai** at 4-734 Kuhio Hwy. (just north of Coconut Plantation Marketplace), Kapaa (✆ **800/262-7725** or 808/823-9433; www.snorkelbob.com); in Koloa, Snorkel Bob's is at 3236 Poipu Rd. (just south of Poipu Shopping Village), near Poipu Beach (✆ **808/742-2206**).

For general advice on the activities listed below, see "The Active Vacation Planner," in chapter 3.

BOATING

One of Hawaii's most spectacular natural attractions is Kauai's **Na Pali Coast.** Unless you're willing to make an arduous 22-mile hike (p. 189), there are only two ways to see it: by helicopter (see "Helicopter Rides over Waimea Canyon & the Na Pali Coast," p. 205) or by boat. Picture yourself cruising the rugged Na Pali coastline in a 42-foot ketch-rigged yacht under full sail, watching the sunset as you enjoy a tropical cocktail, or speeding through the aquamarine water in a 40-foot trimaran as porpoises play off the bow.

When the Pacific humpback whales make their annual visit to Hawaii from December to March, they swim right by Kauai. In season, most boats on Kauai—including sail and powerboats—combine **whale-watching** with their regular adventures.

Kauai has many freshwater areas that are accessible only by boat, including the Fern Grotto, Wailua State Park, Huleia and Hanalei national wildlife refuges, Menehune Fishpond, and numerous waterfalls. For sportfishing charters, see "Fishing," below. For tours of the Fern Grotto, see p. 209.

Captain Andy's Sailing Adventures ★ Captain Andy operates a 55-foot, 49-passenger catamaran out of two locations on the south shore. The **snorkel/picnic cruise,** a 5½-hour cruise to the **Na Pali Coast,** from May to October, costs $139 for adults and $99 for children 2 to 12, and includes a deli-style lunch, snorkeling, and drinks. There's also a 4-hour Na Pali Coast **dinner sunset cruise** that sets sail for $105 for adults and $80 for children, and a 2-hour pupu **cocktail sunset sail** with drinks and pupu for $69 adults and $50 children. They also offer a 6-hour Na Pali Zodiac cruise on inflatable boats for $139–$159 adults and $99–$109 children ages 5 to 12. Book 7 days in advance for $10 off.

Kukuiula Small Boat Harbor, Poipu; and Port Allen, Eleele. ✆ **800/535-0830** or 808/335-6833. www.napali.com. Prices vary depending on trip.

Holoholo Charters This outfitter has taken over several boats and features both swimming/snorkeling sailing charters as well as powerboat charters to the Na Pali Coast. The 5-hour sailing trips take place on a 50-foot catamaran called *Leila* and is offered both in the morning (with a continental breakfast and lunch) for $139 adults, $99 children. In the afternoon there is a 2-hour dinner cruise for adults only ($79). The 7-hour powerboat trip is on the 65-foot vessel *Holoholo,* and it not only cruises the Na Pali Coast but then crosses the channel to the forbidden island of Niihau, where they stop to snorkel. A continental breakfast, buffet lunch, and snorkel equipment are included in the price: $179 adults, $129 children. Afternoons, there is a 3½-hour sunset tour with heavy appetizers, $99 adults and $79 children. (Check for web deals.)

Port Allen, Eleele. ✆ **800/848-6130** or 808/335-0815. www.holoholocharters.com. Prices and departure points vary depending on trip.

Liko Kauai Cruises ★ Kids Liko offers more than just a typical whale-watching cruise; this is a 4 ½-hour combination Na Pali Coast tour/fishing/historical lecture/whale-watching extravaganza with lunch. It all happens on a 49-foot power catamaran (with only 32 passengers). In addition to viewing the whales, you'll glimpse sea caves, waterfalls, lush valleys, and miles of white-sand beaches; you'll also make stops along the way for snorkeling.

Kekaha Small Boat Harbor, Waimea. ✆ **888/732-5456** or 808/338-0333. Fax 808/443-0881. www.liko-kauai.com. Na Pali trips $140 adults, $95 children 4–12 (lunch included).

BODYBOARDING (BOOGIE BOARDING) & BODYSURFING

The best places for bodysurfing and boogie boarding are **Kalapaki Beach** (near Lihue) and **Poipu Beach. Snorkel Bob's** (see above) rents boogie boards for just $26 a week.

FISHING

DEEP-SEA FISHING Kauai's fishing fleet is smaller and less well-recognized than others in the islands, but the fish are still out there. All you need to bring are your lunch and your luck. The best way to book a sportfishing charter is through the experts; the best booking desk in the state is **Sportfish Hawaii ★** (✆ **877/388-1376** or 808/396-2607; www.sportfishhawaii.com), which books boats not only on Kauai but on all the islands. These fishing vessels have been inspected and must meet rigorous criteria to guarantee that you will have a great time. Prices are $1,250 to $1,495 for a full-day exclusive charter (you and five of your closest friends get the entire boat to yourself), $950 to $1,195 for a three-quarter day exclusive, and $675 to $795 for a half-day exclusive.

Tips Not So Close! They Hardly Know You

In your excitement at seeing a whale or a school of dolphins, don't get too close—both are protected under the Marine Mammals Protection Act. Swimmers, kayakers, and windsurfers must stay at least 100 yards away from all whales, dolphins, and other marine mammals. And yes, visitors have been prosecuted for swimming with dolphins! If you have any questions, call the **National Marine Fisheries Service** (✆ **808/541-2727**) or the **Hawaiian Islands Humpback Whale National Marine Sanctuary** (✆ **800/831-4888**).

FRESHWATER FISHING Freshwater fishing is big on Kauai, thanks to its dozens of "lakes," which are really man-made reservoirs. Regardless, they're full of large-mouth, small-mouth, and peacock bass (also known as *tucunare*). The **Puu Lua Reservoir,** in Kokee State Park, also has rainbow trout and is stocked by the state every year. Fishing for rainbow trout in the reservoir has a limited season: It begins on the first Saturday in August and lasts for 16 days, after which you can only fish on weekends and holidays through the last Sunday in September.

Before you rush out and get a fishing pole, you have to have a **Hawaii Freshwater Fishing License,** available through the **State Department of Land and Natural Resources,** Division of Aquatic Resources, 3060 Eiwa St., Lihue, HI 96766 (✆ **808/274-3346**). To purchase online or find license agents, go to http://hawaii.gov/dlnr/dar/licenses_permits.html. A 7-day license costs $10; a 1-month license costs $20. When you get your license, pick up a copy of the booklet *State of Hawaii Freshwater Fishing Regulations.* If you would like a guide, **Sportfish Hawaii ★** (✆ **877/388-1376** or 808/396-2607; www.sportfishhawaii.com) has guided bass fishing trips starting at $265 for 1-2 people for a half-day and $375 per person for a full day.

KAYAKING

Kauai is made for kayaking. You can take the Huleia River into **Huleia National Wildlife Refuge** (located along the eastern portion of Huleia Stream, where it flows into Nawiliwili Bay). It's the last stand for Kauai's endangered birds, and the only way to see it is by kayak. The adventurous can head to the Na Pali Coast, featuring majestic cliffs, empty beaches, open-ocean conditions, and monster waves. Or you can just paddle around Hanalei Bay.

Kayak Kauai ★, a mile past Hanalei Bridge on Highway 560, in Hanalei (✆ **800/437-3507** or 808/826-9844; www.kayakkauai.com), has a range of tours for independent souls. The shop's experts will be happy to take you on a guided kayaking trip or to tell you where to go on your own. Equipment rental starts at $29 for a one-person kayak and $54 for a two-person ocean kayak per day. Kayak lessons are $50 per person per hour. Tours (some including snacks) start at $60 per person and include transportation and lunch for the all-day excursion. Kayak Kauai also has its own private dock in Hanalei (the only one on Kauai) for launching kayaks and canoes.

Rick Haviland, who gained fame after he was mentioned in Paul Theroux's book *The Happy Isles of Oceania,* is the owner of **Outfitters Kauai ★**, 2827A Poipu Rd. (at Poipu Plaza, a small five-shop mall before the road forks to Poipu/Spouting Horn), Poipu (✆ **888/742-9887** or 808/742-9667; www.outfitterskauai.com), which offers several kayaking tours. A full-day trip along the entire Na Pali Coast (summer only) costs $225 per person and includes a guide, lunch, drinks, and equipment. Another kayak tour takes you up a jungle stream and involves a short hike to waterfalls and a swimming hole; it's $110 (children ages 5–14, $98) including lunch, snacks, and drinks. Outfitters Kauai also rents river kayaks by the day ($40).

In the winter, mid-September to mid-May, **Outfitters Kauai ★** has launched a new **South Shore Sea Kayak Tour.** This 8-mile tour, from Poipu to Port Allen, lets you explore secluded bays and beaches that you can only get to by the sea. Along the way, the guided tour stops for coffee and snacks and later for lunch. This fabulous tour is not for everyone; if you get seasick, you might want to reconsider. Also, the paddling is moderately strenuous and not appropriate for kids under 12. But those adventurous souls, who are somewhat fit and love exploring, will be talking about this tour for a long time. Cost is $148 for adults and $118 for kids ages 12 to 14. Check for new adventures on their website!

You can also rent from **Pedal 'n Paddle,** Ching Young Village Shopping Center, Hanalei (✆ **808/826-9069;** www.pedalnpaddle.com).

PADDLING INTO HULEIA NATIONAL WILDLIFE REFUGE Ride the Huleia River through Kauai's 240-acre Huleia National Wildlife Refuge, the last stand of Kauai's endangered birds, with **True Blue,** Nawiliwili Harbor (✆ **888/245-1707** or 808/246-6333; www.kauaifun.com). You paddle up the picturesque Huleia (which appeared in *Raiders of the Lost Ark* and the remake of *King Kong*) under sheer pinnacles that open into valleys full of lush tropical plants, bright flowers, and hanging vines. Look for great blue herons and Hawaiian gallinules taking wing. The 4½-hour voyage, which starts at Nawiliwili Harbor, is a great trip for all—but especially for movie buffs, birders, and great adventurers under 12. It's even safe for nonswimmers. Wear a swimsuit, T-shirt, and boat shoes. The cost is $89 for adults, $36 for children 8 to 12. The prices include a picnic snack, juice, kayak, life vest, and guide services.

SCUBA DIVING

Diving on Kauai is dictated by the weather. In winter, when heavy swells and high winds hit the island, diving is generally limited to the more protected south shore. Probably the best-known site along the south shore is **Caverns,** located off the Poipu Beach Resort area. This site consists of a series of lava tubes interconnected by a chain of archways. A constant parade of fish streams by (even shy lionfish are spotted lurking in crevices), brightly hued Hawaiian lobsters hide in the lava's tiny holes, and turtles swim past.

In summer, when the north Pacific storms subside, the magnificent North Shore opens up. You can take a boat dive locally known as the **Oceanarium,** northwest of Hanalei Bay, where you'll find a kaleidoscopic marine world in a horseshoe-shaped cove. From the rare (long-handed spiny lobsters) to the more common (taape, conger eels, and nudibranchs), the resident population is one of the more diverse on the island. The topography, which features pinnacles, ridges, and archways, is covered with cup corals, black-coral trees, and nooks and crannies enough for a dozen dives.

Because the best dives on Kauai are offshore, we recommend booking a two-tank dive off a dive boat. **Bubbles Below Scuba Charters,** 6251 Hauaala Rd., Kapaa (✆ **808/332-7333;** www.aloha.net/~kaimanu), specializes in highly personalized, small-group dives, with an emphasis on marine biology. The 35-foot dive boat, *Kaimanu,* is a custom-built Radon that comes complete with a hot shower. Two-tank boat dives cost $125 ($25 more if you need gear); nondivers can come along for the ride for $80. In summer (May–Sept), Bubbles Below offers a three-tank trip for experienced divers only to the "forbidden" island of Niihau, 90 minutes by boat from Kauai. You should be comfortable with vertical drop-offs, huge underwater caverns, possibly choppy surface conditions, and significant currents. You should also be willing to share water space with the resident sharks. The all-day, three-tank trip costs $295, including tanks, weights, dive computer, lunch, drinks, and marine guide (if you need gear, it's $25 more).

On the south side, call **Fathom Five Adventures,** 3450 Poipu Rd. (next to the Chevron), Koloa (✆ **808/742-6991;** www.fathomfive.com).

GREAT SHORE DIVES FROM KAUAI If you want to rent your own equipment for shore dives, it will probably cost around $30 to $45 a day. Try **Dive Kauai,** 4-976 Kuhio Hwy., Kapaa (✆ **808/822-0452;** www.kascuba.com); or **Fathom Five Adventures,** 3450 Poipu Rd. (next to the Chevron), Koloa (✆ **808/742-6991; www.fathomfive.com**).

Spectacular shoreline dive sites on the North Shore include **Kee Beach/Haena Beach Park** (where the road ends), one of the most picturesque beaches on the island. On a calm summer day, the drop-off near the reef begs for underwater exploration. Another good bet is **Tunnels Beach,** also known as Makua Beach. It's off Highway 560, just past mile marker 8; look for the short dirt road (less than a half mile) to the beach. The wide reef here makes for some fabulous snorkeling and diving, but again, only during the calm summer months. **Cannons Beach,** east of Haena Beach Park (use the parking area for Haena, located across the street from the Dry Cave near mile marker 9 on Hwy. 560), has lots of vibrant marine life in its sloping offshore reef.

On the south shore, if you want to catch a glimpse of sea turtles, head to **Tortugas** (located directly in front of Poipu Beach Park). **Koloa Landing** has a horseshoe-shaped reef teeming with tropical fish. **Sheraton Caverns** (located off the Sheraton Kauai) is also popular, due to its three large underwater lava tubes, which are usually filled with marine life.

SNORKELING

For rental equipment, see the intro to this section for locations of **Snorkel Bob's.**

For great shoreline snorkeling, try the reef off **Kee Beach/Haena Beach Park,** located at the end of Highway 560. **Tunnels Beach,** about a mile before the end of Highway 560 in Haena, has a wide reef that's great for poking around in search of tropical fish. Be sure to check ocean conditions—don't go if the surf is up or if there's a strong current. **Anini Beach,** located off the northern end of Kalihiwai Road (between mile markers 25 and 26 on Kuhio Hwy., or Hwy. 56), just before the Princeville Airport, has a safe, shallow area with excellent snorkeling. **Poipu Beach Park** has some good snorkeling to the right side of Nukumoi Point—the tombolo area, where the narrow strip of sand divides the ocean, is best. If this spot is too crowded, wander down the beach in front of the old Waiohai resort; if there are no waves, this place is also hopping with marine life. **Salt Pond Beach Park,** off Highway 50 near Hanapepe, has good snorkeling around the two rocky points, home to hundreds of tropical fish.

SURFING

Hanalei Bay's winter surf is the most popular on the island, but it's for experts only. **Poipu Beach** is an excellent spot at which to learn to surf; the waves are small and—best of all—nobody laughs when you wipe out. Check with the local surf shops or call the **Weather Service** (✆ **808/245-3564**) to find out where surf's up.

Surf lessons are available for $150 for a 2-hour session for 1 or 2 people, including use of equipment (board and wetsuit top), from **The Surf Clinic of Hanalei,** in Hanalei (✆ **808/826-6924**). Poipu is also the site of numerous surfing schools; the oldest and

Kids Especially for Kids

Surfing with an Expert (p. 175) If seven-time world champ Margo Oberg, a member of the Surfing Hall of Fame, can't get your kid—or you—up on a board riding a wave, nobody can. She promises same-day results even for klutzes.

Paddling up the Huleia River (p. 173) Indiana Jones ran for his life up this river to his seaplane in *Raiders of the Lost Ark*. You and the kids can venture down it yourself in a kayak. The picturesque Huleia winds through tropically lush Huleia National Wildlife Refuge, where endangered species like great blue herons and Hawaiian gallinules take wing. It's ideal for everyone.

Climbing the Wooden Jungle Gyms at Kamalani Playground Located in Lydgate State Park, Wailua, this unique playground has a maze of jungle gyms for children of all ages. You can whip down slides, explore caves, hang from bars, and climb all over. It's a great place to spend the afternoon.

Cooling Off with a Shave Ice (p. 147) On a hot, hot day, stop by **Brennecke's Beach Broiler,** across from Poipu Beach Park (✆ **808/742-7588**), and order a traditional Hawaiian shave ice. This local treat consists of crushed ice stuffed into a paper cone and topped with a tropical-flavored syrup. If you can't decide on a flavor, go for the "rainbow"—three different flavors in one cone.

Exploring a Magical World (p. 213) **Na Aina Kai Botanical Gardens,** located on about 240 acres sprinkled with some 70 life-size (some larger than life-size) whimsical bronze statues and hidden off the beaten path of the North Shore, is perfect for kids. The tropical children's garden features a gecko hedge maze, a tropical jungle gym, a treehouse in a rubber tree, and a 16-foot-tall Jack and the Bean Stalk Giant with a 33-foot wading pool below. Na Aina Kai is only open 3 days a week, so book before you leave for Hawaii to avoid disappointment.

Experiencing a Hands-On Learning Adventure The **Kauai Children's Discovery Museum,** located in Kapaa (✆ **808/823-8222;** www.kcdm.org), resulted from a grass-roots community effort. The exhibits offer activities ranging from playing with Hawaiian musical instruments to participating in virtual reality television to hiding out in a "magic treehouse" and reading a book. There's even an area for kids 4 and under. There are also Keiki Camps (Children's Camps) where you can leave the kids all day. The kids will be taken on outings to the beach and other points of interest.

best is **Margo Oberg's School of Surfing** (✆ **808/332-6100;** www.surfonkauai.com). Margo charges $68 for 2 hours of group instruction, including surfboard and leash; she guarantees that by the end of the lesson, you'll be standing and catching a wave. Equipment is available for rent (ranging from $5 an hour or $20 a day for "soft" beginner boards to $7.50 an hour or $30 a day for hard boards) from **Nukumoi Surf Shop,** across from Brennecke's Beach, Poipu Beach Park (✆ **888/384-8810** or 808/742-8019); and **Hanalei Surf Co.,** 5-5161 Kuhio Hwy. (across from Zelo's Beach House Restaurant in Hanalei Center), Hanalei (✆ **808/826-9000**).

TUBING

Back in the days of the sugar plantations, on really hot days, if no one was looking, local kids would grab inner tubes and jump in the irrigation ditches crisscrossing the cane fields for an exciting ride. Today you can enjoy this (formerly illegal) activity by "tubing" the flumes and ditches of the old Lihue Plantation through **Kauai Backcountry Adventures** (✆ **888/270-0555** or 808/245-2506; www.kauaibackcountry.com). Passengers are taken in four-wheel-drive vehicles high into the mountains above Lihue and see vistas generally off-limits to the public. At the flumes, you will be outfitted with a giant tube, gloves, and headlamp (for the long passageways through the tunnels). All you do is jump in the water, and the gentle gravity-feed flow will carry you through forests, into tunnels, and finally to a mountain swimming hole, where a picnic lunch is served. The 3-hour tours are $100 and appropriate for anyone ages 5 to 95. Swimming is not necessary, since all you do is relax and drift downstream.

WATER-SKIING

Hawaii's only freshwater water-skiing is on the Wailua River. Ski boats launch from the boat ramp in Wailua River State Park, directly across from the marina. **Kauai Water Ski & Surf Co.,** Kinipopo Shopping Village, 4-356 Kuhio Hwy., Kapaa (✆ **808/822-3574**), rents equipment and offers lessons and guided ski. A half-hour trip costs $75; an hour-long trip costs $140.

WINDSURFING

Windsurfing lessons are available for $100 for a 3-hour session, including use of equipment (board and sail, wetsuit top), from **Windsurf Kauai,** in Hanalei (✆ **808/828-6838**).

3 HIKING & CAMPING

Kauai is an adventurer's delight. The island's greatest tropical beauty isn't easily accessed (more than 90% of Kauai is inaccessible by road); you have to head out on foot and find it. Trails range from a 10-minute nature loop from your car and back to check out Mother Nature without too much fuss, to several days of trekking requiring stamina and fitness. Those interested in seeing the backcountry—complete with virgin waterfalls, remote wilderness trails, and quiet meditative settings—should head for Waimea Canyon and Kokee Park or for the Na Pali Coast and the Kalalau Trail. Most trails are well marked and maintained, but occasionally, after a heavy rainy season, markers are down and the vegetation has taken over. Always ask about a trail before you go.

Camping on Kauai can be extreme (it's cold at 4,000 ft. in Kokee) or benign (by the sea). It can be wet, cold, and rainy, or hot, dry, and windy—often all on the same day. If you're heading for Kokee, bring rain gear, warm clothes, T-shirts, and shorts. (You will use everything.)

For more information on Kauai's hiking trails, contact the **State Division of Parks,** 3060 Ewa St., Lihue, HI 96766 (✆ **808/274-3446;** www.hawaiistateparks.org); the **State Division of Forestry and Wildlife,** 3070 Ewa St., Lihue, HI 96766 (✆ **808/274-3077** or 808/587-0166; www.dofaw.net); **Kauai County Parks and Recreation,** 4444 Rice St., Lihue, HI 96766 (✆ **808/241-4460;** http://www.kauai.gov/default.aspx?tabid=515); or the **Kokee Lodge Manager,** P.O. Box 367, Waimea, HI 96796 (✆ **808/335-6061**).

Tips A Warning About Flash Floods

When it rains on Kauai, the waterfalls rage and rivers and streams overflow, causing flash floods on roads and trails. If you're hiking, avoid dry streambeds, which flood quickly and wash out to sea. Before going hiking, camping, or sailing, especially in the rainy season (Nov–Mar), check the weather forecast by calling ✆ **808/245-6001.**

Kayak Kauai ★, a mile past Hanalei Bridge on Highway 560 in Hanalei (✆ **800/437-3507** or 808/826-9844; fax 808/822-0577; www.kayakkauai.com), is the premier all-around outfitter on the island. It's staffed by local experts who keep track of weather forecasts and sea and trail conditions; they have a lot of pertinent information that hikers, campers, and other backcountry adventurers need to know. Plus they have guided hiking tours starting at $81 per person. If you don't plan to bring your own gear, you can rent it here or at **Pedal 'n Paddle,** in Hanalei (✆ **808/826-9069**). If you want to buy camping equipment, head for **Ace Island Hardware,** at Princeville Shopping Center (✆ **808/826-6980**).

GUIDED HIKES You can join a guided hike with the Kauai chapter of the **Sierra Club,** P.O. Box 2577, Honolulu, HI 96813 (✆ **808/538-6616;** www.hi.sierraclub.org), which offers four to seven different hikes every month. The hikes vary from an easy family moonlit beach hike to a moderate 4-mile trip up some 1,100 feet, to 8-mile-plus treks for serious hikers only. The club also does guided hikes of **Kokee State Park** (see below), usually on weekends. Because there's no staffed office, the best way to contact the chapter is to check the website; outings are usually listed 3 to 6 months in advance, with complete descriptions of the hike, the hike leader's phone number, and what to wear and bring. You can also check the daily newspaper, the *Garden Island,* for a list of hikes in the Community Calendar section. Generally, the club asks for a donation of $5 per person per hike for nonmembers, $1 for members. It also does service work (clearing trails, picking up trash) on the hikes, so you may spend an hour doing service work, then 2 to 3 hours hiking. Last year, the club took three service-work trips along the Na Pali Coast trail to help maintain it.

During the summer, **Kokee Natural History Museum** (✆ **808/335-9975**) offers **"Wonder Walks,"** a series of guided hikes throughout Kokee State Park for a donation. This is a great way to learn more about the unusual flora and fauna in this high mountain area and to meet new people. Space is limited, so you have to call in your reservation. Hikers are advised to eat lunch before the hike and to bring light rain gear, water, snacks, sunscreen, protective clothing, and hiking boots. The hike leaves promptly at 12:15pm.

Hawaiian Wildlife Tours ★ (✆ **808/639-2968;** www.hawaiianwildlifetours.com) is environmental education in action. Biologist Dr. Carl Berg will take you out into the woods and down to the shoreline to see Kauai's native and vanishing species, from forest birds and flora to hoary bats, monk seals, and green sea turtles. His personalized tours last from 1 hour to a week and are tailored around the season and weather, your physical abilities, and what you want to see. He leads tours to Hanalei taro fields to see wetland birds, to Crater Hill to see nene geese, to Mahaulepu to see wildflowers in the sand dunes, to Kilauea Lighthouse to see oceanic birds, and much more. Rates are $50 per couple, per hour.

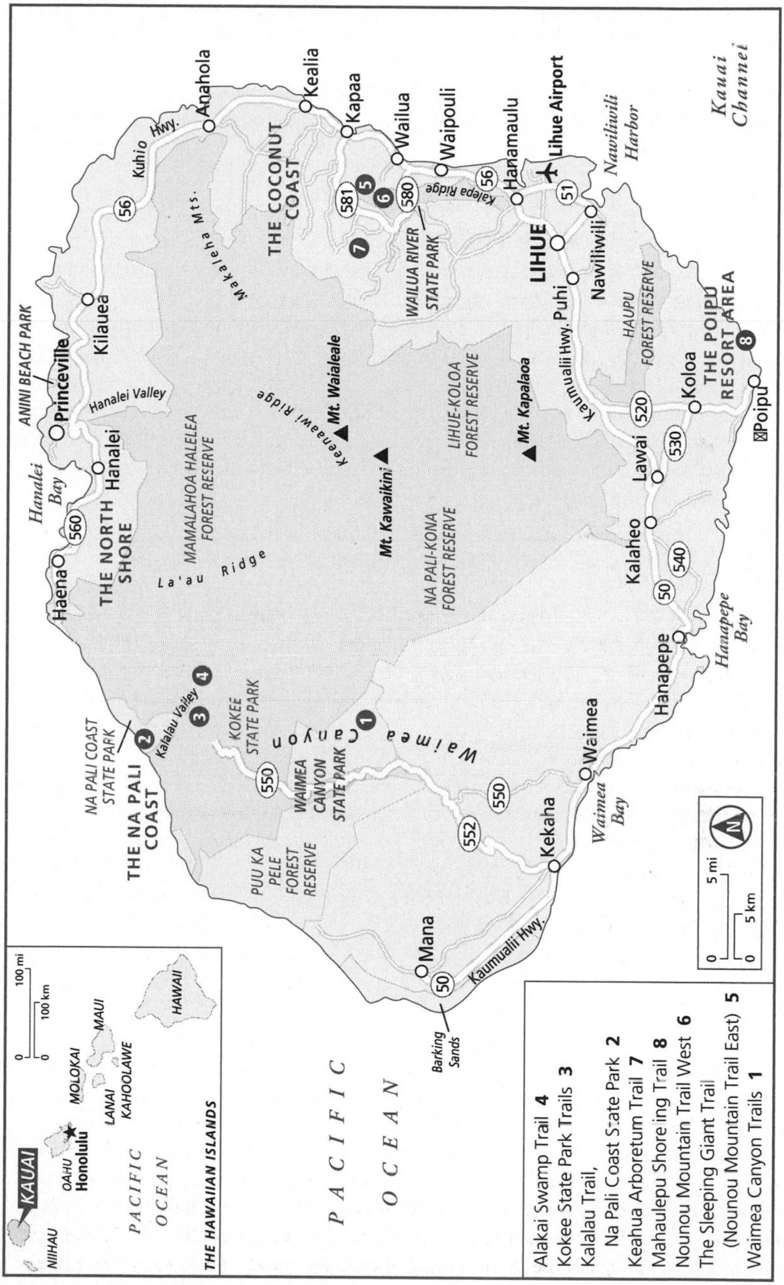

FUN IN THE SURF & SUN 7 HIKING & CAMPING

Other options for guided hikes include **Princeville Ranch Adventures** (✆ **888/955-7669** or 808/826-7669; www.adventureskauai.com), which offers various hikes on 2,000 acres of private property, such as a 3-hour hike to a waterfall (plus another hour spent swimming) for $129; and **Kauai Nature Tours** (✆ **888/233-8365** or 808/742-8305; www.kauainaturetours.com), which offers a geological-history excursion, a tour of Kauai's environments from the mountains to the ocean, and a Mahaulepu coast hike. All Kauai Nature Tours are led by scientists and range from $125 to $140 for adults and $95 to $115 for children ages 7 to 12.

THE POIPU RESORT AREA

Mahaulepu Shoreline Trail ★

The shoreline along Kauai's south coast offers an easy 4-mile round-trip in spectacular scenery, ancient sites, petroglyphs, or, as Kauai geologist Dr. Chuck Blay says: "A heritage landscape revealing 5 million years of continuous history—a living museum, a research site, and a habitat for rare and endangered plants and animals."

The Poipu Beach Foundation, with help from the Hawaii Tourism Authority, has produced a free interpretive map and guide to learn about the sites and features of this area.

The hike begins at Shipwreck Beach Park at Keoneloa Bay and ends at the remote Mahulepu Beach. The map and guide (along with the website) detail 9 different sites and 10 environmental features found only in this area. For more information check out www.hikemahaulepu.org, or for a copy of the guide, contact **Poipu Beach Resort Association** (✆ **888/744-0888;** www.poipubeach.org).

The trail head begins on the east end of Shipwreck Beach, past the Grand Hyatt. It's an easy 10-minute walk up to Makawehi Point; after you take in the big picture, keep going uphill along the ridge of the sand dunes (said to contain ancient Hawaiian burial sites), past the coves frequented by green sea turtles and endangered Hawaiian monk seals, through the coastal pine forest, and past World War II bunkers to the very top.

Moments Zipping Through the Forest

The latest adventure on Kauai is ziplining. From a high perch, participants outfitted in harnesses and helmets attach themselves to a cable, which is suspended above the ground from one point to another a hundred or so feet away. The zippers, attached only by a cable, zoom through the air, above treetops, at speeds of up to 35 mph from one end of the cable to the other. It's an adrenaline rush you will not forget. One of our favorite zipline tours is done by **Outfitters Kauai ★**, 2827A Poipu Rd., Poipu (✆ **888/742-9887** or 808/742-9667; www.outfitterskauai.com). Their **Kipu Falls Zipline Trek** starts with a 1/4-mile hike through the jungle to a steep valley with a 150-foot waterfall. Zippers climb up one side of the valley, attach themselves to the cable some 50 feet above the earth, step off the platform, and usually holler with ear-to-ear grins as they zip along the cable over the forest canopy, rivers, and waterfalls. Even first-time zippers run as quickly as their legs will carry them back up the trail to do it all over again. If you get your fill of zipping, there are hikes, a swimming hole, and rope swings to fill up the 3-hour adventure. Cost is $138 for adults and $118 for children ages 7 to 14.

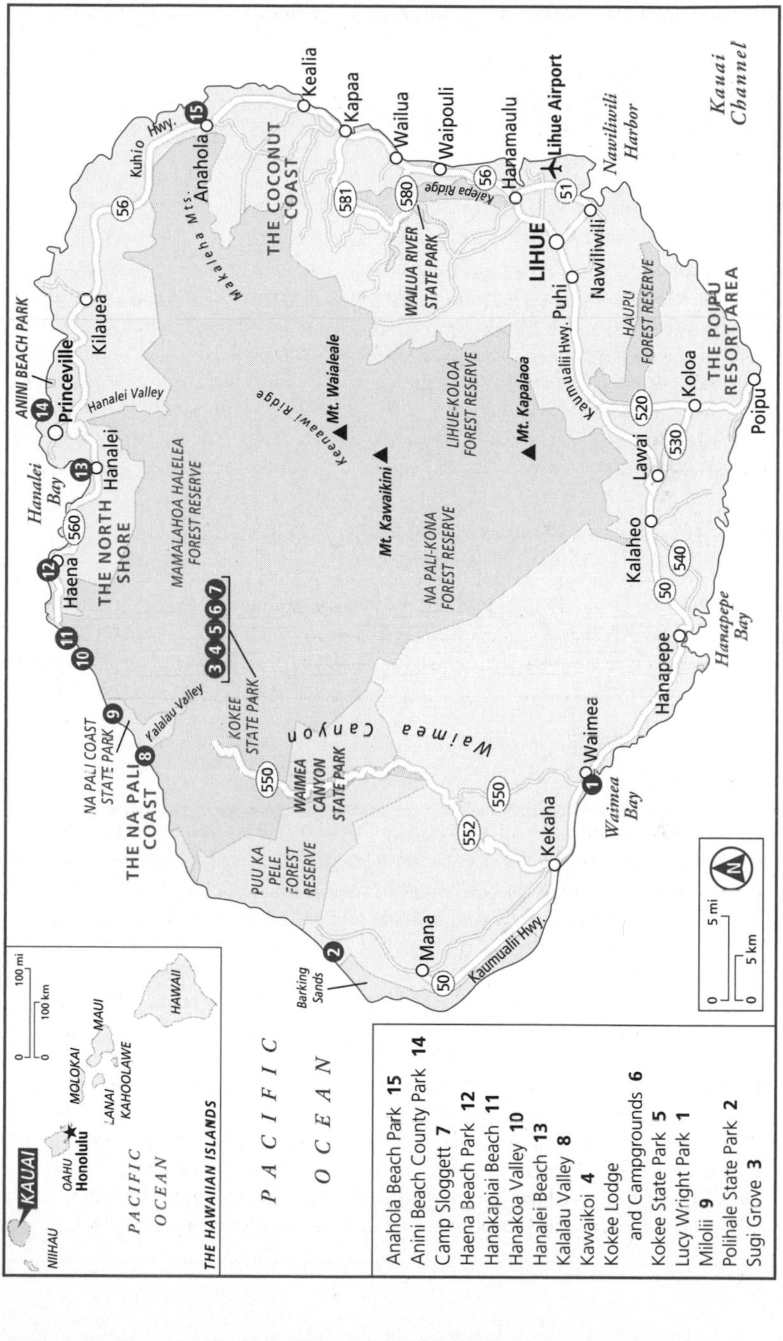
Anahola Beach Park 15
Anini Beach County Park 14
Camp Sloggett 7
Haena Beach Park 12
Hanakapiai Beach 11
Hanakoa Valley 10
Hanalei Beach 13
Kalalau Valley 8
Kawaikoi 4
Kokee Lodge and Campgrounds 6
Kokee State Park 5
Lucy Wright Park 1
Milolii 9
Polihale State Park 2
Sugi Grove 3
THE HAWAIIAN ISLANDS
NIIHAU
KAUAI
OAHU
Honolulu
MOLOKAI
LANAI
KAHOOLAWE
MAUI
HAWAII
PACIFIC OCEAN
0 100 mi
0 100 km
PACIFIC
OCEAN
Barking Sands
Mana
Kaumualii Hwy.
Kekaha
Waimea Bay
Waimea
Hanapepe
Hanapepe Bay
Kalaheo
Lawai
Koloa
Poipu
THE POIPU RESORT AREA
HAUPU FOREST RESERVE
Kaumualii Hwy.
Puhi
Nawiliwili
LIHUE
Lihue Airport
Nawiliwili Harbor
Kauai Channel
Hanamaulu
Kalepa Ridge
WAILUA RIVER STATE PARK
Waipouli
Wailua
Kapaa
Kealia
THE COCONUT COAST
Anahola
Makaleha Mts.
Kuhio Hwy.
Kilauea
Princeville
ANINI BEACH PARK
Hanalei Valley
Hanalei
Hanalei Bay
THE NORTH SHORE
Haena
MAMALAHOA HALELEA FOREST RESERVE
Mt. Waialeale
Keanawi Ridge
Mt. Kawaikini
LIHUE-KOLOA FOREST RESERVE
Mt. Kapalaoa
NA PALI-KONA FOREST RESERVE
KOKEE STATE PARK
Yalalau Valley
NA PALI COAST STATE PARK
THE NA PALI COAST
Waimea Canyon
WAIMEA CANYON STATE PARK
PUU KA PELE FOREST RESERVE
0 5 mi
0 5 km
N

Now you can see Haupu Ridge and its 2,297-foot peak, the famously craggy ridgeline that eerily resembles Queen Victoria's profile and, in the distance, Mahaulepu Beach, one of the best looking in Hawaii. Inland, three red craters dimple the green fields; the one in the middle, the biggest, Puu Huni Huni, is said to have been the last volcano to erupt on Kauai—but it was so long ago that nobody here can remember when.

WESTERN KAUAI

Waimea Canyon Trails

On a wet island like Kauai, a dry hike is hard to find. But in the desert-dry gulch of Waimea Canyon, known as the Grand Canyon of the Pacific (once you get here, you'll see why—it's pretty spectacular), you're not likely to slip and slide in the muck as you go.

CANYON TRAIL You want to hike Hawaii's Grand Canyon, but you don't think you have time? Well, then, take the Canyon Trail to the east rim for a breathtaking view into the 3,000-foot-deep canyon. Park your car at the top of Halemanu Valley Road (located between mile markers 14 and 15 on Waimea Canyon Rd., about a mile down from the museum). Walk down the not very clearly marked trail on the 3.5-mile round-trip, which takes 2 to 3 hours and leads to Waipoo Falls (as does the hike below) and back. We suggest going in the afternoon, when the light is best.

HIKE TO WAIPOO FALLS ★ The 3-hour round-trip hike to Waipoo Falls is one of Kauai's best hikes. The two-tiered, 800-foot waterfall that splashes into a natural pool is worth every step it takes to get here. To find the trail, drive up Kokee Road (Hwy. 550) to the Puu Hina Hina Outlook; a quarter mile past the lookout, near a NASA satellite-tracking station on the right, a two-lane dirt road leads to the Waipoo Falls trail head. From here, the trail winds gently through a jungle dotted with wild yellow orchids and flame-red torch ginger before it leads you out onto a descending ridgeback that juts deep into the canyon. At the end of the promontory, take a left and push on through the jungle to the falls; reward yourself with a refreshing splash in the pool.

Kokee State Park

At the end of Highway 550, which leads through Waimea Canyon to its summit, lies a 4,640-acre state park of high-mountain forest wilderness (3,600–4,000 ft. above sea level). The rainforest, bogs, and breathtaking views of the Na Pali Coast and Waimea Canyon are the draws at Kokee. This is the place for hiking—among the 45 miles of maintained trails are some of the best hikes in Hawaii. Official trail maps of all the park's trails are for sale for 50¢ at the **Kokee Natural History Museum** (**© 808/335-9975**).

A few words of advice: Always check current trail conditions. Up-to-date trail information is available on a bulletin board at the Kokee Natural History Museum. Stay on established trails; it's easy to get lost here. Get off the trail well before dark. Carry water and rain gear—even if it's perfectly sunny when you set out—and wear sunscreen.

For complete coverage of the state park, see p. 205.

AWAAWAPUHI TRAIL This 3.25-mile hike (6.5 miles round-trip) takes about 3 hours each way and is considered strenuous by most, but it offers a million-dollar view. Look for the trail head at the left of the parking lot, at mile marker 17, between the museum and Kalalau Lookout. The well-marked and maintained trail now sports quarter-mile markers, and you can pick up a free plant guide for the trail at the museum. The trail drops about 1,600 feet through native forests to a thin precipice right at the very edge of the Na Pali cliffs for a dramatic and dizzying view of the tropical valleys and blue Pacific 2,500 feet below. It's not recommended for anyone with vertigo (although a railing will keep you from a major slip and fall). Go early, before clouds obscure the view, or go late in the day; the chiaroscuro sunsets are something to behold.

The Awaawapuhi can be a straight out-and-back trail or a loop that connects with the **Nualolo Trail** (3.75 miles), which provides awesome views and leads back to the main road between the ranger's house and the Kokee cabins, about a mile and a half from where you started. So you can hike the remaining 1.5 miles along the road or hitch a ride if you decide to do the entire loop but can't make it all the way.

PIHEA TRAIL This is the park's flattest trail, but it's still a pretty strenuous 7.5-mile round-trip. A new boardwalk on a third of the trail makes it easier, especially when it's wet. The trail begins at the end of Highway 550 at Puu o Kila Lookout, which overlooks Kalalau Valley; it goes down at first, then flattens out as it traces the back ridge of the valley. Once it enters the rainforest, you'll see native plants and trees. It intersects with the Alakai Swamp Trail (below). If you combine both trails, figure on about 4 hours in and out.

ALAKAI SWAMP TRAIL ★ If you want to see the "real" Hawaii, this is it—a big swamp that's home to rare birds and plants. The trail allows a rare glimpse into a wet, cloud-covered wilderness preserve where 460 inches of rainfall a year is common. This 7-mile hike used to take 5 hours of sloshing through the bog, with mud up to your knees. Now a boardwalk protects you from the shoe-grabbing mud. Come prepared for rain. (The silver lining is that there are no mosquitoes above 3,000 ft.)

The trail head is off Mohihi (Camp 10) Road, just beyond the Forest Reserve entrance sign and the Alakai Shelter picnic area. From the parking lot, the trail follows an old World War II–era four-wheel-drive road. Stick to the boardwalk; this is a fragile eco-area (not to mention the mud). At the end of the 3.5-mile slog, if you're lucky and the clouds part, you'll have a lovely view of Wainiha Valley and Hanalei from Kilohana Lookout.

Campgrounds & Wilderness Cabins in Kokee

CABINS & TENT CAMPGROUNDS Camping facilities include state campgrounds (one next to Kokee Lodge and four more primitive backcountry sites), one private tent area, and the **Kokee Lodge,** which has 12 cabins for rent at very reasonable rates. At 4,000 feet, the nights are cold, particularly in winter. Because no open fires are permitted at Kokee, the best deal is the cabins. (See chapter 5 for details.) The **Kokee Lodge Restaurant** is open daily from 9am to 3:30pm for continental breakfast and lunch. Groceries and gas aren't available in Kokee, so stock up in advance, or you'll have to make the long trip down the mountain.

The **state campground** at Kokee allows tent camping only. Permits can be obtained from a state parks office on any island; on Kauai, it's at 3060 Eiwa St., Room 306, Lihue, HI 96766 (✆ **808/274-3446;** www.hawaiistateparks.org). The permits are $5 per night; the time limit is 5 nights in a single 30-day period. Facilities include showers, drinking water, picnic tables, pavilion with tables, restrooms, barbecues, sinks for dishwashing, and electric lights.

Tent camping at **Camp Sloggett,** owned by the Kauai YWCA, 3094 Elua St., Lihue, HI 96766 (✆ **808/245-5959;** fax 808/245-5961; www.campingkauai.com), is available for $10 per person per night (children under 5 stay free). The sites are on 1½ acres of open field, with a covered pit for fires and a barbecue area, plus volleyball and badminton nets. There are also hostel-style accommodations at the **Weinberg Bunkhouse,** with bunk beds, separate toilets, showers, and kitchenettes ($25 per person). To get here, continue on the highway past park headquarters and take the first right after the Kokee

Hiking Safety

According to a survey done in 2000, 78% of the hikers in Hawaii were from out-of-state. At the same time, Hawaii's search-and-rescue teams are responding to more and more calls from injured, stranded, or missing hikers. The best thing you can do to avoid becoming a statistic is to get Na Ala Hele's (the State of Hawaii's Trail and Access Program) free brochure, ***Hiking Safety in Hawaii*** (from the State Department of Land and Natural Resources, Division of Forestry & Wildlife, 1151 Punchbowl St., Room 325, Honolulu, HI 96813; ✆ **808/587-0166;** or print it off the Web at www.hawaiitrails.org). This free brochure could save your life. It has comprehensive lists of trail safety tips and equipment you'll need; describes what to do in an emergency; and contains other information you should know before you lace up your hiking boots.

If you are not an experienced hiker, consider hiking with a commercial operator (we list several in this chapter), or join a Sierra Club hike. If you have experience hiking, keep these tips in mind when venturing out in Hawaii:

- **Remember you are a guest** in Hawaii and treat the land (especially sacred cultural areas) with respect by following posted signage on the trail. Always start your hikes with clean (well-scrubbed) boots, so you don't unintentionally carry seeds into the island's fragile environment.
- **Practice courtesy** when on a multiple-usage trail. The signs will let you know who to yield to (hikers generally yield to horseback riders, and bikers yield to both hikers and horses).
- **Plan your hike** by informing others where you are going and when you should be back. Learn as much as you can about the hike (the conditions you will encounter and the degree of difficulty) before you set out.

Lodge. Follow the dirt road and look for the wooden CAMP SLOGGETT sign; turn right and follow the bumpy road past the state cabins into a large clearing.

BACKCOUNTRY CAMPING The more primitive backcountry campgrounds include **Sugi Grove** and **Kawaikoi,** located about 4 miles from park headquarters on the Camp 10 Road, an often muddy and steep four-wheel-drive road. Sugi Grove is located across the Kawaikoi Stream from the Kawaikoi campsite. The area is named for the sugi pines, which were planted in 1937 by the Civilian Conservation Corps. This is a shady campsite with a single picnic shelter, a pit toilet, a stream, and space for several tents. The Kawaikoi site is a 3-acre open grass field, surrounded by Kokee plum trees and forests of koa and ohia. Facilities include two picnic shelters, a composting toilet, and a stream that flows next to the camping area. There is no potable water—bring in your own or treat the stream water.

Permits are available from the **State Forestry and Wildlife Division,** 3060 Eiwa St., Room 306, Lihue, HI 96766 (✆ **808/274-3446;** www.hawaiistateparks.org). There's no fee for the permits, but camping is limited to 3 nights. You can also request the *Kauai Recreation Map* (with illustrations of all roads; trails; and picnic, hunting, and camping

- **Hike with a partner.** Never go alone. Dress in layers to protect yourself from Hawaii's intense tropical sun, carry light rain gear, have a brightly colored jacket (not only for weather, but so that if you get lost, people will be able to spot you), and bring a hat, sunglasses, and sunscreen. If you are hiking, you should wear hiking boots with traction and ankle support.
- **Check the weather.** Call ✆ **808/245-6001.** The bright, sunny day can dissolve into wind and rain, and you don't want to be caught in a narrow gully or streambed where flash flooding is possible.
- **Carry water** (2 liters per person per day), a cellphone, and a daypack (holding a whistle, sunscreen, insect repellent, a small flashlight, food, and a basic first-aid kit). Don't drink untreated stream water; *leptospirosis* (a bacterial disease transmitted from animals to humans, which can be fatal) is present in some streams.
- **Stay on the trail** and stay together. Most hikers are injured wandering off the trail or trying to climb rocks.
- **Watch the time.** Being close to the Equator, Hawaii does not have a very long twilight. Once the sun goes down, it's dark. Be sure to allow enough time to return from your hike, and always carry a flashlight.
- **If an emergency arises** (for example, if an injury or illness prevents someone from walking, bad weather hits, it's too dark to see, or you become lost or stranded), call 911 and ask for fire/rescue. Tell them what trail you are on and what happened. Make yourself visible with either bright clothing or a flashlight, and use the whistle. Stay calm and stay put. Keep as warm as you can by getting out of wind and rain and by layering clothing to maintain your body temperature.

areas) by mail; contact the Forestry and Wildlife Division at the number above to find out how.

Beach Camping at Polihale State Park

Polihale holds the distinction of being the westernmost beach in the United States. The beach is spectacular—some 300 feet wide in summer, with rolling sand dunes (some as high as 100 ft.), and the islands of Niihau and Lehua just offshore. Bordered by a curtain of Na Pali Coast cliffs to the north, razor-sharp ridges and steep valleys to the east, and the blue Pacific to the south and west, this is one of the most dramatic camping areas in the state.

The campgrounds for tent camping are located at the south end of the beach, affording privacy from daytime beach activities. There's great swimming in summer (even then, be on the lookout for waves and rip currents—there are no lifeguards), some surfing (the rides are usually short), and fishing. The camping is on sand, although there are some kiawe trees for shade. (***Warning:*** Kiawe trees drop long thorns, so make sure you have protective footwear.) Facilities include restrooms, showers, picnic tables, barbecues, and a spigot for drinking water. You can purchase supplies about 15 miles away in Waimea.

> **Tips** **Safety Tip**
>
> Be sure to see "Staying Healthy," in chapter 3, before you set out on your Kauai adventures. It includes useful information on hiking, camping, and ocean safety, plus how to avoid seasickness and sunburn, and what to do should you get stung by a jellyfish.

Permits, which are $5 per night, are available through the **State Parks Office,** 3060 Eiwa St., Lihue, HI 96766 (✆ **808/241-3446**). You're limited to 5 nights in any 30-day period. To reach the park from Lihue, take Highway 50 west to Barking Sands Pacific Missile Range. Bear right onto the paved road, which heads toward the mountains. There will be small signs directing you to Polihale; the second sign will point to a left turn onto a dirt road. Follow this for about 5 miles; at the fork in the road, the campgrounds are to the left and the beach park is to the right.

Beach Camping at Lucy Wright Park

If you want to camp on the west side but can't get a space at Polihale State Park, the county allows camping at the 4½-acre Lucy Wright Park, located just outside Waimea. Not the best beach park, it's okay for camping in a pinch. The park, located on the western side of the Waimea River, is where Captain Cook first came ashore in Hawaii in January 1778. The park is named after the first native Hawaiian schoolteacher at Waimea, Lucy Kapahu Aukai Wright (1873–1931). The beach here is full of flotsam and jetsam from the river, making it unappealing. On the other side of the Waimea River, across from Lucy Wright Park, is the 17¼-acre Russian Fort, with ruins of a Russian fort built in 1815. Facilities at Lucy Wright include the camping area, restrooms, a pavilion, picnic tables, and (cold) showers. You need a permit to camp at any of the county's seven beach parks. Permits are $3 per person, per night. You can stay at the county parks a maximum of 4 nights (or 12 nights if you go from one county park to another). To apply for the permit, contact Shani Saito in the Permits Division of Kauai County Parks and Recreation, 4444 Rice St., Lihue, HI 96766 (✆ **808/241-4460;** www.kauai-hawaii.com/activities.php). To get to Lucy Wright Park, take Kaumualii Highway (Hwy. 50) to Waimea and turn left on Alawai Road, which leads to the park.

THE COCONUT COAST

The Sleeping Giant Trail (Nounou Mountain Trail East)

This medium-to-difficult hike takes you up Nounou Mountain, known as Sleeping Giant (it really does look like a giant resting on his back), to a fabulous view. The clearly marked trail will gain 1,000 feet in altitude. (Be sure to stay on the trail.) The climb is steadily uphill (remember you are climbing a mountain), but the view at the top is well worth the constant incline. To get to the trail head, turn *mauka* (toward the mountain) off Kuhio Highway (Hwy. 56) onto Haleilio Road (between Wailua and Kapaa, just past mile marker 6); follow Haleilio Road for 1.25 miles to the parking area, at telephone pole no. 38. From here, signs posted by the State of Hawaii Division of Forestry and Wildlife lead you over the 1.75-mile trail, which ends at a picnic table and shelter. The panoramic view is breathtaking. Be sure to bring water—and a picnic, if you like.

Nounou Mountain Trail West

If you would like to venture up Sleeping Giant from the other side of Nounou Mountain, this trail joins up with the east trail. This trail is shorter than the eastern trail, and you're in forest most of the time. To get to the trail head, take Kuhio Highway (Hwy. 56) to Wailua. Turn left onto Kuamoo Road (Hwy. 580) and continue to Kamalu Road (Hwy. 581), where you turn right. Make a left on Lokelani Street and drive to the end of the road, where there's a parking area and trail head. This trail meanders through forests of Norfolk pine, strawberry guava, and, as you climb closer to the top, hala trees. About a quarter mile into the hike you will come to a fork with the Kuamoo Trail; veer left. Continue to climb and you will reach the picnic area and shelter.

Keahua Arboretum Trail

If you are looking for an easy hike for the entire family, this half-mile loop will take you just a half hour. It offers you a chance to swim in a cool mountain stream and maybe enjoy a picnic lunch. To get here, take Kuhio Highway (Hwy. 56) to Wailua. Turn left on Kuamoo Road (Hwy. 580) and continue past the University of Hawaii Agricultural Experimental Station to the Keahua Arboretum. The trail head is on the left just past the stream, across the street from the parking lot. This area gets nearly 100 inches of rain a year, and the colorful painted gum eucalyptus trees at the trail head couldn't be happier. Along the trail you'll see kukui trees (which the Hawaiians used as a light source), *milo* (popular among wood artists), hau, and ohia lehua. As you walk parallel to the stream, be on the lookout for a good swimming area. There are lots of picnic tables and shelters along the trail at which to stop and have lunch.

Beach Camping at Anahola Beach Park

Local residents, who love this park and are here almost every day, say that this is the safest year-round swimming beach and great for small children. Tucked behind Kala Point, the narrow park has a shallow offshore reef that protects the sandy shoreline from the high surf visiting the area. Another plus is that board surfing is prohibited in this area. Surfers have to head to the north end of the beach to the sandbar where surfing is allowed. Tall ironwoods provide relief from the sun. Facilities include a camping area, a picnic area, barbecue grills, restrooms, and cold showers. A part-time lifeguard is on duty. When you camp here, don't leave your valuables unprotected. You must have a permit, which costs $3 per person, per night. You can stay at the county parks a maximum of 4 nights, or 12 nights if you are going from one county park to another. To apply for the permit, contact Shani Saito in the Permits Division of Kauai County Parks and Recreation, 4444 Rice St., Lihue, HI 96766 (© **808/241-4460;** www.kauai-hawaii.com/activities.php#CAMPING). To get to Anahola Beach Park, take Kuhio Highway (Hwy. 56 north) to Anahola, turn right onto Anahola Road, and then turn right onto Manai Road.

THE NORTH SHORE

Anini Beach County Park ★★

This 12-acre park is Kauai's safest beach for swimming and windsurfing. It's also one of the island's most beautiful: It sits on a blue lagoon at the foot of emerald cliffs, looking more like Tahiti than almost any other strand in the islands. One of Kauai's largest beach camping sites, it is very, very popular, especially on summer weekends, when local residents flock to the beach to camp. It's easy to see why: This 3-mile-long, gold-sand beach is shielded from the open ocean by the longest, widest fringing reef in Hawaii. With shallow water 4 to 5 feet deep, it's also the very best snorkeling spot on Kauai, even for beginners. On the northwest side, a channel in the reef runs out to the deep blue water with a 60-foot drop that attracts divers. Beachcombers love it, too: Seashells, cowries, and sometimes even rare Niihau shells can be found here. Anini has a park, a campground, picnic and barbecue facilities, a pavilion, outdoor showers, public telephones, and a boat-launch ramp. Princeville, with groceries and supplies, is about 4 miles away. You must have a permit, which costs $3 per person, per night. You can stay at the county parks a maximum of 4 nights, or 12 nights if you are going from one county park to another. To apply for the permit, contact: Shani Saito in the Permits Division of Kauai County Parks and Recreation, 4444 Rice St., Lihue, HI 96766 (✆ **808/241-4460;** www.kauai-hawaii.com/activities.php#CAMPING). Follow Kuhio Highway (Hwy. 56) to Kilauea; take the second exit, called Kalihiwai Road (the first exit dead-ends at Kalihiwai Beach), and drive a half mile toward the sea; turn left on Anini Beach Road.

Hanalei Beach ★

Camping is allowed at this 2½-acre park on weekends and holidays only. Reserve in advance—this is a very popular camping area. Gentle waves roll across the face of half-moon Hanalei Bay, running up to the wide, golden sand; sheer volcanic ridges laced by waterfalls rise to 4,000 feet on the other side, 3 miles inland. Is there any beach with a better location? Celebrated in song and hula and featured on travel posters, this beach owes its natural beauty to its age—it's an ancient sunken valley with post-erosional cliffs. (See p. 169 for a full review of the beach.)

Facilities include a lifeguard, a pavilion, restrooms, picnic tables, and parking. This beach is always packed with both locals and visitors, but you can usually find your own place in the sun by strolling down the shore; the bay is big enough for everyone. You must have a permit, which costs $3 per person, per night. You can stay at the county parks a maximum of 4 nights, or 12 nights if you are going from one county park to another. To apply for the permit, contact the Permits Division of Kauai County Parks and Recreation, 4444 Rice St., Lihue, HI 96766 (✆ **808/241-4460;** www.kauai-hawaii.com/activities.php#CAMPING).

To get here, take Kuhio Highway (Hwy. 56), which becomes Highway 560 after Princeville. In Hanalei town, make a right on Aku Road just after Tahiti Nui, then turn right again on Weke Road, which dead-ends at the parking lot for the Black Pot section of the beach; the easiest beach access is on your left.

Haena Beach Park

There are a lot of pluses and minuses to this county beach park (next door to Haena State Park, which does not allow camping). One plus is its beauty: The nearly 6-acre park is bordered by the ocean on one side and a dramatic mountain on the other. In fact, old-timers call this beach **Maniniholo,** after the local manini fish, which used to be caught in nets during summer. Across the highway from this park are the dry caves, also called Maniniholo. The caves, really a lava tube, run a few hundred feet into the mountain. The area is great for camping, flat and grassy with palm trees for shade. Now the minuses: This is not a good swimming beach because it faces the open ocean, and Kauai's North Shore can be windy and rainy. However, good swimming and snorkeling are available either a quarter mile east of the campground (about a 5-min. walk) at Tunnels Beach, where an offshore reef protects the bay; or at Kee Beach, about a mile west of the campground. Come prepared for wet weather.

Facilities include the camping area, restrooms, outside screened showers, a pavilion with tables, electric lights, a dishwashing sink, picnic tables, and grills; however, there are no lifeguards. The water here is safe to drink. Supplies can be picked up in Hanalei, 4 miles east. You will need a permit, which costs $3 per person, per night. You can stay at the county parks a maximum of 4 nights, or 12 nights if you are going from one county park to another. To apply for the permit, contact Shani Saito in the Permits Division of Kauai County Parks and Recreation, 4444 Rice St., Lihue, HI 96766 (© **808/241-4460;** www.kauai-hawaii.com/activities.php#CAMPING). To get here, take Highway 56 from Lihue, which becomes Highway 560. Look for the park, 4 miles past Hanalei.

YMCA of Kauai—Camp Naue

Attention, campers, hikers, and backpackers: This is the ideal spot to stay before or after conquering the Na Pali Trail, or if you just want to spend a few days lounging on fabulous Haena Beach. This YMCA campsite, located on Kuhio Highway, 4 miles west of Hanalei and 2 miles from the end of the road, sits right on the ocean, on 4 grassy acres ringed with ironwood and kumani trees and bordered by a sandy beach that offers excellent swimming and snorkeling in the summer (the ocean here turns really rough in the winter). Camp Naue has two bunkhouses overlooking the beach; each has four rooms with 10 to 12 beds, $15 per bunk. The facilities are coed, with separate bathrooms for men and women. There's no bedding here, so bring your sleeping bag and towels. Large groups frequently book the camp, but if there's room, the Y will squeeze you into the bunkhouse or offer tent space, at $15 per person. Also on the grounds is a beachfront pavilion and a campfire area with picnic tables. You can pick up basic supplies in Haena, but it's best to stock up on groceries and other necessities in Lihue or Hanalei. Remember this is the Y, not the Ritz; they only have one employee who handles all the bookings (they don't take reservations) plus everything else related to the Y activities. The best way to find out if they have space available is to call © **808/246-9090.** (And keep calling; they can't return long distance calls.) Don't send email or a letter—the Y simply is not set up to answer mail. Instead, a few months before your trip, call and they will let you know if there is space in the campsite or if the bunkhouse will be available.

Na Pali Coast State Park

Simply put, the Na Pali Coast is the most beautiful part of the Hawaiian Islands. Hanging valleys open like green-velvet accordions, and waterfalls tumble to the sea from the 4,120-foot-high cliffs; the experience is both exhilarating and humbling. Whether you hike in, fly over, or take a boat cruise past, be sure to see this park.

Established in 1984, Na Pali Coast State Park takes in a 22-mile stretch of fluted cliffs that wrap the northwestern shore of Kauai between Kee Beach and Polihale State Park. Volcanic in origin, carved by wind and sea, "the cliffs" (*na pali* in Hawaiian), which heaved out of the ocean floor 200 million years ago, stand as constant reminders of majesty and endurance. Four major valleys—Kalalau, Honopu, Awaawapuhi, and Nualolo—crease the cliffs.

Unless you boat or fly in (see "Boating," on p. 171; or "Helicopter Rides over Waimea Canyon & the Na Pali Coast," on p. 205), the park is accessible only on foot—and it's not easy. An ancient footpath, the **Kalalau Trail,** winds through this remote, spectacular, 6,500-acre park, ultimately leading to Kalalau Valley. Of all the green valleys in Hawaii (and there are many), only Kalalau is a true wilderness—probably the last wild valley in the islands. No road goes here, and none ever will. The remote valley is home to long-plumed tropical birds, golden monarch butterflies, and many of Kauai's 120 rare and endangered species of plants. The hike into the Kalalau Valley is grueling and takes most people 6 to 8 hours one-way.

Despite its inaccessibility, this journey into Hawaii's wilderness has become increasingly popular since the 1970s. Overrun with hikers, helicopters, and boaters, the Kalalau Valley was in grave danger of being loved to death. Strict rules about access have been adopted. The park is open to hikers and campers only on a limited basis, and you must have a permit (though you can hike the first 2 miles, to Hanakapiai Beach, without a permit). Permits are $10 per night and are issued in person at the **Kauai State Parks Office,** 3060 Eiwa St., Room 306, Lihue, HI 96766 (✆ **808/274-3446;** www.hawaiistateparks.org). You can also request one by writing the **Kauai Division of State Parks,** at the address above. For more information, contact the **Hawaii State Department of Land and Natural Resources,** 1151 Punchbowl St., Room 130, Honolulu, HI 96813 (✆ **808/587-0320**).

Hiking the Kalalau Trail ★★

The trail head is at Kee Beach, at the end of Highway 560. Even if you only go as far as Hanakapiai, bring water.

THE FIRST 2 MILES: TO HANAKAPIAI BEACH Do not attempt this hike unless you have adequate footwear (closed-toe shoes at least; hiking shoes are best), water, a sun visor, insect repellent, and adequate hiking clothes. (Shorts and T-shirt are fine; your bikini is not.) It's only 2 miles to Hanakapiai Beach, but the first mile is all uphill. This tough trail takes about 2 hours one-way and dissuades many, but everyone should attempt at least the first half mile, which gives a good hint of the startling beauty that lies ahead. Day hikers love this initial stretch, so it's usually crowded. The island of Niihau and Lehua Rock are often visible on the horizon. At mile marker 1, you'll have climbed from sea level to 400 feet; now it's all downhill to Hanakapiai Beach. Sandy in summer, the beach becomes rocky when winter waves scour the coast. There are strong currents and no lifeguards, so swim at your own risk. You can also hike another 2 miles inland from the beach to **Hanakapiai Falls,** a 120-foot cascade. Allow 3 hours for that one-way stretch.

THE REST OF THE WAY The Kalalau is the most difficult and challenging hike in Hawaii, and one you'll never forget. Even the Sierra Club rates the 22-mile round-trip into Kalalau Valley and back as "strenuous"—this is serious backpacking. Follow the footsteps of ancient Hawaiians along a cliff-side path that's a mere 10 inches wide in some places, with sheer 1,000-foot drops to the sea. One misstep, and it's *limu* (seaweed) time. Even the hardy and fit should allow at least 2 days to hike in and out. (See below for camping information.) Although the trail is usually in good shape, go in summer when it's dry; parts of it vanish in winter. When it rains, the trail becomes super-slippery, and flash floods can sweep you away.

A park ranger is now on-site full time at Kalalau Beach to greet visitors, provide information, oversee campsites, and keep trails and campgrounds in order.

Camping in Kalalau Valley & Along the Na Pali Coast

You must obtain a camping permit; see above for details. The camping season runs roughly from May or June to September (depending on the site). All campsites are booked almost a year in advance, so call or write well ahead of time. Stays are limited to 5 nights. Camping areas along the Kalalau Trail include **Hanakapiai Beach** (facilities are pit toilets, and water is from the stream), **Hanakoa Valley** (no facilities, water from the stream), **Milolii** (no facilities, water from the stream), and **Kalalau Valley** (composting toilets, several pit toilets, and water from the stream). To get a permit, contact the Division of State Parks, 3060 Eiwa St., Suite 306, Lihue, HI 96766 (✆ **808/274-3446;** www.kauai-hawaii.com/activities.php). Generally, the fee for a state park camping permit is $5 per campsite per night, but the Na Pali fee is $10 per campsite per night. You cannot stay more than 5 consecutive nights at one campsite. Keep your camping permit with you at all times.

4 OTHER OUTDOOR PURSUITS

GOLF

For last-minute and discount tee times, call **Stand-by Golf** (✆ **888/645-BOOK;** www.hawaiistandbygolf.com) between 7am and 10pm. Stand-by offers discounted greens fees, guaranteed tee times for same-day or next-day golfing.

In the listings below, the cart fee is included in the greens fee unless otherwise noted.

Lihue & Environs

Kauai Lagoons Golf Courses As we went to press only 18 holes were open on this two-course resort. There were 10 holes open at the **Kauai Kiele Championship Course ★**, for the low handicapper and eight holes open at **Mokihana Course** (formerly known as the Lagoons Course), for the recreational golfer. The 6,942-yard, par-72 Mokihana is a links-style course with a bunker that's a little less severe than Kiele's; emphasis is on the short game. The Kiele is a mixture of tournament-quality challenge and high-traffic playability; it winds up with one of Hawaii's most difficult holes, a 431-yard, par-4 played straightaway to an island green. Both courses are not scheduled to have a full 36 holes until 2011.

Facilities include a driving range, lockers, showers, a restaurant, a snack bar, a pro shop, practice greens, a clubhouse, and club and shoe rental; transportation from the airport is provided.

Kalapaki Beach, Lihue (less than a mile from Lihue Airport). ✆ **800/634-6400** or 808/241-5061. www.kauailagoonsgolf.com. From the airport, make a left on Kapule Hwy. (Hwy. 51) and look for the sign on your left. Greens fees for 18 holes is $175 ($115 for guests of Kauai Marriott; $125 for guests of select hotels and condos).

Puakea Golf Course This former Grove Farm sugar plantation opened up 18 holes in 2003 to rave reviews. The course was in the middle of construction when Hurricane Iniki slammed into it in 1992, rearranging the greens from what golf designer Robin Nelson had originally planned. The first 9 (actually the first 10) holes finally opened in 1997 to many kudos; *Sports Illustrated* named it one of the 10 best 9-hole golf courses in the U.S. The final 8 holes are now open, giving golfers something to think about. The course opens with a fairly standard first couple of holes, and just when you think you have nothing to worry about, you get to the third tee. Now you see the evidence of Nelson's work and the time he spent playing the first 10 holes numerous times. He offers golfers this advice on number three: "The fairway is really wide, and the difficulty of your second shot is really affected by which side of it you're on, because you've got to angle your shot over a lake. Hit your tee shot to the right and you've got a good shot, hit it to the left and it's almost impossible."

 Facilities include lockers, showers, a pro shop, practice greens, a clubhouse, and club and shoe rental.

4150 Nuhou St., Lihue. ✆ **866/773-5554** or 808/245-8756. www.puakeagolf.com. From the airport, take a left onto Kapule Hwy. (Hwy. 51 south). Take another left at the stop sign onto Rice St. (Hwy. 51 south), which becomes Nawiliwili Rd. (or Hwy. 58). Turn left at Borders on Pikake St., then turn left on Nuhou St. Greens fees: $135; twilight fees after 2pm $59.

Wailua Municipal Golf Course This municipal course, Kauai's oldest, was built in 1920 with just 6 holes. Another 3 holes were added, then the 9-hole course was reshaped in 1962, and 9 more holes were added after that. The result is a challenging and popular course. The local residents love this course and book up the tee times. You can book tee times up to a week in advance, and we suggest you do that or risk getting very late times or no time at all. The 6,631-yard, par-72 course gets tough from the 1st hole, where you face a par 5 that not only doglegs to the right, but makes you drive into the wind (generally blowing off the ocean from left to right). If you hit too far to the left, it's into the drink. If you hit too far to the right, better make sure the ball will stick. But regulars here agree that the 1st hole is nothing compared with the par-3, 17th hole. There, you are once again shooting into the wind coming off the ocean, past the numerous bunkers surrounding the green, and up to the seemingly teeny-tiny, skinny hot dog–shaped green. Good luck. Facilities include pro shop, lockers, practice putting green, driving range, and golf cart rental. As we went to press, there was no restaurant, but a lunch wagon is stationed by the practice putting green.

3-5350 Kuhio Hwy., Lihue. ✆ **808/241-6666.** www.kauai.gov/default.aspx?tabid=66. Take Kapule Hwy. (Hwy. 51) north from the airport, which becomes Kuhio Hwy. (Hwy. 56). Just after the 4-mile marker, the course is located on the ocean side of the highway. Greens fees: $32 weekdays, $44 weekends. Twilight rates (after 2pm): $16 weekdays, $22 weekends. Cart rental fee $18.

The Poipu Resort Area

Kiahuna Golf Club This par-70, 6,353-yard Robert Trent Jones, Jr.–designed course plays around four large archaeological sites, ranging from an ancient Hawaiian temple to the remains of a Portuguese home and crypt built in the early 1800s. This Scottish-style course has rolling terrain, undulating greens, 70 sand bunkers, and near-constant winds. The 3rd hole, a par-3, 185-yarder, goes over Waikomo Stream. At any given time, about half the players on the course are Kauai residents, the other half visitors. Facilities include a driving range, practice greens, and a restaurant.

2545 Kiahuna Plantation Dr. (adjacent to Poipu Resort area), Koloa. ✆ **808/742-9595.** www.kiahunagolf.com. Take Hwy. 50 to Hwy. 520, bear left into Poipu at the fork in the road, and turn left onto Kiahuna Plantation Dr. Greens fees: $95; twilight rates $65 (times for twilight rates may vary throughout the year).

Kukuiolono Golf Course (Finds) This is a fun 9-hole course in a spectacular location with scenic views of the entire south coast. You can't beat the price—$8 for the day, whether you play 9 holes or 90. The course is in Kukuiolono Park, a beautiful wooded area donated by the family of Walter McBryde. In fact, you'll see McBryde's grave on the course, along with some other oddities like wild chickens, ancient Hawaiian rock structures, and Japanese gardens. Of course, there are plenty of trees to keep you on your game. When you get to the second tee box, check out the coconut tree dotted with yellow, pink, orange, and white golf balls that have been driven into the bark. Don't laugh—your next shot might add to the decor! This course shouldn't give you many problems—it's excellently maintained and relatively straightforward, with few fairway

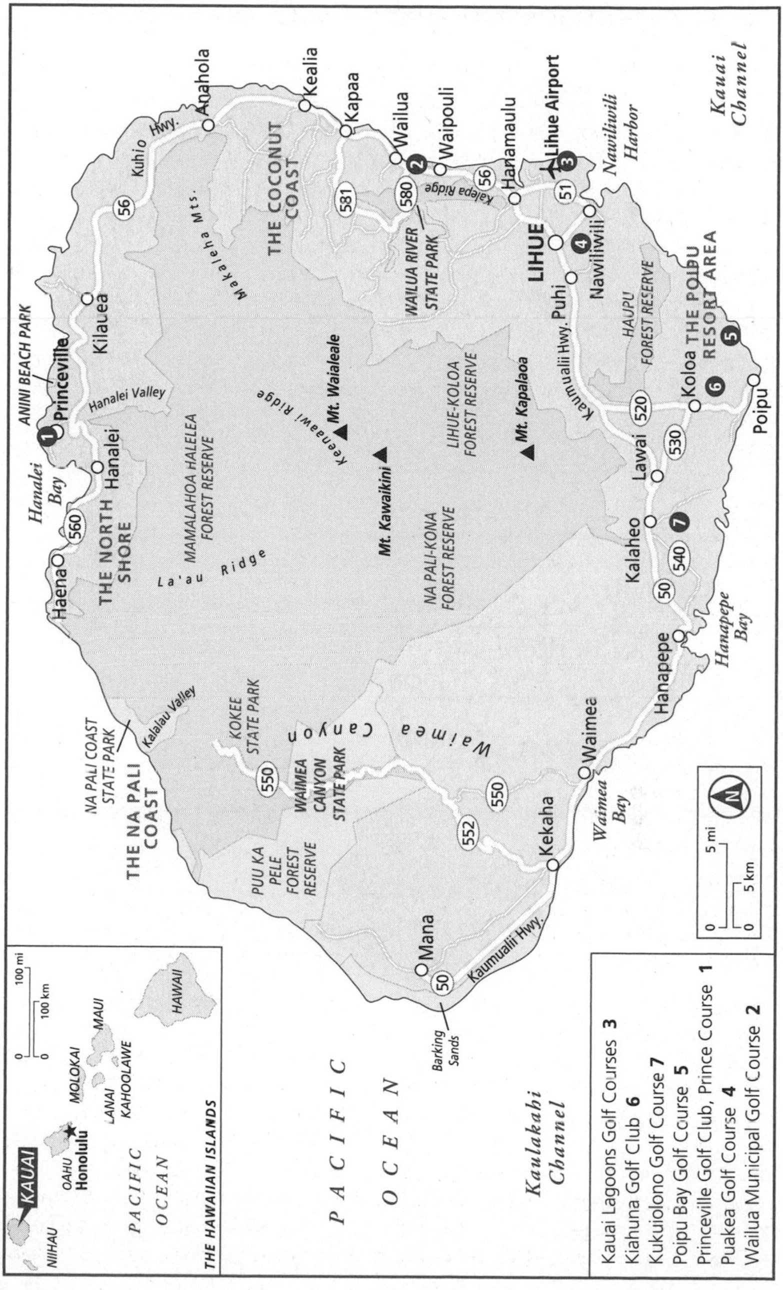

THE HAWAIIAN ISLANDS
NIIHAU
KAUAI
OAHU
Honolulu
MOLOKAI
LANAI
KAHOOLAWE
MAUI
HAWAII
PACIFIC OCEAN
0 100 mi
0 100 km
PACIFIC OCEAN
Kaulakahi Channel
Barking Sands
Mana
Kaumualii Hwy.
Kekaha
Waimea
Waimea Bay
Hanapepe
Hanapepe Bay
Kalaheo
Lawai
Koloa
Poipu
Kaumualii Hwy.
Puhi
LIHUE
Nawiliwili
Nawiliwili Harbor
Lihue Airport
Hanamaulu
Waipouli
Wailua
Kapaa
Kealia
Anahola
Kuhio Hwy.
Kilauea
Princeville
ANINI BEACH PARK
Hanalei Valley
Hanalei
Hanalei Bay
Haena
THE NORTH SHORE
THE NA PALI COAST
NA PALI COAST STATE PARK
Kalalau Valley
KOKEE STATE PARK
WAIMEA CANYON STATE PARK
Waimea Canyon
PUU KA PELE FOREST RESERVE
NA PALI-KONA FOREST RESERVE
MAMALAHOA HALELEA FOREST RESERVE
La'au Ridge
Mt. Kawaikini
Mt. Waialeale
Keenaawi Ridge
Makaleha Mts.
LIHUE-KOLOA FOREST RESERVE
Mt. Kapalaoa
THE COCONUT COAST
WAILUA RIVER STATE PARK
Kalepa Ridge
HAUPU FOREST RESERVE
THE POIPU RESORT AREA
Kauai Channel
50
540
530
520
550
552
560
56
580
581
51
0 5 mi
0 5 km
N
Kauai Lagoons Golf Courses 3
Kiahuna Golf Club 6
Kukuiolono Golf Course 7
Poipu Bay Golf Course 5
Princeville Golf Club, Prince Course 1
Puakea Golf Course 4
Wailua Municipal Golf Course 2

 hazards. Facilities include a driving range, practice greens, club rental, a snack bar, and a clubhouse.

Kukuiolono Park, Kalaheo. ✆ **808/332-9151.** Take Hwy. 50 into the town of Kalaheo; turn left on Papaluna Rd., drive up the hill for nearly a mile, and watch for the sign on your right; the entrance has huge iron gates and stone pillars—you can't miss it. Greens fees: $9 for the day; optional cart rental is $9 for 9 holes.

Poipu Bay Golf Course ★★ This 6,959-yard, par-72 course with a links-style layout was designed by Robert Trent Jones, Jr. This challenging course features undulating greens and water hazards on 8 of the holes. The par-4, 16th hole has the coastline weaving along the entire left side. You can take the safe route to the right and maybe make par (but more likely bogey), or you can try to take it tight against the ocean and possibly make it in two. The most striking (and most disrespectful) hole is the 201-yard, par-3 on the 17th, which has a tee built on an ancient Hawaiian stone formation. Facilities include a restaurant, a locker room, a pro shop, a driving range, and putting greens.

2250 Ainako St. (across from the Grand Hyatt Kauai), Koloa. ✆ **800/858-6300** or 808/742-8711. www.poipubaygolf.com. Take Hwy. 50 to Hwy. 520; bear left into Poipu at the fork in the road; turn right on Ainako St. Greens fees: $220 ($150 Grand Hyatt guests); $135 afternoon play noon–2:30pm; $80 twilight rate after 2:30pm.

The North Shore

Princeville Golf Club, Prince Course ★★ Here's your chance to play one of the best golf courses in Hawaii. This Robert Trent Jones, Jr.–designed devil of a course sits on 390 acres molded to create ocean views from every hole. Some holes have a waterfall backdrop to the greens, others shoot into the hillside, and the famous par-4, 12th has a long tee shot off a cliff to a narrow, jungle-lined fairway 100 feet below. This is the most challenging course on Kauai; accuracy is key here. Most of the time, if you miss the fairway, your ball's in the drink. "The average vacation golfer may find the Prince Course intimidating, but they don't mind because it's so beautiful," Jones says. Facilities include a restaurant, a health club and spa, lockers, a clubhouse, a golf shop, and a driving range.

Princeville. ✆ **800/826-1105** or 808/826-5070. www.princeville.com. Take Hwy. 56 to mile marker 27; the course is on your right. Greens fees: $200 ($155 for Princeville Resort guests and $130 for Princeville Hotel guests) for the Prince Course. As we went to press, the Makai Course was closed for renovations until 2010, fees were unavailable, call for information.

ALL-TERRAIN-VEHICLE (ATV) TOURS

For those who may not have the stamina to go hiking or bicycling or who don't really enjoy horseback riding, now there is a new way to explore Kauai's wilderness: All-Terrain-Vehicle (ATV) tours. Each person is given one of these four-wheel-drive vehicles resembling an oversize motorcycle. Don't think this is for the weak, either. Wrestling with an ATV and learning how to steer, shift gears, maneuver over ruts in the dirt, and charge up and down hills takes some instruction and practice. That's partially why we recommend **Kipu Ranch Adventures** (✆ **808/246-9288;** www.kiputours.com)—they emphasize safety. They start out with a lesson on flat ground, making sure everyone on the tour feels comfortable maneuvering and shifting gears on the 300cc or 350cc Hondas. Off you go on the tour. After about 10 to 15 minutes of pretty easy riding, they take you to a very steep hill that has all kinds of ruts and bumps. Patiently, they teach each person how to ride over the rough terrain. Everyone practices until the instructors give the okay to proceed. Once you have passed this torturous hill test, the rest of the 3-hour tour is a breeze. The second reason we recommend this company is that they are the only operator

Yes, Virginia, There Are Problems in Paradise—Crime & Weather

You may be in paradise, but be aware there is crime on Kauai. Always lock your bicycle (even if you're just leaving it for a minute). You are responsible if it is stolen. Remember that weather in Hawaii is not like your weather back home—an island rainstorm can cause a flash flood. The Kauai Visitors Bureau publishes a free brochure ***Tips for a Safe Vacation*** that recommends the following:

- Never leave valuables in your car, unattended at the beach
- Do not drive into waterfalls or pools of water
- Always wear your seatbelt (the fine for non-compliance is very stiff)
- On a one-way bridge, courtesy calls for only six cars to cross, then yield to opposing traffic

For the free brochure contact the Kauai Visitors Bureau, ✆ **808/245-3971.**

on a 3,000-acre private property never before opened to the public. Here's your chance to see a part of Kauai that even local residents have not seen. Extending from the Huleia River to the top of the Haupu Mountains, this property has been the filming site for numerous movies *(Jurassic Park, Raiders of the Lost Ark, Outbreak, Six Days and Seven Nights).* The tour provides helmets, safety glasses, snacks, juice, water, fruit, and a stop over a swimming hole with a swinging rope. For those who would rather leave the driving to someone else (or who are ages 6–15), they have a "rhino," a four-wheel-drive Kawasaki that holds up to four passengers (2 adults and 2 children). Cost for the ATV tour is $125; the rhino is $125 for the driver, $100 for another adult, $72 for each child 6 to 15, and $100 for seniors over 65.

BIKING

There are a couple of great places on Kauai for two-wheeling: the **Poipu area,** which has wide, flat roads and several dirt-cane roads (especially around Mahaulepu); and the cane road (a dirt road used for hauling sugar cane) between **Kealia Beach** and **Anahola,** north of Kapaa.

The following places rent mountain bikes, from a low of $20 a day for cruisers to $25 to $30 a day for mountain bikes (with big discounts for multiple-day rentals): **Outfitters Kauai,** 2827A Poipu Rd. (look for the small, five-shop mall before the road forks to Poipu/Spouting Horn), Poipu (✆ **808/742-9667;** www.outfitterskauai.com); and **Kauai Cycle and Tour,** 1379 Kuhio Hwy., Kapaa (✆ **808/821-2115;** www.bikehawaii.com/kauaicycle). For a great selection of high-quality mountain bikes at reasonable prices, it's worth the drive to **Pedal 'n Paddle,** in Hanalei (✆ **808/826-9069;** www.pedalnpaddle.com), which has high-grade Marin hybrid road bikes with Shimano components. Rentals start at $20 a day or $80 a week and include helmet and bike lock. The shop also has cruisers. The knowledgeable folks here are more than happy to provide you with free maps and tell you about the best biking spots on the island.

GUIDED BIKE TOURS **Outfitters Kauai** ★ (✆ **808/742-9667;** www.outfitterskauai.com) offers a fabulous downhill bike ride from Waimea Canyon to the ocean. The 12-mile trip (mostly coasting) begins at 6am, when the van leaves the shop in Poipu and heads up to the canyon. By the time you've eaten the fresh-baked muffins and enjoyed the coffee, you're at the top of the canyon, just as the sun is rising over the rim—it's a remarkable moment. The tour makes a couple of stops on the way down for short, scenic nature hikes. You'll be back at the shop around 10am. The sunset trip follows the same route. Both tours cost $98 per adult, $78 per child 12 to 14.

BIRDING

Kauai provides some of Hawaii's last sanctuaries for endangered native birds and oceanic birds, such as the albatross.

At **Kokee State Park,** a 4,345-acre wilderness forest at the end of Highway 550 in southwest Kauai, you have an excellent chance of seeing some of Hawaii's endangered native birds. You might spot the apapane, a red bird with black wings and a curved black bill; or the iwi, a red bird with black wings, orange legs, and a salmon-colored bill. Other frequently seen native birds are the honeycreeper, which sings like a canary; the amakihi, a plain, olive-green bird with a long, straight bill; and the anianiau, a tiny yellow bird with a thin, slightly curved bill. The most common native bird at Kokee is the moa, or red jungle fowl, brought as domestic stock by ancient Polynesians. Ordinarily shy, they're quite tame in this environment. David Kuhn leads custom hikes, pointing out Hawaii's rarest birds on his **Terran Tours** (✆ **808/335-0398**), which range from a half day to 3 days and feature endemic and endangered species.

Kilauea Point National Wildlife Refuge ★, a mile north of Kilauea on the North Shore (✆ **808/828-0168**), is a 200-acre headland habitat that juts above the surf and includes cliffs, two rocky wave-lashed bays, and a tiny islet that serves as a jumping-off spot for seabirds. You can easily spot red-footed boobies, which nest in trees, and wedge-tailed shearwaters, which burrow in nests along the cliffs. You may also see the great frigate bird, the Laysan albatross, the red-tailed tropic bird, and the endangered nene. Native plants and the Kilauea Point Lighthouse are highlights as well. The refuge is open from 10am to 4pm daily (closed on Thanksgiving, Christmas, and New Year's Day); admission is $5. To get here, turn right off Kuhio Highway (Hwy. 56) at Kilauea, just after mile marker 23; follow Kilauea Road to the refuge entrance.

Peaceful Hanalei Valley is home to Hawaii's endangered Koloa duck, gallinule, coot, and stilt. The **Hanalei National Wildlife Refuge** (✆ **808/828-1413;** www.fws.gov/hanalei) also provides a safe habitat for migratory shorebirds and waterfowl. It's not open to the public, but an interpretive overlook along the highway serves as an impressive vantage point. Along Ohiki Road, which begins at the west end of the Hanalei River Bridge, you'll often see white cattle egrets hunting crayfish in streams.

HORSEBACK RIDING

Only in Kauai can you ride a horse across the wide-open pastures of a working ranch under volcanic peaks and rein up near a waterfall pool. No wonder Kauai's *paniolo* (cowboys) smile and sing so much. Near the Poipu area, **CJM Country Stables,** 1731 Kelaukia St. (2 miles beyond the Grand Hyatt Kauai Resort & Spa), Koloa (✆ **808/742-6096;** www.cjmstables.com), offers both 2- and 3-hour escorted Hidden Valley beach rides. You'll trot over Hidden Valley ranch land, past secluded beaches and bays, along the Haupu Ridge, across sugar-cane fields, and to Mahaulepu Beach; it's worth your time and money just to get out to this seldom-seen part of Kauai. The 3-hour "Secret Beach Picnic Ride" with swimming costs $125 and includes lunch. The 2-hour "Scenic Valley Ride" is $98. There's also a 3½-hour swim/beach/picnic ride for $115.

Princeville Ranch Stables, Highway 56 (just after the Princeville Airport), Hanalei (✆ **808/826-6777;** www.princevilleranch.com), has a variety of outings. The 1½-hour country ride takes in views of the Hanalei Mountains and the vista of Anini Beach ($80). The 3-hour or the 4-hour "Waterfall Picnic Ride" crosses ranch land, takes you on a short (but steep) hike to swimming pools at the base of waterfalls, and includes a picnic lunch for $125 to $135. Riders must be in good physical shape, and don't forget to put your swimsuit on under your jeans. The Princeville Ranch Stables also offers other adventures, ranging from the less strenuous wagon rides to a cattle-drive ride.

TENNIS

The **Kauai County Parks and Recreation Department,** 4444 Rice St., Suite 150, Lihue (✆ **808/241-4463**), has a list of the nine county tennis courts around the island, all of which are free and open to the public. Private courts that are open to the public include the **Princeville Tennis Club,** Princeville Hotel (✆ **808/826-3620** www.princeville.com), which has six courts available for $15 per person ($12 for guests) for 90 minutes. On the south side, try **Grand Hyatt Kauai Resort & Spa Poipu Resort** (✆ **808/742-1234;** www.kauai-hyatt.com), which has three courts, available for $25 an hour; and **Kiahuna Swim and Tennis Club,** Poipu Road (just past the Poipu Shopping Village on the left), Poipu Resort (✆ **808/742-9533**), which has eight courts renting for $15 per person per hour.

8

Exploring Kauai

Yes, Kauai has the best beaches in Hawaii, but don't forget the rest of this beautiful island. Get out and discover for yourself why Kauai is called the "Garden Isle." Walk back in history in the capital of Lihue. Make time to see Kauai's incredible botanical world of manicured gardens, the geological wonders of Waimea Canyon, the incredible carved cliffs of the Na Pali Coast, and the enchanted rainforests of the wettest place on Earth. Book a helicopter flight, take a back-roads tour in a four-wheel-drive vehicle, make a pilgrimage to a Hindu temple located on a sacred Hawaiian site, drop the kids off at a children's museum, or sign up for an expedition to Kauai's famous movie sites. There's a lot more to Kauai than its gorgeous beaches, so get out there and discover why visitors become enchanted with this magical island.

1 LIHUE & ENVIRONS

Grove Farm Homestead Museum You can experience a day in the life of an 1860s sugar planter on a visit to Grove Farm Homestead, which shows how good life was (for some, anyway) when sugar was king. This is Hawaii's best remaining example of a sugar-plantation homestead. Founded in 1864 by George N. Wilcox, a Hanalei missionary's son, Grove Farm was one of the earliest of Hawaii's 86 sugar plantations. A self-made millionaire, Wilcox died a bachelor in 1933, at age 94. His estate looks much like it did when he lived here, complete with period furniture, plantation artifacts, and Hawaiiana.

4050 Nawiliwili Rd. (Hwy. 58) at Pikaka St. (2 miles from Waapa Rd.), Lihue. © **808/245-3202.** www.hawaiiweb.com/kauai/html/sites/grove_farm_homestead.html. Requested donation $5 adults, $2 children under 12. Tours offered Mon and Wed–Thurs at 10am and 1pm; reservations required.

Kauai Museum ★ Kids The history of Kauai is kept safe in an imposing Greco-Roman building that once served as the town library. This great little museum is worth a stop before you set out to explore the island. It contains a wealth of historical artifacts and information tracing the island's history, from the beginning of time through Contact (when Capt. James Cook "discovered" Kauai in 1778), the monarchy period, the plantation era, and the present. You'll hear tales of the *menehune* (the mythical, elflike people who were said to build massive stone works in a single night) and see old poi pounders and idols, relics of sugar planters and *paniolo,* a nice seashell collection, old Hawaiian quilts, feather leis, a replica of a plantation worker's home, and much more—even a model of Cook's ship, the HMS *Resolution,* riding anchor in Waimea Bay. Vintage photographs by W. J. Senda, a Japanese immigrant, show old Kauai, while a contemporary video, shot from a helicopter, captures the island's natural beauty.

4428 Rice St., Lihue. © **808/245-6931.** www.kauaimuseum.org. Admission $10 adults, $8 seniors, $3 students 13–17, $1 children 6–12; free for children 5 and under.. Mon–Fri 9am–4pm; Sat 10am–4pm. First Sat of every month is "Family Day," when admission is free.

Allerton Garden of the National Tropical Botanical Garden **25**
Fern Grotto **15**
Grove Farm Homestead Museum **21**
Guava Kai Plantation **10**
Hanalei Bridge **7**
Hanalei National Wildlife Refuge **8**
Hanalei Valley Lookout **9**
Ka Ulu O Laka Heiau **4**
Kauai Children's Discovery Museum **13**
Kauai Museum **19**
Kiki a Ola (Menehune Ditch) **27**
Kilauea Point National Wildlife Refuge **11**
Kilohana **22**
Kokee Natural History Museum **3**
Limahuli Garden of the National Tropical Botanical Garden **5**
Menehune (Alakoko) Fishpond **20**
Na Aina Kai Botanical Gardens **12**
Pacific Missile Range Facility **1**
Prince Kuhio Park **23**
Russian Fort Elizabeth State Historical Park **26**
San Marga Iraivan Temple **16**
Sleeping Giant **14**
Spouting Horn **24**
Wailua Falls **18**
Wailua River State Park **17**
Waimea Canyon **2**
Waioli Mission House Museum **6**

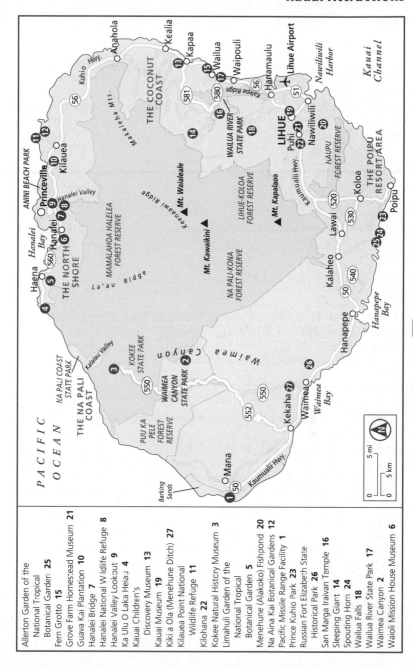

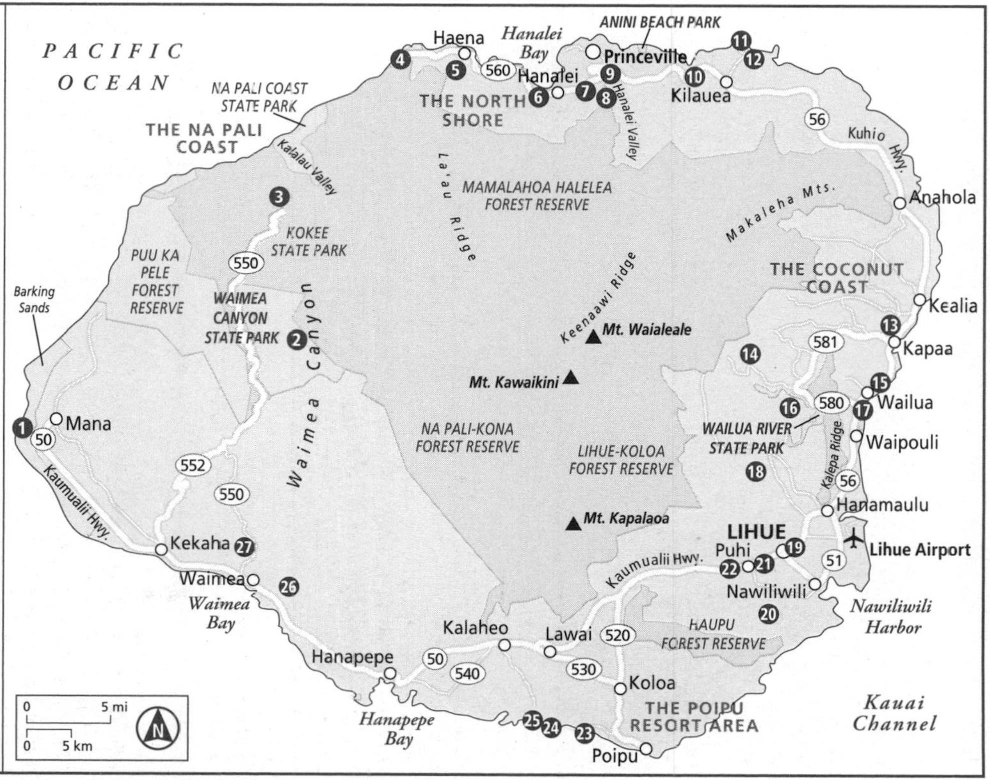

Touring Off the Beaten Path

If you are itching to get off the beaten path and see the "hidden" Kauai, **Aloha Kauai Tours★**, 1702 Haleukana St., Lihue, HI 96766 (✆ **800/452-1113** or 808/245-8809; www.alohakauaitours.com), has a half-day, four-wheel-drive tour that follows a figure-eight path around Kauai, from Kilohana Crater to the Mahaulepu coastline. The tour, done in a four-wheel-drive van, not only stops at Kauai's well-known scenic spots but also travels on sugar-cane roads (on private property), taking you to places most people who live on Kauai have never seen. The guides are well versed in everything from native plants to Hawaiian history. Don't forget your camera. The tour costs $75 adults, $50 children 5 to 12. Reservations are required.

Kauai Plantation Railway ★ Kids The first new railroad to be built in Hawaii in 100 years opened in 2007 after 5 years of work, 6,000 ties, 30,000 hand-driven spikes, and 480,000 pounds of iron rail. The Kauai Plantation Railway is part scenic tour, part-cultural tour, part agricultural tour, part educational tour, and 100% fun for the family. The train, consisting of two refurbished diesel engines and four custom (hardwood floors) passenger cars, travels along a 3-mile figure-eight track through the grounds of Kilohana (see below). The 40-minute tour is narrated by very knowledgeable guides dressed in green *palaka* print shirts like those traditionally worn by plantation workers. They not only weave in Kauai's history but also point out the more than 50 different crops that have been planted along the train route, everything from Hawaii crops like sugar, pineapple, and taro to fruit trees to fragrant plants (ginger, gardenia, plumeria), vegetable plants, and even hardwood trees (*milo,* koa). The train stops briefly at the "animal farm," where some pigs, goats, sheep, chickens, and cows are available for petting. Coming are a train/hike adventure into Kahuna Nui Valley and a "Gourmet Deli Lunch Tour." Check the website for details.

Kilohana, 3-2087 Kaumualii Hwy., Lihue. ✆ **808/245-RAIL.** www.kauaiplantationrailway.com. Admission $18 adult, $14 children 2–12. Mon–Sat 10am–2pm.

Kilohana Plantation This 35-acre Tudor-style estate sprawls across the landscape in Puhi. The best way to see the grounds is on the Kauai Plantation Railway tour (see above). The mansion, built by sugar baron Gaylord Parke Wilcox in 1936, is an architectural marvel that houses a sprinkling of galleries and shops (see p. 218) as well as Gaylord's restaurant (see p. 133). It's worth a stroll around the house to admire the original furnishings and architecture even if you're not interested in shopping or dining here. Kilohana also hosts a luau on Tuesday and Friday (see "A Hawaiian Feast: The Luau" on p. 156).

Kilohana, 3-2087 Kaumualii Hwy., Lihue. ✆ **808/245-5608.** www.kilohanakauai.com.

Menehune (Alekoko) Fishpond Just outside Lihue and Nawiliwili Harbor, on the Huleia River, lies a mystery that still can't be explained: the handiwork of the *menehune* (see "Discovering the Legendary 'Little People,'" below). The pond, called Alekoko ("rippling blood") and today known as the Menehune Fishpond, was an aquacultural feat constructed hundreds of years ago. The builders of this 2,700-foot-long stone wall (that cuts off a bend in the river) were believed to be the mythical people who inhabited Kauai

Fun Facts Discovering the Legendary "Little People"

Like many places in the world, including Ireland with its leprechauns, Hawaii has stories about "little people." According to ancient Hawaiian legend, among Kauai's earliest settlers were the *menehune,* a race of small people who worked at night to accomplish magnificent feats. However, archaeologists say the *menehune* may not be legendary people but in fact non-Polynesian people who once lived on Kauai. These people, believed to be from the Marquesas Islands, arrived in Hawaii between A.D. 0 and 350. When the Polynesians ventured from Tahiti to Hawaii between A.D. 600 and 1100, they fought the *menehune* already living in Hawaii. Some scholars claim the Polynesians were more aggressive and warlike than the Marquesans, and in a series of wars the Tahitians drove the Marquesans north through the island chain to Kauai.

Anthropologists point out that the Tahitian word *manahune,* which means a lower class or a slave, was used to describe the racial hierarchy, not the physical stature of the people already living in Hawaii. In other words, *manahune* (or *menehune*) was used to mean small in the Tahitians' strict caste system, not small in size.

In any case, everyone agrees that these people performed incredible feats, constructing elaborate stonework edifices (without using mortar) that have stood for centuries. One example is the **Menehune Ditch** (Kiki a Ola), along the Waimea River. Only a 2-foot-high portion of the wall can be seen today; the rest of the marvelous stonework is buried under the roadbed. To get here from Hwy. 50, go inland on Menehune Road in Waimea; a plaque marks the spot about 1½ miles up.

Another example lies above Nawiliwili Harbor. The **Menehune Fishpond**—which at one time extended 25 miles—is said to have been built in just 1 night, with two rows of thousands of *menehune* passing stones hand-to-hand. The *menehune* were promised that no one would watch them work, but one person did. When the *menehune* discovered the spy, they stopped working immediately, leaving two gaps in the wall. From Nawiliwili Harbor, take Hulemalu Road above Huleia Stream. Look for the HAWAII CONVENTION AND VISITORS BUREAU marker at a turnoff in the road, which leads to the legendary fishpond. Kayakers can paddle up Huleia Stream to see it up close.

before the Polynesians arrived. The fishpond is located in the Huleia National Wildlife Refuge, 238 acres of river valley that is a habitat for endangered Hawaiian water birds (*ae'o* or Hawaiian stilt, *'alae Ke'oke'o* or Hawaiian coot, *'alae 'ula* or Hawaiian gallinule, and *Koloa maoli* or Hawaiian duck). Although you can see the fishpond and the refuge from the road, the area is not open to the public. Small boats, kayaks, jet skis, windsurfers, and water-skiers use the river.

Hulemalu Rd., Niumalu. From Lihue, take Rice St. to Nawiliwili Harbor. Turn left on Niumalu Rd. and right on Hulemalu Rd. Up the hill is a lookout where you have a view of the pond, Huleia Stream, and Huleia National Wildlife Reserve.

Wailua Falls If you'd like to see cascading waterfalls but don't want to hike into the wilderness to do it, this is your best bet. The journey here, about a 4-mile drive from Lihue, takes you through rolling hills past former sugar-cane fields and across a valley, with majestic mountains in the background. From the Wailua Falls parking lot you can look down at two waterfalls cascading some 80 feet into a large pool. Legend claims that the *alii* (royalty) came to these waterfalls and dived from the cliff into the pool below to show the common people that monarchs were not mere men. Don't try this today.

Maalo Rd. (Hwy. 583), Wailua. From Lihue, take Kaumualii Hwy. (Hwy. 50) north, and turn left on Maalo Rd. (Hwy. 583). After 4 miles, look for the parking area for Wailua Falls on the right.

2 THE POIPU RESORT AREA

No Hawaii resort has a better entrance: On Maluhia Road, eucalyptus trees planted in 1911 as a windbreak for sugar-cane fields now form a monumental **tree tunnel.** The leafy-green, cool tunnel starts at Kaumualii Highway; you'll emerge at the golden-red beach. The **Poipu Beach Resort Association** (✆ **888/744-0888** or 808/742-7444; www.koloaheritagetrail.info) produces a free brochure called the ***Koloa Heritage Trail,*** which is a 10-mile walk, bike ride, or drive that has some 14 historical stops and markers describing the history and culture of this area. The Historic Trail begins at **Spouting Horn** (see below) and finishes at the Koloa Mission Church in Koloa town. The trail is a great idea, but a few of the sites are either no longer there (like site no. 10 on Hapa Rd., where the pre-Contact evidence of ancient Hawaiians is no longer); changed dramatically from what they once were (like site no. 13, the Yamamoto Store and Koloa Hotel, now gone); or difficult to get to (like site no. 9, Pu'uwanawana Volcanic Cone, which you can see in the distance from the highway, but is located on fenced private property).

Allerton Garden of the National Tropical Botanical Garden ★ Discover an extraordinary collection of tropical fruit and spice trees, rare Hawaiian plants, and hundreds of varieties of flowers at the 186-acre preserve known as **Lawai Gardens,** said to be the largest collection of rare and endangered plants in the world. Adjacent **McBryde Garden,** a royal home site of Queen Emma in the 1860s, is known for its formal gardens, a delicious kind of colonial decadence. The garden contains fountains, streams, waterfalls, and European statuary. Endangered green sea turtles can be seen here. (Their home in the sea was wiped out years ago by Hurricane Iniki.) The tours are fascinating for green thumbs and novices alike.

Visitor Center, Lawai Rd. (across the street from Spouting Horn), Poipu. ✆ **808/742-2623.** www.ntbg.org. Admission and tour of Allerton Garden $45 adults, $20 children 10–12 (children 10 years and older only on tour). Guided 2½-hr. tours by reservation only, Mon–Sat at 9am, 10am, 1pm, and 2pm. Self-guided tours of McBryde Garden Mon–Sat 9am–4pm, $20 adults, $10 children 6–12 (trams into the valley leave once an hour on the half-hour; last tram 2:30pm).

Prince Kuhio Park This small roadside park is the birthplace of Prince Jonah Kuhio Kalanianaole, the "People's Prince," whose March 26th birthday is a holiday in Hawaii. He opened the beaches of Waikiki to the public in 1918 and served as Hawaii's second territorial delegate to the U.S. Congress. What remains here are the foundations of the family home, a royal fishpond, and a shrine where tributes are still paid in flowers.

Lawai Rd., Koloa. Just after mile marker 4 on Poipu Rd., veer to the right of the fork in the road; the park is on the right side.

Spouting Horn ★ Kids This natural phenomenon is second only to Yellowstone's Old Faithful. It's quite a sight—big waves hit Kauai's south shore with enough force to send a spout of funneled salt water 10 feet or more up in the air; in winter, the water can get as high as six stories.

Spouting Horn is different from other blowholes in Hawaii, in that an additional hole blows air that sounds like a loud moaning. According to Hawaiian legend, this coastline was once guarded by a giant female lizard (Mo'o); she gobbled up any intruders. One day, along came Liko, who wanted to fish in this area. Mo'o rushed out to eat Liko. Quickly, Liko threw a spear right into the giant lizard's mouth. Mo'o then chased Liko into a lava tube. Liko escaped, but legend says Mo'o is still in the tube, and the moaning at Spouting Horn is her cry for help.

At Kukuiula Bay, beyond Prince Kuhio Park (see above).

3 WESTERN KAUAI

WAIMEA TOWN

If you'd like to take a self-guided tour of this historic town, stop at the **Waimea Library,** at mile marker 23 on Highway 50, to pick up a map and guide to the sites.

Kiki a Ola (Menehune Ditch) Ancient Hawaiians were expert rock builders, able to construct elaborate edifices without using mortar. They formed long lines and passed stones hand over hand, and lifted rocks weighing tons with ropes made from native plants. Their feats gave rise to fantastic tales of *menehune,* elflike people hired by Hawaiian kings to create massive stoneworks in a single night—reputedly for the payment of a single shrimp. (See "Discovering the Legendary 'Little People,'" above.) An excellent example of ancient Hawaiian construction is Kiki a Ola, the so-called Menehune Ditch, with cut and dressed stones that form an ancient aqueduct that still directs water to irrigate taro ponds. Historians credit the work to ancient Hawaiian engineers who applied their knowledge of hydraulics to accomplish flood control and irrigation. Only

Keep Out: Pacific Missile Range Facility

At the end of Kaumualii Highway (Hwy. 50) lies the 42,000-square-mile **Pacific Missile Range Facility (PMRF),** which is technically run by the Navy. Lately it seems as if everyone on the base, from the military to federal agencies, works on "national defense." According to their website, PMRF "supports a variety of training exercises and developmental tests involving space, air, surface, and sub-surface units," such as missile and submarine tracking information. For years, the base shared its beaches with the people of Kauai, but the September 11, 2001, terrorist attacks stopped all that. They still have a (very complex and convoluted) system whereby local residents gain clearance (through a long series of checks by the military and police department) to get a pass to the base's beaches, but it is impossible for visitors to do so. For more information, call ✆ **808/335-4229** or go to www.pmrf.navy.mil/index.html.

a 2-foot-high portion of the wall can be seen today; the rest of the marvelous stonework is buried under the roadbed.

From Hwy. 50, go inland on Menehune Rd.; a plaque marks the spot about 1½ miles up.

Russian Fort Elizabeth State Historical Park Add the Russians to the list of those who tried to conquer Hawaii. In 1815, a German doctor tried to claim Kauai for Russia. He even supervised the construction of a fort in Waimea, but he and his handful of Russian companions were expelled by Kamehameha I a couple of years later. Now a state historic landmark, the Russian Fort Elizabeth (named for the wife of Russia's Czar Alexander I) is on the eastern headlands overlooking the harbor, across from Lucy Kapahu Aukai Wright Beach Park. The fort, built Hawaiian-style with stacked lava rocks in the shape of a star, once bristled with cannons; it's now mostly in ruins. You can take a free, self-guided tour of the site. It affords a keen view of the west bank of the Waimea River, where Captain Cook landed, and of the island of Niihau across the channel.

Hwy. 50 (on the ocean side, just after mile marker 77), east of Waimea.

Sugar Plantation Tours The only sugar tour in Hawaii, this 2-hour guided tour takes you into the fields and through the factory, viewing just how sugar goes from the soil to your dining room table. Along the way you learn the 165-plus-year history of sugar in Hawaii and all the trials and errors the industry went through to establish such a sweet crop in the middle of the Pacific. Also find out why this once powerful industry is now on the downswing.

Gay & Robinson Visitor Center and Museum, Hwy. 50 (on the ocean side, just after mile marker 22), east of Waimea. ✆ **808/335-2824.** www.hawaiimuseums.org/mc/iskauai_gayandrobinson.htm. Tours $30 adults, $21 children 17 and under. Mon–Fri 9am and 1pm.

THE GRAND CANYON OF THE PACIFIC: WAIMEA CANYON ★★★

The great gaping gulch known as Waimea Canyon is quite a sight. This valley, known for its reddish lava beds, reminds everyone who sees it of the Grand Canyon. Kauai's version is bursting with ever-changing color, just like its namesake, but it's smaller—only a mile wide, 3,567 feet deep, and 12 miles long. A massive earthquake sent a number of streams into the single river that ultimately carved this picturesque canyon. Today, the Waimea River—a silver thread of water in the gorge that's sometimes a trickle, often a torrent, but always there—keeps cutting the canyon deeper and wider, and nobody can say what the result will be 100 million years from now.

You can stop by the road and look at the canyon, hike down into it, or swoop through it in a helicopter. For more information, see "Hiking & Camping," in chapter 7, and "Helicopter Rides over Waimea Canyon & the Na Pali Coast," below.

THE DRIVE THROUGH WAIMEA CANYON & UP TO KOKEE

By car, there are two ways to visit Waimea Canyon and Kokee State Park, 20 miles from Waimea. From the coastal road (Hwy. 50), you can turn up Waimea Canyon Drive (Hwy. 550) at Waimea town; or you can pass through Waimea and turn up Kokee Road (Hwy. 55) at Kekaha. The climb is very steep from Kekaha, but Waimea Canyon Drive, the rim road, is narrower and rougher. A few miles up, the two merge into Kokee Road.

The first good vantage point is **Waimea Canyon Lookout,** located between mile markers 10 and 11 on Waimea Canyon Road. From here, it's another 6 miles to Kokee.

There are a few more lookout points along the way that also offer spectacular views, such as **Puu Hina Hina Lookout,** between mile markers 13 and 14, at 3,336 feet; be sure to pull over and spend a few minutes pondering this natural wonder. (The giant white object that looks like a golf ball and defaces the natural landscape is a radar station left over from the Cold War.)

KOKEE STATE PARK

It's only 16 miles from Waimea to Kokee, but the park is a whole different world because it is 4,345 acres of rainforest. You'll enter a new climate zone, where the breeze has a bite and trees look quite continental. You're in a cloud forest on the edge of the Alakai Swamp, the largest swamp in Hawaii, on the summit plateau of Kauai. Days are cool and wet, with intermittent bright sunshine, not unlike Seattle on a good day. Bring your sweater and, if you're staying over, be sure you know how to light a fire. (Overnight lows dip into the 40s [single digits Celsius].)

The forest is full of native plants, such as mokihana berry, ohia lehua, and iliau (similar to Maui's silversword), as well as imports like Australia's eucalyptus and California's redwood. Pigs, goats, and black-tailed deer thrive in the forest, but the moa, or Polynesian jungle fowl, is the cock of the walk.

Right next to Kokee Lodge (which lies on the only road through the park, about a mile before it ends) is the **Kokee Natural History Museum ★** (**© 808/335-9975;** www.kokee.org), open daily from 10am to 4pm (free admission). This is the best place to learn about the forest and Alakai Swamp before you set off hiking in the wild. The museum shop has great trail information and local books and maps, including the official park trail map. We recommend getting the *Pocket Guide on Native Plants on the Nature Trail for Kokee State Park* and the *Road Guide to Kokee and Waimea Canyon State Park.*

A **nature walk** is the best introduction to this rainforest; it starts behind the museum at the rare Hawaiian koa tree. This easy, self-guided walk of about a quarter mile takes about 20 minutes if you stop and look at all the plants identified along the way.

Two miles above Kokee Lodge is **Kalalau Lookout ★**, the spectacular climax of your drive through Waimea Canyon and Kokee. When you stand at the lookout, below you is a work in progress that began at least 5 million years ago. It's hard to stop looking; the view is breathtaking, especially when light and cloud shadows play across the red-and-orange cliffs.

There's lots more to see and do up here: Anglers fly-fish for rainbow trout, and hikers tackle the 45 trails that lace the Alakai Swamp. (See "Watersports" and "Hiking & Camping," in chapter 7.) That's a lot of ground to cover, so you might want to plan on staying over. If pitching a tent is too rustic for you, the wonderful **cabins** set in a grove of redwoods are one of the best lodging bargains in the islands (see chapter 5). The restaurant at **Kokee Lodge** is open for continental breakfast and lunch daily from 9am to 3:30pm.

For advance information, contact the **State Division of Parks,** 3060 Eiwa St., Room 306, Lihue, HI 96766 (**© 808/274-3446**); and the **Kokee Lodge Manager,** P.O. Box 819, Waimea, HI 96796 (**© 808/335-6061**). The park is open daily year-round. The best time to go is early in the morning, to see the panoramic view of Kalalau Valley from the lookout at 4,000 feet, before clouds obscure the valley and peaks.

HELICOPTER RIDES OVER WAIMEA CANYON & THE NA PALI COAST ★★★

Don't leave Kauai without seeing it from a helicopter. It's expensive but worth the splurge. You can take home memories of the thrilling ride up and over the Kalalau Valley on Kauai's wild North Shore and into the 5,200-foot vertical temple of Mount Waialeale,

Moments Taking to the Skies—It's More Than Just a Helicopter Ride

The light on the floor-to-ceiling windshield sparkles dazzlingly. Only the sound of traditional Hawaiian music wafts through the noise-canceling headset as I relax into the plush, comfy seat. Staring at the ground, I notice that it begins to move away, almost like magic, as the helicopter effortlessly rises straight up.

Defying gravity, the high-tech aircraft smoothly glides through the air, like some kind of modern magic carpet. There really is nothing else that can compare to the helicopter's serene motion of floating. It's not a rocking sensation like being on a boat, nor the high-speed forward velocity of an airplane, but a gentle drifting.

Helicopter rides over Kauai are more than just a "ride," but a tour of the island. In fact, the only way to truly see a large percentage of the island is to sail the skies in a helicopter.

"On Kauai, a helicopter is really the only way to see two-thirds of the island because of the remote nature of the terrain," says Casey Riemer, of Jack Harter Helicopters. "You just can't see it any other way."

One of the first questions Hawaii's helicopter tour operators always get asked is, "How safe is flying in a helicopter?" To which most of them respond that statistically, it is more dangerous driving in your car than it is flying in Hawaii's helicopter tours.

"Hawaii's [helicopter tour's] safety record is quite frankly phenomenal," states Riemer. In the past decade, Hawaii has only seen a handful of helicopter accidents despite the hundreds of thousands of hours that helicopters are in the sky touring the state.

In addition, the industry not only meets federal safety standards, but most helicopter companies go beyond federal requirements to ensure the safest ride possible.

Safety, as well as the entire helicopter touring industry, is a pricey business. Helicopters are expensive aircraft (costing from $1 million to nearly $2 million); maintenance is very costly (several parts must be replaced every so many flight hours); and the number of personnel necessary for the air-touring business

the most sacred place on the island and the wettest spot on Earth. (And in some cases, you can even take home a video of your ride.) All flights leave from Lihue Airport.

Blue Hawaiian ★★★ Blue Hawaiian has been the Cadillac of helicopter tour companies on Maui and the Big Island for more than a decade, and recently they have expanded their operations to Kauai. I strongly recommend that you try to book with them first. Their operation is first-class, and they use state-of-the-art equipment: American Eurocopter ECO-Star, which reduces noise in the helicopter by 50% and allows 23% more interior room. Plus the craft has individual Business Class–style seats, two-way communication with the pilot, and expansive glass for incredible views. The 50-minute flights journey first to Hanapepe Valley, then continue on to Mana Waiapuna, commonly referred to as (from the pilot to the mechanics to the dispatchers to the ground personnel to the people who book you) is immense.

The cost of a helicopter tour varies; see below. Yes, it is expensive, but worth every penny for an experience you will remember for a lifetime.

However, don't choose a helicopter tour company based on price alone. Remember that you get what you pay for, and if you are going to pay a few hundred dollars, you might as well get your money's worth. (Cheaper is not necessarily better.)

There are ways to save money. Check the Internet. Generally if you book 7 days in advance on the Internet, you can get 10% to 15% off. One company has an Internet discount as high as 40%.

This is one time that you might want to do the investigative work into the tour yourself—if you go to a booking agency, they may just book the helicopter company that gives them the best commission (and may not have the "right" tour for you). Also beware of timeshare presentations offering greatly discounted rates for helicopter tours only if you first sit through a lengthy presentation.

Tour operators all agree that you should book early in your trip, just in case weather cancels your tour. You will then still have several days remaining in your trip to re-book.

If a tour operator is unable to fly due to weather, then you are not charged for your trip. Some operators tell stories about taking off and then deciding that the trip will not be comfortable for their passengers, so they return them to base without charging them.

However, if you cannot make your flight, you must cancel 24 hours in advance or you could be charged for the flight.

There really is no such thing as a perfect time to fly. Conditions change. On Kauai, the east end of the island gets light early, but the Na Pali Coast, on the west side, gets light later in the day. And yes, helicopters fly when it is cloudy because it nearly always is cloudy somewhere on the island. ***But remember:*** With a helicopter, it is possible to fly over the rainbow.

"Jurassic Park Falls." Next it's up the Olokele Canyon, then on to the Waimea Canyon, the famed "Grand Canyon of the Pacific." Most of the flight will continue along the Na Pali Coast, before heading out to the Bali Hai Cliffs, and the pristine blue waters of Hanalei Bay and the Princeville Resort area. If the weather gods are on your side, then you'll get to see the highest point on Kauai: Mount Waialeale, the wettest spot on Earth, with an average rainfall of 450 to 500 inches annually. Your flight will take you right into the center of the crater with its 5,000-foot walls towering above and its 3,000-foot waterfalls surrounding you—something you will remember forever.

3501 Rice St., Lihue. ✆ **800/745-2583** or 808/245-5800. www.bluehawaiian.com. 55-min. tour $226 ($197 if you book online). Harbor Mall staging area; take off from the Lihue Airport.

Island Helicopters ★ Curt Lofstedt has been flying helicopter tours of Kauai for nearly 3 decades. He personally selects and trains professional pilots with an eye not only to their flying skills but also to their ability to share the magic of Kauai. All flights are in the six-passenger Aerospatiale A STAR, with extra-large windows and stereo headsets to hear the pilot's personal narration. Here's the latest tour option: a 90-minute Manawaiopuna Falls tour with a landing in a private valley and short hike to the 400 foot falls for $349 rack rate, but if you book on their website it's just $299.

Lihue Airport. ✆ **800/829-5999** or 808/245-8588. www.islandhelicopters.com. 55-min. island tour $266. Mention Frommer's and receive 40% off.

Jack Harter ★ The pioneer of helicopter flights on Kauai, Jack was the guy who started the sightseeing-via-helicopter trend. On the 60-minute tour, he flies a four-passenger Hughes 500 with the doors off or a Eurocopter AS350BA A STAR. The 90-minute tour (in the A STAR only) hovers over the sights a bit longer than the 60-minute flight, so you can get a good look, but we found the shorter tour sufficient.

4231 Ahukini Rd., Lihue. ✆ **888/245-2001** or 808/245-3774. www.helicopters-kauai.com. 60-min. tour $239–$259; 90-min. tour $384. (Book on the Internet and save $10–$20.)

Niihau Helicopter This is the only helicopter company offering tours of Niihau, the "Forbidden Island." The half-day tours, on an Agusta 109A twin-engine helicopter, include an aerial tour over the island. The helicopter then lands on Niihau at a beach (the island is generally closed to the public), where you can spend a few hours swimming, snorkeling, beachcombing, or just relaxing and sunbathing. Lunch and refreshments are included. You leave from Port Allen Air Strip.

P.O. Box 690086, Makaweli, HI 96769. ✆ **877/441-3500** or 808/335-3500. www.niihau.us. Half-day tours, with lunch and a stop at a Niihau beach, $365.

Safari Helicopters This family-owned and -run company also flies custom-designed, huge windowed "Super" A STAR helicopters (37% larger than most helicopters) with high-back leather seats. Here, too, the pilot is on the left side of the helicopter (instead of the usual position on the right), which not only allows you better views, but more legroom.

Lihui Heliport, office on Ahukini Rd. ✆ **800/326-3356** or 808/246-0136. www.safariair.com. 55-min. tour $229 ($161 with advance Web booking); 90-min. tour $329 ($247 with advance Web booking).

Sunshine Helicopter Ross and Anna Scott bought out Will Squyres Helicopter tours and have a range of tours from both the Lihue Airport and from the Princeville Airport. You can save a lot of cash by booking through their website, where you have a choice of a 30- to 40-minute tour or a 45- to 55-minute tour.

Lihue Airport. ✆ **866/501-7738** or 808/270-3999. www.helicopters-hawaii.com. Tours start at $199 for 30–40 minutes ($169 if you book on their website).

4 THE COCONUT COAST

The **Kauai Historical Society** (✆ **808/245-3373;** www.kauaihistoricalsociety.org) sponsors a 90-minute **Kapaa History Tour** on Tuesday, Thursday, and Saturday at 10am. Your trained interpretive guide will take you back at least 125 years to a time when King Kalakaua came to Kauai seeking to make a fortune in sugar when pineapple was king, and learn about the various ethnic groups that make Kapaa what it is today. Cost is $15 for adults and $5 for children under 12; be sure to make reservations in advance.

Moments — Make a Pilgrimage to a Hindu Temple

Believe it or not, a sacred Hindu temple is being carved out of rocks from India on the banks of the Wailua River. The **San Marga Iraivan Temple** is being built to last "a thousand years or more," on the 458-acre site of the Saiva Siddhanta Church monastery. In the making for years now and expected to be completed in 2010, the Chola-style temple is the result of a vision by the late Satguru Sivaya Subramuniyaswami, known to his followers as Gurudeva, the founder of the church and its monastery. He specifically selected this site in 1970, recognizing that the Hawaiians also felt the spiritual power of this place. The Hawaiians called it *pihanakalani*, "where heaven touches the Earth."

The concrete foundation is 68 feet×168 feet and 3 feet thick, designed not to crack under the weight of the 3.2-million-pound temple dedicated to the Hindu god Shiva. The granite for the temple is being hand-quarried by some 70 stonemasons in India, then shipped to Kauai for final shaping and fitting on the site. The center of the temple will hold a 700-pound crystal, known as the Sivalingam, now displayed at the monastery's smaller temple on the grounds.

Hindu pilgrims come from around the globe to study and meditate at the monastery. The public is welcome to the monastery temple, open daily from 9am to noon. There also is a weekly guided tour of the grounds that includes the San Marga Iraivan Temple. The weekly tour time varies depending on the retreat schedule at the monastery. For information, call ✆ **808/822-3012** (and hold for visitor information), or go to www.saivasiddhanta.com.

A few suggestions if you plan to visit: Carry an umbrella (it's very rainy here), and wear what the Hindus call "modest clothing" (certainly no shorts, short dresses, T-shirts, or tank tops); Hindu dress is ideal. Also, even though this is a monastery, there are lots of people around, so don't leave valuables in your car.

To get there, turn *mauka* (left, inland) off Kuhio Highway (Hwy. 56) at the lights, just after crossing the bridge, onto Kuamoo Road (between Coco Palms Hotel and the Wailua River). Continue up the hill, for just over 4 miles. A quarter mile past the 4-mile marker, turn left on Kaholalele Road and go 1 block to the end of the road. The Information Center is at 107 Kaholalele. Park on Temple Lane. Enter the open pavilion, where a guide will escort you through the monastery. You can also visit the Sacred Rudraksha Forest at 7345 Kuamoo Road for meditation, open 6am to 6pm; or the Nepalese Ganesha Shrine and Bangalore Gallery, which are located at 107 Kaholalele Rd.

Fern Grotto This is one of Kauai's oldest (since 1946) and most popular tourist attractions. A 157-passenger motorized barge takes people up and downriver on an hour-and-20-minute cruise with a hula show on the return trip. At the Fern Grotto landing, you get off the boat and walk through the rainforest to the lush Fern Grotto, the source of many Hawaiian legends and a popular site for weddings.

Contact Smith's Motor Boats for tours. ✆ **808/821-6895.** www.smithskauai.com. Reservations recommended. Admission $20 adults, $10 children 2–12 (10% off if booked online). Daily 9:30am–3:30pm. Wailua Marina, at the mouth of the Wailua River; turn off Kuhio Hwy. (Hwy. 56) into Wailua Marine State Park.

WAILUA RIVER STATE PARK

Ancients called the Wailua River "the river of the great sacred spirit." Seven temples once stood along this 20-mile river, which is fed by 5,148-foot Mount Waialeale, the wettest spot on Earth. You can go up Hawaii's biggest navigable river by boat or kayak (see "Boating" and "Kayaking," in chapter 7), or drive Kuamoo Road (Hwy. 580, sometimes called the King's Hwy.), which goes inland along the north side of the river from Kuhio Highway (Hwy. 56)—from the northbound lane, turn left at the stoplight just before the ruins of Coco Palms Resort. Kuamoo Road goes past the *heiau* (temple) and historical sites to Opaekaa Falls and Keahua Arboretum, a State Division of Forestry attempt to reforest the watershed with native plants.

SLEEPING GIANT

If you squint your eyes just so as you pass the 1,241-foot-high Nounou Ridge, which makes a dramatic backdrop for the coastal villages of Wailua and Waipouli, you can see the fabled Sleeping Giant. On Kuhio Highway, just after mile marker 7, around the minimall complex of Waipouli Town Center, look *mauka* (inland) and you may see what appears to be the legendary giant named Puni who, as the story goes, fell asleep after a great feast. If you don't see him at first, visualize him this way: His head is Wailua and his feet are Kapaa. For details on an easy hike to the top of the Sleeping Giant, see "The Sleeping Giant Trail," p. 186.

5 PARADISE FOUND: THE NORTH SHORE ★★★

ON THE ROAD TO HANALEI

The first place everyone should go on Kauai is Hanalei. The drive along **Kuhio Highway** (Hwy. 56, which becomes Hwy. 560 after Princeville to the end of the road) displays Kauai's grandeur at its absolute best. Just before Kilauea, the air and the sea change, the light falls in a different way, and the last signs of development are behind you. Now there are roadside fruit stands, a little stone church in Kilauea, two roadside waterfalls, and a long, stiltlike bridge over the Kalihiwai Stream and its green river valley.

Birders might want to stop off at **Kilauea Point National Wildlife Refuge,** a mile north of Kilauea, and the **Hanalei National Wildlife Refuge,** along Ohiki Road, at the west end of the Hanalei River Bridge. (For details, see "Birding," in chapter 7.) In the Hanalei Refuge, along a dirt road on a levee, you can see the **Hariguchi Rice Mill,** now a historic treasure.

Now the coastal highway heads due west, and the showy ridgelines of Mount Namahana create a grand amphitheater. The two-lane coastal highway rolls through pastures of grazing cattle and past a tiny airport and the luxurious Princeville Hotel.

Five miles past Kilauea, just past the Princeville Shopping Center, is **Hanalei Valley Lookout.** Big enough for a dozen cars, this lookout attracts crowds of people who peer over the edge into the 917-acre Hanalei River Valley. So many shades of green: Rice green, taro green, and green streams lace a patchwork of green ponds that back up to green-velvet Bali Hai cliffs. Pause to catch your first sight of taro growing in irrigated ponds; maybe you'll see an endangered Hawaiian black-necked stilt. Don't be put off by the crowds; this is definitely worth a look.

Tips Bridge Etiquette: Showing Aloha on Kauai's One-Lane Bridges

Unlike the aggressive drivers you see on the mainland, Hawaii's drivers are much more laid-back and courteous. Hanalei has a series of one-lane bridges where it is not only proper etiquette to be courteous, but it is also the law. When you approach a one-lane bridge, slow down and *yield* if a vehicle, approaching in the opposite direction, is either on the bridge or just about to enter the bridge. (This is not a contest of chicken.) If you are in a long line of vehicles approaching the bridge, don't just join the train crossing the bridge. The local "rule of thumb" is about seven to eight cars over the bridge, then yield and give the cars waiting on the other side of the bridge a chance to come across. Of course, not everyone will adhere to these rules, but then, not everyone visiting Hawaii truly feels the spirit of aloha.

Farther along, a hairpin turn offers another scenic look at Hanalei town, and then you cross the **Hanalei Bridge.** The Pratt truss steel bridge, pre-fabbed in New York City, was erected in 1912; it's now on the National Registry of Historic Landmarks. If it ever goes out, the nature of Hanalei will change forever; currently, this rusty, one-lane bridge (which must violate all kinds of Department of Transportation safety regulations) isn't big enough for a tour bus to cross.

You'll drive slowly past the **Hanalei River banks** and Bill Mowry's **Hanalei Buffalo Ranch,** where 200 American bison roam in the tropical sun; you may even see buffalo grazing in the pastures on your right. The herd is often thinned to make buffalo patties. (You wondered why there was a Buffalo Burger on the Ono Family Restaurant menu, didn't you?)

Just past Tahiti Nui, turn right on Aku Road before Ching Young Village, then take a right on Weke Road. **Hanalei Beach Park** (see p. 169), one of Hawaii's most gorgeous, is a half-block ahead on your left. Swimming is excellent here year-round, especially in summer, when Hanalei Bay becomes a big, placid lake.

If this exquisite 2-mile-long beach doesn't meet your expectations, head down the highway, where the next 7 miles of coast yield some of Kauai's other spectacular beaches, including **Lumahai Beach** of *South Pacific* movie fame, as well as **Tunnels Beach** (p. 170), where the 1960s puka-shell necklace craze began, and **Haena Beach Park** (p. 170), a fabulous place to kick back and enjoy the waves, particularly in summer. Once you've found your beach, stick around until sundown, then head back to one of the North Shore's restaurants for a mai tai and a fresh seafood dinner. (See chapter 6.) Another perfect day in paradise.

ATTRACTIONS ALONG THE WAY

Ka Ulu O Laka Heiau On a knoll above the boulders of Kee Beach (p. 170) stands a sacred altar of rocks, often draped with flower leis and ti-leaf offerings. The altar is dedicated to Laka, the goddess of hula. It may seem like a primal relic from the days of idols, but it's very much in use today. Often, dancers (men and women) of Hawaii's hula *halau* (schools) climb the cliff, bearing small gifts of flowers. In Hawaiian myths, Lohiau,

Fun Facts Hollywood Loves Kauai

More than 50 major Hollywood productions have been shot on Kauai since the studios discovered the island's spectacular natural beauty. Here are just a few:

- The lush, tropical mountain waterfall and awe-inspiring peaks seen in the *Jurassic Park* films (1993, 1997, and 2001) were not filmed on an island off Costa Rica, but on Kauai at Manawaiopu Falls, Mount Waialeale, and other scenic areas.
- Kauai's verdant rainforests formed a fantastic backdrop for Harrison Ford in both *Raiders of the Lost Ark* (1981) and *Indiana Jones and the Temple of Doom* (1984).
- A pilot and his passenger are forced to land on the classical tropical island, believed to be in French Polynesia, in *Six Days, Seven Nights* (1998); actually, Ivan Reitman filmed Harrison Ford and Anne Heche for 11 weeks on Kauai's spectacular shores.
- Mitzi Gaynor sang "I'm Gonna Wash That Man Right Outta My Hair" on Lumahai Beach in *South Pacific* (1958).
- Jessica Lange, Jeff Bridges, and Charles Grodin tangled with Hollywood's most famous gorilla in Honopu Valley, in the remake of *King Kong* (1976).
- Elvis Presley married costar Joan Blackman near the Wailua River in *Blue Hawaii* (1961).
- Beautiful Kee Beach, on the North Shore, masqueraded as Australia in the miniseries *The Thornbirds* (1983), starring Richard Chamberlain and Rachel Ward.
- Kauai appeared as the backdrop for *Outbreak,* the 1994 thriller about the spread of a deadly virus on a remote tropical island, starring Dustin Hoffman. Hoffman also appeared with Robin Williams and Julia Roberts in *Hook* (1991), in which Kauai appeared as Never-Never Land.
- James Caan, Nicolas Cage, Sarah Jessica Parker, and Pat Morita shared laughs on Kauai (which appeared as itself) in *Honeymoon in Vegas* (1992).

If you are a film buff, you can get more movie trivia about Kauai and the movies in Chris Cook's book, *The Kauai Movie Book,* published by Mutual Publishing, Honolulu. Or log onto www.filmkauai.com, the Kauai Film Commission's website, which has lots of facts about films on the Garden Isle. You can also visit these and other Kauai locations that made it to the silver screen, plus locations from such TV classics as *Fantasy Island* and *Gilligan's Island,* with **Hawaii Movie Tours** (✆ **800/628-8432** or 808/822-1192; www.hawaiimovietour.com). Tickets are $89 for adults for the daily 6-hour tour and $79 for children 11 and under. The 6-hour off-road tour Monday to Friday is $95 for adults and $85 for children ages 9-11 only. Lunch is included on both tours.

a handsome chief, danced here before the fire goddess Pele; their passion became *Haena,* which means "the heat." Sometimes, in a revival of the old Hawaiian ways (once banned by missionaries), a mother of a newborn will deposit the umbilical cord of her infant at this sacred shrine. The site is filled with what Hawaiians call *mana,* or power.

From the west side of Kee Beach, take the footpath across the big rocks almost to the point; then climb the steep grassy hill.

Limahuli Garden of the National Tropical Botanical Garden ★ Out on Kauai's far North Shore, beyond Hanalei and the last wooden bridge, there's a mighty cleft in the coastal range where ancestral Hawaiians lived in what can only be called paradise. Carved by a waterfall stream known as Limahuli, the lush valley sits at the foot of steepled cliffs that Hollywood portrayed as Bali Hai in the film classic *South Pacific.* This small, almost secret garden is ecotourism at its best. It appeals not just to green thumbs but to all who love Hawaii's great outdoors. Here botanists hope to save Kauai's endangered native plants. You can take the self-tour to view the plants, which are identified in Hawaiian and English. From taro to sugar cane, the mostly Polynesian imports tell the story of the people who cultivated the plants for food, medicine, clothing, shelter, and decoration. In addition, Limahuli's stream is sanctuary to the last five species of Hawaiian freshwater fish.

Visitor Center, 1/2 mile past mile marker 9 on Kuhio Hwy. (Hwy. 560), Haena. ✆ **808/826-1053.** Fax 808/826-1053. www.ntbg.org. Admission $15 adults, children under 12 free for self-guided; $30 guided tour, $15 for children (ages 10–12 years only). Open Tues–Sat 9:30am–4pm. Advance reservations required for the 10am 2 1/2-hr. guided tours. During peak seasons of July–Sept, book at least a week ahead.

Na Aina Kai Botanical Gardens ★★★ Finds Do not miss this incredible, magical garden on some 240 acres sprinkled with about 70 life-size (some larger than life-size) whimsical bronze statues. Hidden off the beaten path of the North Shore, and only recently opened, this is the place for both avid gardeners as well as people who think they don't like botanical gardens. These gardens have everything: waterfalls, pools, arbors, topiaries, colonnades, gazebos, a maze you will never forget, a lagoon with spouting fountains, a Japanese teahouse, and an enchanting path along a bubbling stream to the ocean. The imaginary, fairy-tale creativity that has gone into these grounds will be one of your fondest memories of Kauai. A host of different tours is available, from 1½ ($30) to 5 ($75) hours long, ranging from casual, guided strolls, to a ride in the covered CarTram, to treks from one end of the gardens to the ocean. A tropical children's garden is the latest edition: It features a gecko hedge maze, a tropical jungle gym, a treehouse in a rubber tree, and a 16-foot-tall Jack and the Bean Stalk Giant with a 33-foot wading pool below. Na Aina Kai is only open 4 days a week and offers only guided tours; book a tour before you leave for Hawaii to avoid being disappointed.

4101 Wailapa Rd. (P.O. Box 1134), Kilauea, HI 96754. ✆ **808/828-0525.** Fax 808/828-0815. www.naainakai.com. Tues–Fri for specific tour times only. Tours vary. Advance reservations strongly recommended. From Lihue, drive north past mile marker 21 and turn right on Wailapa Rd. At the road's end, drive through the iron gates. From Princeville, drive south 6 1/2 miles and take the 2nd left past mile marker 22 on Wailapa Rd. At the road's end, drive through the iron gates.

Waioli Mission House Museum If you're lucky and time your visit just right, you can see this 150-year-old mission house, which serves today as a living museum. It's a real treasure. Others in Honolulu are easier to see, but the Waioli Mission House retains its sense of place and most of its furnishings, so you can really get a clear picture of what life was like for the New England missionaries who came to Kauai to convert the "heathens" to Christianity.

Most mission houses are small, dark Boston cottages that violate the tropical sense of place. This two-story, wood-frame house, built in 1836 by Abner and Lucy Wilcox of New Bedford, Massachusetts, is an excellent example of hybrid architecture. The house features lanais on both stories and a cookhouse in a separate building. It has a lava-rock chimney, ohia-wood floors, and Hawaiian koa furniture.

Kuhio Hwy. (Hwy. 560), just behind the green Waioli Huia Church, Hanalei. ✆ **808/245-3202.** Free admission (donations gratefully accepted). Tours: Tues, Thurs, Sat 9am–3pm.

THE END OF THE ROAD

The real Hawaii begins where the road stops. This is especially true on Kauai—for at the end of Highway 56, the spectacular **Na Pali Coast** begins. To explore it, you have to set out on foot, by boat, or by helicopter. For details on experiencing this region, see "Hiking & Camping" and "Boating," in chapter 7, and "Helicopter Rides over Waimea Canyon & the Na Pali Coast," earlier in this chapter.

Shopping

Shopping is a pleasure on this island. Where else can you browse vintage Hawaiiana practically in a cane field, buy exquisite home accessories in an old stone building built in 1942, and get a virtual agricultural tour of the island through city-sponsored green markets that move from town to town throughout the week, like a movable feast? At Kauai's small, tasteful boutiques, you can satisfy your shopping ya-yas in concentrated spurts around the island. This is a bonanza for the boutique shopper—particularly one who appreciates the thrill of the hunt.

"Downtown" Kapaa continues to flourish, and Hanalei, touristy as it is, is still a shopping destination. (Ola's and Yellowfish make up for the hurricane of trinkets and trash in Hanalei.) Kilauea, with Kong Lung Store and the fabulous Lotus Gallery, is the style center of the island. The Kauai Heritage Center of Hawaiian Culture & the Arts makes it possible for visitors to escape the usual imitations, tourist traps, and clichés in favor of authentic encounters with the real thing: Hawaiian arts, Hawaiian cultural practices, and Hawaiian elders and artists. What else can you expect on Kauai? Anticipate great shops in Hanalei, a few art galleries and boutiques, and a handful of shopping centers—not much to distract you from an afternoon of hiking or snorkeling. The gift items and treasures you'll find in east and north Kauai, however, may be among your best Hawaiian finds.

To make sure you are getting products made on Kauai go to **www.kauaimade.net** and download the free brochure from the county of Kauai, ***The Official Shopping Guide to Local Products Made with Aloha,*** that identifies and promotes products made on Kauai, by Kauai people, using Kauai materials. The brochure lists the name, address, phone, and Web address of Kauai residents crafting local products using material from Kauai, ranging from apparel and accessories to wood workers, complete with a map listing retailers by regions.

1 GREEN MARKETS & FRUIT STANDS

The county of Kauai sponsors regular weekly **Sunshine Markets** (**© 808/241-6390;** www.kauai.gov) throughout the island, featuring fresh Kauai **Sunrise papayas** (sweeter, juicier, and redder than most), herbs and vegetables used in ethnic cuisines, exotic fruit such as *rambutan* and *atemoya,* and the most exciting development in pineapple agriculture, the low-acid white pineapple called **Sugarloaf,** rarer these days but still spottily available. These markets, which sell the full range of fresh local produce and flowers at rock-bottom prices, present the perfect opportunity to see what's best and what's in season. Farmers sell their bounty from the backs of trucks or at tables set up under tarps.

The biggest market is at **Kapaa New Town Park,** in the middle of Kapaa town, on Wednesday at 3pm. The Sunshine Market in **Lihue,** held on Friday at 3pm at the Vidhina Stadium parking lot, is close in size and extremely popular. The schedule for the other markets: **Koloa Ball Park,** Monday at noon; **Kalaheo Neighborhood Center,**

Fruity Smoothies & Other Exotic Treats

Fruit stands have sprouted on this island, and smoothies are gaining ground as the milkshake of the new millennium. New crops of exotic trees imported from Southeast Asia are maturing on Kauai, creating anticipation among residents and fruitful ideas for the smoothie world. "Everyone's waiting for the mangosteens and durians," comments Joe Halasey, who, with his wife, Cynthia, runs **Banana Joe's** (✆ **808/828-1092**), the granddaddy of Kauai's roadside fruit-and-smoothie stands. "They take about 12 years to start bearing, so there are a lot of maturing trees. We're all waiting for the fruit. *Rambutans* (with a hairy, red exterior and a translucent, litchilike flesh) are good for the farmers here because they're available, and they're a winter fruit. In the summer, mangoes and litchis are always in high demand."

Banana Joe's has been a Kilauea landmark since it opened in 1986 at 52719 Kuhio Hwy., between mile markers 23 and 24 heading north, on the mauka (mountain) side of the street. Sapodilla, star apple (round, purple, and sweet, like a creamy Concord grape), macadamia nuts, Anahola Granola, and home-made breads—like banana and mango-coconut—are among Banana Joe's attractions. The Halaseys have expanded their selection of organic vegetables and exude a quiet aloha from their roadside oasis.

Mangosteens, reputedly the favorite fruit of Queen Victoria, have a creamy, custardy flesh of ambrosial sweetness. When mangosteens start appearing at Hawaii fruit stands, they will no doubt be in high demand, like mangoes and litchis during their summer season. In the meantime, Banana Joe's has a hit on its hands with Sugarloaf, the white, nonacidic, ultrasweet, organically grown pineapple popularized on the Big Island. Whether made into smoothies or frostees (frozen fruit put through the Champion juicer), or just sold plain, fresh, and whole, the Sugarloaf is pineapple at its best. For litchi lovers, who must wait for their summer appearance, new varieties such as Kaimana and Brewster are adding to the pleasures of the season. In addition to fresh fruit, fruit smoothies, and frostees, Banana Joe's sells organic greens, tropical-fruit salsas, jams and jellies, drinking coconuts (young coconuts containing delicious drinking water), gift items, and baked goods such as papaya-banana bread. Its top-selling smoothies are papaya, banana, and pineapple.

Near the Lihue Airport, Pammie Chock at **Kauai Fruit & Flower** (✆ **808/245-1814;** see below) makes a pineapple–passion fruit smoothie that gets my vote as the best on the island.

Papalina Road off Kaumualii, Tuesday at 3pm; **Hanapepe Park,** Thursday at 3pm; **Kilauea Neighborhood Center,** Keneke off Lighthouse Road, Thursday at 4:30pm; and **Kekaha Neighborhood Center,** Elepaio Road, Saturday at 9am. Especially at the Koloa Market, which draws hundreds of shoppers, go early and shop briskly.

On the North Shore, Kilauea is the agricultural heart of the island, with two weekly green markets: the county-sponsored **Sunshine Market,** Thursday at 4:30pm at the Kilauea Neighborhood Center; and the private Kilauea Quality Farmers Association (mostly organic growers) **Farmers Market,** Saturday from 11:30am to 1:30pm behind the Kilauea Post Office. Everything in the wide-ranging selection is grown or made on Kauai, from *rambutan* and long beans to sweet potatoes, corn, lettuce, and salsas and chutneys.

Also on the North Shore, about ¼ mile past Hanalei in an area called Waipa, the **Hawaiian Farmers of Hanalei**—anywhere from a dozen to 25 farmers—gather along the main road with their budget-friendly, just-picked produce. This market is held every Saturday 10am to noon. You'll find unbelievably priced papayas (in some seasons, several for a dollar, ready to eat), organic vegetables, inexpensive tropical flowers, avocados and mangoes in season, and, when possible, fresh seafood. The best of the best, in season, are rose apples, mountain apples, and the orange-colored papaya *lilikoi.*

Another great Kauai-made product that makes an excellent gift from Kauai is **Aunty Lilikoi's passion fruit products** (ranging from jelly to passion fruit mustard, bubble and bath gel, shampoo, even candles). Aunty's shop is located at 9875 Waimea Rd., in Waimea (✆ **808/338-1296;** www.auntylilikoi.com).

2 LIHUE & ENVIRONS

DOWNTOWN LIHUE

The gift shop of the **Kauai Museum,** 4428 Rice St. (✆ **808/245-6931**), is your best bet for made-on-Kauai arts and crafts, from Niihau-shell leis to woodwork, lauhala and coconut products, and more.

About a mile north of the Lihue Airport, on Highway 56 (Kuhio Hwy.), **Kauai Fruit & Flower** is a great stop for flowers, including the rare Kauai maile in season; coconut drums the owner makes himself; Hawaiian gourds *(ipu);* cut flowers for shipping; and Kauai fruit, such as papayas and pineapples. Other products include lauhala gift items, teas, Kauai honey, Kauai salad dressings, jams and jellies, and custom-made gift baskets.

In the **Kukui Grove Center,** at Kaumualii Highway (Hwy. 50) and Old Nawiliwili Road, is the **Kauai Products Store** (✆ **808/246-6753**). It's a fount of local handicrafts (about 60% Kauai artists) and a respectable showcase for made-on-the-island products, such as soaps, paintings, clothing, coffee, Kukui guava jams, fabrics, and Niihau-shell leis. The Hawaiian quilts are made on Kauai and designed by Kauai families. You'll find everything from a $10,750 bronze sculpture to bamboo chairs. Beware of the macadamia-nut fudge, found only at Kauai Products Store: It's rich, sweet, and irresistible.

For a great selection in alohawear—shirts, dresses, pareu—and lots of souvenirs to take to the folks back home, stop by **Hilo Hattie,** 3252 Kuhio Hwy. (Hwy. 50) at Ahukini Road (✆ **808/245-3404**). Their selection of Hawaii-related gift items is immense: food, books, CDs, mugs, key chains, T-shirts, and more. They even offer free hotel pickup from Poipu and Kapaa. If you are on a budget, go to the **Kauai Humane Society Thrift Shop,** Lihue Center, 3-3100 Kuhio Hwy. (✆ **808/245-7387**), where a great selection of "vintage" aloha shirts starts at $5. All the money raised goes to help the Kauai Humane Society continue their excellent work on the island. If you want wooden or coconut buttons for your vintage aloha shirt, stop by **Kapaa Stitchery,** 3-3551 Kuhio Hwy. (✆ **808/245-2281**), and buy a few buttons; you can have an authentic aloha shirt for a quarter of what you would spend in retail stores. Quilters will be in heaven at the Kapaa Stitchery, where they will find a huge selection of Hawaiian quilts, quilting supplies, needlework designs, and lots of fabric.

> **Tips** **Photo Opportunity: Hang Ten Without Getting Wet**
>
> Here's your opportunity to take a photo of your trip to Kauai that will astound and amaze your friends—you on a surfboard. Oh, you don't surf; can't even swim? No problem. Drive down to Hawaiian Trading Post, at the intersection of Koloa Road and Kaumualii Highway. On the side of their building (facing the parking lot) is a fake backdrop with a surfboard and a huge wave (fashioned from plaster) that looks amazingly like the real thing. Bring your own camera (and bathing suit) and snap away.

Another good souvenir store is Paradise Sportswear's **Red Dirt Shirt,** 3-3229 Kuhio Hwy. (✆ **808/246-0224**), with another outlet in Kapaa (see "The Ultimate Kauai Souvenir: The Red Dirt Shirt" on p. 222). Here you'll find zillions of the famous "red dirt" T-shirts in a variety of styles and designs (and sizes all the way to XXXXL).

If you are looking for something more artsy, **Two Frogs Hugging** (✆ **808/246-8777**), just down Kuhio Highway from Hilo Hattie and Paradise Sportswear, is a great place to wander about marveling at their collection of Indonesian arts, crafts, furniture, pottery, and accessories.

If you just need necessities like suntan lotion, film, or a cheap pair of slippers, head for **Kmart,** 4303 Nawiliwili, Lihue (✆ **808/245-7742**). If you need laundry done (and don't want to waste a minute of your vacation doing it), drop it off at **Plaza Laundry,** in the Hanamaulu Plaza Shopping Center, Kuhio Highway (Hwy. 56) and Hanamaulu Road (✆ **808/246-9057**), which offers a full wash, dry, and fold service for just $1.50 a pound.

KILOHANA PLANTATION

Kilohana, the 35-acre Tudor-style estate on Highway 50 between Lihue and Poipu, is an architectural marvel that houses a sprinkling of galleries and shops. At the **Country Store,** on the ground level, you'll find island and American crafts of decent quality, koa accessories, pottery, and Hawaii-themed gift items. On the other side of Gaylord's, the **Artisans Room** and **The Hawaiian Collection Room** offer a mix of crafts and two-dimensional art, from originals to affordable prints, at all levels of taste.

3 THE POIPU RESORT AREA

Expect mostly touristy shops in Poipu, the island's resort mecca; here you'll find T-shirts, souvenirs, black pearls, jewelry, and the usual quota of tired marine art and trite hand-painted silks.

There are exceptions. The formerly characterless **Poipu Shopping Village,** at 2360 Kiahuna Plantation Dr., is shaping up into a serious shopping stop. Also in Poipu Shopping Village, the tiny **Bamboo Lace** boutique lures the fashionistas; its resortwear and accessories can segue from Hawaii to the south of France in one easy heartbeat. Across the courtyard, **Sand People** is great for understated resortwear (such as Tencel Jeans) and Indonesian coconut picture frames. Don't miss out on **Sand Kids,** with its adorable kids' clothes, books, gifts, T-shirts, and jewelry, plus cute stuffed "sea creatures" (like mermaids). It's one

Up and "Rumming:" Koloa Rum Company Tasting Room

There's now another reason to visit the Kilohana Plantation—the recently opened **Koloa Rum Company Tasting Room, Retail Store & Gallery** (next door to the Kilohana Plantation, at 3-2087 Kaumualii Hwy (Hwy. 50), between Lihue and Poipu, ✆ **808/742-1616,** www.koloarum.com). Kauai's first rum distillery makes white, gold, dark, and on occasion, specialty flavors of rum (like coconut and vanilla) using high-grade molasses and sugar from Hawaii's only remaining sugar company (Gay & Robinson) and pure water from Mount Waialeale (one of the wettest spots on Earth). The tasting room is separated from the retail store (where the rum and other Kauai-made products are sold) by a small distillery, where you can see how the rum is made. In addition to sampling this premium rum, you will learn the history of rum and sugar in the islands, ranging from 1778 when Captain Cook, whose ship carried barrels of rum for his sailor's daily ration of "grog," made a landing in Kauai to the 1830s when Kauai built its first sugar mill for sugar cane, which was to become the island's number one agricultural crop.

of the best places to get sunglasses for kids. The newly renovated **Overboard** rides the wave of popularity in alohawear and surf stuff, plus great swimwear, linens, a selection of Tommy Bahama clothing and accessories, and other island-style merchandise. Take a break from all the shopping at **Puka Dog,** serving up a range of island hot dogs (even veggie ones).

The shopping is surprisingly good at the **Grand Hyatt Kauai Resort and Spa,** with the footwear mecca **Sandal Tree, Water Wear Hawaii** for swim stuff, and **Reyn's,** an institution in Hawaii for alohawear. My favorite store here (and it's worth the drive) is the **Kohala Bay Collections,** filled with resort casual clothing with top names like Tommy Bahama, Toes on the Nose, Jams World, and M Mac, all at very wallet-pleasing prices.

Across the street from Poipu Beach, on Hoone Road, **Nukumoi Surf Shop** is a pleasant surprise: It has an excellent selection of sunglasses, swimwear, surf equipment, and watersports regalia, and not just for the under-20 crowd.

In neighboring **Old Koloa Town,** you'll find everything from **Lappert's Ice Cream** and **Island Soap and Candle Works** (where you can watch them make soap and candles), to **Crazy Shirts** and **Sueoka Store** on Koloa's main drag, Koloa Road. Walk the long block for gifts, souvenirs, sunwear, groceries, soaps and bath products, and everyday necessities. You might want to stop in at **Hula Moon,** 5426 Koloa Rd. (✆ **808/742-9298**), which has a unique selection of gifts, especially hand-painted tiles with sayings like "I'd Rather Be On Kauai," or "Please Remove Your Shoes." If you are looking for a beach bag or Hawaiian-print hats, dresses, or T-shirts, **Paradise Clothing,** 5402 Koloa Rd. (✆ **808/742-1371**), has a great selection. Another great place for island-style clothes is **Progressive Expressions,** in Koloa town (✆ **808/742-6041**), which also has every kind of surfboard and surf accessory, as well as a great selection of sunscreens. For more stylish fashions, go to **Jungle Girl,** 5424 Koloa Rd. (✆ **808/742-9649**), which markets their clothes, jewelry, shoes, and artwork as "island funk and flash."

Niihau Shell Lei: The Island's Most Prized Artwork

Because Kauai is so close to Niihau (the "Forbidden Island," where the public is prohibited, is just offshore), it's the best place in the state to buy exquisite Niihau-shell leis. Nothing can match the craftsmanship and the tiny shells in this highly sought-after and highly prized jewelry. Niihau is in the best position to catch the very tiny and very rare shells that roll up from the deep onto the windward shores after a big storm (generally Nov–Mar). When the shells are spotted on a beach, everyone (men, women, and children) on Niihau drops what they are doing and races down to the beach to begin the backbreaking work of collecting them.

The shells are then sorted according to size and color, and only the best are kept. Some 80% of the shells are thrown out because they are chipped, cracked, discolored, or flawed in some way that renders them imperfect. The best shells are the teeny, tiny ones. The best colors are white or the rare gold (the shells can also be yellow, blue, or red).

The shells can be crafted into anything, but leis and necklaces are the most popular items. A necklace may take anywhere from hours to years to complete. Each shell is strung with very small and very intricate knots. The patterns sometimes mimic flower leis, and the length can range from a single-strand choker to a multistrand, 36-inch (or longer) necklace. No two leis are alike. The leis are not cheap; they range from several hundred to several thousand dollars, depending on the length, the shells used, and the intricate work involved.

You can find Niihau shell leis at numerous locations on Kauai. One of our two favorite places is **Hawaiian Trading Post,** Koloa Road and Kaumualii Highway, in Lawai (✆ **808/332-7404**), which carries a range of items from junky souvenirs to excellent Niihau leis. (You have to ask for them to bring out the "good stuff" from the back.) Our other favorite place to buy the leis is at **www.niihau.us** which is owned and operated by Niihau residents. (You can buy direct, so to speak.)

On Poipu Road, between Koloa and Poipu, there is an exceptional place you cannot miss: **Pohaku T's,** 3430 Poipu Rd. (✆ **808/742-7500**), only sells clothing, artwork, T-shirts, and other whimsical things designed and produced by Kauai artists. All the products either have a great sense of humor or promote awareness of Hawaii's cultural and environmental issues. Prices are excellent. Farther down Poipu Road, in the tiny Poipu Plaza, nestled next to **Sea Sport Divers** and **Outfitters Kauai,** is the **Kukuiula Store**—a shop for everything from produce and sushi to paper products, sunscreen, beverages, and groceries. Occasionally, when fishermen drop by, the store offers fresh sliced sashimi and poke, quite delicious and popular with sunset picnickers and nearby condo residents. In Kalaheo, condo dwellers and locals flock to the solitary, nondescript building that is **Medeiros Farms,** 4365 Papalina Rd. (✆ **808/332-8211**), for everything they raise and make: chicken, range-fed beef, eggs, Italian pork, and Portuguese sausages. The meats are hailed across the island, and the prices are good. Medeiros Farms chicken is so good it's mentioned on some of the upscale menus on the island.

You can take paradise home with you—well, at least the outrageously beautiful flowers. The best place to order flowers to be sent home is **Tropical Flowers by Charles,** 3465 Lawailoa Lane, Koloa (✆ **800/699-7984** or 808/332-7984; www.a-tropical-flower.com). Not only is Charles a flower genius (who grows a range of tropical flowers, including some very rare and unusual varieties), but his hardy blooms and his skill at packing means that your little bit of Kauai will live for a long, long time. For all this, at extremely reasonable prices, we highly recommend Charles.

4 WESTERN KAUAI

HANAPEPE

This West Kauai hamlet is becoming a haven for artists, but finding them requires some vigilance. The center of town is off Highway 50; turn right on Hanapepe Road just after Eleele if you're driving from Lihue. First, you'll smell the chips at the sumptuous lavender **Taro Ko Chips Factory ★**, located in an old green plantation house at 3940 Hanapepe Rd., Hanapepe ✆ **808/335-5586**. Cooked in a tiny, modest kitchen at the east end of town, these famous taro chips are handmade by the farmers who grow the taro in a nearby valley. Despite their breakable nature, these chips make great gifts to go. To really impress them back home, get the authentic Hawaiian *li hing mui*–flavored chips.

Our very favorite Hanapepe store is the **Banana Patch Studio,** 3865 Hanapepe Rd. (✆ **808/335-5944;** www.bananapatchstudio.com). For the best prices on the island for tropical plates and cups, hand-painted tiles, artwork, handmade soaps, pillows with tropical designs, and jewelry, this is the place. Plus, they will pack and ship for you anywhere. Farther along, Hanapepe Road is lined with gift shops and galleries, including **Koa Wood Gallery** (✆ **808/335-5483**), with its koa furniture, koa photo albums, and Norfolk pine bowls; and nearby **Kauai Fine Arts** (✆ **808/335-3778**) offers an odd mix that works: antique maps and prints of Hawaii, authentic Polynesian *tapa* (bark cloth), rare wiliwili-seed leis, old Matson liner menus, and a few pieces of contemporary island art. Taking a cue from Maui's Lahaina, where every Friday night is Art Night, Hanapepe's gallery owners and artists recently instituted the **Friday Night Art Walk** from 6 to 9pm. Gallery owners take turns hosting this informal event along Hanapepe Road.

WAIMEA

Neighboring Waimea is filled with more edibles than art. Kauai's favorite native supermarket, **Big Save** (✆ **808/338-1621**), serves as the one-stop shop for area residents and passersby heading for the uplands of Kokee State Park, some 4,000 feet above this sea-level village. For more hard-to-find delicious gourmet items, try the **Ishihara Market** (✆ **808/338-1751**), where they have marinated meats, freshly made poke, and a range of prepared picnic items. A cheerful distraction for lovers of Hawaiian collectibles is **Collectibles and Fine Junque** (✆ **808/338-9855**), on Highway 50, next to the fire station on the way to Waimea Canyon. This is where you'll discover what it's like to be the proverbial bull in a china shop. (Even a knapsack makes it hard to get through the aisles.) Heaps of vintage linens, choice aloha shirts and muumuus, rare glassware (and junque, too), books, ceramics, authentic 1950s cotton chenille bedspreads, and a back room full of bargain-priced secondhand goodies always capture our attention. You never know what you'll find in this tiny corner of Waimea.

Ultimate Kauai Souvenir: The Red Dirt Shirt

If you are looking for an inexpensive, easy-to-pack souvenir of your trip to Kauai or gifts for all the friends and relatives back home, check out the Red Dirt Shirt. Every T-shirt is hand-dyed and unique. The shirts were the result of a bad situation turned into a positive one. The "legend" is that **Paradise Sportswear,** in Waimea (✆ **808/335-5670;** www.dirtshirt.com), lost the roof of their warehouse during Hurricane Iniki in 1992. After the storm passed, employees returned to the building to find all their T-shirts covered with Kauai's red soil. Before throwing out their entire inventory as "too soiled to sell," someone had an idea—sell the shirts as a Kauai "Red Dirt Shirt." The grunge look was just starting to be popular. Unbelievable as it is, people took to these "dirt" shirts. Fast-forward a couple of decades, and the shirts have numerous outlets on Kauai.

There's also an interesting story behind how these T-shirts are dyed. Paradise Sportswear is a true community effort. They employ families who, due to family or disability challenges, prefer to work from home. Their employees take ordinary white T-shirts home and dye the shirts in vats with red dirt collected from valleys on Kauai where centuries of erosion have concentrated red iron oxide into the dirt. It's this red iron oxide that is used in the tinting agent, along with some other organic compounds in the dye solution that ensure that your dirt shirt will keep its red-dirt color.

The best prices on the Red Dirt Shirts can be found at the factory by the Port Allen Small Boat Harbor, open daily 9am to 5pm. You can watch the silk-screening process or purchase a few shirts from the retail shop, which has everything from T-shirts for infants to XXXXL. The deals are on the factory seconds and discontinued designs.

Up in Kokee State Park, the gift shop of the **Kokee Natural History Museum** (✆ **808/335-9975**) is *the* stop for botanical, geographical, historical, and nature-related books and gifts, not only on Kauai, but on all the islands. Audubon bird books, hiking maps, and practically every book on Kauai ever written line the shelves.

5 THE COCONUT COAST

As you make your way from Lihue to the North Shore, you'll pass **Bambulei** (✆ **808/823-8641**), bordering the cane field in Wailua next to Caffè Coco. Bambulei houses a charming collection of 1930s and 1940s treasures—everything from Peking lacquerware to exquisite vintage aloha shirts to lamps, quilts, jewelry, parrot figurines, and zany salt and pepper shakers. If it's not vintage, it will look vintage, and it's bound to be fabulous. Vintage muumuus are often in perfect condition, and dresses go for $20 to $2,000.

Wood-turner **Robert Hamada** (✆ **808/822-3229**) works in his studio at the foot of the Sleeping Giant, quietly producing museum-quality works with unique textures and grains. His skill, his lathe, and his more than 60 years of experience have brought luminous life to the kou, milo, *kauila,* camphor, mango, and native woods he logs himself.

WAILUA

The Kinipopo Shopping Village, on Kuhio Highway just past Wailea Beach, is more of a minimall than a "shopping village," but a few places here are worth a stop. Entering **The Tin Can Mailman** (✆ **808/822-3009**) is like stepping into the past. It's filled with old things Hawaiian, like out-of-print books on Hawaii, rare artifacts, kitschy items from the 1940s, and artwork. **Kauai Water Ski and Surf Co.** (✆ **808/822-3574**) has everything you could possibly need for playing in the water, from swimwear to equipment (fins, mask, snorkel, and so on), all for sale and for rent.

KAPAA

Moving toward Kapaa on Highway 56 (Kuhio Hwy.), don't get your shopping hopes up; until you hit Kapaa town, quality goods are slim in this neck of the woods. The **Coconut Marketplace** features the ubiquitous **Elephant Walk** gift shop, **Gifts of Kauai,** and various other underwhelming souvenir and clothing shops sprinkled among the sunglass huts. Also check out **Ship Store Gallery** (✆ **808/822-7758**) for an unusual collection of nautical artwork, antiques, and contemporary Japanese art.

Nearby, set back from the main road across from Foodland supermarket, is **Marta's Boat** (✆ **808/822-3926**). Once one of the island's more appealing boutiques for children and women, today it's more art and unusual gift items, but you still can find terrific accessories and chic clothing.

Among the green-and-white wooden storefronts of nearby **Kauai Village,** you'll find everything from trite marine art to Yin Chiao Chinese cold pills and organic produce at **Papayas Natural Foods** (✆ **808/823-0190**). Although its prepared foods are way overpriced, Papayas carries the full range of health-food products and is your only choice in the area for vitamins, health foods to go, health-conscious cosmetics, and bulk food items.

Less than a mile away, on the main road, the **Waipouli Variety Store** is Kapaa's version of Maui's fabled Hasegawa General Store—a tangle of fishing supplies, T-shirts, thongs, beach towels, and souvenirs. Fishermen love this store as much as cookie lovers swear by nearby **Popo's Cookies,** the ne plus ultra of store-bought cookies on the island. Popo's chocolate-chip, macadamia-nut, chocolate–macadamia nut, chocolate-coconut, almond, peanut butter, and other varieties of butter-rich cookies are among the most sought-after food items to leave the island.

And Kapaa town is full of surprises. On the main strip, across from Sunnyside Market, you'll find the recently expanded **Kela's Glass Gallery** (✆ **808/822-4527**), the island's showiest showplace for handmade glass in all sizes, shapes, and prices, with the most impressive selection in Hawaii. The gallery now has new owners who display more than 50 artists specializing in glass. Go nuts over the vases and studio glass pieces, functional and nonfunctional. The gallery also has a great collection of hand-carved and hand-painted wooden flowers. Continue on to **Hula Girl** (✆ **808/822-1950**), where the wonderful and the dreamy prevail, with aloha shirts (very pricey), vintage-looking luggage covered with decals of old Hawaii, Patrice Pendarvis prints, zoris, sandals, sunglasses, and shells.

Across the street is the town's favorite fashion stop, **Island Hemp & Cotton** (✆ **808/821-0225**), where Hawaii's most stylish selection of this miracle fabric is sold: gorgeous silk-hemp dresses, linen-hemp sportswear, hemp aloha shirts, Tencel clothing, T-shirts, and wide-ranging, attractive, and comfortable clothing and accessories that have shed the hippie image. It's also a great store for gift items, from Balinese leather goods to handmade paper, jewelry, luxury soaps, and natural-fiber clothing for men and women. A few doors to the north, **Orchid Alley** (✆ **808/822-0486**) gets our vote for most adorable nursery on the island. A narrow alcove opens into a greenhouse of phalaenopsis, oncidiums, dendrobiums, and dozens of brilliant orchid varieties for shipping or carryout.

6 THE NORTH SHORE

Kauai's North Shore is the premier shopping destination on the island. Stylish, sophisticated galleries and shops, such as **Kong Lung,** in a 1942 Kilauea stone building (the last to be built on the Kilauea Plantation) off Highway 56 on Kilauea Road (✆ **808/828-1822**), have launched these former hippie villages into top-drawer shopping spots. Save your time, energy and, most of all, discretionary funds for this end of the island. Kong Lung, through all its changes, including pricier merchandise in every category, remains a showcase of design, style, and quality, with merchandise from top-of-the-line dinnerware and bath products to aloha shirts, jewelry, ceramics, women's wear, stationery, and personal and home accessories. The book selection is fabulous, and the home accessories—sake sets, tea sets, lacquer bowls, handblown glass, pottery—are unequaled in Hawaii. The items are expensive, but browsing here is a joy.

Directly behind Kong Lung is **Lotus Gallery** (✆ **808/828-9898**), a showstopper for lovers of antiques and designer jewelry. Good juju abounds here. The serenity and beauty will envelop you from the moment you remove your shoes and step through the door onto the bamboo floor. The gallery contains gems, crystals, Tibetan art, antiques and sari clothing from India, 12th-century Indian bronzes, temple bells, Oriental rugs, and pearl bracelets—items from $30 to $50,000. Owners Kamalia (jewelry designer) and Tsajon Von Lixfeld (gemologist) have a staggering sense of design and discovery that brings to the gallery such things as Brazilian amethyst crystal (immense and complex); emeralds; a fine, 100-strand lapis necklace ($4,000); and Kamalia's 18-karat pieces with clean, elegant lines and gemstones that soothe and elevate.

Also behind Kong Lung is **Island Soap and Candle Works** (✆ **808/828-1955;** www.handmade-soap.com), which has been making traditional soaps for more than 2 decades. What started as a mom-and-pop operation in 1984, today is still the only soap and candle factory in Hawaii, with two locations on Kauai and a third on Oahu. You can stop by to watch them hand-pour the soap and, depending on which soap they are making that day, see them add coconut, olive, palm, macadamia, or kukui nut oils, as well as herbs and essential oils, to each bar. There is a small retail shop on the property.

In Hanalei, at **Ola's,** by the Hanalei River on the Kuhio Highway (Hwy. 560) after the bridge and before the main part of Hanalei town (✆ **808/826-6937**), Sharon and Doug Britt, an award-winning artist, have amassed a head-turning assortment of American and island crafts, including Doug's paintings and the one-of-a-kind furniture that he makes out of found objects, driftwood, and used materials. Britt's works—armoires, tables, lamps, bookshelves—often serve as the display surfaces for others' work, so look carefully. Lundberg Studio handblown glass, exquisite jewelry, intricately wrought pewter switch plates, sensational handblown goblets, and many other fine works fill this tasteful, seductive shop. Be on the lookout for the wonderful koa jewel boxes by local woodworker Tony Lydgate.

From health foods to groceries to Bakelite jewelry, Hanalei has it all. For quick and healthy lunches or shopping for a week's groceries try **Papaya's Natural Foods**, 5-5161 Kuhio Hwy. (✆ **808/826-0089**). Just across the street the **Ching Young Village Shopping Center,** in the heart of Hanalei, covers a lot of bases. It's more funky than fashionable, but Hanalei, until recently, has never been about fashion. **Hot Rocket** (✆ **808/826-7776)** is ablaze with aloha shirts, T-shirts, Reyn Spooner and Jams sportswear, flamingo china, backpacks, pareu, swimwear, and, for collectors, one of the finest collections of Bakelite accessories you're likely to see in the islands. **Savage Pearls** (✆ **808/826-9397;** www.savagepearls.com) features a terrific collection of Tahitian black pearls, with everything from loose pearls to elegant settings to custom designs (they even repair jewelry).

Next door to Ching Young Village is **On The Road to Hanalei** (✆ **808/826-7360**), which is definitely worth your time to wander around in and check out the unusual T-shirts (great gifts to take home because they don't take up much suitcase space), scarves, pareu, jewelry, and other unique gifts.

Across the street in the **Hanalei Center,** the standout boutique is the **Yellowfish Trading Company** ★ (✆ **808/826-1227**), where owner Gritt Benton's impeccable eye and zeal for collecting are reflected in the 1920s to 1950s collectibles: menus, hula-girl nodders, hula lamps, rattan and koa furniture, vases, bark-cloth fabric, retro pottery and lamp bases, must-have vintage textiles, and wonderful finds in books and aloha shirts.

10

Kauai After Dark

Kauai is known for lots of things: the most beautiful beaches in the state, the magnificent Na Pali Cliffs jutting into the ocean, the incredible rainforests, and the wide panoramas of the Waimea Canyon, but it is not known for a vibrant nightlife. This is a rural island, where work stops when the sun goes down and people go to bed early. There are a few nightlife options, but you pretty much have to search them out and be ready to blend into the island-style choices.

1 LIHUE

The former plantation community and now county seat, Lihue is a place where local residents live and work. For action after sunset, music, dancing, and bars, the hotels and resorts are the primary players. There are a few local places, but generally all is quiet in Lihue after dark.

The **Kauai Marriott Resort & Beach Club,** 3610 Rice St., Nawiliwili (✆ **808/245-5050**), has a host of nightlife activities. **Kukui's Restaurant** has a sunset torch-lighting ceremony on Thursdays. **Duke's Barefoot Bar** (✆ **808/246-9599**) has live traditional and contemporary Hawaiian music on Wednesday through Friday nights that really stirs up the joint. Friday nights, tropical drinks go for $6 from 4 to 6pm.

On the other side of Lihue, the **Hilton Kauai Beach Resort,** 4331 Kauai Beach Dr. (✆ **808/245-1955;** www.hilton.com), has a dinner theater, which currently is showing Rogers and Hammerstein's *South Pacific* every Wednesday night. The 3-hour dinner show includes a dinner buffet, and the show for $85 for adults and $45 for children age 12 and under.

If you are looking for a neighborhood bar, **Rob's Good Time Grill,** in the Rice Shopping Center (✆ **808/246-0311**), is a terrific place to have a beer, shoot some pool, watch the big-screen TV, and display your talent at karaoke. This down-home bar is not fancy, with its Formica tables, but the crowd is friendly, and it's a great place to meet local folks.

If you are up for a movie, the **Kukui Grove Cinemas,** in the Kukui Grove Shopping Center, 4368 Kukui Grove St. (✆ **808/245-5055**), features the latest films at prices a lot cheaper than those in a big city.

For arts and culture, local residents flock to the plays put on by the nonprofessional group the **Kauai Community Players.** Call ✆ **808/245-7700** to find out what the latest production is and where it will be performed. It's not Broadway (or off-Broadway), but it is energetic community theater at its best.

2 POIPU RESORT AREA

The south shore, with its sunset view and miles of white-sand beaches, is a great place for nightlife. At the far end of Poipu, **Stevenson's Library** at the **Grand Hyatt Kauai Resort & Spa,** 1571 Poipu Rd., Koloa (✆ **808/742-1234;** www.kauai-hyatt.com), is the place

Moments It Begins with Sunset . . .

A must-do on your Kauai vacation—take the time every day to stop and enjoy the sunset. You can watch the big yellow ball descend slowly into the blue waters of the Pacific anywhere, from Poipu to Polihale State Park to Kee Beach to the entire Na Pali Coast. Some insist on viewing the sunset with a locally made tropical mai tai. The entire day can be built around the sunset—shopping for the mai tai ingredients, checking the angle of the sun, and swimming with the knowledge that your big, salty thirst will soon be quenched with a tall, homemade mai tai on one of the world's best beaches. When the sun is low, mix your tropical drink using fresh lime juice, fresh lemon juice, fresh orange juice, passion-orange-guava juice, and fresh grapefruit juice, if possible. Pour this concoction on ice in tall, frosty glasses, and then add Meyer's rum, in which Tahitian vanilla beans have been soaking for days. (Add cinnamon if desired, or soak a cinnamon stick with the rum and vanilla beans.) A dash of Angostura bitters, a few drops of Southern Comfort as a float, a sprig of mint, a garnish of fresh lime, and *voilà!*—you have a tropical, homemade mai tai, a cross between planter's punch and the classic Trader Vic's mai tai. As the sun sets, lift your glass and savor the moment, the setting, and the first sip—not a bad way to end the day.

for an elegant after-dinner drink with live jazz nightly from 8 to 11pm. Dress in casual resortwear (no tank tops or flip-flops) for this wood-lined bar with comfy, overstuffed chairs. You can be mesmerized by the fish in the big saltwater aquarium, or engage in activities like pool, billiards, or chess. For those so inclined, tickle the ivories on the grand piano.

Also in Poipu, **Keoki's Paradise,** in the Poipu Shopping Village, 2360 Kiahuna Plantation Dr. (✆ **808/742-7534**), offers live music Monday through Friday evenings (call for times). The cafe menu is available from 11am to 11:30pm. Contemporary Hawaiian music draws the 21-and-over dancing crowd.

The **Poipu Shopping Village** offers free Tahitian dance performances every Tuesday and Thursday at 5pm in the outdoor courtyard.

Down the street at **Sheraton Kauai Resort,** 2440 Hoonani Rd. (✆ **808/742-1661**), **The Point,** on the water, is the Poipu hot spot, featuring live music and dancing Friday to Sunday. Musical styles range from contemporary Hawaiian to good ol' rock 'n' roll.

3 WEST SIDE

For a romantic evening that will linger in your memory as the highlight of your trip, **Capt. Andy's Sailing Adventure** (✆ **800/535-0830** or 808/335-6833; www.napali.com) has a **Na Pali Sunset Dinner,** a 4-hour cruise along the Na Pali Coast, $105 for adults and $80 for kids age 2 to 12 (see website for a discount). Your evening will include commentary on the history and legends of this coast, great views of the island from out at sea (turtles are frequently spotted), live music, and a sumptuous buffet dinner, catered by Mark's Place and Gaylord's Restaurant, offering Kauai garden salad served with sunrise papaya-seed dressing, Teriyaki chicken topped with diced pineapple, Pulehu beef with sautéed mushrooms and onions in garlic sauce, kaffir lime and lemon rice pilaf, and pineapple bars for dessert. It's best enjoyed during the calm summer months, May to September, but they do have cruises during the winter as well.

In the old plantation community of Hanapepe, every Friday is **Hanapepe Art Night** from 5 to 9pm. Each art night is unique. Participating galleries take turns being the weekly "host gallery" offering original performances or demonstrations, which set the theme for that art night. All the galleries are lit up and decked out, giving the town a special atmosphere. Enjoy a stroll down the streets of quaint, historic Hanapepe town and meet the local artists. Also in Hanapepe on Friday night, the **Hanapepe Café,** 3830 Hanapepe Rd. (✆ **808/335-5011**), is open for dinner from 6 to 9pm and has live music.

4 COCONUT COAST

The Coconut Coast towns of Wailua, Waipouli, and Kapaa offer sunset torch-lighting ceremonies, music, and other evening entertainment, but the real action is in the Coconut Marketplace after dark. Every Wednesday, starting at 5pm, and every Saturday at 1pm, the **Coconut Marketplace,** 4-484 Kuhio Hwy. (✆ **808/822-3641**), features a free hula show performed by local residents ranging from the hula troop of tiny dancers who still don't have their permanent teeth, to lithe young women and men gracefully performing this ancient Hawaiian art, to grandmothers who have been dancing for decades.

The **Hukilau Lanai Restaurant,** in the Kauai Coast Resort, located *makai* (oceanside) of the Coconut Marketplace (✆ **808/822-0600;** www.gaylordskauai.com), features live music Sunday, Tuesday, and Friday 6:30 to 9:30pm.

If you are just looking for a place to have a drink and wind down, try **Pau Hana Bar and Grill,** Kauai Village Shopping Center (✆ **808/821-2900**).

5 THE NORTH SHORE

Kilauea generally rolls up the sidewalks at night, with the exception of the **Lighthouse Bistro** (✆ **808/828-0480**) in the Kong Lung Center, which has live music (from classical guitar to Hawaiian music to African) during dinner nightly.

Hanalei has some action, primarily at **Bouchons Restaurant and Sushi Bar** (formerly **Sushi & Blues),** in Ching Young Village (✆ **808/826-9701**). Reggae, rhythm and blues, rock, and good music by local groups draw dancers and revelers Thursday through Sunday from 7:30pm on. The format changes often here, so call ahead to see who's playing.

Across the street, **Hanalei Gourmet,** in the Old Hanalei Schoolhouse, 5-5161 Kuhio Hwy. (✆ **808/826-2524**), has live music Wednesday, and Friday through Sunday. Down the road, **Tahiti Nui** (✆ **808/826-6277**) is a great place to "experience" Old Hawaii. Stop by for an exotic drink, and "talk story" with the family of Louise Marston. Louise, who was from Tahiti, has passed away, but she started the talk story tradition. The restaurant/bar is family-friendly, and someone always seems to drop in and sing and play music, just like they used to do in the "old days."

Watch for the Green Flash

If you have been on the island for a few days, you'll notice that people seem to gather outside and watch the sunset. After the sun has set, several people may call out, "Green flash!"

No, they haven't had too many mai tais or piña coladas. They are referring to a real, honest-to-God phenomenon that happens after sunset—there is a "green flash" of light.

The romantic version of the story is that the green flash happens when the sun kisses the ocean good night. (Honeymooners love this version.) The scientific version is not quite as dreamy; it goes something like this: Light bends as it goes around the curve of the Earth. When the sun dips beneath the horizon, it is at the far end of the spectrum. So this refraction of the sun's light, coupled with the atmosphere at the extreme angle of the sunset on the horizon, causes only the color green to be seen in the color spectrum just before the light disappears.

Here's how to view the green flash: First, the day has to be clear, with no clouds or haze on the horizon. Keep checking the sun as it drops. (Try not to look directly into the sun; just glance at it to assess its position.) If the conditions are ideal, just as the sun drops into the blue waters, a "flash" or laserlike beam of green will shoot out for an instant. That's the flash. May it be with you on your vacation.

Every week, **Ki Hoalu, Slack Key Guitar Music of Hawaii** (✆ **808/826-1469;** www.alohaplentyhawaii.com) performs at the Hanalei Community Center, usually Fridays at 4pm and Sundays at 3pm. In addition to old-style slack-key guitar, they also feature stories and legends of Hawaii. Cost is $20 for adults and $15 for seniors and children.

11

Fast Facts

1 FAST FACTS: KAUAI

AREA CODE All the Hawaiian Islands are in the **808** area code. Note that if you're calling one island from another, you'll have to dial 1 then 808 first.

AUTOMOBILE ORGANIZATIONS Auto clubs will supply maps, suggested routes, guidebooks, accident and bail-bond insurance, and emergency road service. The **American Automobile Association (AAA)** is the major auto club in the United States. Kauai does **not** have an American Automobile Association (AAA) office. Some car-rental agencies now provide auto club–type services, so you should inquire about their availability when you rent your car. If you belong to an auto club in your home country, inquire about AAA reciprocity before you leave. You may be able to join AAA even if you're not a member of a reciprocal club; to inquire, call AAA (✆ **800/222-4357**). AAA is actually an organization of regional auto clubs, so look under "AAA Automobile Club" in the White Pages of the telephone directory. AAA has a nationwide emergency road service telephone number (✆ **800/AAA-HELP**).

BUSINESS HOURS Most offices are open from 8am to 5pm. The morning commute usually runs from 6 to 8am, and the evening rush is from 4 to 6pm. Bank hours are Monday through Thursday from 8:30am to 3pm, Friday from 8:30am to 6pm; some banks are open on Saturday. Shopping centers are open Monday through Friday from 10am to 9pm, Saturday from 10am to 5:30pm, and Sunday from 10am to 5 or 6pm.

DRINKING LAWS The legal drinking age in Hawaii is 21. Bars are allowed to stay open daily until 2am; places with cabaret licenses are able to keep the booze flowing until 4am. Grocery and convenience stores are allowed to sell beer, wine, and liquor 7 days a week. Proof of age is required and often requested at bars, nightclubs, and restaurants, so it's always a good idea to bring ID when you go out.

Do not carry open containers of alcohol in your car or any public area that isn't zoned for alcohol consumption. The police can fine you on the spot. And nothing will ruin your trip faster than getting a citation for DUI ("driving under the influence"), so don't even think about driving while intoxicated.

DRIVING RULES See "Getting Around," p. 51.

ELECTRICITY Like Canada, the United States uses 110–120 volts AC (60 cycles), compared to 220–240 volts AC (50 cycles) in most of Europe, Australia, and New Zealand. Downward converters that change 220–240 volts to 110–120 volts are difficult to find in the United States, so bring one with you.

EMBASSIES & CONSULATES All embassies are located in the nation's capital, Washington, D.C. Some consulates are located in major U.S. cities, and most nations have a mission to the United Nations in New York City. If your country isn't listed below, call for directory information in **Washington, D.C.** (✆ **202/555-1212**) or check www.embassy.org/embassies.

The embassy of **Australia** is at 1601 Massachusetts Ave. NW, Washington, DC 20036 (✆ **202/797-3000;** usa.embassy.gov/au).

The embassy of **Canada** is at 501 Pennsylvania Ave. NW, Washington, DC 20001 (✆ **202/682-1740;** www.canadianembassy.org). Other Canadian consulates are in Buffalo (New York), Detroit, Los Angeles, New York City, and Seattle.

The embassy of **Ireland** is at 2234 Massachusetts Ave. NW, Washington, DC 20008 (✆ **202/462-3939;** www.irelandemb.org). Irish consulates are in Boston, Chicago, New York City, San Francisco, and other cities. See website for complete listing.

The embassy of **New Zealand** is at 37 Observatory Circle NW, Washington, DC 20008 (✆ **202/328-4800;** www.nzembassy.com). New Zealand consulates are in Los Angeles, Salt Lake City, San Francisco, and Seattle.

The embassy of the **United Kingdom** is at 3100 Massachusetts Ave. NW, Washington, DC 20008 (✆ **202/588-7800;** www.britainusa.com). Other British consulates are in Atlanta, Boston, Chicago, Cleveland, Houston, Los Angeles, New York City, San Francisco, and Seattle.

EMERGENCIES Dial ✆ **911** for police, fire, and ambulance service.

GASOLINE (PETROL) At press time, in the U.S., the cost of gasoline (also known as gas, but never petrol), is abnormally high, but still lower than prices in Europe. Gas prices in Hawaii are consistently higher than in the U.S. mainland. Taxes are already included in the printed price. One U.S. gallon equals 3.8 liters or .85 imperial gallons. Taxes are already included in the printed price. Fill-up locations are known as gas stations or service stations.

HOLIDAYS Banks, government offices, post offices, and many stores, restaurants, and museums are closed on the following legal national holidays: January 1 (New Year's Day), the third Monday in January (Martin Luther King, Jr., Day), the third Monday in February (Presidents' Day), the last Monday in May (Memorial Day), July 4 (Independence Day), the first Monday in September (Labor Day), the second Monday in October (Columbus Day), November 11 (Veterans Day/Armistice Day), the fourth Thursday in November (Thanksgiving Day), and December 25 (Christmas). The Tuesday after the first Monday in November is Election Day, a federal government holiday in presidential-election years (held every 4 years, and next in 2012).

In addition Hawaii celebrates Prince Kuhio Day on March 26, King Kamehameha Day on June 11, and Admissions Day (when Hawaii became a state on August 21, 1959) on the third Friday in August. Banks and state and county offices may be closed during these dates.

For more information on holidays see "Kauai Calendar of Events," inchapter 3.

HOSPITAL The island's only hospital, **Wilcox Hospital,** 3420 Kuhio Hwy., Lihue (✆ **808/245-1100**), has emergency services available round-the-clock.

INSURANCE It is a good idea to have some sort of medical coverage—if you do not have health insurance, some doctor's offices may refuse to see you. For information on traveler's insurance, trip cancellation insurance, and medical insurance while traveling please visit www.frommers.com/planning.

INTERNET ACCESS See staying connected (p. 73).

LANGUAGE Hawaii is the 50th state of the United States and everyone speaks English. However, you might find it helpful to see the "Life and Language" section in chapter 2 to peruse the Hawaiian words you will encounter on your trip.

LEGAL AID If you are "pulled over" for a minor infraction (such as speeding), never attempt to pay the fine directly to a police officer; this could be construed as attempted bribery, a much more serious crime. Pay fines by mail, or directly into the hands of the clerk of the court. If accused of a more serious offense, say and do nothing before consulting a lawyer. Here the burden is on the state to prove a person's guilt beyond a reasonable doubt, and everyone has the right to remain silent, whether he or she is suspected of a crime or actually arrested. Once arrested, a person can make one telephone call to a party of his or her choice. International visitors should call their embassy or consulate.

MAIL At press time, domestic postage rates were 28¢ for a postcard and 44¢ for a letter. For international mail, a first-class postcard or letter of up to 1 ounce costs 98¢ (75¢ to Canada and 79¢ to Mexico). For more information go to **www.usps.com** and click on "Calculate Postage."

If you aren't sure what your address will be in the United States, mail can be sent to you, in your name, c/o General Delivery at the main post office of the city or region where you expect to be. (Call ✆ **800/275-8777** for information on the nearest post office.) The addressee must pick up mail in person and must produce proof of identity (driver's license, passport, and so on). Most post offices will hold your mail for up to 1 month and are open Monday to Friday from 8am to 6pm, and Saturday from 9am to 3pm.

Always include zip codes when mailing items in the U.S. If you don't know your zip code, visit www.usps.com/zip4.

NEWSPAPERS & MAGAZINES The daily newspaper is the ***Garden Island News,*** available online at www.kauaiworld.com and at newsstands on island. Dozens of visitor magazines ranging from dining to shopping are available on newsstands throughout the island.

PASSPORTS See www.frommers.com/planning for information on how to obtain a passport. See "Embassies & Consulates," above, for whom to contact if you lose yours while traveling in the U.S. For other information, please contact the following agencies:

For Residents of Australia Contact the **Australian Passport Information Service** at ✆ **131-232,** or visit the government website at www.passports.gov.au.

For Residents of Canada Contact the central **Passport Office,** Department of Foreign Affairs and International Trade, Ottawa, ON K1A 0G3 (✆ **800/567-6868;** www.ppt.gc.ca).

For Residents of Ireland Contact the **Passport Office,** Setanta Centre, Molesworth Street, Dublin 2 (✆ **01/671-1633;** www.irlgov.ie/iveagh).

For Residents of New Zealand Contact the **Passports Office** at ✆ **0800/225-050** in New Zealand or 04/474-8100, or log on to www.passports.govt.nz.

For Residents of the United Kingdom Visit your nearest passport office, major post office, or travel agency or contact the **United Kingdom Passport Service** at ✆ **0870/521-0410** or search its website at www.ukpa.gov.uk.

For Residents of the United States To find your regional passport office, either check the U.S. State Department website or call the **National Passport Information Center's** toll-free number (✆ **877/487-2778**) for automated information.

POLICE Dial ✆ **911** for police.

SMOKING It's against the law to smoke in public buildings in Hawaii, including airports, shopping malls, grocery stores, retail shops, buses, movie theaters, banks, convention facilities, and all government buildings and facilities. There is no smoking in restaurants, bars, and nightclubs. Most bed-and-breakfasts prohibit smoking indoors, and more and more hotels and resorts are becoming nonsmoking even in public areas. Also there is no smoking within 20 feet of a doorway, window, or ventilation intake (no hanging around outside a bar to smoke—you must go 20 ft. away). Some beaches also prohibit smoking.

TAXES The United States has no value-added tax (VAT) or other indirect tax at the national level. Every state, county, and city may levy its own local tax on all purchases, including hotel and restaurant checks and airline tickets. These taxes will not appear on price tags. Hawaii's sales tax is 4%. As we went to press, the hotel-occupancy tax is 8.25% and will go up to 9.25% on July 1, 2010. Plus hoteliers are allowed by the state to tack on an additional 4.1666% excise tax. Thus, expect taxes of about 12.42% (13.42% after July 1, 2010) to be added to your hotel bill.

TELEPHONE Generally, hotel surcharges on long-distance and local calls are astronomical, so you're better off using your **cellphone** or a **public pay telephone.** Many convenience groceries and packaging services sell **prepaid calling cards** in denominations up to $50; for international visitors these can be the least expensive way to call home. For more information see "Staying Connected" on p. 73.

TIME The continental United States is divided into **four time zones:** Eastern Standard Time (EST), Central Standard Time (CST), Mountain Standard Time (MST), and Pacific Standard Time (PST). Alaska and Hawaii have their own zones. Hawaii is 2 hours behind Pacific Standard Time and 5 hours behind Eastern Standard Time. In other words, when it's noon in Hawaii, it's 2pm in California and 5pm in New York during standard time on the mainland.

Daylight saving time takes effect at 2am the second Sunday in March and ends at 1am on the first Sunday in November, except in Arizona, Hawaii, the U.S. Virgin Islands, and Puerto Rico. Daylight saving moves the clock 1 hour ahead of standard time. When daylight saving time is in effect on the mainland, Hawaii is 3 hours behind the West Coast and 6 hours behind the East Coast; when it's noon in Hawaii, it's 3pm in California and 6pm in New York.

Hawaii is east of the international date line, putting it on the same day as the U.S. mainland and Canada, and a day behind Australia, New Zealand, and Asia.

TIPPING Tips are a very important part of certain workers' income, and gratuities are the standard way of showing appreciation for services provided. (Tipping is certainly not compulsory if the service is poor!) In hotels, tip **bellhops** at least $1 per bag ($2–$3 if you have a lot of luggage) and tip the **chamber staff** $1 to $2 per day (more if you've left a disaster area for him or her to clean up). Tip the **doorman** or **concierge** only if he or she has provided you with some specific service (for example, calling a cab for you or obtaining difficult-to-get theater tickets). Tip the **valet-parking attendant** $1 every time you get your car.

In restaurants, bars, and nightclubs, tip **service staff** 15% to 20% of the check, tip **bartenders** 10% to 15%, tip **checkroom attendants** $1 per garment, and tip **valet-parking attendants** $1 per vehicle.

As for other service personnel, tip **cab-drivers** 15% of the fare; tip **skycaps** at airports at least $1 per bag ($2–$3 if you have a lot of luggage); and tip **hairdressers** and **barbers** 15% to 20%.

TOILETS You won't find public toilets or "restrooms" on the streets in most U.S. cities, but they can be found in hotel lobbies, bars, restaurants, museums, department stores, railway and bus stations, and service stations. Large hotels and fast-food restaurants are often the best bet for clean facilities. If possible, avoid the toilets at parks and beaches, which tend to be dirty;

some may be unsafe. Restaurants and bars in resorts or heavily visited areas may reserve their restrooms for patrons.

USEFUL PHONE NUMBERS

- Emergency: ✆ 911
- Time of Day: ✆ 808/245-0212
- Kauai Bus: ✆ 808/241-6410
- Kauai Visitor Bureau: ✆ 808/245-3971
- U.S. Agricultural Inspections: ✆ 808/245-2831
- Marine Weather Forecast: ✆ 808/245-3564
- Land Weather Forecast: ✆ 808/245-6001

VISAS For information about U.S. Visas go to **http://travel.state.gov** and click on "Visas." Or go to one of the following websites:

Australian citizens can obtain up-to-date visa information from the **U.S. Embassy Canberra,** Moonah Place, Yarralumla, ACT 2600 (✆ **02/6214-5600**) or by checking the U.S. Diplomatic Mission's website at **http://usembassy-australia.state.gov/consular**.

British subjects can obtain up-to-date visa information by calling the **U.S. Embassy Visa Information Line** (✆ **0891/200-290**) or by visiting the "Visas to the U.S." section of the American Embassy London's website at **www.usembassy.org.uk**.

Irish citizens can obtain up-to-date visa information through the **Embassy of the USA Dublin,** 42 Elgin Rd., Dublin 4, Ireland (✆ **353/1-668-8777**); or by checking the "Visas to the U.S." section of the website at **http://dublin.usembassy.gov**.

Citizens of **New Zealand** can obtain up-to-date visa information by contacting the **U.S. Embassy New Zealand,** 29 Fitzherbert Terrace, Thorndon, Wellington (✆ **644/472-2068**), or get the information directly from the website at **http://wellington.usembassy.gov**.

VISITOR INFORMATION The **Kauai Visitors Bureau** is located on the first floor of the Watumull Plaza, 4334 Rice St., Suite 101, Lihue, HI 96766 (✆ **808/245-3971;** fax 808/246-9235; www.kauaidiscovery.com). For a free official *Kauai Vacation Planner* or recorded information, call ✆ **800/262-1400.** The **Poipu Beach Resort Association,** P.O. Box 730, Koloa, HI 96756 (✆ **888/744-0888** or 808/742-7444; www.poipu-beach.org), will also send you a free guide to accommodations, activities, shopping, and dining in the Poipu Beach area.

If you'd like to learn more about Kauai before you go, contact the **Kauai Historical Society,** 4396 Rice St., Lihue, HI 96766 (✆ **808/245-3373;** khs@hawaiian.net). The group maintains a video-lending library that includes material on a range of topics.

To find out more about state parks on Kauai and Molokai, contact the **Hawaii State Department of Land and Natural Resources,** P.O. Box 1671, Lihue, HI 96766 (✆ **808/274-3446;** www.state.hi.us/dlnr/dsp/kauai.html), which provides information on hiking and camping and will send you free topographic trail maps on request.

For information on Maui County Parks, contact **Kauai County Parks and Recreation,** 4444 Rice St., Lihue, HI 96766 (✆ **808/241-6670;** www.kauai.gov/Government/Departments/ParksRecreation/ParkFacilities/tabid/105/Default.aspx).

WATER The County water on Kauai is safe to drink. If you are camping, do not drink water out of streams without purifying it first.

2 AIRLINE, HOTEL & CAR RENTAL WEBSITES

MAJOR AIRLINES

American Airlines
www.aa.com

American West
www.americawest.com

Hawaiian Airlines
www.hawaiianair.com

United Airlines
www.united.com

INTERISLAND AIRLINES

go!
www.iflygo.com

Hawaiian Airlines
www.hawaiianair.com

Mokulele Airlines
www.mokuleleairlines.com

MAJOR HOTEL & MOTEL CHAINS

Best Western International
www.bestwestern.com

Castle Resorts
www.castleresorts.com

Embassy Suites
www.embassysuites.com

Hilton Hotels
www.hilton.com

Hyatt
www.hyatt.com

Marriott
www.marriott.com

Outrigger Resorts
www.outrigger.com

Sheraton Hotels & Resorts
www.starwoodhotels.com/sheraton

CAR RENTAL AGENCIES

Alamo
www.alamo.com

Avis
www.avis.com

Budget
www.budget.com

Dollar
www.dollar.com

Hertz
www.hertz.com

National
www.nationalcar.com

Thrifty
www.thrifty.com

INDEX

See also Accommodations and Restaurant indexes, below.

General Index

AAA (American Automobile Association), 230
AARP, 63
Access-Able Travel Source, 62
Accessibility, 62
Accessible Vans of Hawaii, 62
Accommodations, 75–79, 96–131. *See also* Accommodations Index
- B&B etiquette, 113
- bargaining on prices, 78
- best, 8–11
- "cleaning fees," 108
- the Coconut Coast, 116–125
- environmentally-friendly, 68
- family-friendly, 98–99
- Lihue and environs, 96–101
- nickel-&-dime charges at high-priced hotels, 78
- the North Shore, 125–131
- Poipu Resort Area, 101–115
- super-cheap sleeps
  - the Coconut Coast, 124
  - Kalaheo, 115
  - Lihue area, 101
  - the North Shore, 131
- timeshares, 118
- types of, 75–78
- western Kauai, 115–116

Ace Island Hardware, 178
Active vacation planner, 69–71
Activities and Attractions Association of Hawaii Gold Card, 71
Activities desks, 70–71
Ae'o, 29
African tulip trees, 26
Agricultural screening at the airports, 50
Air Canada, 48
Air Canada Vacations, 72
Airfarewatchdog.com, 49
Air New Zealand, 48
Air Pacific, 48
Air Tickets Direct, 50
Air travel
- health concerns, 51
- to Kauai, 48–51
- staying comfortable on long flights, 40

AITO (Association of Independent Tour Operators), 68
Alakai Swamp Trail, 183
Alala, 29
Alekoko (Menehune) Fishpond, 200–201
All Angels Jazz Festival (Lihue), 43
Allerton Garden of the National Tropical Botanical Garden, 5, 202
All Nippon Airways, 48
***All Stings Considered: First Aid and Medical Treatment of Hawaii's Marine Injuries,* 57, 59, 60**
All-Terrain-Vehicle (ATV) tours, 194–195
All Woman's Koloa Rodeo (Poipu), 45
Aloha Festivals, 45–46
Aloha Kauai Tours, 200
Amakihi, 29
Amberjack, 31
American Airlines, 49
American Airlines FlyAway Vacations, 72
American Automobile Association (AAA), 230
American Express Travel, 72
American Express traveler's checks, 54
America West, 49
Anahola Beach Park, 169
- beach camping, 187

ANARA Spa (Koloa), 101
Angelfish, 30
Angel's trumpets, 26
Anianiau, 29
Animal Quarantine Facility, 62
Anini Beach, 83, 175
Anini Beach County Park, 2, 169, 187–188
Annual Coconut Festival, 46
Annual Family Ocean Fair (Kilauea National Wildlife Refuge), 44
Annual Festival of Lights (Lihue), 46
Annual Hula Exhibition (Lihue), 44
Annual Royal Paina (Lihue), 43
Annual Taste of Hawaii (Kapaa), 43–44
Annual Visitor Industry Charity Walk (Lihue), 43
Anthuriums, 26
Apapane, 29
***A Pocket Guide to Hawaii's Birds,* 34**
Area code, 230
Art galleries, Hanapepe, 221
A Simple Marriage, 64
Association of Independent Tour Operators (AITO), 68
ATMs (automated-teller machines), 53, 54
ATV (All-Terrain-Vehicle) tours, 194–195
Aunty Lilikoi's passion fruit products (Waimea), 217
Australia
- customs regulations, 48
- embassy of, 231
- green travel resources, 68
- passports, 232
- visas, 234

Avis, 52, 62
A Vow Exchange, 64
Awaawapuhi Trail, 182–183

Backcountry camping, 184–185
Bali Hai Photo (Hanalei), 75
Bambulei (Wailua), 222
Banana Joe's, 216
Banana Patch Studio (Hanapepe), 221
Banana Poka Roundup (Kokee State Park), 44
Banyan trees, 26
Barking Sands Beach, 2, 168
Beach camping
- Anahola Beach Park, 187
- Lucy Wright Park, 186
- Polihale State Park, 185–186

Beaches, 161–171
- Anahola Beach Park, 169
- Anini Beach County Park, 2, 169
- Barking Sands Beach, 2, 168
- best, 1–2
- the Coconut Coast, 168–169
- Haena Beach, 2
- Haena Beach Park, 170, 188–189
- Hanakapiai Beach, 190–191
- Hanalei Beach, 2, 188
- Hanamaulu Beach Park, 164
- Kalapaki Beach, 1–2, 161–162
- Kee Beach State Park, 170–171
- Lihue and environs, 161–164
- Lumahai Beach, 170
- Lydgate State Park, 168
- Mahaulepu Beach, 164
- Ninini Beach, 162
- Niumalu Beach Park, 162
- the North Shore, 169–171
- Poipu Beach Park, 2, 164–165
- Poipu Resort Area, 164–167
- Polihale State Park, 2, 168
- Prince Kuhio Park, 165–166
- Queen's Pond, 168
- safety, 59
- Salt Pond Beach Park, 168
- sustainable tourism, 66
- trespassing and, 60
- Tunnels Beach, 170
- Wailua Beach, 168–169
- western Kauai, 168

Bed & breakfasts (B&Bs), 77–79. *See also* Accommodations
- best, 10–11

Bento, 23
Bergeron, Vic, 18
Big Island, 25
Big Save (Waimea), 221
Biking, 195–196
Billfish, 31
Birds, 29
Birds-of-paradise, 26
Bird-watching, 34, 196
Bisexual/Transgender/Gay/Lesbian Community Bulletin Board, 62
Black Pot, 169
Blennies, 30
***Blue Hawaii* (film), 36**
Blue Hawaiian, 206–207
Boating (rentals, charters, and cruises), 171–172
Bodyboarding (boogie boarding) and bodysurfing, 172
Bonefish, 31
Booking agencies for accommodations, 79
Books, recommended, 33–35
Bottom fish, 145
Bouchons Restaurant and Sushi Bar (Hanalei), 228
Bougainvillea, 26–27
Box jellyfish, 59
Breadfruit trees, 27
Bridge etiquette, 211
Bromeliads, 27
Bubbles Below Scuba Charters, 174–175
Bucket shops (consolidators), 50
Budget, 52
Bugs, 55–57
Burns Supper (Waimea), 42
Business hours, 230
Business Support Services (Kapaa), 75
Bus travel, 53
Butterfly fish, 30
***By Wind, By Wave: An Introduction to Hawaii's Natural History*, 34**

Calling cards, prepaid, 73
Campgrounds and wilderness cabins, 177
- backcountry, 184–185
- at beaches
  - Anahola Beach Park, 187
  - Lucy Wright Park, 186
  - Polihale State Park, 185–186
- Kokee State Park, 183–185
- Polihale State Park, 185–186

Camp Sloggett, 183
Canada
- customs regulations, 48
- embassy of, 231
- green travel resources, 68
- passports, 232

Cannons Beach, 175
Canyon Trail, 182
Captain Andy's Sailing Adventures, 172, 227
Captain Cook Fun Run (Waimea), 43
Carbonfund, 68
Carbon Neutral, 68
Car insurance, 52
Car rentals, 51–52
Carrying capacity of the Hawaiian Islands, 67
Car travel, 51, 67
Caverns, 6, 174
Cellphones, 73
Centipedes, 55–57
Cheapflights.com, 49
Chickens and roosters, wild, 111
Children, families with, 63
- hotels, 98–99
- restaurants, 142–143
- sights and activities, 176
- suggested itinerary, 90–93
- sun protection, 58

China Airlines, 48
Ching Young Village Shopping Center (Hanalei), 225
Christmas Parade, Waimea Lighted, 46
CJM Country Stables (Koloa), 196
"Cleaning fees," 108
Clinton, Bill, 20
The Coconut Coast, 80
- accommodations, 116–125
- beaches, 168–169
- brief description of, 82
- hiking and camping, 186–187

The Coconut Coast *(cont.)*
nightlife, 228
restaurants, 143, 148–153
vegetarian-friendly, 151
shopping, 222–224
sights and attractions, 208–210
Coconut Coast Weddings & Honeymoons, 64
Coconut Festival, 46
Coconut Marketplace (Kapaa), 223
nightlife, 228
Coffee, 27
Collect calls, 73
Collectibles and Fine Junque (Waimea), 221
Concert in the Sky (Lihue), 44
Condos, 76
Conger eels, 30
Connection kit, 75
Consolidators (bucket shops), 50
Consulates, 230–231
Continental Airlines Vacations, 72
Cook, Capt. James, 16, 81
Coral, 30
Coral cuts, 60
Country Store (Kilohana), 218
Credit cards, 53
Crime, 61, 195
Cuisine, 21–24
green markets and fruit stands, 215–217
Cultural renaissance, 19–20
Customs regulations, 47–48
Cuts, 60

David Kalakaua, King, 17
Daylight saving time, 43, 46, 233
Debit cards, 53
Deep vein thrombosis (economy-class syndrome), 40
Delta Dream Vacations, 72
Dim sum, 23
Dining, 132–160. ***See also*** **Food and cuisine; Restaurants Index**
best, 11–13
the Coconut Coast, 143, 148–153
vegetarian-friendly, 151
environmentally-friendly, 68
family-friendly, 142–143
Lihue and environs, 132–137
vegetarian-friendly, 150
for luaus, 156–157
the North Shore, 143, 154–160
plate lunches, 134–135
Poipu Resort Area, 138–145
family-friendly, 142
vegetarian-friendly, 150
vegetarian-friendly, 150–151
western Kauai, 146–148
Disabilities, travelers with, 62
Discount-tickets.com, 49
Dive Kauai, 175
Dole, Sanford, 17
Dollar, 52
Donovan's Reef **(film), 35**
Drinking laws, 230
Driving rules, 52
Duke's Barefoot Bar (Nawiliwili), 226

Eco Directory, 68
Ecosystem problems, 32–33
Ecotourism, 65–68
Ecotourism Australia, 68
Edwards, Webley, 18
Elderhostel, 63
Electricity, 230
'Elepaio, 29
Embassies and consulates, 230–231
Emergencies, 231
Environmental guide, 24–32
Environmentally Friendly Hotels, 68
Eo E Emalani Festival (Kokee State Park), 46
E-Passport, 47
Etiquette
bed & breakfasts (B&Bs), 113
bridge, 211
outdoor, 71
Expedia.com, 49

Families with children, 63
hotels, 98–99
restaurants, 142–143
sights and activities, 176
suggested itinerary, 90–93
sun protection, 58
Family Ocean Fair (Kilauea National Wildlife Refuge), 44
Farecast.com, 49
Farmers Market (Kilauea), 217
Fathom Five Adventures, 175
Fauna, 28–33
books about, 34
Fern Grotto, 209
Festival of Lights (Lihue), 46
50 First Dates **(film), 36**
Film Festival, Hawaii International, 46
Films, 35–37
shot on Kauai, 212
Fireworks display, New Year's Eve (Poipu), 46
Fishing, 66, 172–173
Flash floods, 178
Flights.com, 50
Flights International, 49
Flora, 26–28, 32
books about, 34
FlyCheap, 50
FlyerTalk, 50
Food and cuisine, 21–24
green markets and fruit stands, 215–217
4th Annual All Angels Jazz Festival (Lihue), 43
4th Annual Kauai Orchid and Art Festival (Hanapepe), 43
4th of July Celebration, Kekaha Town, 44
Frequent-flier clubs, 50
Frequent-flier credit cards, 50
Friday Night Art Walk (Hanapepe), 221
From Here to Eternity **(film), 36**
Frommer's favorite Kauai experiences, 166–167

Game fish, 31
Garden Island, **64, 178**
Garden Isle Artisan Faire (Lihue), 44

Gardens, 5
Allerton Garden of the National Tropical Botanical Garden, 5, 202
Limahuli Garden of the National Tropical Botanical Garden, 213
Na Aina Kai Botanical Gardens, 213
Gasoline, 231
Gays and lesbians, 62–63
GayWired Travel Services, 62
Geckos, 30
Geography, 25–26
Ginger, 27
Go!, 49
Goatfish, 31
Godfrey, Arthur, 18
Gold Card, Activities and Attractions Association of Hawaii, 71
Golden Week, 38
Golf, 191–194
best courses, 6–7
Grand Hyatt Kauai Resort & Spa, 7
Kauai Lagoons Golf Courses, 6, 191
Kauai Marriott Resort & Beach Club, 7
Kiahuna Golf Club, 7, 192
Kukuiolono Golf Course, 192, 194
the North Shore, 194
Poipu Bay Golf Course, 7, 194
Princeville Golf Club, 7, 194
Puakea Golf Course, 7, 191–192
Wailua Municipal Golf Course, 192
Grand Canyon of the Pacific (Waimea Canyon), 4, 6, 204–205
Grand Hyatt Kauai Resort and Spa (Poipu), 7
Business Center at, 75
nightlife, 226–227
shopping, 219
tennis, 197
The Green Directory, 68
Green flash, 229
Greenhotels, 68
Green markets and fruit stands, 215–217
Green Pages, 68
Green travel resources, 68
Grove Farm Homestead Museum (Lihue), 198
GSM (Global System for Mobile Communications) wireless network, 73

Haena, 83
Haena Beach Park, 2, 6, 170, 175, 188–189, 211
Hala (pandanus), 28
Halo Halo Shave Ice (Lihue), 147
Hamada, Robert, 222–223
Hanakapiai Beach, 190–191
Hanakapiai Falls, 190
Hanakoa Valley, 191
Hanalei, 83
Hanalei Bay, 83
surfing, 175
Hanalei Beach Park, 2, 6, 188, 211
beaches, 169
Hanalei Bridge, 211
Hanalei Buffalo Ranch, 211
Hanalei Center, 225
Hanalei Gourmet (Hanalei), 228
Hanalei National Wildlife Refuge, 196, 210
Hanalei North Shore Properties, 125
Hanalei River banks, 211
Hanalei Surf Co., 176
Hanalei Valley Lookout, 210
Hanamaulu Beach Park, 164
Hanapepe
brief description of, 81
shopping, 221
Hanapepe Art Night, 228
Hanapepe Café, 228
Hanauma Bay (Oahu), 32
Hariguchi Rice Mill, 210
Harter, Jack, 208
***Hawaii* (film), 36**
Hawaiiana Festival (Poipu), 46
Hawaiian Airlines, 49
***Hawaiian Antiquities,* 34**
Hawaiian Blizzard (Kapaa Shopping Center), 147
Hawaiian culture, 19–20, 69
Hawaiian Farmers of Hanalei, 217
***Hawaiian Folk Tales,* 34**
***Hawaiian Heritage Plants,* 34**
Hawaiian language, 20–21
The Hawaiian Language Web Site, 79
Hawaiian monk seal, 29
Hawaiian music, 37
Hawaiian Slack-Key Guitar Festival (Lihue), 46
***Hawaiian Reef Fish: The Identification Book,* 34**
Hawaiian Slack-Key Guitar Festival (Lihue), 46
***Hawaiian Sovereignty: Do the Facts Matter?,* 35**
Hawaiian Trading Post (Lawai), 220
Hawaiian Wildlife Tours, 178
Hawaii Beachfront Vacation Homes, 79
Hawaii Center for Independent Living, 62
Hawaii Condo Exchange, 79
Hawaii Freshwater Fishing License, 173
Hawaii Geographic Society, 53
Hawaii International Film Festival, 46
Hawaii Movie Tours, 212
Hawaii's Best Bed & Breakfasts, 79
***Hawaii's Story by Hawaii's Queen Liliuokalani,* 35**
Hawaii State Department of Land and Natural Resources, 234
Hawaii Visitors and Convention Bureau, 64, 79
Hawaii Wildlife Fund, 66
Health concerns, 55–60
jet lag, 51
Health insurance, 60
***Heiaus,* 69**
Heliconia, 27
Helicopter tours, 4–5
Niihau, 82
over Waimea Canyon & The Na Pali Coast, 205–208
Hertz, 52, 62
Hibiscus, 27
High season, 38
Hiking, 5, 66, 177–191. *See also specific trails*
guided, 178, 180
Poipu Resort Area, 180, 182
safety, 61, 184–185
western Kauai, 182–183
Hilo Hattie (Lihue), 217
Hilton Kauai Beach Resort (Lihue), 226
History of Hawaii, 16–20
books about, 34–35

Hoary bat, 29
Holiday Hula Celebration (Lihue), 46
Holidays, 41–42, 231
Holoholo Charters, 172
Home exchanges, 77–78
The Honolulu Advertiser, 35
Honolulu Stories: Two Centuries of Writing, 34
Horseback riding, 196
Hospital, 231
Hotel Association of Canada, 68
Hotels, 75–79, 96–131. *See also* Accommodations Index
  B&B etiquette, 113
  bargaining on prices, 78
  best, 8–11
  "cleaning fees," 108
  the Coconut Coast, 116–125
  environmentally-friendly, 68
  family-friendly, 98–99
  Lihue and environs, 96–101
  nickel-&-dime charges at high-priced hotels, 78
  the North Shore, 125–131
  Poipu Resort Area, 101–115
  super-cheap sleeps
    the Coconut Coast, 124
    Kalaheo, 115
    Lihue area, 101
    the North Shore, 131
  timeshares, 118
  types of, 75–78
  western Kauai, 115–116
Hot Rocket (Hanalei), 225
House rentals, 77
Hukilau Lanai Restaurant (Kauai Coast Resort), 228
Hula, 4, 20
  Holiday Hula Celebration (Lihue), 46
Hula Exhibition (Lihue), 44
Hula Girl (Kapaa), 223
Hula Moon (Old Koloa Town), 219
Huleia National Wildlife Refuge, 174

Ice cream, 140
Iiwi, 29
Insects, 55–57
Inside Flyer, 50
Insurance, 52, 231
International calls, 73
International Gay & Lesbian Travel Association (IGLTA), 62
Internet access, 74–75
Internet Service Provider (ISP), 75
InTouch USA, 73
Ireland
  embassy of, 231
  passports, 232
  visas, 234
Ishihara Market (Waimea), 221
Island Helicopters, 208
Island Hemp & Cotton (Kapaa), 223–224
Islands in the Stream (film), 35
Island Soap and Candle Works (Kilauea), 224
Island Weddings & Blessings Dream Wedding, 65
Itineraries, suggested, 84–95
  for the adventurous, 93–95
  for families, 90–93
  one-week, 84–87
  two-week, 87–90

Jacaranda, 28
Jack Harter, 208
Japan Air Lines, 48
Jet lag, 51
Jungle Girl (Koloa town), 219
Jurassic Park (film), 35

Kaahumanu, Queen, 17
Kalaheo/Lawai, brief description of, 81
Kalalau Lookout, 205
Kalalau Trail, 189–190
Kalalau Valley, 191
  camping, 190–191
Kalapaki Beach, 1–2, 161–162
Kamehameha I, King, 17
Kanahele, George, 19
Kapaa
  brief description of, 82
  shopping, 223–224
Kapaa New Town Park, 215
Kapaa Stitchery (Lihue), 217
The Karate Kid, Part II (film), 35
Kauai, 26
Kauai: Island of Discovery, 79
Kauaian Days, 42
Kauai Backcountry Adventures, 177
Kauai Beach Guide, 165
Kauai Bus, 53
Kauai Community Players, 226
Kauai Concert Association's 3rd Annual Red Clay Jazz Festival (Lihue), 44
Kauai County Farm Bureau Fair (Lihue), 45
Kauai County Parks and Recreation, 234
Kauai Cycle and Tour, 195
Kauai Educational Association for the Study of Astronomy, 171
Kauai Fine Arts (Hanapepe), 221
Kauai Fruit & Flower (near Lihue Airport), 216, 217
Kauai Harley Davidson, 53
Kauai Historical Society, 208, 234
Kauai Humane Society Thrift Shop (Lihue), 217
Kauai Lagoons Golf Courses, 6, 191
Kauai Marriott Resort & Beach Club (Nawiliwili), 7, 226
Kauai Mokihana Festival, 46
The Kauai Movie Book, 212
Kauai Museum (Lihue), 198
  gift shop, 217
Kauai Museum Lei Day Celebrations (Lihue), 43
Kauai Music Festival (Lihue), 45
Kauai Nature Tours, 180
Kauai Plantation Railway (Lihue), 200
Kauai Products Store (Lihue), 217
Kauai Taxi Company, 53
Kauai Village, 223
Kauai Visitors Bureau (Lihue), 234
Kauai Water Ski and Surf Co. (Wailua), 171, 177, 223
Kauai Wedding Professional Association, 64
Ka Ulu O Laka Heiau, 211–213
Kawaikoi Campground, 184
Kayak.com, 49
Kayaking, 173–174

Kayak Kauai, 171, 173, 178
Keahua Arboretum Trail, 187
Kee Beach/Haena Beach Park, 6, 170–171, 175
Kekaha Neighborhood Center, 216
Kekaha Town 4th of July Celebration, 44
Kela's Glass Gallery (Kapaa), 223
Kendrick, John, 17
Keoki's Paradise (Poipu), 227
Kiahuna Golf Club, 7, 192
Kiahuna Swim and Tennis Club, 197
Kids, 63
hotels, 98–99
restaurants, 142–143
sights and activities, 176
suggested itinerary, 90–93
sun protection, 58
Ki Hoalu, Slack Key Guitar Music of Hawaii (Hanalei), 229
Kiki a Ola (Menehune Ditch), 201, 203–204
Kilauea, 83
Kilauea Point National Wildlife Refuge, 44, 196, 210
Kilauea Volcano, 18
Kilohana Long-Distance Canoe Race (Waimea), 43
Kilohana Plantation (Lihue), 200, 218
King Kamehameha Celebration Ho'olaule'a, 44
Kipu Falls Zipline Trek, 180
Kipu Ranch Adventures, 194
Kmart (Lihue), 218
Koa Wood Gallery (Hanapepe), 221
Kokee Lodge, 183, 205
Kokee Natural History Museum, 205, 222
Wonder Walks, 178
Kokee State Park, 178
bird-watching, 196
campgrounds and wilderness cabins in, 183–185
hiking, 182
sightseeing, 205
Koloa, brief description of, 81
***Koloa Heritage Trail,* 202**
Koloa Landing, 104, 175
Koloa Plantation Days (Koloa and Poipu), 44
Koloa Rum Company Tasting Room, Retail Store & Gallery (Kilohana Plantation), 219
Kong Lung (Kilauea), 224
Korean Airlines, 48
Kuhio Highway, 210
Kukui Grove Center (Lihue), 217
Kukui Grove Cinemas, 226
Kukuiolono Golf Course, 192, 194
Kukui's Restaurant (Nawiliwili), 226
Kukui'ula Village Shopping Center (off Ala Kalanikaumaka), 104
Kukuiulu Development (between Poipu and Lawai Valley), 104

Ladyfish, 31
Lanai, 26
Language, 20–21, 231
Laundry, 39
Lawai Gardens, 202
Leather-fish, 31
Legal aid, 231–232
***The Legends and Myths of Hawaii,* 35**
Lei Day Celebrations (Lihue), 43
Leis, 74
Niihau shell, 220
Liberty Travel, 72
Lighthouse Bistro (Kilauea), 228
Lihue Airport, arriving at, 49
Lihue and environs
accommodations, 96–101
beaches, 161–164
brief description of, 80–81
golf, 191–192
nightlife, 226
restaurants, 132–137
vegetarian-friendly, 150
shopping, 217–218
sights and attractions, 198–202
Liko Kauai Cruises, 172
Liliuokalani, Queen, 17
Lima-huli, 5
Limahuli Garden of the National Tropical Botanical Garden, 213
Literature, 33–35
Lodging, 75–79, 96–131. *See also* Accommodations Index
B&B etiquette, 113
bargaining on prices, 78
best, 8–11
"cleaning fees," 108
the Coconut Coast, 116–125
environmentally-friendly, 68
family-friendly, 98–99
Lihue and environs, 96–101
nickel-&-dime charges at high-priced hotels, 78
the North Shore, 125–131
Poipu Resort Area, 101–115
super-cheap sleeps
the Coconut Coast, 124
Kalaheo, 115
Lihue area, 101
the North Shore, 131
timeshares, 118
types of, 75–78
western Kauai, 115–116
Lost luggage, 56
***The Lost World: Jurassic Park* (film), 35**
Lotus Gallery (Kilauea), 224
Luaus, 156–157
Lucy Wright Park, beach camping, 186
Lumahai Beach, 170, 211
Lydgate State Park, 168

Macadamia, 28
Mahaulepu Beach, 164
Mahaulepu Shoreline Trail, 180
Mahimahi, 31
Mail, 232
Mail2web, 75
Malama Hawaii, 66
Manapua, 23
Maniniholo, 188
Maps, 52–53
Margo Oberg's School of Surfing, 176
Marine life, 30–32
ecosystem problems and, 32
sustainable tourism, 66
Marriage, 63–65
Marriage License Office, 64
Marta's Boat (Kapaa), 223

MasterCard traveler's checks, 55
Maui, 25
McBryde Garden, 202
Meadow Gold Dairies, 140
Medeiros Farms (Kalaheo), 220
Medical insurance, 60
Medical requirements for entry, 48
Menehune (little people), 201
Menehune Ditch (Kiki a Ola), 201, 203–204
Menehune (Alekoko) Fishpond, 200–201
Michener, James A., 33
Microclimates, 39
Milolii, 191
Missionaries, 17, 20
Moa (wild chickens), 29, 111
Mokulele Airlines, 49
Molokai, 25–26
Molokai: The Story of Father Damien (film), 36
Molokini, 32
Money and costs, 53–55
Monkeypod trees, 28
Monk seals, 66, 164
Moray eels, 30
More Hawaii For Less, 72
Mosquitoes, 55–57
MossRehab ResourceNet, 62
Motorcycle rentals, 53

Na Aina Kai Botanical Gardens, 5, 213
Na Pali Coast, 4–5, 214
 boating, 171–172
 brief description of, 83–84
 camping, 190–191
Na Pali Coast State Park, 189
Na Pali Explorer (Waimea), 75
Na Pali Sunset Dinner, 227
National, 52
National Weather Service, 61
Nation Within: The Story of America's Annexation of the Nation of Hawaii, 35
Native Planters in Old Hawaii: Their Life, Lore, and Environment, 34
Nene, 29
Newspapers and magazines, 232–233
New Year's Eve Fireworks (Poipu), 46
New Zealand
 customs regulations, 48
 embassy of, 231
 passports, 232
 visas, 234
Night-blooming cereus, 28
Nightlife, 226–229
 the Coconut Coast, 228
 Lihue and environs, 226
 the North Shore, 228–229
 Poipu Resort Area, 226–227
Niihau, 82
Niihau Helicopter, 82, 208
Niihau shell leis, 220
Ninini Beach, 162
9th Annual Kauai Polynesian Festival: Heiva I Kauai Ia Orana Tahiti (Kapaa), 45
Niumalu Beach Park, 162
None But the Brave (film), 35–36
The North Shore, 80
 accommodations, 125–131
 beaches, 169–171
 brief description of, 83
 golf, 194
 hiking and camping, 187–190
 nightlife, 228–229
 restaurants, 143, 154–160
 shopping, 224–225
 sights and attractions, 210–214
Nounou Mountain Trail East (The Sleeping Giant Trail), 186
Nounou Mountain Trail West, 187
Nualolo Trail, 183
Nudity, 60
Nukumoi Surf Shop (Poipu Beach Park), 176, 219

Oahu, 25
Obon Days & Festival (Koloa), 44
Obon Festival, 45
Oceanarium, 6, 174
Ocean safety, 57
Odyssey Publishing, 52
Official Kauai Travel Planner, 64
Off seasons, 38
Ola's (Hanalei), 224
Old Koloa Town, shopping, 219
On The Road to Hanalei, 225
Opaekaa Falls, 5
Opodo, 49
Orbitz.com, 49
Orchid Alley (Kapaa), 224
Orchid and Art Festival (Hanapepe), 43
Orchids, 28
Out and About, 62–63
Outdoor etiquette, 71
Outfitters, 69–70
Outfitters Kauai, 173–174, 180, 195–196
Outrigger Canoe Season, 43
Outrigger Hotel and Resorts chain, 72

Pacific Missile Range Facility (PMRF), 203
Pacific Ocean Holidays, 62
Package deals, 71–73
Pandanus (hala), 28
Papayas Natural Foods (Hanalei), 225
Papayas Natural Foods (Kapaa), 223
Paradise Clothing (Old Koloa Town), 219
Paradise Sportswear (Waimea), 222
The Parrish Collection (Koloa), 107
Parrotfish, 31
Passports, 47, 232
Pau Hana Bar and Grill (Kauai Village Shopping Center), 228
Peacock, W. C., 18
Pearl Harbor, 18
Pearl Harbor (film), 36
Pedal 'n Paddle, 174, 178, 195
Pedestrians, 52
People Attentive to Children (PATCH), 63
Petrol, 231
Philippine Airlines, 48
Picture Bride (film), 36–37
Pidgin, 21
Pihea Trail, 183
Pili Mai at Poipu, 105
Pineapples, 17
Planning your trip to Kauai, 38–79
 active vacation planner, 69–71
 calendar of events, 42–46

entry requirements, 47–48
getting married, 63–65
health concerns, 55–60
money and costs, 53–55
package deals, 71–73
safety concerns, 60–61
specialized travel resources, 62–63
traveling to Kauai, 48–51
when to go, 38–39
Plate lunches, 22–23, 134–135
Plaza Laundry (Lihue), 218
Pleasant Hawaiian Holidays, 49
Plumeria, 28
PMRF (Pacific Missile Range Facility), 203
Pohaku T's (between Koloa and Poipu), 220
The Point (Poipu), 227
Poipu Aina Estates, 105
Poipu Bay Golf Course, 7, 194
Poipu Beach Estates, 105
Poipu Beach Park, 2, 164–165, 175
surfing, 175
Poipu Beach Resort Association, 180, 202, 234
Poipu Resort Area, 80
accommodations, 101–115
beaches, 164–167
brief description of, 81
golf, 192–194
hiking, 180, 182
nightlife, 226–227
projects currently under construction in, 104–105
restaurants, 138–145
family-friendly, 142–143
vegetarian-friendly, 150–151
shopping, 218–221
sights and attractions, 202–203
Poipu Shopping Village, 218–219
Tahitian dance performances, 227
Poipu Shopping Village Phase II, 105
Police, 232
Polihale State Park, 2, 168
beach camping at, 185–186
Popo's Cookies (Kapaa), 223
Portuguese man-of-war, 59
Prepaid calling cards, 73
Prescription medications, 60
Priceline.com, 49
Prince Kuhio Celebration of the Arts (Lawai), 43
Prince Kuhio Park, 165–166, 202
Princeville, 83
Princeville Golf Club, 7, 194
Princeville Ranch Adventures, 180
Princeville Ranch Stables (Hanalei), 196–197
Princeville Tennis Club, 197
Progressive Expressions (Koloa town), 219
Protea, 28
Puakea Golf Course, 7, 191
Public libraries, 75
Pueo, 29
Punctures, 59
Puu Hina Hina Lookout, 205
Puu Lua Reservoir (Kokee State Park), 173
Puuwai, 82

Qantas, 48
Queen's Pond, 168

***Raiders of the Lost Ark* (film), 36**
Rainbow runner, 31
The Ready Mapbook of Kauai, 52
Red Dirt Shirt (Lihue), 218
Reef fish, 30
Reefs, 32
Resorts and hotels, 75, 75–79, 96–131. *See also* Accommodations Index
B&B etiquette, 113
bargaining on prices, 78
best, 8–11
"cleaning fees," 108
the Coconut Coast, 116–125
environmentally-friendly, 68
family-friendly, 98–99
Lihue and environs, 96–101
nickel-&-dime charges at high-priced hotels, 78
the North Shore, 125–131
Poipu Resort Area, 101–115
super-cheap sleeps
the Coconut Coast, 124
Kalaheo, 115
Lihue area, 101
the North Shore, 131
timeshares, 118
types of, 75–78
western Kauai, 115–116
Responsible Travel, 68
Restaurants, 132–160. *See also* Restaurants Index
best, 11–13
the Coconut Coast, 143, 148–153
vegetarian-friendly, 151
environmentally-friendly, 68
family-friendly, 142–143
Lihue and environs, 132–137
vegetarian-friendly, 150
for luaus, 156–157
the North Shore, 143, 154–160
plate lunches, 134–135
Poipu Resort Area, 138–145
family-friendly, 142
vegetarian-friendly, 150
vegetarian-friendly, 150–151
western Kauai, 146–148
Reversed-charge calls, 73
Road maps, 52–53
Robinson, Bruce, 82
Rob's Good Time Grill (Lihue), 226
Rosewood Kauai, 125
Royal Paina (Lihue), 43
Russia, 81
Russian Fort Elizabeth State Historical Park, 204

Safari Helicopters, 208
Safety concerns, 60–61, 70, 195
at beaches, 165
hiking, 184–185
Salt Pond Beach, 175
Salt Pond Beach Park, 168
San Marga Iraivan Temple, 209
Savage Pearls (Hanalei), 225
Scheffer, George Anton, 81
Scorpion fish, 31
Scorpions, 55–57
Scuba diving, 6, 174–175
Sea bass, 31
Seafood, 23–24

Sea life, 30–32
ecosystem problems and, 32
sustainable tourism, 66
Seasickness, 57
Seat belts, 52
Sea urchins, 59–60
Seeing Eye dogs, 62
Seniors, 63
Sharks, 32, 57
Shave ice, 23, 147
Shave Ice Paradise (Hanalei Center), 147
Sheraton Caverns, 175
Sheraton Kauai Resort (Poipu), nightlife, 227
Ship Store Gallery (Kapaa), 223
Shopping, 215–225
best, 13
the Coconut Coast, 222–224
green markets and fruit stands, 215–217
Lihue and environs, 217–218
the North Shore, 224–225
Poipu Resort Area, 218–221
western Kauai, 221–222
***Shore Fishes of Hawaii,* 34**
Sidestep.com, 49
Sierra Club, 70, 178
Sights and attractions, 198–214
the Coconut Coast, 208–210
Lihue and environs, 198–202
the North Shore, 210–214
Poipu Resort Area, 202–203
western Kauai, 203–208
Silversword, 28
Sinclair, Eliza, 82
Site59.com, 49
***Six Days Seven Nights* (film), 36**
Sleeping Giant, 210
The Sleeping Giant Trail (Nounou Mountain Trail East), 186
SmarterTravel.com, 49
Smoking, 42, 60–61, 232
Smoothies, 216
Snapper, 31
Snorkel Bob's Kauai, 171
Snorkeling, 4, 175
***South Pacific* (film), 36**
Sovereignty, 20
Spas, best, 14–15
Sportfish Hawaii, 172, 173
Spouting Horn, 202, 203
Spouting Horn Beach Park, 166–167
Stand-by Golf, 191
Stargazing, 171
Statehood, 19
STA Travel, 50
Stevenson's Library (Koloa), 226
Stings, 59
***Stories of Old Hawaii,* 34**
Sugar, 17–18
Sugar Plantation Tours, 204
Sugi Grove Campground, 184
Summer, 39
Sunglasses, 58
Sun protection, 39, 58
Sunscreen, 58
Sunset viewing, 4, 227
Sunshine Helicopter, 208
Sunshine Market, 215, 216
SunTrips, 49
The Surf Clinic of Hanalei, 175–176
Surfing, 175–176
Surgeonfish, 31
Sustainable tourism, 65–68
Sustainable Travel International, 68
Sustain Lane, 68

Tahiti Nui (Hanalei), 228
Tanning tips, 58
Taro, 28
Taro Ko Chips Factory (Hanapepe), 221
Taste of Hawaii (Kapaa), 43–44
Taxes, 233
Taxis, 53
Telephone, 233
Telephones, 73
Temperature, 39
Tennis, 197
Terran Tours, 196
TerraPass, 68
***This Week Magazine,* 52**
Threadfin, 31
Thrifty, 52
Timeshares, 118
Time zones, 233
The Tin Can Mailman (Wailua), 223
Tipping, 233
***Tips for a Safe Vacation,* 165, 195**
Toilets, 233
***Tora! Tora! Tora!* (film), 37**
Tortugas, 175
Tourism, 18, 19
Tourism Concern, 68
Traffic problems, 52
Traveler's checks, 54–55
Travelocity.com, 49
Tread Lightly, 68
Trespassing, 60
Trevally, 31
Tropical Flowers by Charles (Koloa), 221
***Tropicals,* 34**
True Blue, 174
Tubing, 177
Tuna, 31
Tunnels Beach, 170, 175, 211
Turtles, 66, 164
Twain, Mark, 33
21st Annual Concert in the Sky (Lihue), 44
Two Frogs Hugging (Lihue), 218

United Airlines, 49
United Kingdom
customs regulations, 48
embassy of, 231
green travel resources, 68
passports, 232
visas, 234
United Vacations, 72
University of Hawaii Press maps, 53
University of Hawaii Sea Grant College Program, 66

Vacation rentals, 77
Vegetarian-friendly restaurants, 150–151
Village at Poipu Phase I, 105
Visas, 47, 234
Visa traveler's checks, 55
Visa Waiver Program (VWP), 47
Visitor Industry Charity Walk (Lihue), 43
Visitor information, 234
Vog, 61
Voice-over Internet Protocol (VoIP), 73
***Voices of Wisdom: Hawaiian Elders Speak,* 33**
Volunteering, 66
Volunteer International, 68

Wahoo, 31
Waialeale, Mount, 26
Waikiki, A History of Forgetting and Remembering, 35
Wailua, shopping, 223
Wailua Beach, 168–169
Wailua Falls, 202
Wailua Municipal Golf Course, 192
Wailua River State Park, 210
Waimea Canyon (Grand Canyon of the Pacific), 204–205
Waimea Canyon Lookout, 204
Waimea Canyon Trails, 182
Waimea Library, 203
Waimea Lighted Christmas Parade, 46
Waimea Town
- brief description of, 81
- shopping, 221–222
- sights and attractions, 203–204

Waimea Town Celebration, 43
Wainani at Kiahuna, 105
Waioli Mission House Museum (Hanalei), 213–214
Waipoo Falls, hike to, 182
Waipouli Variety Store (Kapaa), 223
Wana, 59–60
Water, drinking, 234
Waterfalls, 5
Water-skiing, 177
Watersports, 171–177
Waterworld (film), 36
Weather, 39
Web access, 75
Websites, Hawaii-specific, 79
Wedding planner, 64
Weddings, 63–65
Weedon, W. C., 18
Weinberg Bunkhouse, 183–184
Western Kauai
- accommodations, 115–116
- beaches, 168
- brief description of, 81
- hiking, 182–183
- restaurants, 146–148
- shopping, 221–222
- sights and attractions, 203–208

Whale and Dolphin Conservation Society, 68
Whales, 31
Whale-watching, 171
Wheelchair accessibility, 62
Wi-Fi access, 74–75
Wilcox Hospital (Lihue), 231
Wildlife refuges, 5
Windsurfing, 177
Windsurf Kauai, 177
World War II, 18
Wrasses, 31

Yahoo! Mail, 75
Yee, Harry, 18
Yellowfish Trading Company (Hanalei), 225
YMCA of Kauai-Camp Naue, 189

Ziplining, 180

Accommodations

Aloha Estates at Kalaheo Plantation, 115
Aloha Sunrise Inn/Aloha Sunset Inn (Kilauea), 126, 128
Aston Aloha Beach Resort (Kapaa), 119–120
Aston Kauai Beach at Makaiwa, 116, 118
Bamboo Jungle (Kalaheo), 113–114
Bed, Breakfast & Beach at Hanalei Bay, 129
Best Western Plantation Hale Suites (Kapaa), 120
Brennecke's Beach Bungalow (Poipu Beach), 108–109
Ellie's Koloa House (Koloa), 109
Garden Island Inn (Lihue), 100–101
Garden Isle Cottages Oceanfront (Koloa), 106
Grand Hyatt Kauai Resort & Spa, 98
Grand Hyatt Kauai Resort & Spa (Koloa), 101–102
Hale Ho'o Maha (Hanalei), 128
Hale Ikena Nui (Kalaheo), 114
Hale Kua (Lawai), 114
Hale Lani Bed & Breakfast (Kapaa), 120–121
Hale Luana (Kilauea), 129
Hale O Kuawa (Kilauea), 130
Hale Pohaku (Koloa), 109
Hanalei Bay Resort & Suites (Princeville), 126
Hanalei Colony Resort, 98, 128–129
Hanalei Inn, 130
Hanalei Surf Board House, 129
Hideaway Cove Poipu Beach, 106–107
Hilton Kauai Beach Hotel Resort (Lihue), 97–99
Honua Lani Gardens (Kapaa), 121
Hotel Coral Reef (Kapaa), 121
Inn Paradise (Kapaa), 121
Inn Waimea, 115–116
Kaha Lani Resort (Lihue), 99–100
Kakalina's Bed and Breakfast (Kapaa), 122
Kalaheo Inn (Koloa), 98, 114–115
Kapaa Sands, 122
Kapaa Shores, 122
Kauai Banyan Inn (Lawai), 109
Kauai Beach Villas (Lihue), 100
Kauai Country Inn (Kapaa), 122–123
Kauai Cove (Poipu), 110
Kauai International Hostel (Kapaa), 124
Kauai Marriott Resort & Beach Club (Lihue), 96–97
Kauai Sands (Kapaa), 123
Kiahuna Plantation Resort (Koloa), 99, 105–106
Ko'a Kea Hotel & Resort (Poipu), 102
Kokee Lodge (Waimea), 116
Lae Nani Outrigger Resort Condominium (Kapaa), 119
Lani-keha (Kapaa), 124
Mahina Kai (Anahola), 120
Makahuena (Poipu), 107
Mana Yoga Vacation Rental (Hanalei), 130
Mango Cottage (Koloa), 110
Marjorie's Kauai Inn, 110
Mohala Ke Ola Bed & Breakfast (Kapaa), 123
Motel Lani (Lihue), 101
Nihi Kai Villas (Koloa), 110–111
North Country Farms (Kilauea), 130–131

Opaeka'a Falls Hale, 116
Outrigger Waipouli Beach Resort & Spa (Kapaa), 119
The Palmwood (Kilauea), 126
Poipu Crater Resort, 111
Poipu Kapili Resort, 107–108
Poipu Plantation, 111–112
Princeville Bed & Breakfast, 131
Pua Hale at Poipu, 112
Rosewood Bed & Breakfast (Kapaa), 123–124
St. Regis Resort Princeville (Princeville), 125–126
Seaview Suite (Kalaheo), 115
Sheraton Kauai Resort (Koloa), 99, 102, 104
Surf & Ski Cottage (Kapaa), 124
Surf Song (Poipu Beach), 112
Tip Top Motel (Lihue), 101
Turtle Cove Suites (Poipu Beach), 108
Waikomo Stream Villas, 112–113
Wailua Bayview (Kapaa), 124
Waimea Plantation Cottages, 99, 116
Whaler's Cove (Koloa), 106
YMCA of Kauai-Camp Naue, 131

Restaurants

Bar Acuda (Hanalei), 154
The Beach House (Poipu), 138, 150
Bouchons Restaurant and Sushi Bar Hanalei, 154, 156
Brennecke's Beach Broiler (Poipu), 141, 142, 150
Brick Oven Pizza (Kalaheo), 142–144
Bubba Burgers (Hanalei), 159
Bubba Burgers (Kapaa), 143, 152
The Bull Shed (Waipouli), 148
Café Portofino (Lihue), 135–136
Caffè Coco (Wailua), 148
Casa Blanca at Kiahuna (Poipu), 141–142, 150
Casa di Amici (Poipu), 138
Dani's Restaurant (Lihue), 136
Dondero's (Koloa), 138, 140
Duane's Ono-Char Burger (Anahola), 143, 154
Duke's (Lihue), 136
Duke's Canoe Club (Nawiliwili), 150
Federico's (Princeville), 159
Fish Express (Lihue), 134–135
Garden Island BBQ (Lihue), 135
Gaylord's (Lihue), 133, 150
Genki Sushi (Lihue), 136
Grinds Café (Eleele), 146
Hamura's Saimin Stand (Lihue), 136–137
Hanalei Dolphin Restaurant & Fish Market, 157
Hanalei Gourmet, 158
Hanalei Wake-up Café, 159
Hanamaulu Restaurant, 137, 142
Hanapepe Café (Hanapepe), 146, 151
Hukilau Lanai (Kapaa), 148
Java Kai (Hanalei), 159
Joe's on the Green (Poipu), 145
Kalaheo Café & Coffee Co., 145, 151
Kalamaku (Kilohana), 157
Kalapaki Beach Hut (Nawiliwili), 137, 142, 150
Kilauea Bakery & Pau Hana Pizza, 151, 158
Kilauea Fish Market, 160
The King and I (Kapaa), 152
Koloa Fish Market, 134
Kountry Kitchen (Kapaa), 152
Lighthouse Bistro Kilauea (Kilauea), 154
Mark's Place (Puhi Industrial Park), 135
Mediterranean Gourmet (Hanalei), 158–159
Mema (Kapaa), 150–151
Mermaids Café (Kapaa), 151-152
Norberto's El Cafe (Kapaa), 153
Ocean Front Luau (Haena), 157
Olympic Café (Kapaa), 153
Ono Family Restaurant (Kapaa), 143, 153
Plantation Gardens Restaurant (Kiahuna), 150
Plantation Gardens Restaurant (Koloa), 140
Poipu Beach Broiler, 142, 143–144
Pomodoro (Kalaheo), 144
Pono Market (Kapaa), 135
Po's Kitchen (Lihue), 135
Postcards Cafe (Hanalei), 151, 159
Red Salt (Koloa), 140
Restaurant Kiibo (Lihue), 137
Roy's Poipu Bar & Grill, 140–141, 150–151
Sheraton Kauai (Poipu Beach), 157
Shrimp Station (Waimea), 147
Smith's Tropical Paradise Garden Lu'au (Wailua), 156–157
Sukhothai Restaurant (Kapaa), 153
Tidepool Restaurant (Koloa), 141
Tidepool Restaurant (Poipu), 151
Tihati Production's "Havaiki Nui" (Poipu), 157
Tip Top Café/Bakery (Lihue), 137, 142
Toi's Thai Kitchen (Eleele), 147
Tomkats Grille (Old Koloa Town), 144
Tropical Taco (Hanalei), 143, 160
Wailua Marina Restaurant, 152
Waimea Brewing Company, 146
Wong's Restaurant (Hanapepe), 147–148
Wrangler's Steakhouse (Waimea), 146
Yum Cha (Poipu), 144

NOTES

NOTES